W9-AWR-341

The Democratization of American Christianity

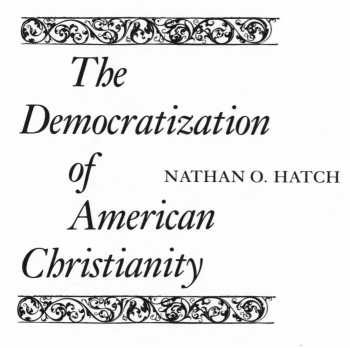

The
Democratization
of NATHAN O. HATCH
American
Christianity

Yale University Press : New Haven and London

The Albert C. Outler Prize
in Ecumenical Church History
of the American Society of Church History

Copyright © 1989 by Yale University.
All rights reserved.
This book may not be reproduced, in whole
or in part, including illustrations, in
any form (beyond that copying permitted by
Sections 107 and 108 of the U.S. Copyright
Law and except by reviewers for the public
press), without written permission from the
publishers.

Designed by James J. Johnson
and set in Janson Roman type.
Printed in the United States of America.

Library of Congress Cataloging-in-Publication Data

Hatch, Nathan O.
   The democratization of American Christianity / Nathan O. Hatch.
      p. cm.
   Bibliography: p.
   Includes index.
   ISBN 0–300–04470–4 (cloth)
         0–300–05060–7 (pbk.)
      1. United States—Church history—19th century. 2. Democracy—Religious aspects—
Christianity—History of doctrines—19th century. I. Title.
BR525.H37 1989
277.3'081—dc19   89–5439
                                                                                    CIP

The paper in this book meets the guidelines for
permanence and durability of the Committee on
Production Guidelines for Book Longevity of the
Council on Library Resources.

19 18 17 16 15 14 13 12 11

To
Julie and Gregg,
David and Beth,
with love

"Tendencies, which had found no political room to unfold themselves in other lands, wrought here without restraint. . . . Every theological vagabond and peddler may drive here his bungling trade, without passport or license, and sell his false ware at pleasure. What is to come of such confusion is not now to be seen."

PHILIP SCHAFF,
The Principle of Protestantism, 1844

Contents

Illustrations

Acknowledgments

This project had a curious origin a decade ago while I enjoyed fellowships at the Charles Warren Center for Studies in American History at Harvard University and the American Antiquarian Society. I am grateful for the support of these organizations, particularly since my original project, a study of Federalist ideology, quickly gave way to a different one. My focus shifted to the very people whom the Federalists attacked for subverting the republic's moral foundations. Unlearned "enthusiasts" like Elias Smith, James O'Kelly, and Lorenzo Dow turned out to be fascinating and important characters in a story of social and religious change. Throughout this study, the University of Notre Dame and its Department of History have remained an immensely supportive academic home. I also appreciate the excellent service of the Microtext Department and the Interlibrary Loan Department of the Theodore M. Hesburgh Library.

Many friends and scholars in the historical profession have shown remarkable patience in listening to me drone on about democracy and American Christianity. I am particularly thankful to those who provided comments on drafts of this manuscript: Jon Butler, Jay Dolan, David Hempton, George Marsden, Mark Noll, Richard Pointer, George Rawlyk, Jan Shipps, Richard Shiels, Harry Stout, Grant Wacker, Anne Wotring, Robert Wiebe, and Gordon Wood. Chuck Grench, Executive Editor of Yale University Press, offered valuable encouragement and advice on frequent occasions. Meighan Pritchard added skilled editorial assistance. Mittie Hatch, an astute wordsmith, graciously proofed these pages.

Portions of chapters 4, 5, and 6 appeared in different form as essays in the *Journal of American History*, in William L. Joyce et al., *Printing and*

Society in Early America (Worcester, Mass., 1983), and in Nathan O. Hatch and Mark A. Noll, eds., *The Bible in America: Essays in Cultural History* (New York, 1982). I am grateful to this journal and to the American Antiquarian Society and Oxford University Press for permission to use this material.

I am indebted to Mike Loux and Roger Skurski, colleagues in administration at the University of Notre Dame. Over a two-year span, they saw much less of me in the dean's office than they had a right to expect, my preoccupation with this book compounding their workload. Yet neither ever voiced a word of complaint. In fact, on more than one occasion, Mike Loux whisked me out of the dean's office with the impertinent question, "How many pages have you written today?" I am thankful for the generous commitment of these colleagues to my continued scholarly development.

I am also grateful to three splendid colleagues in the Institute for Scholarship in the Liberal Arts. Under their influence, our offices became graced with many gifts, among them laughter. This crew went the extra mile in effective service, yet they always leavened hard work with humor and good fun. Somehow our fate could not seem grimly serious after Bob Burke, Irish Catholic to the core, arrived from Boston to take a job at Notre Dame—only to find himself surrounded by three Protestants. Bob, we shall long remember your clear exposition of the proper distinction between schismatic, heretic, and infidel.

Each of these co-workers also contributed to the completion of this book: Bob Burke gave up a holiday—and saved me from cardiac arrest—by fixing a computer disk that flashed "unrecoverable error." Behind Valerie Friedline's warm and generous manner lurks a ruthless critic of prose. She took a special interest in my writing and, page after page, straightened many crooked paths. Carol Bryant brought her marvelous skill for organization to a complex array of sources, notes, and drafts. Carol, I await the completion of your quest to trace Lorenzo Dow's exact pilgrimage.

Mike Hamilton, a superb graduate student, did become an itinerant of sorts, crisscrossing the landscape of religious sources from the early republic. Time and again, he would return from forays into the evidence bearing a wealth of fresh material and new insight. A more imaginative and enjoyable junior colleague I could not hope to find. In particular, I appreciate his work in tracing the growth of population and of clergy in the early republic (chapter 1), in estimating the age of death and length of service of Methodist itinerants (chapter 4), and in assisting with the appendix and the index.

Finally, a word of gratitude to my family. Beth, David, and Gregg have cheerfully put up with hasty dinners, trips back to the office, and a father often preoccupied even at home. Their mother has remained a strong source of love, patience, understanding, and wise counsel for us all. Julie—best friend and wisest critic—you are richly deserving of this dedication.

I. Context

CHAPTER ONE

Introduction: Democracy and Christianity

All Christendom has been decomposed, broken in pieces, and resolved into new combinations and affinities.

HARRISON GRAY OTIS, *1836*

This book is about the cultural and religious history of the early American republic and the enduring structures of American Christianity. It argues both that the theme of democratization is central to understanding the development of American Christianity, and that the years of the early republic are the most crucial in revealing that process. The wave of popular religious movements that broke upon the United States in the half century after independence did more to Christianize American society than anything before or since. Nothing makes that point more clearly than the growth of Methodist and Baptist movements among white and black Americans. Starting from scratch just prior to the Revolution, Methodism in America grew at a rate that terrified other more established denominations. By 1820 Methodist membership numbered a quarter million; by 1830 it was twice that number. Baptist membership multiplied tenfold in the three decades after the Revolution; the number of churches increased from five hundred to over twenty-five hundred. The black church in America was born amidst the crusading vigor of these movements and quickly assumed its own distinct character and broad appeal. By the middle of the nineteenth century, Methodist and Baptist churches had splintered into a score of separate denominations, white and black. In total these movements eventually constituted two-thirds of the Protestant ministers and church members in the United States.[1]

Between the American Revolution and 1845, the population of the United States grew at a staggering rate: two and a half million became

3

twenty million in seventy years. This unprecedented growth was due to a high birth rate and the availability of land, rather than to heavy immigration. The population of the United States, less than half of England's in 1775, was growing three times faster than England's in the early 1800s. By 1845 Americans outnumbered the English by five million. Despite this dramatic growth, life in the United States remained overwhelmingly rural. Even in New England, population density did not match Great Britain's. The ratio of people to land barely doubled while the number of Americans expanded tenfold.[2]

Amidst this population boom, American Christianity became a mass enterprise. The eighteen hundred Christian ministers serving in 1775 swelled to nearly forty thousand by 1845. The number of preachers per capita more than tripled; the colonial legacy of one minister per fifteen hundred inhabitants became one per five hundred. This greater preaching density was remarkable given the spiraling population and the restless movement of peoples to occupy land beyond the reach of any church organization. The sheer number of new preachers in the young republic was not a predictable outgrowth of religious conditions in the British colonies. Rather, their sudden growth indicated a profound religious upsurge and resulted in a vastly altered religious landscape. Twice the number of denominations competed for adherents, and insurgent groups enjoyed the upper hand. For example, an upstart church such as the Freewill Baptists had almost as many preachers in the early republic as did the Episcopalians. Antimission Baptist preachers far outnumbered both Roman Catholic priests and Lutheran pastors. One new denominational cluster, the Christians and the Disciples of Christ, had an estimated four thousand preachers, equalling the number of clergy serving Presbyterian denominations. The Congregationalists, which had twice the clergy of any other American church in 1775, could not muster one-tenth the preaching force of the Methodists in 1845.[3]

This book examines five distinct traditions, or mass movements, that developed early in the nineteenth century: the Christian movement, the Methodists, the Baptists, the black churches, and the Mormons. Each was led by young men of relentless energy who went about movement-building as self-conscious outsiders. They shared an ethic of unrelenting toil, a passion for expansion, a hostility to orthodox belief and style, a zeal for religious reconstruction, and a systematic plan to realize their ideals. However diverse their theologies and church organizations, they all offered common people, especially the poor, compelling visions of individual self-respect and collective self-confidence. Like the Populist movement at the end of the nineteenth century, these movements took shape around magnetic leaders who were highly skilled in communication and group mobilization.

Abstractions and generalities about the Second Great Awakening as a conservative force have obscured the egalitarianism powerfully at work in the new nation. As common people became significant actors on the religious scene, there was increasing confusion and angry debate over the purpose and function of the church. A style of religious leadership that the public deemed "untutored" and "irregular" as late as the First Great Awakening became overwhelmingly successful, even normative, in the first decades of the republic. Ministers from different classes vied with each other to serve as divine spokesmen. Democratic or populist leaders associated virtue with ordinary people and exalted the vernacular in word, print, and song.[4]

The canon of American religious history grows out of traditions that are intellectually respectable and institutionally cohesive. Yet American Protestantism has been skewed away from central ecclesiastical institutions and high culture; it has been pushed and pulled into its present shape by a democratic or populist orientation. At the very time that British clergy were confounded by their own gentility in trying to influence working-class culture, America exalted religious leaders short on social graces, family connections, and literary education. These religious activists pitched their messages to the unschooled and unsophisticated. Their movements offered the humble a marvelous sense of individual potential and of collective aspiration.

Religious populism has been a residual agent of change in America over the last two centuries, an inhibitor of genteel tradition and a recurring source of new religious movements. Deep and powerful undercurrents of democratic Christianity distinguish the United States from other modern industrial democracies. These currents insure that churches in this land do not withhold faith from the rank and file. Instead, religious leaders have pursued people wherever they could be found; embraced them without regard to social standing; and challenged them to think, to interpret Scripture, and to organize the church for themselves. Religious populism, reflecting the passions of ordinary people and the charisma of democratic movement-builders, remains among the oldest and deepest impulses in American life.

The Church in an Age of Democratic Revolution

The American Revolution is the most crucial event in American history. The generation overshadowed by it and its counterpart in France stands at the fault line that separates an older world, premised on standards of deference, patronage, and ordered succession, from a newer one that continues to shape our values. The American Revolution and the beliefs flowing from it created a cultural ferment over the meaning of freedom. Turmoil swirled around the crucial issues of authority, organization, and leadership.[5]

Above all, the Revolution dramatically expanded the circle of people who considered themselves capable of thinking for themselves about issues of freedom, equality, sovereignty, and representation. Respect for authority, tradition, station, and education eroded. Ordinary people moved toward these new horizons aided by a powerful new vocabulary, a rhetoric of liberty that would not have occurred to them were it not for the Revolution. In time, the issue of the well-being of ordinary people became central to the definition of being American, public opinion came to assume normative significance, and leaders could not survive who would not, to use Patrick Henry's phrase, "bow with utmost deference to the majesty of the people." The correct solution to any important problem, political, legal, or religious, would have to appear to be the people's choice.[6] "In the early nineteenth century," Sean Wilentz has written, "to be an American citizen was by definition to be a republican, the inheritor of a revolutionary legacy in a world ruled by aristocrats and kings."[7]

This book argues that the transitional period between 1780 and 1830 left as indelible an imprint upon the structures of American Christianity as it did upon those of American political life.[8] Only land, Robert Wiebe has noted, could compete with Christianity as the pulse of a new democratic society. The age of the democratic revolutions unfolded with awesome moment for people of every social rank. Not since the English Civil War had such swift and unpredictable currents threatened the traditions of Western society. It was not merely the winning of battles and the writing of constitutions that excited apocalyptic visions in the minds of ordinary people but the realization that the very structures of society were undergoing a democratic winnowing. Political convulsions seemed cataclysmic; the cement of an ordered society seemed to be dissolving. People confronted new kinds of issues: common folk not respecting their betters, organized factions speaking and writing against civil authority, the uncoupling of church and state, and the abandonment of settled communities in droves by people seeking a stake in the back country. These events seemed so far outside the range of ordinary experience that people rushed to biblical prophecy for help in understanding the troubled times that were upon them.[9]

Amidst such acute uncertainty, many humble Christians in America began to redeem a dual legacy. They yoked strenuous demands for revivals, in the name of George Whitefield, with calls for the expansion of popular sovereignty, in the name of the Revolution. Linking these equally potent traditions sent American Christianity cascading in many creative directions in the early republic. Church authorities had few resources to restrain this surge of movements fueled by the passions of ordinary people. Nothing illustrates this better than the way in which American Methodism veered sharply away from the course of British Methodism during these years. The heavy, centralizing hand of Jabez Bunting kept British Methodism firmly grounded in traditional notions of authority and leadership. It was unthinkable to British church leaders that a radical and eccentric revivalist like the American itinerant Lorenzo Dow should be allowed to influence their congregations, and after 1800 the British leadership successfully barred Dow from their meetings. This sort of control was impossible in America. Despite the misgivings of American bishops and elders, Dow took the camp-meeting circuit by storm. His popular support prevented them from mounting a direct challenge to his authority.

A diverse array of evangelical firebands went about the task of movement-building in the generation after the Revolution. Intent on bringing evangelical conversion to the mass of ordinary Americans, they could rarely divorce that message from contagious new democratic vocabularies and impulses that swept through American popular cultures. Class structure was viewed as society's fundamental problem. There was widespread disdain for the supposed lessons of history and tradition, and a call for reform using the rhetoric of the Revolution. The press swiftly became a sword of democracy, fueling ardent faith in the future of the American republic.

At the same time, Americans who espoused evangelical and egalitarian convictions, in whatever combination, were free to experiment with new forms of organization and belief. Within a few years of Jefferson's election in 1800, it became anachronistic to speak of dissent in America—as if there were still a commonly recognized center against which new or emerging groups defined themselves. There was little to restrain a variety of new groups from vying to establish their identity as a counterestablishment. The Christian movement, the Methodists, and the Mormons all commonly referred to all other Protestant denominations as "sectarians."

The fundamental history of this period may be, as Roland Berthoff suggests, a story of things left out.[10] Churches and religious movements after 1800 operated in a climate of withering ecclesiastical establishments. The federal government, a "midget institution in a giant land," had almost no internal functions.[11] And a rampant migration of people continued to snap old networks of personal authority. American churches did not face the kind of external social and political pressures that in Great Britain often forced Christianity and liberty to march in opposite directions. Such isolation made it possible for religious outsiders to see their own destiny as part and parcel of the meaning of America itself. If the earth did belong to the living, as President Jefferson claimed, why should the successful new-comer defer to the claims of education, status, and longevity?[12]

Christianity in England, on the other hand, endured powerful buffet-ings early in the nineteenth century. Beset by radical attacks against the institutional church, by industrial strife and overt class conflict, the church battened down its conservative hatches. Anglicanism, locked in its defense of deference and paternalism, avoided the industrial areas of the Midlands and the North. The conservative alliance of squire and parson remained a distinctive feature of English life. The inescapable aura of gentility, Alan Gilbert has written, served as "a millstone around the neck of the Victorian Church in its ministrations to the masses of working and lower-middle-class people."[13]

During these years Methodist leaders in Britain were also forging alliances with the forces of law and order. In the wake of the political unrest of the French Revolution and the social disquiet of industrial workers, Methodist preachers realized that their preaching privileges depended upon their continued loyalty to the civil government. Officials continued to remind them that religious liberty was a privilege dissenters enjoyed at the discretion of magistrates. At the same time, Methodists confronted a pe-riod of social upheaval and industrial strife from which their American cousins were largely exempt. Few Americans had to make the difficult choice of being radical or loyal to the church, as English Methodists did when faced with Luddite discontent. By 1819, official Methodist state-ments made it impossible to be both a Methodist and a radical.[14] The resulting social divide within the movement thrust the poor and radical on one side and the preacher in alliance with "the leading friends" on the other.[15] Dominant leaders of Victorian Methodism in England took every opportunity to diminish popular expression and disown populist leader-ship.

Meanwhile, in America, Francis Asbury claimed it was his duty to condescend to people of low estate, and Peter Cartwright, dispensing with the trappings of respectability, recast the gospel in a familiar idiom. Most important, they welcomed hundreds of common people into the ministry, creating a cadre of preachers who felt and articulated the interests of ordinary people. In America, established religious institutions linked to the upper classes remained too weak to make a whole society accept their language and analysis. The field remained open for the repeated onslaughts of religious populists.

A Passion for Equality

America's nonrestrictive environment permitted an unexpected and often explosive conjunction of evangelical fervor and popular sovereignty. It was this engine that accelerated the process of Christianization within American popular culture, allowing indigenous expressions of faith to take hold among ordinary people, white and black. This expansion of evangelical Christianity did not proceed primarily from the nimble response of religious elites meeting the challenge before them. Rather, Christianity was effectively reshaped by common people who molded it in their own image and who threw themselves into expanding its influence. Increasingly assertive common people wanted their leaders unpretentious, their doctrines self-evident and down-to-earth, their music lively and singable, and their churches in local hands. It was this upsurge of democratic hope that characterized so many religious cultures in the early republic and brought Baptists, Methodists, Disciples of Christ, and a host of other insurgent groups to the fore. The rise of evangelical Christianity in the early republic is, in some measure, a story of the success of common people in shaping the culture after their own priorities rather than the priorities outlined by gentlemen such as the framers of the Constitution.[16]

It is easy to miss the democratic character of the early republic's insurgent religious movements. The Methodists, after all, retained power in a structured hierarchy under the control of bishops. The Mormons reverted to rule by a single religious prophet and revelator. And groups such as the Disciples of Christ, despite professed democratic structures, were eventually controlled by such powerful individuals as Alexander Campbell, who had little patience with dissent. As ecclesiastical structures, these movements often turned out to be less democratic than the congregational structure of the New England Standing Order. The rise of popular sovereignty, as Edmund S. Morgan suggests, often has involved insurgent leaders glorifying the many as a way to legitimate their own authority.[17]

The democratization of Christianity, then, has less to do with the specifics of polity and governance and more with the incarnation of the church into popular culture. In at least three respects the popular religious movements of the early republic articulated a profoundly democratic spirit. First, they denied the age-old distinction that set the clergy apart as a separate order of men, and they refused to defer to learned theologians and traditional orthodoxies. All were democratic or populist in the way they instinctively associated virtue with ordinary people rather than with elites, exalted the vernacular in word and song as the hallowed channel for communicating with and about God, and freely turned over the reigns of power.[18] These groups also shared with the Jeffersonian Republicans an overt rejection of the past as a repository of wisdom.[19] By redefining leadership itself, these movements reconstructed the foundations of religion in keeping with the values and priorities of ordinary people.

Second, these movements empowered ordinary people by taking their deepest spiritual impulses at face value rather than subjecting them to the scrutiny of orthodox doctrine and the frowns of respectable clergymen. In the last two decades of the century, preachers from a wide range of new religious movements openly fanned the flames of religious ecstasy. Rejecting the Yankee Calvinism of his youth in 1775, Henry Alline found that his soul was transported with divine love, "ravished with a divine ecstasy beyond any doubts or fears, or thoughts of being then deceived."[20] What had been defined as "enthusiasm" was increasingly advocated from the pulpit as an essential part of Christianity. Such a shift in emphasis, accompanied by rousing gospel singing rather than formal church music, reflected the common people's success in defining the nature of faith for themselves. In addition, an unprecedented wave of religious leaders in the last quarter of the eighteenth century expressed their openness to a variety of signs and wonders, in short, an admission of increased supernatural involvement in everyday life. Scores of preachers' journals, from Methodists and Baptists, from north and south, from white and black, indicated a ready acceptance to consider dreams and visions as inspired by God, normal manifestations of divine guidance and instruction. "I know the word of God is our infallible guide, and by it we are to try all our dreams and feelings," conceded the Methodist stalwart Freeborn Garrettson. But he added, "I also know, that both sleeping and waking, things of a divine nature have been revealed to me." Volatile aspects of popular religion, long held in check by the church, were recognized and encouraged from the pulpit. It is no wonder that a dismayed writer in the *Connecticut Evangelical Magazine* countered in 1805: "No person is warranted from the word of God to publish to the world the discoveries of heaven or hell which he supposes he has had in a dream, or trance, or vision."[21]

The early republic was also a democratic movement in a third sense. Religious outsiders, flushed with confidence about their prospects, had little sense of their limitations. They dreamed that a new age of religious and social harmony would naturally spring up out of their efforts to overthrow coercive and authoritarian structures.[22] This upsurge of democratic hope, this passion for equality, led to a welter of diverse and competing forms, many of them structured in highly undemocratic ways. The Methodists under Francis Asbury, for instance, used authoritarian means to build a church that would not be a respecter of persons. This church faced the curious paradox of gaining phenomenal influence among laypersons with whom it would not share ecclesiastical authority. Similarly, the Mormons used a virtual religious dictatorship as the means to return power to illiterate men. Yet despite these authoritarian structures, the fundamental impetus of these movements was to make Christianity a liberating force; people were given the right to think and act for themselves rather than depending upon the mediations of an educated elite. The most fascinating religious story of the early republic is the signal achievements of these and other populist religious leaders—outsiders who used democratic persuasions to reconstruct the foundations of religious authority.

The strands of this story can be traced through the remarkable, if largely ignored, record of these leaders' values and goals and of the religious cultures they built. These populist religious leaders were intoxicated with the potential of print. The rise of a democratic religious culture in print after 1800 put obscure prophets such as Elias Smith, Lorenzo Dow, and Theophilus Gates or black preachers such as Richard Allen or Daniel Coker on an equal footing with Jonathan Edwards or Timothy Dwight. Many of these popular figures also published far more material in their lifetimes than did America's august divines. They certainly commanded broader audiences.

Historians have often overlooked the flood of print produced by persons depicted as stalwarts of enthusiasm and anti-intellectualism.[23] Yet this material offers an unusual opportunity to enter minds unlike our own, to explore the assumptions, beliefs, and rhetorical strategies of obscure Americans who played significant roles in the religious affairs of the nation. This book seeks to plumb the pamphlets, booklets, tracts, hymnbooks, journals, and newspapers that inundated popular culture in the early republic. Particularly illuminating are the biographical accounts and journals that Methodist itinerants kept on the advice of Wesley and Asbury and that Baptists and other revivalists wrote in the tradition of Whitefield. These sources give splendid testimony to the conviction of unlearned preachers and show that their own spiritual experience had as much to commend it to the public as that of the most learned. This book grows out of the wealth and diversity of these sources and the popular ideologies they poignantly convey.

Populist Leaders and Democratic Movements

This is a book about popular religion which focuses, ironically, upon elites—or at least upon those persons who rose to leadership positions in a wide range of popular American churches and religious movements. Using democratic leadership as an organizing principle complements other approaches: the evolution of individual denominations; the clash of theological debate; the outworking of ethnic and regional patterns; the dynamics of recurring revival; or the flourishing of popular religion outside Christian institutions. The theme of democratic leadership brings into sharper focus certain deep and recurring patterns in American religious history.

At the outset, it is important to note several things that such a book about leaders and movements is not. First, it is not primarily a denominational study. Instead, it cuts across the popular culture of the years 1780 to 1830 in order to pose questions about the relationship between leaders and constituents that may be common to a variety of religious groups. In addressing themes common to this era, I risk slighting the particularities of individual religious traditions. Although Roman Catholicism in this period experienced a measure of democratic ferment, this book has an explicit Protestant focus in order to trace the rise of a full-fledged populist clergy.[24]

In the same vein, I focus on common developments rather than those characteristic of a given region such as the South, the "Burned-Over District," the frontier, or of a local town or county. The choice to study common developments springs from a conviction that certain underlying cultural dynamics of this period are not reducible to distinct regional characteristics.[25] The flowering of Methodism, of the Christian movement, or of black Christianity cannot be explained by focusing attention on a single section of the country. This is not to say that certain common impulses, such as a clamor to retain local authority, did not reinforce regional perspectives. Yet no section of the new nation was exempt from a democratic upsurge in religious matters.

This study also does not attempt to trace the social composition of religious groups: who joined churches, under what conditions, and with what effect. Instead of concentrating on the background of constituents, this work focuses upon the religious leaders themselves, particularly those who mastered the democratic art of persuasion and on that rock built significant religious movements. The agitations of these insurgents brought into being new churches and denominations in which authority depended not on education, status, ordination, or state support, but on the ability to move people and retain their confidence. The reality of lay preachers confused the carefully wrought distinction between pulpit and pew.

I have chosen to focus this study on issues of religious leadership and movement-building. The most unusual feature of Christianity in this era is its remarkable set of popular leaders. Not since the crusading vigor of the early Puritans or of first-generation Methodists had an English-speaking culture produced a generation of so many rootless, visionary young preachers. Alienated from conventional religious forms, these bold intruders pursued their divergent courses with remarkably similar dispositions. Their faces set like flint, they proclaimed the gospel with an amazing energy, self-sacrifice, and missionary zeal. Henry Alline, for instance, a farmer and tanner from Rhode Island, unleashed his fiery evangelism upon the whole of Nova Scotia on the eve of the American Revolution. He died in 1784 at the age of thirty-five after less than a decade of relentless labor and driving asceticism. Recalling his experience in the Kentucky Revival at the turn of the century, Richard McNemar, a Methodist-turned-Presbyterian-turned-Christian-turned-Shaker, captured his generation's fervor:

> As full of zeal and pure desire
> As e're a coal was full of fire
> I flash'd & blazed by day and night
> a burning & a shining light.[26]

Leaders without formal training (Barton Stone, the Christian; William Miller, the Adventist; Francis Asbury, the Methodist; John Leland, the Baptist; Richard Allen, the African Methodist Episcopal; and Joseph Smith, the Latter-Day Saint) went outside normal denominational frameworks to develop large followings by the democratic art of persuasion. These are inherently interesting personalities, unbranded individualists, who chose to storm heaven by the back door. Widely diverse in religious convictions, they were alike in their ability to portray, in compelling terms, the deepest hopes and aspirations of popular constituencies. It was said that Joseph Smith had "his own original eloquence, peculiar to himself, not polished, not studied, not smoothed and softened by education and refined by art."[27] A New England clergyman, who resented uneducated and unrefined greenhorns presuming to speak in the Lord's name, put it this way: "They measure the progress of religion by the numbers who flock to their standards, not by the prevalence of faith and piety, justice and charity and the public virtues in society in general."[28] This new style of gospel minister, remarkably attuned to popular sentiment, amazed Tocqueville. "Where I expect to find a priest," he said, "I find a politician."[29]

These individuals were reacting to deep cultural shifts transforming the relationship between leaders and people; focusing on the issue of leadership allows a clear view of this process. Most important, it shows that the fundamental religious debates in the early republic were not merely a clash of intellectual and theological differences but also a passionate social struggle with power and authority. Deep-seated class antagonism separated clergy from clergy.[30] The learned and orthodox disdained early Methodism's new revival measures, notions of free will, and perfectionism. But they despaired that the wrong sort of people had joined Methodism— people who rejected social authority's claim to religious power.[31] While the eighteenth century had seen a steady growth of authority based on popular appeal, particularly in various forms of religious dissent, the Revolution quickened the pace. Those who defended clerical authority as the right of a gentry minority were pitted against rough-hewn leaders who denied the right of any one class of people to speak for another. The early republic witnessed a popular displacement of power from the uncommon man, the man of ideas in American politics and religion. It is the intent of this study to tell at least part of this complicated story: how ordinary folk came to distrust leaders of genius and talent and to defend the right of common people to shape their own faith and submit to leaders of their own choosing.

This story also provides new insight into how America became a liberal, competitive, and market-driven society. In an age when most ordinary Americans expected almost nothing from government institutions and almost everything from religious ones, popular religious ideologies were perhaps the most important bellwethers of shifting worldviews. The passion for equality during these years equaled the passionate rejection of the past. Rather than looking backward and clinging to an older moral economy, insurgent religious leaders espoused convictions that were essentially modern and individualistic. These convictions defied elite privilege and vested interests and anticipated a millennial dawn of equality and justice. Yet, to achieve these visions of the common good, they favored means inseparable from the individual's pursuit of spiritual and temporal well-being. They assumed that the leveling of aristocracy, root and branch, would naturally draw people together in harmony and equality. In this way, religious movements eager to preserve the supernatural in everyday life had the ironic effect of accelerating the break-up of traditional society and the advent of a social order of competition, self-expression, and free enterprise. In this moment of democratic aspiration, religious leaders could not foresee that their assault upon mediating structures could produce a society in which grasping entrepreneurs could erect new forms of tyranny in religious, political, and economic institutions.[32]

A study of popular religious leadership illuminates the dynamics of church growth during the so-called Second Great Awakening.[33] Studies of Christian advance in this era, like those of eighteenth-century revivals, have focused on the latent conditions present in the social structure of given communities. The age, gender, income, and kinship patterns of individuals and the population, size, and location of churches have been used to explain varying responses to revivalism. This approach makes good sense given an identifiable community in which there are a limited number of social variables and a stable system of communications. The parish structure of New England in the century after 1730 provides a superb laboratory for this kind of study.[34]

The expanding republic, though, bore little resemblance to the New England town with its steady habits and social continuities. In a pluralistic, mobile, and competitive religious environment, an audience-oriented inter-pretation has only limited value, particularly in studying the rise of dissi-dent movements whose preachers and audiences were characteristically mobile. In a climate of volatile audiences and innovative communications, it is instructive to analyze matters from the perspective of those religious entrepreneurs who worked to capture popular attention. With the rise of fierce religious competition, movements that employed more aggressive measures prospered. Churches reluctant to compete on the same terms declined. A recent study of the Second Great Awakening in Baltimore, for instance, concludes that variables on the supply rather than the demand side of the religious equation best explained the dynamics of revivalism. Evangelical religion prospered "largely because the price was right and the streets were filled with vendors."[35]

This book is organized topically and chronologically. It is divided into four sections, each consisting of two chapters. The two middle sections are topical assessments of the heyday of religious populism from 1800 to 1830. This material is bracketed by chapters (2 and 7) that construe the story on a more chronological axis. Chapter 2 assesses the conditions that triggered this democratic upsurge, the currents of democratic dissent that churned angrily in America from the debate over the Constitution to the election of Jefferson. A widespread crisis of authority alienated many common folk from gentry culture and its churches and gave them new expressions of the supernatural and new vocabularies of popular sovereignty. A tangle of diverse roots nourished the formation of new religious movements.

While all of Christian history is, in some sense, a dialectic between atomization and authority, the early republic was the most centrifugal epoch in American church history. It was a time when the momentum of events pushed toward the periphery and subverted centralized authority and professional expertise. Yet the white-hot intensity of early Disciples,

Methodists, Baptists, and Mormons grew cool over time. Cultural alienation gave way to a pilgrimage toward respectability. By 1840 populist dissent had diminished in American Christianity, but the democratic revolution had left a permanent imprint on the denominational landscape. Chapter 7 considers the threefold process that shaped denominational structures in America at the close of the period in question: the continuing influence of democratic persuasions upon established traditions, the taming effects of respectability upon insurgents, and, in reaction, the fresh appeal of democratic firebrands.

Religious populism has remained a creative, if unsettling, force at the fringes of major Protestant denominations. More than lawyers or physicians, American clergy have remained subject to democratic forces. In the first third of the nineteenth century, a stiff democratic challenge shattered the professional monopoly of educated elite over law, medicine, and the church. State laws permitted almost anyone to practice law, and various brands of medical practice were allowed to compete for the public's attention. Yet in the twentieth century, doctors and lawyers have reasserted their professional prerogatives. The American Medical Association and the American Bar Association now serve as powerful monopolies. A free-market economy continues in the field of religion, however, and credentialing, licensing, or statutory control is absent. This hands-off position is sacrosanct because of fixed notions about the separation of church and state and because of the long-standing voluntary principle within churches.

The rise of democratic Christianity in the early United States is riddled with irony, unrealistic hope, and unfulfilled expectations. A central theme of the chapters that follow is the unintended results of people's actions. Attempting to erase the difference between leaders and followers, Americans opened the door to religious demagogues. Despite popular acclaim, these leaders could exercise tyranny unimagined by elites in the more controlled environment of the colonial era. Likewise, a deep sensitivity to audience resulted in values of the audience shaping the message's contours. The quest for unity that drove people to discard formal theology for the Scriptures drove them further asunder. Yet Americans continue to maintain their right to shape their own faith and to submit to leaders they have chosen. Over the last two centuries, an egalitarian culture has given rise to a diverse array of powerful religious leaders, whose humble origins and common touch seem strangely at odds with the authoritarian mantle that people allow them to assume. The tapestry of American Protestantism is richly colored with interwoven strands of populist strength and authoritarian weakness.

CHAPTER TWO

The Crisis of Authority
in Popular Culture

> *"But alas I felt like one wandering and benighted in an unknown wilderness, that wants both a light and guide. The bible was like a sealed book, so mysterious I could not understand it, and in order to hear it explained, I applied to this person and that book; but got no satisfactory instruction, I frequently wished I had lived in the days of the prophets or apostles, that I could have had sure guides."*
>
> LORENZO DOW, *1804*

By 1814 Timothy Dwight, the president of Yale, had ample cause for good cheer. Under his tutelage, a remarkable coalition of talented leaders had developed and were now coming to maturity across New England. Innovative and forward looking, Dwight's disciples were revitalizing Calvinism as both an intellectual and a spiritual force. The collaborations of activists such as Lyman Beecher and Asahel Nettleton and theologians such as Moses Stuart and Nathaniel William Taylor gave evangelical Calvinism a firmer foundation than it had known since the days of Dwight's grandfather, Jonathan Edwards. The founding of Andover Seminary in 1808 stood as a strategic outpost for orthodoxy; new magazines and voluntary societies mobilized the faithful; and religious revivals were revitalizing congregations across New England, by one estimate in as many as one hundred and fifty towns.[1]

Buoyed by these local prospects, a contingent of like-minded Yankees used the occasion of Yale's commencement in 1814 to broaden their endeavors. They convened in New Haven to establish a new charitable society. The organization's immediate aim was to provide scholarships for poorer young men to attend Yale; its ultimate goal was to spread proper religious instruction across the expanding republic. On this occasion, Lyman Beecher addressed the full leadership corps of what would come to be known as New England's Second Great Awakening. Among them were

Timothy Dwight, Tapping Reeve, Nathaniel W. Taylor, Jedediah Morse, Herman Humphreys, and Bennett Tyler.

At one level Beecher's address was entirely predictable. He set before his peers the unprecedented number of new ministers required to serve the young nation and challenged the men of Yale to provide financial assistance for worthy candidates. Yet there was also a puzzling undercurrent in Beecher's remarks. It was not simply his tone of pessimism as he cast his eye over the broad expanse of America and found "a scene of destitution and wretchedness little realized by the people of this state."[2] One might well expect an anguished tone as this stern Yankee looked beyond Connecticut's borders to assess a sprawling republic whose citizens often thumbed their noses at the steady habits of New England religious life. Yet neither the outright rejection of orthodoxy nor the religious vacuum of the frontier drew Beecher's direct fire.

Instead, what agitated Beecher was that a certain kind of Christianity was flourishing. After declaring that the whole of the United States could boast only "3000 educated ministers of the Gospel," Beecher called for five thousand new recruits, men who could train at a place such as Yale and thus rescue the people of America from another kind of religious leader who presumed to speak about matters divine: "There may be, perhaps, 1500 besides who are nominally ministers of the Gospel. But they are generally illiterate men, often not possessed of a good English education, and in some instances unable to read or write. By them, as a body, learning is despised. With few exceptions they are utterly unacquainted with theology and like other men are devoted through the week to secular employment, and preach on the Sabbath, with such preparation as such an education and such avocations allow." Beecher went on to spell out the grave effects of people being "exposed to the errors of enthusiastic and false teachers." Illiterate teachers could not stand as pillars of civilization and moral influence, nor could they command the attention of "that class of the community which is above their own," wielding "that religious and moral and literary influence which it belongs to the Ministry to exert."[3] Ordinary vessels who attempted to proclaim the gospel would certainly incur scorn and contempt, in Beecher's opinion. "When its chosen advocates are ignorant and unlettered men," Beecher reasoned, the gospel is "totally incompetent" to arrest human depravity. "Illiterate men have never been the chosen instruments of God to build up his cause." As an afterthought to this assertion, and as if to anticipate an obvious objection, Beecher explained that the twelve disciples were instructed by Christ himself for three years "to supply the deficiency of an education."[4]

At the opening of Andover Seminary a few years earlier, Timothy

Dwight had sounded the same note of alarm. While Andover may have been created to serve as a citadel to defend theological orthodoxy, Dwight chose the occasion of its inaugural sermon to sight his cannons elsewhere. His opening remarks were a sustained volley against the ignorant teacher, the mere "Empiric" who professed to communicate what he did not possess, offering hearers chaff instead of wheat. Dwight denounced those persons

> who declare, both in their language and conduct, that the desk ought to be yielded up to the occupancy of Ignorance. While they demand a seven-years apprenticeship, for the purpose of learning to make a shoe, or an axe; they suppose the system of Providence, together with the numerous, and frequently abstruse, doctrines and precepts, contained in the Scriptures, may be all comprehended without learning labour, or time. While they insist, equally with others, that their property shall be managed by skilful agents, their judicial causes directed by learned advocates, and their children, when sick, attended by able physicians; they were satisfied to place their Religion, their souls, and their salvation, under the guidance of quackery.[5]

Timothy Dwight, like Beecher, linked the fate of Christianity to the reputation of its ministers. He assumed that the clergy were to be a separate order of men capable of elevating "mankind at large" by their respectability, seriousness, intelligence, and piety—"the decorum and dignity, which are indispensable in the desk." By the same token, if ministers appeared contemptible, ignorant, and vulgar, religion itself would sink to a sordid level and "be regarded, not by superior minds only, but ultimately by the people at large, as a system of groveling doctrines, and debasing precepts, lowering the character of man to a degree, beneath even his natural degradation." In this vein, Dwight was delighted that Andover had established one of its five professorships in "the eloquence of the Desk."[6]

It is difficult to understand the intensity of Beecher's and Dwight's reactions apart from the radically different conceptions of the ministry that had come to be proclaimed boldly in their own backyard. Even as Beecher spoke in New Haven, his own parish of Litchfield, Connecticut, was being besieged by the Methodist firebrand Billy Hibbard. The son of a tanner and shoemaker whose father had played an active role in Shays's Rebellion, Hibbard boasted three hundred converts in 1814 alone on the Litchfield circuit.[7] Hibbard took considerable offense that Beecher would dwell on the "wretchedness" of America's people and slander uneducated ministers as "worse than nothing." In response, he published a lengthy rebuttal in which he challenged the very foundations of traditional New England religious life, including the "habit of believing the testimonies of great men that bear sacred titles."[8]

Billy Hibbard was not the only Methodist itinerant to take note of Beecher's aspersion of common preachers. In his discourse *On Church Government*, Lorenzo Dow found in Beecher's condescension "a Snake in the grass." "I see no gospel law that authorizes any man, or set of men, to forbid, or put up bars to hinder or stop any man from preaching the gospel." Denying the right of church authority to coerce the individual, Dow appealed to two simple criteria: divine evidence in the soul and the effectiveness and power of demonstrated preaching. Freeborn Garrettson also interpreted Beecher's address as a direct attack upon the Methodists. He countered with membership statistics to show how well the Methodists had evangelized those areas that Beecher labeled religiously destitute.[9]

But it was the actual preaching of Hibbard, Garrettson, and Dow, rather than the sparrings with Beecher, that was so powerfully effective. In his memoirs, written in the 1850s, Samuel Goodrich, the publisher of Boston's first daily newspaper, recalled the terrific stir that Dow created when he invaded a parish in Ridgefield, Connecticut, where Goodrich's father served as minister: "Lorenzo was not only uncouth in his person and appearance, but his voice was harsh, his action hard and rectangular. It is scarcely possible to conceive of a person more entirely destitute of all natural eloquence. But he understood common life, and especially vulgar life—its tastes, prejudices, and weaknesses; and he possessed a cunning knack of adapting his discourses to such audiences."[10] Goodrich recalls the grave concern of his father and other respectable clergymen as they watched people straying into new folds and identifying with commoners who preached. His account of the preaching of one "gifted Poundtext" illustrates why the evangelical stalwarts of Yale were gravely concerned:

> What I insist, upon my brethren and sisters, is this: larnin isn't religion, and eddication don't give a man the power of the Spirit. It is grace and gifts that furnish the real live coals from off the altar. St. Peter was a fisherman—do you think he ever went to Yale College? No, no, beloved brethren and sisters. When the Lord wanted to blow down the walls of Jericho, he didn't take a brass trumpet, or a polished French horn: no such thing; he took a ram's horn—a plain, natural ram's horn—just as it grew. And so, when he wants to blow down the walls of the spiritual Jericho, my beloved brethren and sisters, he don't take one of your smooth, polite, college larnt gentlemen, but a plain, natural ram's-horn sort of man like me.[11]

During these years, Yale men were not the only ones bewildered by commoners deigning to speak in God's name. In Salem, Massachusetts, even the tolerant Jeffersonian diarist, William Bentley, was shocked at the religious assault on well-bred and high-toned culture. As late as 1803, Bentley had confided smugly that Essex County remained virtually free of sects. During the next five years, however, he watched with dismay as the lower orders of his community championed "religious convulsions," "domestic fanaticism," and "Meeting-Mania." Chronicling the parade of sects that won attention—Baptist, Freewill Baptist, Methodist, Universalist, and Christian—Bentley noted the first field meeting in the county since George Whitefield, preaching by blacks and illiterate sailors, and servants angering their employers by frequenting night lectures "as in Mother [Anne] Hutchinson's time." What Bentley found most appalling was that "the rabble" not only noised abroad strange doctrine but actually went beyond what they were told in the attempt "to explain, commend and reveal" religious matters. The people, he groaned, were doing theology for themselves.[12]

In Virginia, the evangelical Episcopalian Devereux Jarratt was beset with the same woes. A devoted friend of evangelical causes prior to the Revolution, by the 1790s Jarratt has come to fear the volatile mix of things evangelical and egalitarian. Bemoaning the leveling spirit in "our high republican times," he recoiled from new expressions of Christianity "under the supreme control of tinkers and tailors, weavers, shoemakers, and country mechanics of all kinds."[13] A similar assessment of turn-of-the-century religious conditions in Kentucky and Ohio was made by David Rice, a former student of Samuel Davies in Virginia and the first permanent Presbyterian minister in the state of Kentucky. At the request of the Presbyterian General Assembly, he wrote two reports in which he deplored the "unrestrained freedom" that had turned the western country into a "hot-bed of every extravagance of opinion and practice."[14] Rice took particular offence at the audacity of young people who reshaped the faith in their own hands without recourse to age and experience.[15] Rice warned that such a spirit of ignorance and vanity "has led others to think themselves called of God to preach the gospel, and to go on, relying on their inward call, and neglecting almost every ministerial qualification required in the sacred Scriptures. Some of them utter a strange mixture of sense and non-sense, truth and error, medicine and poison, with as much confidence as if all been [sic] inspired by infinite wisdom. No preachers less qualified, and none more confident."[16]

These incidents are graphic illustrations that the religious history of the early republic is anything but evolutionary and consensual. To be sure, staid Presbyterian and Congregational churchmen did gradually develop a more active, voluntaristic style to accord with disestablishment, and the function of the ministry did shift almost imperceptibly from that of an office to that of a profession.[17] Yet focusing only on these developments masks the turbulence and bitter struggles for authority that characterize American Christianity from 1790 to 1820. The challenge of adjusting existing denominations to the realities of disestablishment paled before this fundamental debate about religious authority.[18] To the consternation of respectable clergymen, the terms of that debate were set largely by people who had not known status, influence, or power. This stringent populist challenge to the religious establishment included violent anticlericalism, a flaunting of conventional religious deportment, a disdain for the wrangling of theologians, an assault on tradition, and an assertion that common people were more sensitive than elites to the ways of the divine. In order to understand the dynamics of this complicated struggle for religious authority, it will be helpful to consider the broader crisis of authority that dominated popular culture in the years after the Revolution.

Ferment over Who Should Rule at Home

In 1776, John Adams posed the question that would preoccupy his generation of Americans and the next. "It is certain, in theory," he mused, "that the only moral foundation of government is, the consent of the people. But to what extent shall we carry this principle?" The Revolution brought an accent of reality to the sovereignty of the people, a new self-evident truth, which Edmund Morgan has described as a "political fiction." For the founding fathers the fiction of popular sovereignty bore some resemblance to the facts, but they fully expected the governed and the governors to "join in a benign conspiracy to suspend disbelief," that is, to believe it rhetorically rather than literally. The people were not so kind. From Adams to Jackson a shrill and unending debate weighed how seriously this fiction should be taken.[19]

A number of scholars have recently explored the dimensions of this cultural ferment over the meaning of freedom. In the wake of the American and French revolutions, Americans witnessed the rapid growth of voluntary organizations and popular newspapers, the formation of organized political parties amid heated popular debate, the armed protest of unprotected economic groups, sharp attacks upon elite professions and slavery, and new ideas of citizenship, representation, old age, and women's identity.[20] Three times during these years Americans deliberated on fundamental propositions about government. Each time—during the Revolution, during the debate over the Constitution, and during the political passion of the 1790s—the issue of popular participation in government flared up with greater intensity. Pressing questions about liberty, authority, and popular sovereignty became "deadly business" for everyone.[21] Historians are presently paying more attention to how violent, messy, and decisive the American Revolution was. The rejection of an ancient regime and the struggle to establish a new social and political order involved intense social strain and dislocation toward the end of the eighteenth century. John Murrin suggests that the Revolution reversed the dominant integrative trend of eighteenth-century America, shattering the most venerable habits, customs, and loyalties. This vast transformation, this shift away from the Enlightenment and classical republicanism toward vulgar democracy and materialistic individualism in a matter of decades, was the real American Revolution. For many Americans the cultural crisis was severe as any in American history and they fought strenuously over the fundamentals of their own revolution in the midst of profound changes in economic, social, and political life.[22]

This crisis of confidence in a hierarchical, ordered society demanded fundamental reform in politics, communications, law, medicine, and religion. In each of these areas, radical Jeffersonians, seizing upon issues close to the hearts of the people, resurrected "the spirit of 1776" to protect elite control and the force of tradition. Rhetoric that had once unified people across the social spectrum now drove a powerful wedge between rich and poor, elite and commoner, privileged classes and the people. Federalists, members of the bar, and the professional clergy heard the wisdom of the ages ridiculed as mere connivances of the powerful to maintain the status quo. They heard challenges to any authority that did not spring from volitional allegiance.[23]

The violence of politics from 1780 to 1800 gave sharp definition to egalitarian impulses in American society. From the Revolution onward, republican equality became the rallying cry for a people who challenged every kind of political authority. Incidents in South Carolina, Massachusetts, and New York illustrate how thoroughly the "virtue" of subjection and deference was giving way to an itching, smarting, writhing awareness of inferiority. In 1784, the South Carolina legislature threatened William Thompson, a tavern keeper, with banishment from the state for insulting the eminent John Rutledge. Thompson responded with a newspaper article that blasted the claims of "self-exalted" characters such as Rutledge who had "conceived me his inferior." Thompson refused to "comprehend the *inferiority*" and denied the right of a conspicuous few to speak for the people.[24] During the debate over the Constitution, Anti-Federalists turned repeatedly to such arguments. At the Massachusetts ratification convention, for example, the self-taught Worcester County farmer Amos Singletary denounced the Constitution as a plot to consolidate the influence of the great: "these lawyers and men of learning, and moneyed men . . . talk so finely, and gloss over matters so smoothly, to make us poor illiterate people swallow down the pill. . . . They expect to be the managers of this Constitution, and get all the power and all the money into their own hands. And then they will swallow up us little fellows, like the great Leviathan."[25]

A decade later the urban democratic leader William Keteltas was able to shake Federalist control of New York City by a shrewd media campaign depicting politics as a clash between rich and poor. Ketaltas touted the case of two Irish-born ferrymen whom Federalist magistrates punished summarily for reportedly insulting one of their number. Dramatizing this cause célèbre in the popular press, Ketaltas attacked the New York assembly for not impeaching the responsible magistrates. This led to his own arrest by the Federalist legislature on a charge of breach of privilege. When Ketaltas appeared before the assembly, a crowd of several thousand gathered in protest. His release from a brief prison sentence prompted a grand celebration in which the people pulled Ketaltas through the streets in a carriage decked with American and French flags, a cap of liberty, and a picture of a man being whipped with the inscription, "What you rascal, insult your superiors?" By championing the cause of the ferrymen, which he described as "the most flagrant abuse of [the people's] rights since Independence," Ketaltas effectively mobilized the common people of New York to challenge Federalist domination.[26]

Such repeated attacks on the capacity of a conspicuous few to speak for the whole society struck at the root of traditional conceptions of society.[27] Extending the logic of Anti-Federalists, radical Jeffersonians came to ridicule the assumption that society was an organic hierarchy of ranks and degrees. They argued that it was a heterogeneous mixture of many different classes, orders, interest groups, and occupations. In such a society the elites could no longer claim to be adequate spokesmen for people in general. In this climate, it took little creativity for some to begin to reexamine the social function of the clergy and to question the right of any order of men to claim authority to interpret God's Word. If opinions about politics and society were no longer the monopoly of the few, why could not people begin to think for themselves in matters of religion?

These reforms gained a new intensity toward the close of the century with the rapid expansion of a Jeffersonian press of vigorous dissent. The American Revolution made newspaper reading a way of life for many.[28] At the same time, freedom of the press increasingly stood less for impartial reporting and more for taking tough stands against tyranny in whatever form. In short, the Revolution had seen the press expand its role as a medium to express a politics of tension and dissent.[29] Against this backdrop, the Sedition Act, clamping down on the dissent that had become the hallmark of the press during the Revolution, made the issue of freedom of the press anything but an abstract constitutional issue in the election of 1800. Threats against a free press riveted the attention of many on the necessity of countering Federalist propaganda with a literature of the people.[30]

One has only to sample the Jeffersonian press in the decade after 1798 to note how many average Americans came to see it as a patriotic duty to begin speaking their own minds and breaking into print. A writer identifying himself as "Baptist" wrote in *The Patriot, or Scourge of Aristocracy* (Stonington-Port, Connecticut) in 1801 to explain how he could no longer remain "neuter in opinion in politics. I have formerly been what is generally called a federalist, a lover of order . . . duped to believe that we must follow the old beaten track laid down by our rulers and priests, without examining whether it was right or wrong." The tyranny he perceived in John Adams's administration, however, convinced him to move beyond a posture of deference: "But of late I began to suspect that every class of people have a right to shew their opinions on points which immediately concern them."[31] In the same journal, another writer argued that because "the people are the ultimate judges" of government, they must interpret freedom of the press to mean the actual process of disseminating information.[32]

Between 1790 and 1810 the United States witnessed an explosive growth in the number of newspapers—from 90 to 370. More important, an overt popularization changed the very character of the medium. Responding to a wider democratic public, papers increasingly employed communication strategies that conspired against any form of social distinction: blunt and vulgar language, crude oratory, and sharp ridicule of lawyers, physicians, and clergymen.[33] Studies by Alfred F. Young and Howard B. Rock have demonstrated the crucial role that the press played in New York City, drawing mechanics into the political process and firing them with a new sense of electoral power and self-esteem.[34] Given these qualitative changes within journalism, it is little wonder that gentlemen such as Timothy Dwight came to equate the reading of newspapers with tavern-haunting, drinking, and gambling.[35]

The career of the Boston radical Benjamin Austin, Jr., superbly captures the interrelated protests against elite control of politics, law, religion, and the press. As successor to Samuel Adams as the leader and favorite of the Boston crowd, Austin held various town offices during the 1780s and frequently contributed to the popular press. He opposed the Constitution in 1787, led a democratic club, and sat in the state Senate. During the 1790s, this "Democratic *enragee*" incurred the wrath of Federalists more than any other man in Massachusetts on account of his talents as a writer—he was probably the ablest polemicist in the state. Austin gained national reputation in 1786 for a series of articles attacking the legal profession in Boston's *Independent Chronicle*. Later published as *Observations on the Pernicious Practice of the Law*, Austin's articles became the single most effective protest in the broader move for legal reform.[36]

Throughout the 1790s, Austin kept egalitarian principles before the people with regular articles in the *Independent Chronicle*. He continued to argue for "the benevolence and dignity of the people" and to assail the tyranny of the Federalists and the legal profession. Yet by the late 1790s he had identified another threat to democracy. He redirected his fire toward the Standing Order of New England, which had aligned the cause of God with that of high-toned Federalism. Austin called for common people to throw off the yoke of "proud priests" who attempted to enslave their conscience: "It is degrading to an American to take every thing on trust, and even the young farmer and tradesman should scorn to surrender their right of judging either to *lawyers or priests*."[37] With an exegesis of Scripture that bordered on a class analysis of society, Austin insisted that the people had always had an instinct for truth and virtue. The multitude had received Christ with great acclaim, with shouts of hosanna, while "the *monarchical, aristocratical* and *priestly* authorities cried crucify him." The Scribes and Pharisees would have killed Jesus sooner, "but they feared the people." In this scenario, the elites were the ones prone to evil and poised to violate principles of social order.[38] What underscores the significance of Austin's polemic is clear evidence that people—common people—were listening.

The case of William Manning serves as a graphic illustration of the influence of Austin's *Independent Chronicle* upon common people. Manning's essay *The Key of Libberty* represents the rarest kind of historical evidence, a window on the mind of a man who would generally be considered among "the inarticulate." An uneducated farmer from Billerica, Massachusetts, Manning put pen to paper in 1798—forming letters one by one like a child—to protest a supposed Federalist plot to renege on the principles of the American Revolution. Manning, who admitted to "have bin a Constant Reader of publick Newspapers," hoped to have the piece published in the *Independent Chronicle*, the primary catalyst of his own thought.[39] Too crude and too radical even for that out-and-out Jeffersonian paper, the manuscript illustrates the power of the popular press to crystallize for common people impulses they may not have had vocabularies to express. To a remarkable degree, Manning's indictment of elites in the name of the American Revolution parallels the views of *Chronicle* publicists such as Benjamin Austin.

In the first place, Manning insisted that what troubled the republic was a fundamental conflict between the few and the many, "a Conceived Difference of Interests Between those that Labour for a Living & those that git a Living without Bodily Labour." Manning was incensed that those who did an honest day's work stood powerless before the well-organized "ordirs": "the marchent, phesition the lawyer and divine and all the literary walkes of Life, the Jutical & Executive oficeers & all the rich who live without bodily labour." What Manning found most galling was the condescension of these gentlemen: "the ordirs of men generally associate together and look down with too much contempt on those that labour. . . . they cant bare to be on a leavel with their fellow cretures." In order to destroy free government, Manning argued, common people had only to continue the pattern that had been drummed into them, to submit to "a few leeding men." Most of all, this agitated soul feared that people would continue to recognize authorities, "to take for truth whatever they [the elites] say without examining for themselves."[40]

His conviction that people had the task of sorting out truth for themselves led Manning to propose new forms of organization and new means of communication. Impressed by the power of association, Manning proposed that "the many" follow the lead of the elites in banding together for a common purpose. He even went so far as to suggest that farmers and laborers use the Society of the Cincinnati as a model for their own organizations. Manning hoped that these popular associations would be instrumental in bringing about a communications revolution; he charged them to bypass the regular press—too expensive and too Federalist for the multitudes—and "to invent the cheapest & most expeditious method of conveying "knowledge to the people. These plans projected upon society the same process of political awakening that Manning had experienced through the popular press.[41]

Revolt against the Professions

The 1790s also witnessed fundamental challenges to the legal profession, orthodox medicine, and the ministry as an office. Richard E. Ellis has documented the strident attacks against the legal system that surfaced in the popular press and in serious political movements to reform the law in Kentucky, Pennsylvania, and Massachusetts.[42] Radical republicans such as Boston's Austin denounced the legal profession for needlessly confusing court cases in order to charge high fees, deliberately making the law inaccessible to laymen, bartering justice to those who could afford to pay, and monopolizing legislative and judicial posts. Early in the new century, legal reform also became a heated issue in the middle states after Delaware's Jesse Higgins led a crusade against the common law and the aristocracy of the legal profession in a series of articles in the *Aurora* and then republished them as a pamphlet.[43]

Those who called for radical legal reform addressed three primary issues. First, they demanded a simplified and easily accessible legal process, "a system of laws of our own, dictated by the genuine principles of Republicanism and made easy to be understood to every individual in the community."[44] Second, they attempted to replace the common law—authority by precedent—with fresh legal codes designed for the new republic. For many of these radicals, the common law conjured up images of complexity, mystery, intolerance, and bias in favor of the elite: "Shall we be directed by reason, equity, and a few simple and plain laws, promptly executed, or shall we be ruled by volumes of statutes and cases decided by the ignorance and intolerance of former times?"[45] Third, having jettisoned the "monkist priesthood" of lawyers and the "absurdity of the common law," those who sought root-and-branch reform exhibited great faith in the ability of ordinary citizens to ascertain and dispense justice before the law. "Any person of common abilities," said Austin, "can easily distinguish between right and wrong" and "more especially when the parties are admitted to give a plain story, without any puzzle from lawyers."[46]

In retrospect, this faith in democratic, personalized, and simplified law appears hopelessly naive. Yet it reflects a moment of historical optimism, a time when many in politics, law, and religion, flushed with the promise of the American Revolution, found it reasonable to take literally the meaning of *novus ordo seclorum* and to declare a decisive expatriation from the past.[47]

Popular disillusionment with orthodox medicine also blossomed at the turn of the century. The clearest example is that of Samuel Thomson, an uneducated practitioner of natural remedies who learned his botanic medicine in rural New Hampshire at the close of the eighteenth century. After 1800 he extended his practice into Essex County, Massachusetts, where he became embroiled in a series of personal and legal conflicts with the regular medical profession. At the behest of one of their number, a grand jury indicted Thomson for murder in 1809 after one of his patients died. Although the Supreme Judicial Court of Massachusetts acquitted Thomson of the charges, he resolved to broadcast his defiance of the medical profession.[48] In 1816 he began work on an autobiographical narrative describing his system of botanic family medicine. His partner in the publishing venture was the indomitable preacher Elias Smith, who also was active in the protest against the established medical profession.[49] Although Smith and Thomson quarreled repeatedly and in the early 1820s developed competing systems of natural medicine, both championed the idea that Americans must throw off the oppressive yoke of clergymen, lawyers, and physicians. Americans, argued Thomson, "should in medicine, as in religion and politics, act for themselves."[50] Returning to natural remedies, common people were to break the stranglehold of the medical profession and resist such treatments as bleeding and blistering and such drugs as mercury and opium.

By the 1830s Thomsonian medicine was challenging the medical establishment in every state beyond the eastern seaboard. What is significant for our purposes are the methods Thomson hammered out early in the century to advance the cause of democratic medicine. In a flurry of pamphlets and journals, Thomsonians made their case by weaving together powerful democratic themes. In the first place, their system drew upon folk beliefs of rural society, where a great deal of medical practice was inevitably domestic. Lobelia, for instance, Thomson's primary medicine, had been used as an emetic by the Penobscot Indians, who communicated knowledge of its functions to Yankee settlers.[51] What made the system appear anything but traditional, however, was that it was linked to the egalitarian rhetoric of the Revolution and flouted the authority of elites and the "speculative" norms of traditional medical education—"the refined taste of the learned Latin and Greeklings of this learned age."[52] Thomsonians also expressed a buoyant faith that, in medicine, "people are certainly capable of judging for themselves."[53] In the end, each person had the potential to become his or her own physician.

The rise of Thomsonian medicine suggests the affinity in the early republic between sectarian medicine, republican politics, and religious dissent. Thomson espoused republican politics in no uncertain terms. One of his defenders made the claim that opposition to him in Essex County stemmed from his daring "to be a republican in a hot bed of federalism."[54] Thomson, for his part, once suggested that it was as impossible "that one of the learned professions can be a republican, as it is for ice to produce heat."[55] Given this posture, it is hardly surprising to find that Thomson's practice in Essex County thrived among religious dissenters. Elias Smith and Lorenzo Dow became significant promoters of sectarian medicine. John Leland openly despised the pretensions of orthodox physicians. A prominent Methodist itinerant included both lawyers and doctors under the "wo" of prophecy. And the Mormon prophet Joseph Smith and his successor Brigham Young aligned the early Mormon movement closely with the Thomsonian botanic system.[56] Physicians, like lawyers, could no longer take for granted popular respect for their office—a problem most acute as professionals moved into the hinterland.

Backcountry Dissent

After the Revolution, a single generation of Americans rushed to occupy more land than their forefathers had subdued during the entire colonial period. By 1790 counties that had been virtually unpopulated before the American Revolution claimed one third of the nation's population; ten years later, land unsettled before 1760 claimed over 40 percent of the nation's total, an increase of over 75 percent since 1790. The free population of western Pennsylvania, for instance, increased almost three-fold—from 33,000 to 95,000—from the end of the Revolution to the turn of the century. In the fifteen years after 1775, the population of Kentucky and Tennessee grew from almost nothing to about 75,000 and 35,000 respectively. After his extensive analysis of this population shift, Alan Taylor has estimated that not since the seventeenth century had such a high proportion of the white population lived in newly settled communities.[57]

Unfortunately, economic prosperity and autonomy in the backcountry failed to keep pace with this unprecedented growth. Whatever common causes backcountry settlers and seaboard authorities shared during the Revolution, their differences intensified in the years that followed. The root of the problem was that economic growth failed to match the aspirations that the Revolution fired and that an increasingly competitive society sustained. Most marginal farmers in the backcountry watched their economic prospects deteriorate during the last two decades of the century even as a free market raised expectations of unlimited good.[58] Between 1780 and 1795, for instance, the percentage of rural landholders in western Pennsylvania declined by 59 percent while absentee owners from the east greatly enhanced their holdings. In 1784, even George Washington was involved in a legal case evicting Scottish settlers from a tract of land he owned in Washington County, Pennsylvania.[59]

In many cases, the plight of western yeomen rekindled the same burning grievances that Americans had experienced under British authority: the access of speculators to land, unfair taxation, heavy-handed courts, excessive legal fees, insensitivity to local conditions, and lack of representation. During the late 1770s, settlers in the New Hampshire Grants and in western Pennsylvania and North Carolina petitioned the Continental Congress to form the separate states of Vermont, Westsylvania, and Watauga.

By 1784, delegates gathered from the western counties of North Carolina had formed the short-lived state of Franklin. One man rose, took out a copy of the Declaration of Independence, and angrily paralleled the grievances of the Declaration and those of frontiersmen.[60]

During the 1780s, western Massachusetts became a cauldron of rural protest against cosmopolitan politicians. In 1778, the Berkshire constitutionalists voted by a six-to-one margin against the opening of courts where debt cases were heard. "We esteem it a matter of great grievance," a county convention declared in 1781, "that *excise* should be paid on any articles of consumption in a free republic." By 1786, farmers in the western part of the state, angered by higher taxes, lower prices, and the legislature's insistence that taxes be paid in hard currency, marched on courts en masse to block the execution of hundreds of foreclosures. What became known as Shays's Rebellion was a spontaneous protest of poor farmers against an eastern-dominated legislature. In an "Address to the Yeomanry of Massachusetts" in Boston's *Independent Chronicle*, one Bristol County farmer, George Brock, complained that their hard-earned liberties were being subverted by new enemies, "the placemen, the pensioners, and above all that aristocratical people too generally prevalent among the wealthy men of the state."[61]

The defeat of Daniel Shays did not silence rural disorder in the new nation. In western Pennsylvania, on the Maine frontier, and along the New York–Connecticut border, organized resistance continued as hundreds of poor families, many of whom had settled these lands during and immediately after the war, refused to acknowledge the claims of nonresident proprietors and land speculators. Pennsylvania's "Wild Yankees," New York's "Anti-renters," and Maine's "Liberty-Men" believed that the American Revolution had put an end to ancient claims in favor of squatter rights, securing land for those who had risked their lives in the defense of liberty and improved it with the sweat of their brow. Taking the opposite view, wealthy proprietors such as Washington's secretary of war, Henry Knox, expected the new republic to safeguard all prerevolutionary laws and contracts. These fundamentally incompatible views of the Revolution's meaning involved a standoff between defiant localism and a concern to centralize, and between radically different assessments of the significance of ordinary mortals. A petition from 151 Maine farmers to the Massachusetts General Court in 1793 put the issue well: "What ought to entitle General Knox to a grant [of] a tract of Land superior in extent to any Lord in Europe or America, has he done more for his Country than hundreds of us, no verily."[62]

During the century's final two decades this agrarian unrest was tightly linked to a vein of radical religious protest. In fact, one of the untold stories of American religious history is the wave of charismatic religious innovators who served as heralds and prophets in these agrarian movements. A hostile critic of Yankee squatters in New York compared the religious ferment with that of the English Civil War. The Yankees were

A set of fierce republicans, if anything sneaking and drawling may be so called, whom litigious contention had banished from their native province. . . . Among this motley crew there was no regular place of worship, nor any likely prospect that there should, for their religions had as many shades of difference as the leaves of autumn; and every man of substance who arrived, was a preacher and magistrate to his own little colony. To hear their people talk, one would think time had run back to the days of the levellers.[63]

Egalitarian religious leaders were also an integral part of protest movements in Pennsylvania, Massachusetts, Maine, and Vermont.[64] In Pennsylvania, for almost two decades after the Revolution, the radical preacher and visionary Herman Husband decried the appearance of a national economic elite and the increasing power of merchants, lawyers, and land speculators. He wrote scathing pamphlets against the proposed Federal Constitution on the grounds that it would centralize power and insure the return of aristocracy.[65] With striking apocalyptic imagery, Husband likened those who prepared the Constitution to "the old forms of a beast's head" and denounced the parade celebrating Pennsylvania's ratification as the pomp of Nebuchadnezzar.[66] After 1789, Husband lost faith in his earlier prediction that all of the American states would be a part of the New Jerusalem; he confined its boundaries to the "Western country," interpreting Genesis 49:26 to mean that the "spiritual sons" of Abraham would live in the "everlasting Western hills, and mountainous land of the Columbian continent."[67] In the 1790s, Husband opposed Hamilton's funding plan and played a minor role in the Whiskey Rebellion. For these activities, he was imprisoned in Philadelphia during the winter of 1794–95 and died within days of his release.[68]

Samuel Ely was an equally fierce preacher of dissent who championed the cause of backcountry folk in three states. A Yale graduate of 1764, Ely pastored a church briefly and unsuccessfully in Somers, Connecticut, took part in the Battle of Bennington, and ended up in Hampshire County, Massachusetts. Timothy Dwight deemed Ely an unusually talented demagogue who everywhere declared himself "the friend of the suffering and oppressed and the champion of violated rights. Wherever he went, he industriously awakened the jealousy of the humble and ignorant against all men of superior reputation as haughty, insolent and oppressive."[69] In 1782, he was arrested in Northampton for vigorously fomenting popular uprisings against the courts in western Massachusetts. After a mob of one hundred fifty broke into the jail in Springfield to free him, he fled to Vermont. A decade later, Ely resurfaced in Maine, where he became a principal spokesman for the squatters who sought to resist the claims of the Proprietors of the Plymouth and Waldo Patents. Ely justified the resistance as divinely sanctioned and argued for the rights of the poor being infringed upon in the name of the Revolution: "We fought for liberty, but despots took it, whose little finger is thicker than George's loins; the cry of violence and wrong; O that George held the claim still! for, before the war, it was better with us than now."[70]

In Maine, Ely was not the only prophet who denounced established authority in the name of God and the Revolution. According to Alan Taylor, all the leaders of the movement spoke in a religious vein and claimed religious authority: Nathan Barlow, a desperately poor illiterate farmer, emerged as a leader in driving off sheriffs and surveyors after recounting to his neighbors a remarkable vision of heaven and hell.[71] Daniel Brackett, an obscure laborer, led Maine's "white Indians" in resisting the proprietary claims of Henry Knox, among others. He described his efforts as part of the larger, cosmic plan to "Cut Down all poopery and kill the Devil and give the world of mankind some piece by stopping the progres of Rogues and Deceivers and helping every man to his right and privilidges and libertys."[72] William Scales, who attended Harvard on a charity scholarship and graduated in 1771 with a social standing next to last in his class, left Cambridge in disgust at the worldly curriculum and high style he witnessed there. Concluding that God would be found within the individual soul rather than in church structures, he spent his career attempting to promote liberation from "spiritual and temporal task masters." He declared that the Maine proprietary patents were marks "of the beast" that advanced the Antichrist's drive to deprive yeomen of the right to live in peace.[73] A delegate to the Massachusetts state convention to ratify the Constitution, William Jones was a staunch Anti-Federalist and Methodist leader. By 1793, he found even the Methodists restrictive but remained a religious seeker adamantly committed to the identification of the Lord with the poor and the humble. This theology gave him every reason to oppose the wealthy and well-educated proprietors.[74] Finally, another defender of the resistance, James Shurtleff, argued that the movement could be placed in the cosmic millennial drama between Christ and the Antichrist. He imagined that Satan was furious because the squatter's success imperiled his control:

Yet know 'tis disputed, for what do I hear?
Strange rumor of late, which alarms and affrights,
Strange rumor of freedom, and human rights;
Tho' men are but squatters, vile squatters, you see,
Who settle on earth, holding not under me;
But, alas! human rights, as urg'd by the squatter,
Makes my kingdom and hell's foundation to totter.[75]

These expressions of egalitarian Christianity, however volatile and short-lived, remain striking evidence of the uncertainty of the times, of unexpected influences upon religious belief, and of the gravitation of common folk to forms of Christianity antagonistic to received authority. These religious leaders were fierce independents and localists, embodying the gospel in populist forms that went considerably beyond the sacred cause of the Revolution as defined by established clergy. Their gospel of the back-country resonated with powerful Anti-Federalist and Jeffersonian persuasions. It challenged the right of a natural elite to speak for the people and empowered those who could claim no real stake in the promise of America.

Blurring of Worlds

The democratic revolution of the early republic sent external religious authority into headlong retreat and elicited from below powerful visions of faith that seemed more authentic and self-evident. These new expressions of faith, fed by passions of ordinary men and women, did not merely diverge from received authority; increasingly they failed even to take into account the standard theological categories that served as guides for religious experience and formed the common denominator of theological discussion between disputants—Old Lights and New Lights, Baptists and Anglicans, or Presbyterians and Quakers. Dissenting evangelicals such as George Whitefield, Samuel Davies, Gilbert Tennant, and Isaac Backus had defined their dissent against an accepted tradition. Despite his lack of formal education, Backus had clung to an undiluted Edwardsian theology, the authority of ordained clergymen, and the necessity of strict church discipline.[76] In the wake of the Revolution, dissenters confounded the establishment with an approach to theological matters that was nothing short of guerilla warfare. The coarse language, earthy humor, biting sarcasm, and commonsense reasoning of their attacks appealed to the uneducated but left the professional clergy without a ready defense. The very ground rules of religious life were at stake.

As preachers from the periphery of American culture came to reconstruct Christianity, three distinct tendencies became evident. First, they mingled diverse, even contradictory sources, erasing distinctions that the polite culture of the eighteenth century had struggled to keep separate. The crucible of popular theology combined odd mixtures of high and popular culture, of renewed supernaturalism and Enlightenment rationalism, of mystical experiences and biblical literalism, of evangelical and Jeffersonian rhetoric. At the same time, this environment accelerated this splintering of Christianity, what George Rawlyk calls "a fragmenting evangelical ethos."[77] As increased numbers of these theological neophytes attempted to explicate religious matters for themselves, the overall range of religious options multiplied. Populist preachers could differ from each other as easily as they could from the establishment. This was particularly true given the clarion message that rang out above all their diversity: the primacy of the individual conscience. This emphasis relates to a third distinguishable pattern: an inversion of the traditional modes of religious authority. Instead of revering tradition, learning, solemnity, and decorum, as did Timothy Dwight and Lyman Beecher, a diverse array of populist preachers exalted youth, free expression, and religious ecstasy. They explicitly taught that divine insight was reserved for the poor and humble rather than the proud and learned.

One of the most prevalent assumptions about the religious history of the early republic is that its central story line involves a contest between evangelicals and rationalists, between forces of the revival and those of the Enlightenment, between revealed and natural religion, between the heart and the head. Conventional wisdom holds that, after flirting briefly with the rationalism of the Enlightenment, Americans embraced revivalism with a vengeance. In the words of Perry Miller, "the invincible persistence of the revival technique" became the dominant theme in American cultural life after 1800.[78] From this perspective, the Second Great Awakening became the Thermidor of the American Enlightenment, the working out of opposite impulses.[79]

A dual problem follows this emphasis on a sharply defined intellectual cleavage between rationalists and evangelicals. First, its focus on intellectual and theological divisions obscures the fact that the most profound religious debates in the early republic followed social and class lines rather than merely intellectual ones. For understanding the long-term course of American religious history, the debate between Lyman Beecher and Lorenzo Dow looms larger than the one between Beecher and, say, William Ellery Channing.

The tendency to see the Second Great Awakening as a self-contained movement has also made it difficult to appreciate the eclectic character of popular faiths. Apocalyptic themes long resonant in the popular culture reappeared laced with Jeffersonian political thought, even heavy doses of Jefferson's prose; traditional resistance to elite positional codes and to local religious taxes took on the ideological imperative of Enlightenment attacks against a state religion and against the use of all religious creeds. The revolution in print late in the eighteenth century allowed ordinary people to gain smatterings of knowledge about that which had been the exclusive preserve of the educated. Such egalitarian circumstances also gave freer reign to subterranean folk beliefs and to unregulated displays of fervency and religious ecstasy. Under such fluid conditions, it was increasingly difficult to differentiate between science and superstition, naturalism and supernaturalism, medicine and quackery. It was a golden age both of empiricism and of imposters and counterfeiters.[80] This blurring of worlds is superbly illustrated in the rhetoric of religious supernaturalism and egalitarian militancy in the Methodist itinerant Lorenzo Dow.

"Crazy" Lorenzo Dow played a significant role in the growth of American Methodism even as he operated independent of the movement itself. Licensed or not, Dow barnstormed throughout the republic at a frenetic pace. One observer may have exaggerated only slightly in noting that Dow preached with a restlessness without parallel in human history.[81] In the year 1804, for instance, he spoke at between five and eight hundred meetings; the following year he traveled some ten thousand miles. Three times he itinerated in the British Isles, and his personal impact there was the most important single factor in generating bitter debate over the issue of American-style "camp meetings" within British Methodism. In 1807 he journeyed from New England to Florida, from Mississippi to New England; in 1808 through the West; in 1809 through Louisiana; and in 1810 through Georgia, North Carolina, and back to New England.[82] Between 1800 and 1835, over seventy editions of a score of his writings were published throughout the union. There is no question that he preached to more people, traveled more miles, and consistently attracted larger audiences to camp meetings than any preacher of his day. From New York City to the wilds of Alabama, many attested that Dow was the most memorable preacher they had ever heard.

The most striking thing about Dow was that he was both a holy man, who cultivated the image of John the Baptist, and a radical Jeffersonian, who could begin a sermon by quoting Tom Paine. Dow sought the conversion of sinners at the same time that he railed at tyranny and priest-craft and the professions of law and medicine.[83] He openly claimed to be guided by dreams and visions and implied that he possessed visionary powers to know the secrets of the heart and to foretell the fate of individuals. When asked to leave Saint Stephens, Alabama, for instance, he prophesied that, within a century, the town would become a roosting place for bats and owls and that no stone would lie upon another. He took great pains to make dramatic last-minute appearances at preaching appointments set up months in advance. And stories were rife of his uncanny power to pick out of an audience an undetected thief, rogue, or murderer.[84]

Yet Dow also championed popular sovereignty and the responsibility of independent persons to throw off the shackles of ignorance and oppression. In his pamphlet *Analects upon the Rights of Man*, Dow grounded all human rights upon "the great and universal 'law of nature.'" He condemned the radical distinction between "gentlemen or nobility" on the one hand and "peasants" on the other. "The first will possess the country," he suggested, "and feel and act more than their own importance; while the latter are put on a level with the animals, and treated as an inferior race of beings, who must pay these lords a kind of divine honor, and bow, and cringe and scrape."[85] After questioning how such differences came to exist between persons, Dow responded with vigorous Jeffersonian rhetoric:

> By what rule of right can one man exercise authority with a command over others? Either it must be the gift of God, or, secondly, it must be delegated by the people—or less, thirdly, it must be ASSUMED!
>
> A power without a right, is assumption; and must be considered as a piece of unjust tyranny. . . .
>
> But if all men are 'BORN EQUAL,' and endowed with unalienable RIGHTS by their CREATOR, in the blessings of life, liberty, and the pursuit of happiness—then there can be no just reason, as a cause, why he may or should not think, and judge, and act for himself in matters of religion, opinion, and private judgment.[86]

Dow's appeal had much to do with his bizarre appearance—long hair parted like a woman's, weather-beaten face, flashing eyes, harsh voice, crude gestures, and disheveled clothes.[87] He was also a captivating performer and remarkable storyteller who could evoke laughter and tears. Most important, he was able to touch two deep, and apparently contradictory, nerves within popular culture. He was able to depict his times as an "Age of Inquiry," in which individuals had to think for themselves and take matters into their own hands; and as an "Age of Wonders," in which the divine continued to permeate everyday life.[88] Dow had a deep-seated aversion to traditional authority—he took "much delight in provoking the ribald mirth" of religious skeptics by exposing the pretensions of genteel

LORENZO DOW.

Fig. 1. Lorenzo Dow, lithograph by Childs and Lehman, 1834

Fig. 2. Lorenzo Dow, engraving by A. Willard, 1832, from painting by Lucius Munson, 1821

clergymen.[89] Yet this egalitarian representative also embodied the continuing presence of the supernatural in everyday affairs, as the observer John Francis noted:

> His weapons against Beelzebub were providential interpositions, wondrous disasters, touching sentiments, miraculous escapes, something after the method of John Bunyan. . . . In his field exercises, at camp meetings, and the like, a raging storm might be the forerunner of God's immediate wrath; a change of elements might betoken Paradise restored, or a new Jerusalem. He might be farcical or funereal. He had genius at all times to construct a catastrophe.[90]

Dow openly trusted his own instincts by virtue of his Jeffersonian convictions and his willingness to see the supernatural unveiled in his daily ministry. The net effect for him, as for many similar pilgrims, was a sharpened reliance on the dictates of the individual conscience.

Individualization of Conscience

Caleb Rich was the most important leader of Universalism in rural New England during the last quarter of the eighteenth century. Born in Sutton, Massachusetts, in 1750 and raised as a separatist Baptist, Rich recalled that as a teenager he was tortured on the rack of Calvinist doubt: "My situation appeared more precarious than a ticket in a lottery, where there was a hundred blanks to one prize." At the same time he was bewildered by the claims of competing churches. He questioned the wisdom of God "for ever suffering the world to be thus enveloped in such a dilemma, and overwhelmed in such impenetrable darkness." These difficulties set Rich on a course to seek his own answers. He came to a "firm and fixed resolution" not to rely on the testimony of any other person but to take up the Bible for himself with attention and diligence.[91]

In 1771 Rich moved with his two brothers to Warwick, Massachusetts, a rural town in the hill country along the New Hampshire border. Here he experienced conversion but also began having a series of visionary experiences in which celestial persons counseled him to avoid all other denominations and all other human advice. This combination of personal Bible study and divine encounters convinced him that all persons would be saved, for which conclusion he was banished from the Warwick Baptist Church. Convinced by an angel that there was no existing church "that stood in the Apostolic rectitude or that contended for the faith once delivered to the saints," Rich began preaching and organizing new societies in 1773. His message of universal salvation contradicted Calvinist orthodoxy in a number of respects. In style and demeanor he attempted to avoid "anything that savours in the least degree of pomposity or worldly grandeur" in a gospel minister. In his mind the real distinctive of his convictions was that God had chosen to reveal his ways directly: "I could say in truth that the gospel that was preached by me, was not after man; for I neither received it of man, neither was I taught it by man, but by revelation of Jesus Christ, through the medium of the Holy Spirit in opening my understanding to understand the scripture."[92]

The experience of Caleb Rich illustrates well the pervasive crisis of authority within popular religion in America in the years after the Revolution. His experience suggests the stages of a pilgrimage that confronted many Christians during this period. Rich came to find traditional religious systems no longer credible and to experience deep intellectual turmoil in groping for new verities. He eventually insisted that his own interpretation of Scripture should not be mediated by any other authority, historical or ecclesiastical—a conviction steeled by the competing claims of rival denominations and a new openness to visionary experiences. He resolved his struggle for assurance by insisting that the unfettered conscience must encounter for itself the *ipse dixit* of the New Testament. The experiences of five other persons also illustrate this individualization of conscience.

A man with little formal schooling but with a near photographic memory, Elhanan Winchester in 1780 was reputed to be one of the best Baptist preachers in America. He served several churches in his native Massachusetts, a congregation in Welch Neck, South Carolina, and after 1780, a burgeoning Baptist church in Philadelphia. The largest church building in the city was often filled to capacity by those who had come to hear him preach.[93]

Upon his arrival in Philadelphia, Winchester began to waver on his commitment to Calvinism. What he found alluring was an idea advocated by Universalists—that all persons would eventually be saved. His ambivalence on this issue brought on a crisis in his church in 1781 and forced him to defend or deny the idea of a universal restoration. Winchester chose to resolve his conflict in the following manner: "I shut myself up chiefly in my chamber, read the Scriptures, and prayed to God to lead me into truth, and not suffer me to embrace any error; and I think with an upright mind, I laid myself open to believe whatsoever the Lord had revealed. It would be too long to tell all the Teaching I had on this head; let it suffice, in short, to say, that I became so well persuaded of the truth of Universal Restoration, that I determined never to deny it."[94] Winchester expressed great emotional release after this experience and set out to champion the cause of Universalism. What is significant for our purposes is his method of resolving theological perplexity: locking the door and coming to grips with Scripture for himself.[95]

The two founders of New England's Christian Connection, Elias Smith and Abner Jones, also experienced personal crises of authority with Calvinist orthodoxy. Each resolved their struggle for assurance by stripping away all authority but that of the individual. At the turn of the century, Elias Smith lost his religious bearings completely and left the pastorate of the Baptist Church in Woburn, Massachusetts. "My mind was ensnared," he confessed, "and I felt myself in a situation from which it was not in my power to extricate myself." He finally resolved his dilemma one day as he pitted the claims of Calvinism against those of Universalism: "While meditating upon these doctrines [Calvinism and Universalism] and my own situation, and saying what shall I do? there was a gentle whisper to my understanding in these words: *Drop them both and search the scriptures.* This command was immediately consented to; and instantly my mind was free from the entanglement before experienced. . . . Having lost all my system, my mind was prepared to search the scriptures."[96]

Abner Jones, an associate of Elias Smith in the Christian Connection, came to his religious convictions in Bridgewater, Vermont, by asserting an equally independent path. Unsatisfied with the views and creeds of those around him, Jones resolved to launch his own "serious investigation." Accordingly, he "took the Bible, and that alone, and without consulting any individual, or receiving sympathy from any living being, commenced a prayerful and careful examination of the sacred pages." In 1801, Jones sought ordination from the Freewill Baptists on the condition that he retain complete independence: "I will never be subject to one of your rules; but if you will give me the right hand as a brother, and let me remain a *free man*, just as I am, I should be glad." On these grounds, the Freewill Baptists agreed to ordain Jones "a free man."[97]

In one nine-month stretch in 1802 and 1803, William Smythe Babcock estimated he traveled fifteen hundred miles and preached two hundred ninety-seven sermons as an itinerant minister in the hill country of New Hampshire and Vermont. History would have entirely swallowed the memory of this folk preacher had he not kept an extensive journal of his travels and preaching between 1801 and 1809. Babcock founded a Freewill Baptist Church in Springfield, Vermont, in 1801 and from there launched extensive preaching forays throughout upper New England.[98]

Babcock proclaimed a message that revolved around the issue of bondage and liberty. The sentiments of this man are aptly summarized in a poem he attributed to a nine-year-old girl in his congregation.

Know then that every soul is free
To choose his life and what he'll be;
For this eternal truth giv'n,
That God will force no man to heav'n.

He'll draw, persuade, direct him right;
Bless him with wisdom, love and light;
In nameless ways be good and kind,
But never force the human mind.[99]

The Freewill Baptist Connection exercised no real authority over Babcock, yet he repeatedly expressed the fear of relying too much on other men or of being coerced by them. By 1809 even the slight contact that he did have with other churches became unbearable. He unilaterally severed all ties with the Monthly Meeting of the Freewill Baptists. "I told them that I now stood alone, unconnected to or with any one." The members of Babcock's congregation followed his lead and agreed to renounce all denominations and set up a church "independent in itself, free from control or of domination of any other churches whatever."[100] They agreed to defer to only one authority, the rule and guide of the Scriptures. Pressing the notion of Christian freedom to its logical conclusion, Babcock could not abide anyone having the right to suggest to him the parameters of biblical teaching.

Lucy Mack Smith, mother of Joseph Smith, the founder of the Mormons, also grew up in the hill country of New Hampshire and Vermont at the end of the eighteenth century. Lucy married Joseph Smith, Sr., in 1802, and they struggled to make a living and raise a family in Randolph, New Hampshire. Lucy wrestled interminably with the problems of competing denominations, each of which seemed to invalidate the claims of the others. "If I remain a member of no church," she wrote, "all religious people will say I am of the world; and if I join some one of the different denominations, all the rest will say I am in error." After one disillusioning experience in a Presbyterian church, Lucy Smith returned home and came to the following conviction: "I said in my heart that there was not then upon earth the religion which I sought. I therefore determined to examine my Bible, and taking Jesus and the disciples as my guide, to endeavor to obtain from God that which man could neither give nor take away. . . . The Bible I intended should be my guide to life and salvation." Lucy Smith sealed this individualization of conscience by finding a minister who would agree to baptize her as a solitary Christian without attachment to any congregation.[101]

Inversion of Authority

The fundamental religious quarrel of the late eighteenth century was not between Calvinist and Arminian, orthodox and Unitarian, evangelical and freethinker but between radically different conceptions of the Christian ministry. As respectable clergymen in these turbulent years reiterated their confidence in learning and civility, potent strains of anticlericalism welled up within the bounds of the church, challenging the right of any special order to mediate the gospel. This virulent anticlericalism resembled the kinds of dissent that were endemic to Protestants from the English Civil War through the Great Awakening. Sustained volleys of criticism about pride, spiritual apathy, and love of station and wealth continued to discomfit clergymen. Yet forms of anticlericalism at the end of the eighteenth century gained sharper focus and broader appeal for two distinct reasons.

In the first place, they became an integral part of a profound upsurge to erase the distinction between gentleman and commoner, privileged classes and the people. These attacks upon the clergy portrayed society as horizontally polarized, reflecting the same fundamental division between those who believed in the right of a natural aristocracy to speak for the people and those who did not. Gordon S. Wood suggests that this issue was the essence of the struggle between Federalist and Anti-Federalist. Like the Anti-Federalists, these religious dissenters were obsessed with aristocracy because they refused to accept the "authority of names" and the "influence of the great." A sharp-tongued layman, Simon Hough of Berkshire County, Massachusetts, offered a class analysis of society in 1792, identifying clergymen as the oppressors of the poor. Hough had been excommunicated from the Congregational Church in Richmond by pastor David Perry for his efforts to awaken the world to Christ's immediate return. In a 1799 pamphlet, Hough thundered against the distinctions and the wealth of the clergy, "these great MEN OF RENOWN, viz. D.D.REV.&c. which must have so much more than common men; and must be maintained like Princes and addressed as gods." Interpreting the earthquake of Revelation 11 as "the downfall of titles of honor," Hough issued a solemn warning to America's "Ecclesiastic Giants" who demanded "ten, fifteen, twenty and twenty-five times as much to maintain them as common men." He foresaw coming judgment: "Woe unto you that bind such heavy burthens on the shoulders of your fellow-citizens. . . . Woe unto you who have exclaimed against tyranny, and are tyrants yourselves."[102]

In an equally radical attack on the oppression of the poor, the Rogerene Quaker Timothy Waterous wrote a pamphlet entitled *The Battle-Axe*, which he printed on a homemade press after no printer in the vicinity of Mystic, Connecticut, would publish it. In this highly apocalyptic pamphlet, Waterous yoked republican politics and a class analysis of society to the coming of the end. On several occasions Elias Smith used passages from *The Battle-Axe* in his paper, the *Herald of Gospel Liberty*, one of them a poem entitled "Priest-Craft Float Away":

> Why are we in such slavery, to men of that degree;
> Bound to support their knavery when we might all be free;
> They'r nothing but a canker, we can with boldness say;
> So let us hoist the anchor, left Priest-craft float away.[103]

At the same time, obscure Christians without social grace and literary education went beyond merely denying the right of the clergy to ascribe authority to themselves. They began to piece together a popular theology that inverted the traditional assumption that truth was more likely to be found at the upper rather than at the lower reaches of society. This perspective sprang from an intensely egalitarian reading of the New Testament. The emphasis was on Christ as a carpenter's son, the Apostles as poor and uneducated, and the crowd shouting hosannah while the rich and powerful sought his death. These popular theologies appropriated Christ's teaching that power in the church should emanate from below, that the first should be last, and that the chief should not lord it over others but become a servant of all. Sharp questions were raised about why the clergy did not live in poverty as Christ did. How could salaried gentlemen claim to imitate the man who had nowhere to lay his head, lived upon the charity of his followers, worked a miracle to have money to pay tribute, washed the feet of his disciples, and "for our sakes became poor"?[104] It was Simon Hough's view that poor Christians who took affairs into their own hands at the end of the eighteenth century would fare little better:

> Now this was intolerable, that such a poor criminal should rail so on God's high Priest. . . . Now if a man was thus openly to confront the Presidents of our Colleges, and the swarms of hirelings that come from them yearly, and call Antichrists, as I believe they mostly if not all are, would he not be in danger? . . . for you reject the poor if they teach truth, and will have none but the learned and worldly wise, not more than they; nay you deny the power of the Holy Ghost, to furnish men for teachers, unless they are college learnt, and in so doing you despise Christ and his Apostles, for they were not college learnt.[105]

These strains of egalitarian theology made sense in the 1790s, a time when the swirl of events moved radical republicans to deny outright that opinions about politics—or any issue of ultimate concern—were the monopoly of the educated few. The republican vision of the 1790s, as portrayed by Joyce Appleby, defended the same classless view of society, hostility to rank and privilege, rejection of the wisdom of the ages, and buoyant confidence in the "newly discovered capacity of human beings to develop constructively under the conditions of freedom."[106] Just as it was ordinary people who ensured the defeat of aristocratic values in American politics under Jeffersonian banners, so it was outsiders, interlopers, and marginal men who created the turmoil, defined the issues, formed the organizations, and preached the gospel that captured the hearts and minds of so many citizens in the following century.

These visions of a Christianity of the people were well served by the structural looseness of American society in the next generation. From many unexpected quarters, populist religious leaders felt the call to step forward and proclaim a faith inviting to all. The methods by which these leaders championed the gospel brought dark and threatening clouds to the horizons of such men as Lyman Beecher. His orthodox gospel of respectability had difficulty standing up to these aggressive measures, the contrast between them easily resembling "flat tranquility against passion; dry leaves against the whirlwind; the weight of gunpowder against its kindled force."[107]

II. Mass Movements

CHAPTER THREE

Storming Heaven by the Back Door

And I turned to [Joseph] Smith, and said, "Are you not ashamed of such pretensions? You, who are no more than any ignorant plough-boy of our land! Oh! blush at such abominations! and let shame, forever cover your face!"

He only replied, by saying, "The gift has returned back again as in former times, to illiterate fishermen."

NANCY TOWLE, *1833*

In May of 1806, Bishop Francis Asbury paused long enough in New York City to send a report to his English colleague, Thomas Coke, on the state of American Methodism. His four thousand–mile pilgrimage in the preceding eight months had taken him through fifteen states, from Vermont to Georgia, from Massachusetts to Kentucky. These travels left Asbury more confident than ever of the role of the Methodists in converting the New World. He spoke glowingly of the hundreds of gospel ministers under his charge, of the 8273 new members added during the last year, and of the pervasive sense that God's work was accelerating at an unprecedented rate.

Asbury took great delight in the rousing success of the American camp meeting. Describing the "overwhelming power" of a four-day meeting twenty miles northeast of New York, he estimated that three thousand persons and one hundred preachers attended the sessions four times a day. Asbury found the level of activity so intense, with "weeping on all sides," that he was unable to sleep for the duration of the meeting. He also wrote approvingly of the presiding elder in Delaware who, in the summer of 1806, had scheduled "100 days and nights to be in the woods." Asbury was a bold advocate of the camp meeting, boasting five years later that these occasions brought together three to four million Americans annually—an estimated one-third of the total population. "Campmeetings! Campmeetings!" he exclaimed. "The battle ax and weapon of war, it will break down walls of wickedness, part of hell, superstition, [and] false doctrine."[1]

Thomas Coke and other leaders of British Methodism disapproved of Asbury's effusive praise of the camp meeting. In fact, the very institution that Asbury extolled as a chief means of grace they found alarming, even terrifying—so much so that when they printed Asbury's letter in the *Methodist Magazine*, they chose to delete any reference to camp meetings.[2] The reason for this judgment is not hard to see. Since the turn of the century the issue of protracted meetings involving unlicensed preachers had become a storm center within British Methodism. At the very time of the correspondence, the ungovernable American revivalist Lorenzo Dow had been barnstorming through Ireland and northwest England encouraging large crowds to spend whole days in preaching, praying, exhorting, and singing. Thomas Coke, suspicious of Dow's eccentric appearance, fervent republicanism, and refusal to swear allegiance to George III, threatened to report the American to Lord Castlereagh, Chief Secretary for Ireland.[3] In the spring of 1807, Dow's preaching in Straffordshire inspired the dissident Methodist Hugh Bourne and his brother James to organize a camp meeting based on the American model. Armed with Dow's pamphlets and songbooks, they convened several day-long meetings during the summer of 1807, the most famous one in May at a place called Mow Cap. Faced with this challenge, the Methodist Conference reacted swiftly and decisively: "It is our judgment, that even supposing such meetings to be allowable in America, they are highly improper in England, and likely to be productive of considerable mischief: and we disclaim all connection with them."[4]

For the next five years Methodist authorities in England worked to destroy the camp meeting. Their nerves were strained by popular activism that threatened the fragile nature of religious toleration for the Methodists.[5] They also perceived a manifest subversiveness in the form and structure of the camp meeting itself, which openly defied ecclesiastical standards of time, space, authority and liturgical form.[6] Camp meetings moved beyond the once-radical field preaching that Wesley and Whitefield had instituted, shifting attention from conspicuous preaching performances to congregational participation. Those who led the meeting made overt attempts to have the power of God "strike fire" over a mass audience; they encouraged uncensored testimonials by persons without respect to age, gender, or race; the public sharing of private ecstasy; overt physical display and emotional release; loud and spontaneous response to preaching; and the use of folk music that would have chilled the marrow of Charles Wesley. Asbury's comments to Coke about the New York camp meeting made it clear that the institution was volatile, subject to shifting currents swelling

Fig. 3. "Camp Meeting," attributed to Alexander Rider, early nineteenth
century

up in the assembled multitude: "We felt God was so great in the praying exercises we could not call off the people to preaching."[7]

Why did Methodist leaders in America not perceive the same subversive implications in the camp meeting? Why did they continue to welcome Lorenzo Dow's public participation in their movement even while censoring him behind closed doors? American camp meetings certainly were not less noisy and extravagant than similar events in Great Britain. It was at least a generation before American Methodists domesticated these religious festivals. In the early republic, the testimony of camp meeting critics and supporters alike pointed to the intense enthusiasm of congregated masses, the unbridled communal force and overwhelming power that swept over these occasions. A critical William Bentley bemoaned the "brutal attempts to excite the passions," noting the cacophony of "fainting, shouting, yelling, crying, sobbing, and grieving."[8] A supportive Ezekiel Cooper, on the other hand, did not underestimate the meetings' high voltage but attributed it to a different source: "Sinners were struck as with hammer and fire, or like as if thunder flashes had smitten them. A general cry began, so that I was forced to stop preaching. I stood upon the stand and looked on, and saw them in every part of the congregation with streaming eyes, and groaning for mercy, while others were shouting praises to God for delivering grace." James B. Finley described a similar scene of "heavenly fire" brought down upon a camp meeting in Ohio by the singing of the preacher Robert Manley: "Before he had finished singing the fourth verse, the *power of God* came down, and pervaded the vast assembly, and it became agitated—swelling and urging like the sea in a storm."[9]

The great American architect and engineer Benjamin Henry Latrobe visited a camp meeting in Georgetown, Virginia, in 1809. He drew a sketch of the preacher, "Bunn, the black smith," a commoner whom Latrobe described as "one of the most eminent Preachers of the Methodists," a man with a powerful and effective message:

> Then he spoke of the judgement to come, "that's the pinch, the judgement to come, when the burning billows of hell wash up against the Soul of the glutton and the miser, what good do all his Victuals and his wine, and his bags of gold; do they allay the fiery torment, the thirst that burns him, the parching that sears his lips, do they frighten away old Satan who is ready to devour him, think of that: this is the judgement to come, when hell gapes, and the fire roars, Oh pour sinful damned souls, poor sinful souls all of ye, will ye be damned, will ye, will ye, will ye be damned, no, no, no, no, don't be damned, now ye pray and groan and strive with the spirit." (a general groaning and

Fig. 4. "Bunn the Blacksmith at a Camp Meeting near Georgetown," pen sketch
by Benjamin Henry Latrobe, 1809

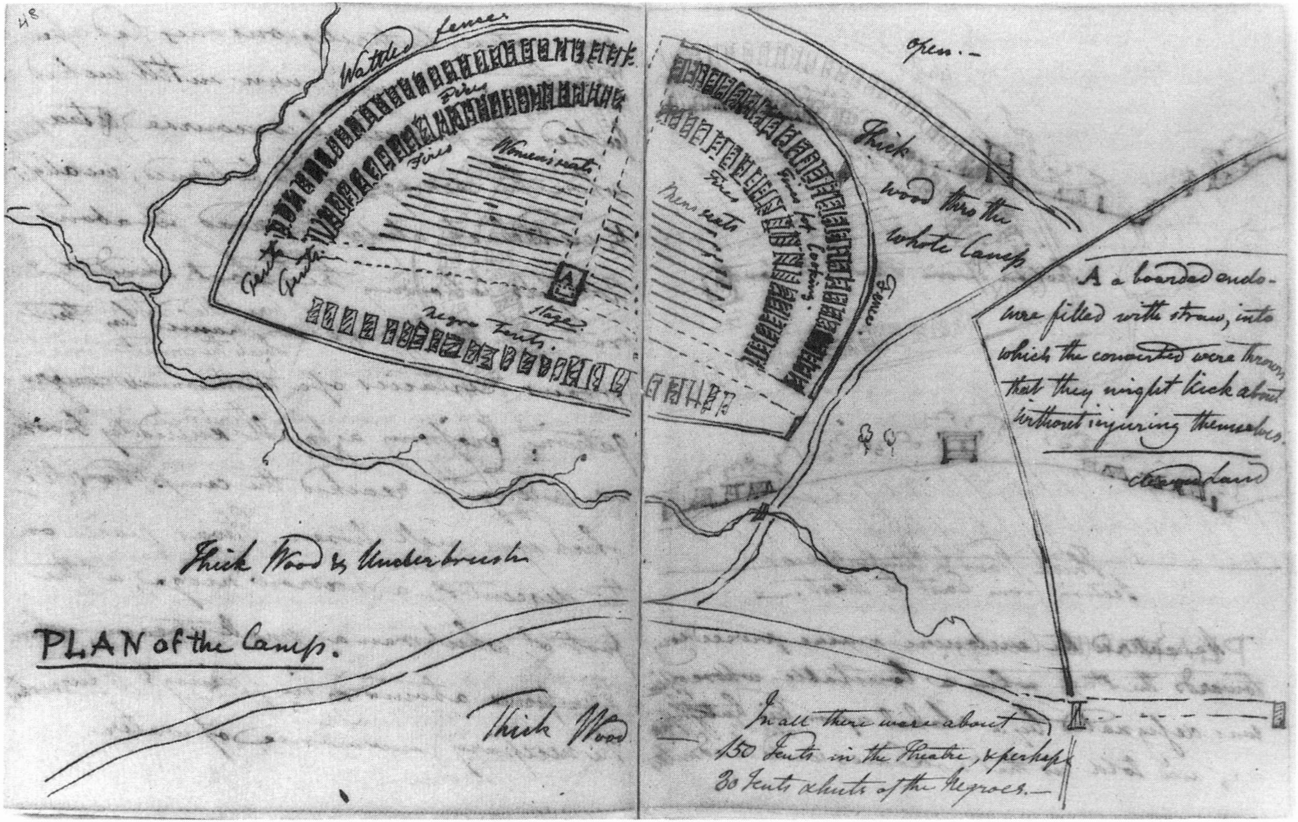

Fig. 5. "Plan of the Camp," sketch by Benjamin Henry Latrobe, 1809

shrieking was now heard from all quarters which the artful preacher immediately suppressed by turning to his text.)

Departing this scene, which he dismissed as rank enthusiasm, Latrobe took note of the "uncommon bustle, and cry" of persons crowding the stage to seek conversion.[10]

American camp meetings were awesome spectacles indeed, conjuring up feelings of supernatural awe in some, "the air of a cell in Bedlam" in others.[11] American followers of John Wesley found it easy to forget his advice never to scream and never to raise the voice above its natural pitch. Instead, they promoted thunderous meetings that were subject to stinging criticism. After watching one Methodist elder "with a voice like thunder" whip up an audience "until they had drowned his own voice," one New England skeptic asked: "Must a man draw his mouth out of all shape, and bellow like a bull, in order to become a Christian?" These attacks notwithstanding, Asbury's promotion of camp meetings persisted. He vowed in 1807 that he would battle all earth and hell to defend field meetings and would sooner suffer death than give them up.[12]

Americans continued to champion the camp meeting, turbulence and all, for a simple reason: it was a phenomenally successful instrument for popular recruitment. Asbury referred to them as "fishing with a large net."[13] In the very years that Methodist leadership in Great Britain seemed willing to forego numerical growth as the supreme object of Methodist polity, accepting numerical losses in order to preserve discipline, American Methodists remained ruthlessly committed to arousing a following and creating new societies.[14] Increasingly, the core of Methodist leaders were, in the words of Donald G. Mathews, "professional organizers" sent out to call churches into existence, not to wait for churches to call them. Invetrate propagandists, these roving evangelists would go from house to house, if necessary, looking for anyone who would listen.[15] Methodists in the shadow of Asbury took seriously the first *Discipline:* "You have nothing to do but to save souls. Therefore, spend and be spent in this work." William M'Kendree's description of the preaching of John Easter, under whom he was converted, seems to be typical: "He never indulged in metaphysical discussions, and rarely in doctrinal expositions. His themes were repentance, salvation by faith in Jesus Christ, and the Witness of the Spirit. . . . He was full of his subject, and intent only upon the rescue of sinners from impending wrath."[16]

In the early republic, the Methodists had no exclusive claim on zealous and uncompromising leaders intent on vast mobilization of people. A whole range of rootless and visionary preachers, spurning conventional religious

establishments and genteel social routines, championed religious movements devoted to reaching people at large. Characteristically bold, self-
educated, self-confident, and inventive, this dedicated corps of charismatic
leaders developed an array of religious movements that differed radically in
theological outlook and organizational intent. Yet, whether they came to fix
their identity as Methodist or Baptist, Universalist or Disciple, Mormon or
Millerite, these unusually strong personalities all shared a passion for
expansion, a hostility to orthodox belief and style, a zeal for religious
reconstruction, and a systematic plan to labor on behalf of that ideal. In the
era of the Second Great Awakening, the most distinctive feature of American Christianity was not the surge of an impersonal force called revivalism,
descending like manna from heaven, but a remarkable set of popular leaders
who proclaimed compelling visions of individual self-respect and collective
self-confidence. This story is not one of established clergy fretting about
loss of social authority but rather the demand of religious insurgents to be
recognized as the latest advance of Christ's kingdom.

Wreckers, Architects, and Builders

In his highly suggestive book *The Revolution of the Saints*, Michael
Walzer explores the character of the Puritan "saint," the stalwart figure of
burning zeal who ignored age-old customs and traditional loyalties to
reconstruct the social order of seventeenth-century England. Walzer suggests that the saint's personality itself was his most radical innovation.
Hardened and disciplined by a compelling ideology, the saint could offer
his own vision and pattern of life as an alternative to traditional social
forms. What made the cadre of Puritan saints so formidable, and in Walzer's view so similar to the modern revolutionary, was their extraordinary
capacity to mobilize people for a cause and to build organizations sustained
by ideological bonds rather than ties of residence, family, and patronage.[17]

In a similar fashion the social and intellectual ferment of the early
republic gave rise to a generation of populist "saints." "The earth, with all
its boasted wealth, had no remaining charm for me," asserted the young
convert Nancy Towle on her decision in 1820 to follow the inward impulse
to preach for the Christian Connection. "I put my hand to the Gospel
Plough, never more to turn again."[18] Such alienation from the established
order matched an aptitude for mobilizing people. This drive set these saints
apart from the generation of George Whitefield and Gilbert Tennant, who
labored to revive lukewarm establishments but left the creation of new

institutional forms to the will of providence and the discretion of those who pursued a New Light call. In the main, the creation of new congregations was an unintended and episodic consequence of the preaching of the Great Awakening.

Dissent in America after the Revolution was characterized by a shift from seeking conversions to movement building from the ground up. A battery of young leaders without elite pedigree constructed fresh religious ideologies around which new religious movements coalesced. W. R. Ward has noted that Francis Asbury was an entrepreneur in religion, a man who perceived a market to be exploited. The itinerant-based machine he set in motion was less a church in any traditional sense than "a military mission of short term agents."[19] Similarly, the founder of the Churches of Christ, Barton W. Stone, eschewed normal pastoral duties and dedicated himself utterly to the pursuit of "causes" in religion. Elias Smith went so far as to define religious liberty as the right to build a movement by itinerating without constraint.[20] All of these leaders eventually defined success not by the sheer number of converts but by the number of those who identified themselves with a fledgling movement. This quest for organization lay at the heart of Methodism's success. One unfriendly critic observed that the movement produced such great results "because it took hold of the doctrines which lay in the minds of all men here, and wrought them with the steam, levers, and pulleys of a new engine."[21]

Above all, these upstarts were radically innovative in reaching and organizing people. Passionate about ferreting out converts in every hamlet and crossroads, they sought to bind them together in local and regional communities. They continued to refashion the sermon as a popular medium, inviting even the most unlearned and inexperienced to respond to a call to preach. These initiates were charged to proclaim the gospel anywhere and every day of the week—even to the limit of their physical endurance. The resulting creation, the colloquial sermon, employed daring pulpit storytelling, no-holds-barred appeals, overt humor, strident attack, graphic application, and intimate personal experience. These young framers of religious movements also became the most effective purveyors of mass literature in the early republic, confronting people in every section of the new nation with the combined force of the written and spoken word. In addition, this generation launched bold experiments with new forms of religious music, new techniques of protracted meetings, and new Christian ideologies that denied the mediations of religious elite and promised to exalt those of low estate.[22]

The result of these intensive efforts was nothing less than the creation of mass movements that were deeply religious and genuinely democratic at the same time. Lawrence Goodwyn has suggested that the building of significant mass democratic movements involves a sequential process of recruitment, education, and involvement that allows a "movement culture" to develop. This new plateau of social possibility, based on self-confident leadership and widespread methods of internal communication, permits people to conceive of acting in self-generated democratic ways, to develop new ways of looking at things less clouded by inherited assumptions, and to defend themselves in the face of adverse interpretations from the orthodox culture. Like the later Populist movement that Goodwyn studies, insurgent religious movements such as the Methodists, a variety of Baptists, the Christians and Disciples, and the Mormons dared to aspire grandly, to surmount rigid cultural inheritances, to work together in order to be free individually. If nothing else, these movements were collective expressions of self-respect, instilling hope, purpose, meaning, and identity in thousands of persons whom the dominant culture had defined as marginal.[23]

All of these movements challenged common people to take religious destiny into their own hands, to think for themselves, to oppose centralized authority and the elevation of the clergy as a separate order of men. These religious communities could embrace the forlorn and the uprooted far more intensely than any political movement and offer them powerful bonds of acceptance and hope. As one new Methodist convert recalled, "I now found myself associated with those who loved each other with a pure heart fervently, instead of being surrounded by those with whom friendship was a cold commerce of interest."[24] These new movements could also impart to ordinary people, particularly those battered by poverty or infirmity, what Martin Luther King called "a sense of somebodiness"—the kind of consolation that another Methodist found so appealing in a worship service held in a log cabin: "an abiding confidence that he was a subject of that powerful kingdom whose Prince cared for his subjects."[25] These movements also allowed common people to trust their own religious impulses. They were encouraged to express their faith with fervent emotion and bold testimony. In the most democratic gesture of all, some preachers took their cues from evidence of divine power in the audience. During a camp meeting on an island in Chesapeake Bay, Lorenzo Dow was interrupted by a woman who began clapping her hands with delight and shouting "Glory! Glory!" In a response that was the opposite of condescension, Dow proclaimed to the audience: "The Lord is here! *He is with that sister*."[26] Given these dynamics, Michael Chevalier may have been more perceptive than he knew in referring to American camp meetings as "festivals of democracy."[27]

The Withering of Establishments

For all their own foresight and energy, these mass religious movements prospered for another reason: they did not have to face intense opposition by a powerful establishment. Most struggles to create significant popular movements have faced imposing cultural roadblocks and have involved intense cultural conflict, with many built-in advantages accruing to the partisans of the established order.[28] Protestant dissenters from Luther to the Puritans to the stalwarts of the Great Awakening had always challenged forces of religious orthodoxy occupying the most culturally sanctioned command posts. As late as the 1770s, Baptist preachers in Virginia were still being thrown in jail, and well into the nineteenth century the popular wing of Methodism in Great Britain faced entrenched opposition by the combined forces of church and state. What is striking about the period after the Revolution in America is not disestablishment per se but the impotence of Congregational, Presbyterian, and Episcopalian churches in the face of dissent. At the turn of the century, their own houses lay in such disarray that movements such as the Methodists, Baptists, and Christians were given free rein to experiment.

In New England the Anti-Jeffersonian alliance between the Congregational clergy and the Federalist party became a cause célèbre in the popular press and worked powerfully to discredit the established clergy. By the late 1790s, Jeffersonian papers such as Benjamin Austin's *Independent Chronicle* and William Duane's *Aurora* were attacking the New England clergy as an intolerant clerical-political aristocracy. They ridiculed unmercifully the crusade of Jedidiah Morse and Timothy Dwight to expose the supposed foreign conspiracy of the "Bavarian Illuminati."[29] Such exaggerated efforts to reassert the clergy's moral authority played into the hands of Jeffersonians, who tarred and feathered Yankee clergymen with the same language of tyranny and oppression that the "Black regiment" had coined to oppose Great Britain. The same Standing Order, which had been extolled as the Revolution's most stalwart defender of liberty, became subjects to the most abusive outpouring of anticlericalism that American history has known.

At the same time, the Congregationalists as a denomination were singularly ill prepared to organize churches for the raw and unsettled communities that Yankees were creating on the frontier. At the same time that an unprecedented number of new settlements were springing up on the fringes of New England, fewer young men from upstanding families were entering the ministry, and graduates of Harvard and Yale were less willing to opt for the hardship and poor pay of a backcountry parish. In 1780, Ezra Stiles, the president of Yale, counted sixty "destitute" parishes in Vermont, sixty in New Hampshire, and eighty in Massachusetts and Maine, most of them in rural areas and new settlements. In 1790, only twelve of Maine's sixty communities had organized a Congregational church, and only one of these churches was in the backcountry. Even by 1800, only one in every twenty backcountry settlements sustained the Standing Order. Compounding the problem of Congregational authority was that many of the clergymen who settled in these new communities were poorly trained or tainted with personal scandal—in short, those who could not find employment elsewhere. Stephen Marini has concluded that these multiple difficulties caused the most serious degeneration of the parish system in New England history.[30]

At the turn of the century, the Episcopalian church in the South found itself in even worse straits. In Virginia, no more than forty of the one hundred seven Episcopal parishes existing in 1784 were able to support ministers during the decade of 1802 to 1811. In 1802, an act of the General Assembly declared that the title of the colonial property of the church belonged to the state at large and directed that even the glebe farms be seized for public benefit. This created a financial collapse of the diocese at a time when very few young men were willing to serve the church. Bishop James Madison, who presided over this dissolution from 1790 to 1812, ordained only one deacon for the entire state in the first decade of the new century and witnessed only three young men in training for the priesthood. By 1805 Madison was so despondent that he went into seclusion, leaving the church too weak and badly organized to contemplate the challenge of moving forward in the growing West.[31] While the church in Maryland was able to keep its lands, half of its parishes remained vacant at the turn of the century, and the General Convention was informed in 1808 that "the Church in Maryland is still in a deplorable condition."[32] In 1816, on the entire Delmarva Peninsula there were only twelve Episcopal clergymen to compete with thirty Methodist itinerants and more than two hundred local preachers.[33] When the well-known minister Nathaniel Blount died in North Carolina in 1816, no clergyman of the Episcopal church was resident within the boundaries of that state.[34] Ralph Morrow had noted that, for many years after its organization in 1789, the Protestant Episcopal Church more "closely resembled an executor settling the bankrupt estate of the old Anglican establishment than the heir of a rich and vital religious tradition."[35]

The Presbyterian Church faced the new century far more stable institutionally and far more capable of concerted efforts for missionary expansion. Yet its initial sortie into the state of Kentucky served as a stark reminder that, under such fluid conditions, no church could presume to be accorded a commanding position. Between 1803 and 1809, the turbulence of revivalism swept away more than half of the Presbyterian clergy and lay members in Kentucky, including the complete Springfield Presbytery. This was followed in 1813 by another major defection, that of the entire Cumberland Presbytery.[36]

The melancholy experience of David Rice, the "father" of Kentucky Presbyterianism, is indicative of the altered relationship between clergy and people. Converted under the Presbyterian revivalist Samuel Davies, educated at Princeton, and married to the daughter of the respected Samuel Blair, David Rice seemed destined for a distinguished career. After serving several Virginia pulpits, welcoming the American Revolution, and helping to found Hampden-Sidney College, Rice moved to Mercer County, Kentucky, in 1783, where he pastored three rustic congregations at Danville, Cane Run, and the Forks of Dick's River. In 1797, he became involved in a salary dispute with his Danville parishioners and made the rash judgment of refusing to administer the sacrament unless the congregation met their financial obligations. The result was a terrific uproar that utterly destroyed Rice's reputation and forced him to resign. In the process, he became the butt of jokes and noisy songs in local taverns. One of Danville's town drunks, Tom Johnson, amused himself by writing a satire in doggerel about Rice, which he published in a volume that was in its fourth edition by 1821.[37] In 1805, at the request of the Presbyterian General Assembly, Rice traveled throughout Kentucky and Ohio to assess religious conditions. His two reports are a deeply disillusioned account of the disintegration of frontier Presbyterianism, made more poignant by his own unswerving evangelical convictions and his lifelong belief that the Presbyterian church should be the primary civilizing force in Kentucky.[38]

The malaise each of these respectable denominations faced at the turn of the century was temporary, to be sure, and each reemerged with new vitality after necessary adjustments to the temper of the times. Yet the point to emphasize is that, in a democratic and rapidly expanding nation, they could no longer assume that they stood at the center of the culture, their very presence giving definition to various shades of dissent. Like everyone else, they had to earn the right to be heard—just as the young Federalists learned after watching the successful communication strategies of the Jeffersonians.[39] The profound concessions to a popular evangelical style made by churchmen such as Lyman Beecher, Albert Barnes, George Duffield, and William Meade indicates the extent to which people at large no longer recognized the place of a disinterested, enlightened elite. If America was becoming a democratic marketplace of equally competing individuals with interest to promote, it is not difficult to understand the appeal of insurgent religious movements who claimed to take a place at the center of culture by virtue of their popular following.[40]

"A Sea of Sectarian Rivalries"

Religious historians have breathed a collective sigh of relief at the Second Great Awakening's unexpected appearance at the turn of the nineteenth century. For them, revivalism rescued the infant nation from the brink of disaster. Christians, faced with church decline in settled communities and moral chaos on the frontier, sought to muster a counteroffensive. They rediscovered revival and forged it into a heroic weapon. Thus, most historical accounts conclude, the revival became the dominant theme in antebellum history, the key to the pervasive Christianization that impressed Tocqueville, the wellspring of reform, the cornerstone of a righteous empire—in short, a powerfully integrating and cohesive force.[41]

This positive historical assessment has much to commend it. Its tone matches the confident rhetoric of such men as Lyman Beecher and Horace Bushnell about the early triumph of Christian civilization in America. But it fails to do justice to a darker, foreboding side of American civilization and its religious underpinnings that troubled even these men. A good example of this tension is found in the address that Bushnell gave to the American Home Missionary Society in 1847. His speech's final lines sound a note of millennial hope. Historians have often quoted them to show that by mid-century America had been saved from ruin: "The wilderness shall bud and blossom as the rose before us; and we will not cease, till a Christian nation throws up its temples of worship on every hill and plain . . . and the bands of a complete Christian commonwealth are seen to span the continent."[42]

Bushnell's visionary lines were appended, however, to the address "Barbarism the First Danger." It was a grim assessment of the religious state of affairs in the expanding republic; west of Connecticut, prospects for the advance of the Kingdom were not bright. Quoting a passage from the book of Judges about a time when "the people have run wild," Bushnell fretted over the tendency of young and mobile societies to devolve rather than progress. He warned that immature societies, bereft of the organic ties of tradition and custom, often fall into "moral and social disorganization" and "ignorance, wildness and social confusion." Under these conditions, even religious expression becomes "narrow and crude." America's present danger, Bushnell concluded, was that the wrong kind of religion was thriving: "It is the wild chant of Deborah, or better still it is the nail that was driven by Jael's hammer—not the ointment ministered by the graceful hand of Mary."[43]

The ominous tone of Bushnell's description of America raises a broader question: whether historians have been overly sanguine about the religious cohesiveness of the young nation, what Perry Miller termed "the centripetal power of the Revival."[44] While the rhetoric of unity was omnipresent in American churches, centrifugal forces had never been more acute. The chief culprit was the democratic dissent that this study attempts to analyze. Between 1800 and 1830 a wildly diverse religious culture made both denominational identity and authority fragile creations. Outside of the face-to-face discipline exercised in local churches, many denominations maintained their authority only by seldom exercising it.

Hans Kohn once observed that American nationalism began without a name, without a common ethnic identity, and without a common religion.[45] To become an American simply meant to identify oneself with a particular idea of liberty. A South Carolinian and a New England Yankee, for instance, could draw upon few common traditions in defining their Americanness. The United States could not even take pride in the English language. In spite of Noah Webster's efforts to create a distinctly American version of the language through his dictionary and his "American" translation of the Bible, the best examples of cultured speech still came from across the Atlantic.

Three realities about life in the early republic intensified anxiety and self-consciousness as Americans sought to create a viable national tradition. All were also important issues confronting popular Protestant denominations in their formative years. The first was the terrible fear that the Union might not work. John M. Murrin suggests that this concern prompted much of the rhetorical insistence that Americans were one people who shared a glorious past. In fact, American national identity was an impromptu and artificial creation of the Revolution. It had few pillars of support other than the revered principles of the Founding Fathers:

> In the architecture of nationhood, the United States had achieved something quite remarkable. . . . Americans had erected their constitutional roof before they put up the national walls. Hovering there over a divided people, it aroused wonder and awe, even ecstasy. Early historians rewrote the past to make the Constitution the culminating event of their story. . . . Orators plundered the language in search of fitting praise. Someone may even have put the document to music. This spirit of amazement, this frenzy of self-congratulation, owed its intensity to the terrible fear that the roof could come crashing down at almost any time. Indeed, the national walls have taken much longer to build.[46]

If fear of regional fragmentation was one reason that Americans clung to an idealized version of the Revolutionary achievement, a second was the seething mobility that cut Americans off from the roots of family, church, and community. Alexis de Tocqueville pointed out in 1840 that for Americans "there are no traditions, or common habits, to forge links between their minds." In 1790, 94 percent of the population lived in the original thirteen colonies; in 1850, only about half of them did. Taking note of this movement, Tocqueville concluded that Americans, plunging into the West, were "adventurers impatient of any sort of yoke, greedy for wealth, and often outcasts from the States in which they were born. They arrive in the depth of the wilderness without knowing one another. There is nothing of tradition, family feeling, or example to restrain them." He also noted the constant, unpredictable social mobility in America: "New families continually arrive from nothing while others fall, and nobody's position is quite stable. The woof of time is broken and the track of past generations lost."[46]

The splintering of American Protestantism compounded this sense of rootlessness and fragmentation, particularly for devout Christians. The first third of the nineteenth century experienced a period of religious ferment, chaos, and originality unmatched in American history. Few traditional claims to religious authority could weather such a relentless beating. There were competing claims of old denominations and a host of new ones. Wandering prophets appeared dramatically, and supremely heterodox religious movements gained followings. People veered from one church to another. Religious competitors wrangled unceasingly, traditional clergy and self-appointed preachers foremost in the fray. And new and passionate causes sprang up within the church's walls around the issues of freemasonry, temperance, slavery, women's rights, and health reform. Julian Sturtevant, a Yale graduate and Congregational missionary to Illinois, found a "realm of confusion and religious anarchy" when he arrived in Jacksonville in 1829: "In Illinois I met for the first time a divided Christian community, and was plunged without warning or preparation into a sea of sectarian rivalries which was kept in constant agitation, not only by real differences of opinion, but by ill-judged discussions and unfortunate personalities among ambitious men."[48]

Whatever common spirit bound Protestants together in this period, it came to rest in few stable institutions. Recurring dissent blasted any semblance of organizational coherence. The array of denominations, mission boards, reform agencies, newspapers, journals, revivalists, and colleges is at best an amorphous collectivity, an organizational smorgasbord.

Power, influence, and authority were radically dispersed, and the most successful came by way of popular appeal.

The democratic winnowing of the church produced not just pluralism but also striking diversity. The flexibility and innovation of religious organizations made it possible for an American to find an amenable group no matter what his or her preference in belief, practice, or institutional structure. Churches ranged from egalitarian to autocratic and included all degrees of organizational complexity. One could be a Presbyterian who favored or opposed the freedom of the will, a Methodist who promoted or denounced democracy in the church, a Baptist who advocated or condemned foreign missions, and a member of virtually any denomination that upheld or opposed slavery. One could revel in Christian history with John W. Nevin or wipe the slate clean with Alexander Campbell. One could opt for traditional piety or join a perfectionist sect. Religious options in the early republic seemed unlimited: one could worship on Saturday, practice foot washing, ordain women, advocate pacifism, prohibit alcohol, or toy with spiritualism, phrenology, or health reform.

The nature of extreme dissent in the republic gives the most telling evidence of these churning centrifugal forces. The Mormons, the Shakers, and the Oneida community, for instance, did not lash out at some combination of Protestant churches and voluntary societies that had gained hegemony over the nation's spiritual destiny. Instead, their passion for a new order grew out of the perception that there was no authoritative center. The entire religious world, perched upon shifting sand, cried out for prophets who could recover the missing bedrock. Lawrence Foster has suggested that the acute crisis of authority that haunted each of these groups motivated them to reconstitute sexual and family life. John Humphrey Noyes was particularly jarred by the cacophony of ideas and causes surrounding him. He feared an unraveling of the entire social order and concluded that he was uniquely responsible for achieving a new social and religious synthesis. He declared in a letter in 1837: "God has set me to cast up a highway across this chaos, and I am gathering out the stones and grading the track as fast as possible."[49]

By appealing to abstract principles such as the Bible alone and the ancient order of things, Christian churches were constructing roofs over their heads. But they lacked the ecclesiastical walls of liturgy, governance, theology, and instruction that are normative in a given church tradition. This was an age in which tradition, to use Ralph Morrow's words, "suffered the perverse fortune of having only the case against it presented fully and explicitly."[50] Once people had left the faith of their mothers and fathers and joined the Disciples, the Universalists, the Baptists, or the Methodists, the real job of building the walls began. In these institutions, the problems of authority were acute, given the tension between their professed first principles and the realities of human organization. This crisis of authority, first kindled in popular culture, rapidly engulfed all of American Protestantism. In a democracy premised on religious liberty, not even those clergymen whose fathers had launched the errand into the wilderness were exempt from what Harrison Gray Otis in 1836 called "the fiery furnace of democracy."[51]

CHAPTER FOUR

Thundering Legions

God's ministers like flames of fire
Are passing thro' the land,
The voice is here; "Repent and fear,
King Jesus is at hand!"

EARLY AMERICAN METHODIST SONG

Thus the Methodists for example have a ministry admirably adapted, as regards
their mode of action, to the new West—a kind of light artillery that God has
organized to pursue and overtake the fugitives that flee into the wilderness from his
presence.

HORACE BUSHNELL, 1847

The democratic religious movements of the early republic all took root in the same soil, an environment that favored certain approaches, answers, and leadership styles. Competition in the religious marketplace muted the appeal of orthodox churches and amplified the message of insurgents. A variety of disparate movements manifested a common style and demeanor.

At the same time, these distinct religious movements need to be understood on their own terms. Each of the five treated in this chapter is a complicated stream of diverse interests and tendencies, and each stands apart from others in theological emphasis and organizational structure. John Leland and Alexander Campbell, for instance, favored democratic church government, while Francis Asbury and Joseph Smith insisted on direction from the top. Leland and Asbury threw themselves into the cause of enthusiastic revivalism. Campbell and Smith found this emphasis misguided, Campbell opting for Biblical rationalism, Smith trusting only a new word from heaven. Leland remained an adamant opponent of slavery, a position that Asbury favored but could not enforce. Smith found little room in his kingdom for people of color, even as Richard Allen insisted that blacks be granted equal opportunity to frame the gospel in their own terms and under their own authority. Campbell, Leland, and Asbury all watched

67

second-generation leaders of their movements yearn to be pillars of American society; having set his face toward building a tangible Zion, Joseph Smith never bowed to the dominant culture's idols of respectability.

For all this fragmentation, one could not have designed a system more capable of Christianizing a people in all of its social, geographic, and ethnic diversity. The collective dynamism of these groups is related to the degree of pluralism and dissent that they represent and to their ability to communicate with a variety of persons high and low, rich and poor, urban and rural, slave and free. Even as society became more stratified, few Americans were untouched by the diverse strains of the gospel being proclaimed.[1]

The Christian Movement

In the fall of 1814 an alarmed Stephen Porter, the Presbyterian minister of Ballston, New York, called together his congregation to warn them of the "awful delusions" that were spreading among them. Two objects drew his fire: the band of "false teachers" that railed against orthodoxy, "aiming the poisoned arrows of ridicule and reproach against all the regular ministers of Christ," and the wholesale distribution of books and pamphlets that reinforced their message. Porter vented his wrath against one publication entitled *A New Testament Dictionary*, a "pocket volume" that offered people the chance to discover for themselves the true "meanings of more than eleven hundred words as they are used in the New Testament." The book also dismissed all Protestant denominations as limbs of the Antichrist.[2]

After Mr. Porter finished reading his sermon and pronounced the benediction, those Presbyterians in the audience who had heard only secondhand about these dissenters had the chance to see them in action. Jabez King of Woodstock, Vermont, one sectarian who had deigned to attend the service, rose and began to sing. Despite repeated interruptions, including an incident in which "one man shook his fist at him, [and] another collared him, to prevent his singing," Jabez King proceeded with the song "The World Turned Upside Down." This crude ballad derided hide-bound priests for their greed and for their oppression of people who organized their own churches.[3]

Calling themselves merely "Christians," these dissenters followed the banner of one Elias Smith, a self-taught Yankee and devout Jeffersonian who sought a radical simplification of the gospel. Smith became a central figure in a loose network of religious radicals who between 1790 and 1815 chose the name "Christian" or "Disciples of Christ." They demanded, in light of the American and French revolutions, a new dispensation free from the trammels of history, a new kind of church based on democratic principles, and a new form of biblical authority calling for common people to interpret the New Testament for themselves. The central figures in the reform movement—Elias Smith in New England, James O'Kelly in Virginia, Barton Stone in Kentucky, and Alexander Campbell in Pennsylvania—were a motley crew with few common characteristics, but they all moved independently to similar conclusions within a fifteen-year span. A Calvinist Baptist, a Methodist, and two Presbyterians all found traditional sources of authority anachronistic and groped toward similar definitions of egalitarian religion. In a culture that increasingly balked at vested interests, symbols of hierarchy, and timeless authorities, a remarkable number of people awoke one morning to find it self-evident that the priesthood of all believers meant just that—religion of, by, and for the people.

There were few characters in Jeffersonian America more inherently interesting than Elias Smith, a man of egalitarian passion and unremitting energy, who made significant innovations as preacher, healer, publicist, and composer of religious folk songs. William Bentley, the Jeffersonian diarist and Congregational minister, had no use for religious enthusiasts in Salem at the opening of the nineteenth century. He saved his sharpest barbs for the "notorious" Elias Smith. Bentley noted that Smith regularly barnstormed through Essex County, preaching in the open air, singing in the streets, and accosting people to question their spiritual state. If this was not enough to discomfit the respectable citizens, Smith kept the pot boiling by leaving behind bundles of his tracts and pamphlets.[4]

For all its parallels with the dissent of a Whitefield or an Isaac Backus, Smith's gospel for the people did have one different twist. It was laced with the language of politics and reflected the experience of a man whose radical pilgrimage began with a political conversion. Until 1800 Smith filled the pulpit of the respectable Baptist Church in Woburn, Massachusetts, and gave little attention to political questions of the day. During the election of 1800, however, he fell under the influence of the radical Jeffersonian publicist Benjamin Austin, Jr., who wrote regularly for Boston's *Independent Chronicle*. Smith quickly imbibed the heady wine of Austin's writings, which made much of the right of common people to think and act for themselves. Resigning from his church as a manifesto of his own liberty and denouncing formal religion of every kind, Smith began to translate the sovereignty of the people to the sphere of religion.[5] "Let us be republicans indeed," he declared in 1809. "Many are *republicans* as to *government*, and yet are but half republicans, being in matters of religion still bound to a catechism, creed, covenant or a superstitious priest. Venture to be as independent in things of religion, as those which respect the government in which you live."[6] From Portsmouth, New Hampshire, Smith launched the first religious newspaper in the United States, a fortnightly *Herald of Gospel Liberty*, which he edited from 1808 to 1818. From that forum, and in scores of pamphlets and sermons, he and a band of fifty or so itinerants who called themselves merely Christians carried on a blistering attack against Baptists, Congregationalists, Methodists, and Federalists of any religious persuasion. By 1815, the *Herald of Gospel Liberty* had fourteen hundred subscribers and over fifty agents around the country and was a vehicle of communication for other individuals who were independently reaching conclusions similar to Smith's.[7]

From Virginia came word of James O'Kelly's Republican Methodists, founded in 1794 to undo the "ecclesiastical monarchy" in the Methodist church. An early leader among Virginia Methodists, O'Kelly could not abide the bishopric of Francis Asbury and withdrew with over thirty ministers to form a connection that had as many as twenty thousand members when it merged with Smith's Christians in 1809.[8] "Episcopacy makes a bad appearance in our republican world," O'Kelly argued in 1798. "Francis was born and nurtured in the land of Bishops and Kings and what is bred in the bone, is hard to get out of the flesh."[9] O'Kelly, who had taken up arms in the Revolution and was briefly a British captive, argued that he was "too sensible of the sweets of liberty, to be content any longer under British chains. . . . As a son of America, and a Christian," he declared to Asbury, "I shall oppose your political measures and contend for the Saviour's government. I contend for Bible government, Christian equality, and the Christian name."[10]

Barton W. Stone was an equally interesting figure who had ventured upon much the same pilgrimage prior to the appearance of the *Herald of Gospel Liberty*. In 1802, in the wake of the Cane Ridge Revival in Kentucky, Stone decided he could no longer live under Presbyterian doctrine or church organization. A year later, he and five other ministers pushed this idea to its logical extreme and proclaimed that it was not just the Presbyterians who were wrong: all church structures were suspect. Signing a document entitled "The Last Will and Testament of Springfield Presbytery," these men vowed to follow nothing but the Christian name and the New Testament.[11]

Scholars have generally viewed Stone's beliefs as the product of the rough-and-tumble context of the frontier and of the rampant emotionalism of the Great Revival.[12] Stone was a rawboned character, no doubt, but his formative years were those of the American Revolution, and his theology of "gospel-liberty" reflected this early experience. "From my earliest recollection I drank deeply into the spirit of liberty," he confessed late in life, "and was so warmed by the soul-inspiring draughts, that I could not hear the name of British, or Tories, without feeling a rush of blood through the whole system. . . . I confess their magic influence to this advanced day of my life." It was not without deep connotation that Stone characterized his break with the Presbyterians as the "declaration of our independence."[13]

The final member of this quartet of reformers is the Scottish immigrant Alexander Campbell, the only college graduate among the four and the only one not to participate in the American Revolution.[14] Whatever Alexander Campbell may have brought to America of his Scottish and Presbyterian heritage, he discarded much of it for an explicitly American theology. Writing to his uncle back in Scotland in 1815, he described his seven years in the United States: "During this period of years my mind and circumstances have undergone many revolutions. . . . I have . . . renounced much of the traditions and errors of my early education." He described the change elsewhere in these words: "My mind was, for a time, set loose from all its former moorings. It was not a simple change: but a new commencement . . . the whole landscape of Christianity presented itself to my mind in a new attitude and position."[15] By 1830 Alexander Campbell's quest for primitive Christianity led his movement, the Disciples of Christ, to unite with Stone's Christians. By 1860 their denomination claimed about two hundred thousand adherents, the fifth largest Protestant body in the United States.[16] More important, his movement followed an unmistakable pattern emerging in the early republic. Smith, O'Kelly, and Stone all knew what Campbell meant when he proclaimed that July 4, 1776, was "a day to be remembered as was the Jewish Passover. . . . This revolution, taken in all its influences, will make men free indeed."[17]

In many ways the message of the Christians built upon the kind of radical piety that Americans had known since the Great Awakening of the 1740s. These new reformers hammered relentlessly at the simple themes of sin, grace, and conversion; they organized fellowships that resisted social distinctions and welcomed spontaneous experience; and they denounced any religion that seemed bookish, cold, or formal. What sets the Christians apart from earlier revivalists is the extent to which they wrestled self-consciously with the loss of traditional sources of authority and found in democratic political culture a cornerstone for new foundations. Taking seriously the mandate of liberty and equality, the Christians espoused reform in three areas. First, they called for a revolution within the church to place laity and clergy on an equal footing and to exalt the conscience of the individual over the collective will of any congregation or church organization. Second, they rejected the traditions of learned theology altogether

Fig. 6. Alexander Campbell, founder of the Disciples of Christ, from *Frank Leslie's Illustrated Newspaper*, July 14, 1883

and called for a new view of history that welcomed inquiry and innovation. Finally, they called for a populist hermeneutic premised on the inalienable right of every person to understand the New Testament for him- or herself.

A zeal to dismantle mediating elites within the church, more than anything else, triggered the Christians' revolt against tradition. O'Kelly broke with Asbury when the Methodist bishop refused to put up with representative government in the church. Smith bade farewell to Isaac Backus and the Warren Association after influential colleagues criticized his plain dress and suggested that the respectable parishioners of Woburn, Massachusetts, deserved more formality. Both Stone and Thomas Campbell (Alexander's father, who had preceded him to America) withdrew from the Presbyterian church when their orthodox colleagues began to clamp down on their freedom of inquiry concerning Presbyterian standards. Before their respective separations, each of these men in his own way had offered stern opposition to received tradition, yet their dissent was contained within assumed cultural boundaries. Once they had severed organization ties, however, formerly mild questions reappeared as seething hostility, and suggestions for reform turned to ecclesiastical defiance.

The Christians excelled at popular communication. They ferreted out converts with an unremitting itinerancy and cranked out an avalanche of pamphlet and newspaper copy, which, in its form and content, conspired against social distinction.[18] Smith was aware of his innovative role when he began the first religious newspaper in the United States; he confessed on its opening page that the utility of such a paper had been suggested to him by the explosion of popular print all around. "In a short and cheap way," he asserted, "a general knowledge of our affairs is diffused through the whole." While his paper did include accounts of revivals of religion throughout the world, its overall strategy showed little resemblance to previous revival periodicals such as the *Christian History* of the Great Awakening, largely an intramural communication among the clergy. By promoting in common language the idea that "right is equal among all," Smith knew that he would be judged as "stirring up the people to revolt" and "turning the world upside down."[19] Just as he expected, the established clergy found his "vulgar stories and malicious sarcasm" totally beneath them, but they could hardly ignore the popularity of his "poisoned arrows of ridicule and reproach."[20]

The style of Smith's communication is well illustrated in one of his early pamphlets, *The Clergyman's Looking-Glass*, a stinging attack on men of the cloth that went through at least a dozen printings. Smith juxtaposed passages of the New Testament with satirical jibes at the contemporary clergy in mock-scripture style. After quoting from I Peter the instructions

HERALD OF GOSPEL LIBERTY.

BY ELIAS SMITH.

NO. 1.] THURSDAY EVENING, SEPTEMBER 1, 1808. [VOL. I

" FROM REALMS FAR DISTANT, AND FROM CLIMES UNKNOWN ; WE MAKE THE KNOWLEDGE OF OUR KING YOUR OWN."

ADDRESS TO THE PUBLIC.

To the Subscribers for this paper, and to all who may hereafter read its contents.

BRETHREN AND FELLOW CITIZENS,

THE age in which we live may certainly be distinguished from others in the history of Man, and particularly, as it respects the people of these *United States*, the increase of knowledge is very great in different parts of the world, and of course there is an increase of *Liberty* among the people, and an increasing desire among *certain individuals*, accompanied with their fruitless exertions, to prevent them from enjoying what they have been taught belongs to them, as a right given by their *Creator*, and guaranteed by the government of the country in which we live.

The struggle which has and still continues to convulse the nations in the old countries, are in a great measure over here. *Liberty* as men, is what many are now making violent exertions to obtain, and others (though few in numbers) by every possible mean are endeavouring to prevent.

This *Liberty* is in a great measure obtained in this country, to the great advantage of *Millions* and the grief of thousands, "who care not for the people ;" but while we glory in being a free people, and of being independent of the nations which endeavoured to deprive us of the rights which God has given us in common with all nations, multitudes are enslaved with the principles bro't from Europe by those who first settled this country. Had *George the third*, when he withdrew his troops from this country, withdrawn all the principles respecting civil and religious affairs, which are in opposition to the rights of mankind, we should have been a much more united and happy people than we now are ; but alas ! they are left among us like the Canaanites in ancient times, to be overcome by little and little ; and like the army of Gog, which fell upon the mountains of Israel they are to be buried by men employed for that purpose, while every passenger is to erect a monument, wherever he finds a bone in his way. It is not now a tyrannical government which deprives us of *liberty* ; but the highly destructive principles of tyranny which remain in a good government ; and though these principles are not protected by law, yet men's attachment to them, in a free government, prevents the enjoyment of *Liberty* which God has given us, and which all might enjoy according to the Constitution of the United States. A member of Congress said to me not long ago (while speaking upon the state of the people in this country, as it respects Religious Liberty) to the amount, "the people in this country are in general free, as to political matters ; but in things of religion, multitudes of them are apparently ignorant of what Liberty is :" This is true, MANY who appear to know what belongs to them as citizens, and who will contend for their rights ; when they talk or act upon things of the highest importance, appear to be guided wholly by the opinions of designing men, who would bind them in the chains of ignorance all their days, and entail the same on all their posterity.— The design of this paper is to shew the *liberty* which belongs to men, as it respects their duty to God, and each other.

It is an established principle with me, that the man who appears in any public service and is faithful to his trust, will have a double character ; by the unjust and them who judge from the testimony of such, he will be considered a disturber of the peace, as turning the world upside down, and stirring up the people to revolt ; but by the well informed lovers of truth, he will be considered a light to them who otherwise would set in darkness. There is no doubt in my mind but many will be displeased at what may appear in this paper from time to time, unless they own that, *right is equal among all*.

How difficult the task may be, which is now undertaken, is unknown to me, experience will shew this ;—this however is my design, to have a steady and persevering regard to truth, and the general good of men ; and to treat every thing in a fair and manly way ; not scandalizing any, or doing any thing by partiality. Should any scandalize themselves by bad conduct ; let them not charge it to me. If men do not wish to have bad things said of them, let them not do bad things. It is my design in the following numbers to give a plain description of the rights of men, and to shew the principle on which they are founded, and likewise to shew the opposite. There are many things taking place in the present day respecting religion, which will be noticed as they occur. A particular attention will be paid to the accounts of revivals of religion in different parts of the world, among the various denominations who call Jesus Lord, as far as it can be obtained.

A religious News-paper, is almost a new thing under the sun ; I know not but this is the first ever published to the world.

The utility of such a paper has been suggested to me, from the great use other papers are to to the community at large. In this way almost the whole state of the world is presented to us at once. In a short and cheap way, a general knowledge of our affairs is diffused through the whole ; and by looking into a News-paper, we often look at the state of nations, and see them rise into importance, or crumble into ruin. If we are profited in political affairs in this way, I do not see why the knowledge of the Redeemer's kingdom may not be promoted or increased in the same way. It appears to me best to make the trial. The liberal subscriptions for this work in these trying times, has encouraged me to begin it, hoping that others will find an advantage in forwarding the work by adding their names to the list of those who have already wished such a work to appear in the world.

There are many things which will be taken up which are not new, but are important, and which if stated to the rising generation will serve to give them a knowledge of that liberty for which their fathers bled, and for which they ought to contend.

It is the design of the Editor, in describing the nature of civil and religious *Liberty*, to come to the capacities of those whose advantages have been small, as to acquiring a general knowledge of the world.

It may be that some may wish to know why this paper should be named the " HERALD OF GOSPEL LIBERTY." This kind of Liberty is the only one which can make us happy, being the glorious Liberty of the sons of God which Christ proclaimed ; and which all who have, are exhorted to stand fast in, being that which is given and enjoyed by the law of Liberty ; which is the law of the spirit of life in Christ Jesus, which makes free from the law of sin and death.

In this place, I give the meaning of the word *Herald*. This word is derived from the Saxon word *Herehault*, and by abbreviation, *Heralt*, which in that language signifies the Champion of an army, and growing to be a name of office, it was given to him who, in the army, had the special charge to denounce war, to challenge to battle and combat, to proclaim peace, and to execute martial messages. The business of an Herald in the English government is as follows—" To marshal, order, and conduct all royal cavalcades, ceremonies at coronations, royal marriages, installations, creations of Dukes, Marquisses, Earls, Viscounts

Fig. 7. Opening page of Elias Smith's *Herald of Gospel Liberty*

that elders were to serve God's flock "not for filthy lucre . . . neither as being lords over God's heritage," Smith gave his Petrine rendition of the modern clergy:

> The reverend clergy who are with me I advise, who am also a clergy-man, and a D.D. a member of that respectable body, who are numerous, and "who seek honor one of another;" and a partaker of the benefit of it; feed yourselves upon the church and parish, over which we have settled you for life, and who are obliged to support you, whether they like you or not; taking the command by constraint, for filthy lucre, not of a ready mind, as lords over men's souls, not as ensamples to them, and when commencement day shall appear, you shall receive some honorary title, which shall make you appear very respectable among the reverend clergy.[21]

In a similar vein, Alexander Campbell used his first newspaper, the *Christian Baptist*, to mock the pretensions of the clergy. In a burlesque "Third Epistle of Peter," a document purportedly discovered by a Roman Catholic monk, he instructed preachers to live well, wear the best clothes, adorn themselves with high-sounding titles, drink costly wine, and fleece the people.[22] Evangelicals in the past had often questioned the spiritual state of individual clergymen; the Christians now took the liberty of slandering the entire profession as money-grubbing tyrants.

This kind of billingsgate journalism was appealing in two powerful ways. In the first place, it portrayed society as horizontally polarized: the people were arrayed against elites of all kind: military, legal, civic, and religious. In an early edition of the *Herald of Gospel Liberty*, Smith sketched a revealing dialogue between the people and the privileged class. "The picture, is this: two companies standing in sight of each other, one large, the other small. The large containing every profession useful to society, the other small, wearing marks of distinction, appearing as though they did no labour, yet in rich attire, glittering with gold and silver, while their plump and ruddy countenances, prove them persons of leisure and riches." Seething with resentment, the people of Smith's dialogue happen to overhear what the privileged are saying to each other: "To mix and place ourselves on a level with the *common people*, would be beyond all measure degrading and vilifying. What! are they not born to serve us? and are we not men of a totally distinct blood and superior pedigree?" In response, the people insist that they are going "to take the management of our affairs into our own hands. . . . When the people declare themselves free, such *privileged classes* will be as useles[s] as candles at noonday."[23]

Abel M. Sargent, another radical figure associated with the Christians, used his paper, the *Halcyon Itinerary and True Millennium Messenger*, to present a virtual class analysis of society. Writing in 1807 to extol Thomas Jefferson as the forerunner of a new millennial age, Sargent demanded that life, liberty, and happiness be extended to "the oppressed who have been deprived of them." His images of society bristle with the ongoing conflict between the powerful and the oppressed:

> How often do we see it the case in earthly courts, under the dominion of the beast, that the power and influence of money and false Agency over-balance equity and right; so that the poor have but a dull chance to obtain Justice in carnal courts; and again, how often is the poor industrious and honest labourer, reduced to the absolute necessity of yielding up his rights and falling a prey to cruelty and injustice, merely for want of money enough to discharge the fees of those whose interest and livings (like the wolf and raven) depend on the ruin and destruction of others.[24]

In addition to this bombast against the privileged, these writings also contained a second appeal. They appropriated the rhetoric of civil and religious liberty that the respectable clergy had made popular during the Revolution and marshaled it for an entirely new purpose: to topple its very architects. The Christians exploited the potent themes of tyranny, slavery, and the Antichrist; they regaled their audiences with the latest chapter in the saga of the beast and the whore of Babylon. Simply put, the Antichrist now worked his evil machinations through elites of all kind, particularly the clergy. In a splendid example of the multivalence of language, rhetoric that had seemed benign when used by respectable clergymen during the Revolution came to have radical connotations when abstracted from a restricted context and transferred to people who had reason to lash out at vested interests.[25]

But what end did the Christians have in view when decrying ecclesiastical authority? What positive implications did they wring out of the notion of religious liberty? Smith came right to the point in an early issue of the *Herald of Gospel Liberty* when he contrasted the mere separation of church and state with "being wholly free to examine for ourselves, what is truth." He argued that every last Christian had the "unalienable right" to follow "the scripture wherever it leads him, even an equal right with the Bishops and Pastors of the churches . . . even though his principles may, in many things, be contrary to what the Reverend D.D.'s call Orthodoxy."[26] Using the same language, Alexander Campbell pressed for "the inalienable right of all laymen to examine the sacred writings for themselves." This logic, brimming with conspiratorial notions of how clergymen of every stripe had "hoodwinked" the people, eventually led each of these Christian leaders to demand that the traditional distinction between clergy and laity be abolished and that any leadership in the local church function according to new rules: "liberty is no where safe in any hands excepting those of the people themselves."[27] With demands for this sort of liberation afoot, it is little wonder that Congregational and Presbyterian clergymen came to view the Christians as but another tentacle of the Bavarian Illuminati's conspiracy to overthrow authority in church and state.[28]

The Christian idea of religious liberty stands in marked contrast to the eighteenth-century notion that religious liberty meant the civil right to choose or not to choose affiliation with a church. The religious dissent that had come out of the Great Awakening, despite its popular sources, had never begun to suggest that power should be surrendered to the people in this fashion. The Baptists in Virginia set themselves off from the culture of gentlemen by striving for more order, more discipline, and more social control within the local congregation.[29] In New England as well, Baptists and Separatists called for closed communion and a tighter discipline within the pure church. By the 1760s, they were educating their clergy, forming associations to regulate doctrine and local disputes, and, as their people began to drift away to other sects during the Revolution, actually imposing stiff creedal tests upon local churches. Backus did not long for some new order that leveled the clergy and exalted the laity; he reminisced, instead, about the pious fathers of early New England. He argued time and again that his Baptists agreed "with the most eminent fathers of New England, except in sprinkling infants upon the faith of their parents and calling it baptism."[30] The same point has been made about the Separatists of New England: "they were reformers, not rebels; . . . they wished to fulfill their history as Puritans, not repudiate it."[31]

In contrast, the Christians called for the abolition of organizational restraints of any kind. Recall that Barton Stone and his colleagues not only separated from the Presbyterian church but also dissolved their own association. Only by renouncing all institutional forms could "the oppressed . . . go free, and taste the sweets of gospel liberty."[32] Alexander Campbell did not even want to hear the words *church government*: "We have no system of our own, or of others, to substitute in lieu of the reigning systems. We only aim at substituting the New Testament."[33] In a similar vein, Stone and his associates declared that the attempt "to impose any form of government upon the church . . . should be justly abandoned by every child of gospel liberty." They went on to say that any human form of government would be "like binding two or more dead bodies together" and coercing people "like parts of a machine."[34] The organization of Protestant churches, which in colonial culture had been seen as vibrant and alive—the very body of Christ—now smacked of death and machines.

By their appeal to "Bible government," the Christians removed the issue of power and authority from any concrete application. They opposed all ecclesiastical names not found in the New Testament, advocated the right of the individual to withdraw unilaterally from church membership, and refused to adhere to creeds as tests of fellowship, to undergo theological examinations, or to offer a confession of faith upon joining a church. In short, no human organization could exist that did not spring from the uncoerced will of the individual. When pressed by Bishop Asbury to heed the scriptural injunction, "Obey them that have rule over you," O'Kelly responded; "Rule over, is no more than for the church to follow those guides who delivered unto them the Word of God." O'Kelly was suggesting that submitting to the New Testament meant never doffing his hat to any mere mortal.[35]

Several women became powerful preachers within the Christian Connection. Nancy Gove Cram, who died in 1815 after less than four years of active preaching, created a remarkable stir in frontier New York. After her prayer at a funeral in Charleston greatly affected the audience, she was invited to hold a meeting. She preached from that point on, and crowds assembled to hear her in barns and out-of-doors. When converts wished to begin a Christian church, the unordained Cram returned to Vermont to seek elders to organize the church and administer sacraments. Cram quickly drew the fire of offended Presbyterian pamphleteers. The Presbyterian minister Gilbert McMaster, who pastored churches in Galway and Duanesburgh, found Cram an aggressive, crude "pioneer," an "outrage upon the decencies and happiness of life": "She is remarkable, neither for the delicacy of mind, which is the ornament of her sex, nor for that information and good sense, by which so many of them are characterized. She is abundantly gifted with that spirit of her head, which opposes literature, order, and whatever christians usually have considered, as of vital importance to the interests of religion. . . . [S]he never studies, and *compliments* her Maker with being the author of crude invectives." David Millard, a prominent second-generation leader of the Christian church, was converted under Cram's influence in Ballstown, New York, in 1814. He later claimed that at least seven active ministers in the Christian church were awakened under her preaching.[36]

An equally bold itinerant was Nancy Towle, a young New Hampshire schoolteacher. She was converted in 1818 under the preaching of Christian exhorter Clarissa H. Danforth. Like Elias Smith and Lorenzo Dow, Towle was a relentless preacher on the move. She estimated she had traveled fifteen thousand miles in a decade of preaching. Her three hundred–page memoir, published in 1833, chronicled her encounters with a score of women preachers among Christians, Freewill Baptists, Universalists, and Methodists and called for more female laborers in the "Gospel harvest-field."

Nancy Towle's call to preach is a superb example of an ordinary person learning to trust her own religious impulses. After her conversion, Towle dreamed that she had been chosen to preach the gospel throughout the world. The intensity of her call rose to fever pitch over the next two years, steeled by a conviction that "the preaching of the Gospel by females was justifiable." She found no support for her position among family and community, however, and experienced "perpetual conflicts of my mind." Finally, in April of 1821, she determined to turn her back on "country and kindred," as Abram did. She declared, "With the fond paternal roof, I now renounce you, once for all!" Nancy Towle's lonely path as a roving preacher encountered dramatic opposition and dramatic success. This ordinary woman of meager prospects found explosive potential in the settled conviction that she was called to thwart social convention and to accomplish great and mighty things.[37]

Joseph Thomas, the "White Pilgrim," was another fascinating character associated with the Christians. Born in poverty in Orange County, North Carolina, in 1791, Thomas was converted at a camp meeting at the age of fifteen. He dedicated his life to preaching after reporting that the prophet Isaiah had given him this charge in a vision. When he considered joining a church, Thomas found Methodist polity too arbitrary, Baptist doctrine too restrictive, and Presbyterian ordination requirements too highbrow. Learning of James O'Kelly's Christian church, Thomas attended a meeting of Christian preachers in Raleigh in 1807. Immediately thereafter he set out on a preaching tour in North Carolina—at the ripe age of sixteen. Three years later, the well-known "boy preacher" expanded his horizons with an eighteen-month, seven-thousand-mile journey to the West. Traveling first through Tennessee, Kentucky, and southern Ohio, he met Stone, whose movement represented, by Thomas's estimate, thirteen thousand persons and over a hundred preachers.[38]

In the first edition of his autobiography, published in 1812, Thomas recounted the "uncontrollable power" of popular religion in the West.[39] In Monroe County, Kentucky, he was amazed by the preaching exploits of a woman: "I was no little astonished at her flow of speech and consistency of ideas." The woman was probably Nancy Mulkey, the daughter of Christian preacher John Mulkey. Another account described her as "a shouter": "She would arise with zeal on her countenance and fire in her eyes, and with a pathos that showed the depth of her soul, and would pour forth an exhortation lasting from five to fifteen minutes, which neither father nor brother could *equal*, and which brought tears from every feeling eye. She was remarkable in this respect."[40] Thomas then traveled widely in the East, particularly in Virginia and in the area around Philadelphia, where he worked briefly with Elias Smith.

Joseph Thomas's quest for apostolic simplicity came to a head in 1815. To protest ease and worldliness, he sold his horse and took up a pilgrimage on foot, dressed in a white robe—anticipating the meeting with "those who are clothed in white around the throne of God." For the next twenty years, the "White Pilgrim" traveled and preached relentlessly. Like so many of his contemporaries, he extended the range of his homespun message through songwriting and extensive publication of spiritual journals, songbooks, and sermons.[41]

The legacy of the Christian movement is riddled with irony. Instead of taking America by storm, the Christian Connection under Smith and O'Kelly vanished into insignificance, while the Disciples of Christ under Stone and Campbell grew into a major denomination only by practicing the kind of organization the reformers had once hoped to stamp out. Instead of calming sectarian strife and restoring edenic harmony, the Christians engendered controversy at every step and had to put up with chronic factionalism within their own ranks.[42] Instead of offering a new foundation for certainty, the Christian approach to knowledge, which made no man the judge of another's conscience, had little holding power and sent many early advocates scrambling for surer footing.[43] Instead of erecting a primitive church free from theological tradition and authoritarian control, the Christians came to advocate their own sectarian theology and to defer to the influence and persuasion of a dominant few. These ironies suggest that the real significance of the Christian movement is not to be found in its institutional development or in the direct influence of Smith, O'Kelly, Stone, and Alexander Campbell. The movement does specify, however, a moment of wrenching change in American culture that had great import for popular religion. Many followed the path even if they did not know its trailblazers.

The Christian movement illustrates, in the first place, the intensity of religious ferment at work in a period of chaos and originality unmatched, perhaps, since the religious turbulence of seventeenth-century England.[44] As in England a century and a half before, common folk in America at the dawn of the nineteenth century came to scorn tradition, relish novelty and experimentation, grope for fresh sources of authority, and champion an array of millennial schemes, each in its own way dethroning hierarchy and static religious forms.[45] The resulting popular culture pulsated with the claims of supremely heterodox religious groups, with people veering from one sect to another, and with the unbridled wrangling of competitors in a "war of words."[46] Scholars have only begun to assess the fragmentation that beset American religion in the period generally referred to as the Second Great Awakening, which they have too often viewed as a conservative response to rapid social change. This was a religious environment that brought into question traditional authorities and exalted the right of the people to think for themselves. The result, quite simply, was a bewildering world of clashing opinion. The erstwhile Shaker pilgrim Richard McNemar took up verse to capture the spirit of his times:

> Ten thousand Reformers like so many moles
> Have plowed all the Bible and cut it [in] holes
> And each has his church at the end of his trace
> Built up as he thinks of the subjects of grace.[47]

The Christians also illustrate the exaltation of public opinion as a primary religious authority. They called for common folk to read the New Testament as if mortal man had never seen it before. People were expected to discover the self-evident message of the Bible without any mediation from creeds, theologians, or clergymen not of their own choosing. This explicit faith that biblical authority could emerge from below, from the will of the people, was the most enduring legacy of the Christian movement. By the 1840s one analyst of American Protestantism concluded, after surveying fifty-three American sects, that the principle "No creed but the Bible" was the distinctive feature of American religion. John W. Nevin surmised that this emphasis grew out of a popular demand for "private judgment" and was "tacitly if not openly conditioned always by the assumption that every man is authorized and bound to get at this authority in a direct way for himself, through the medium simply of his own single mind."[48] Many felt the exhilarating hope that democracy had opened an immediate access to biblical truth for all persons of good will. Americans found it difficult to realize, however, that a commitment to private judgment could drive people apart, even as it raised beyond measure their hopes for unity.

The Spartan Mission of Francis Asbury

It is one of the odd twists of American history that the Methodist Episcopal church, in the firm grip of Bishop Francis Asbury, outstripped the explicitly democratic Christian movement. The very church that most adamantly refused to share ecclesiastical authority with the laity actually came to have the greatest influence among them. James O'Kelly, the first of many to decry Methodism's dread hierarchy, denounced Asbury's unilateral and arbitrary decisions as tyranny and popery. Even Asbury's friends did not deny his autocratic tendencies. John Wesley had been shocked in 1788 when Asbury took upon himself the title of bishop. Devereux Jarratt spoke of Asbury's "strong passion for superiority and thirst for domination," and Nicholas Snethen, who traveled with Asbury and worked to rebut O'Kelly, admitted that Asbury's devotion to duty left little room to accommodate flesh-and-blood people.[49] Asbury never apologized for being domineering, for the government of the church remaining the exclusive province of itinerant preachers, or for this cadre being bound together by strict rule and discipline under one leader, a sort of religious military order.

In fact, in 1814, as Asbury neared the end of his career, he devoted his valedictory address to a defense of the episcopal system as the backbone of the Methodist movement in America—an ecclesiastical offspring so successful that it was rapidly surpassing its English parent. Asbury defended episcopacy by inverting its most common claim of an uninterrupted chain of apostolic succession. Following Wesley's lead, he dismissed the "crooked, muddy succession" of episcopacy and chose to defend his own authority by linking it directly to the apostolic age, transcending the corruptions of the intervening centuries. Like so many of his American counterparts, he made explicit appeal to return to "the apostolic order of things," which had been lost in the first century "when Church governments were adulterated and had much corruption attached to them." Asbury even discounted the Reformation, which "only beat off a part of the rubbish" and only temporarily halted "the rapid increase of absurdities." Supremely confident of his own divine call and mission, Asbury made a simple empirical appeal to the fact that the Methodists, more than any other church, had restored the "primitive order" of the New Testament: "the same doctrine, the same spirituality, the same power in ordinances, in ordination, and in spirit." To those who doubted the possibility of returning to former apostolic days, he replied, "But I say that we can; I say we must; yea, I say we have."[50]

The Methodists were distinctive and uniquely apostolic in Asbury's view because their entire organizational structure, from bishop to circuit rider, was resolutely committed to an apostolic order of sacrifice and itinerancy. The son of a country gardener, Asbury defended his authoritarian rule not as a way to keep the people in their place but as a way to check the professional pretensions of the clerical office—"men going into the ministry by their learning, sent by their parents or moved by pride, the love of ease, money or honor." Asbury warned of the growing evil of preachers, elders, and bishops locating in towns where the wealthy and influential "setttle themselves to purchase ministers." Too often, he concluded, this collusion was a two-way street: ministers "of gifts and learning intend to set themselves to sale."[51]

By contrast, Asbury rested his claim to apostolic authority on the primitive simplicity of the Methodist Connection. He thought the Methodist economy paralleled the early church in two striking ways. First, the Methodists had witnessed a massive outpouring of power upon unlettered men, enabling them to preach the gospel just as fishermen and tax collectors had done in the early church. While Asbury did not disparage learning as such, he despised the way that in modern times a college education had become a crutch for the church and a sure ticket for persons seeking a calling of "more ease and greater emoluments." The prophetic lesson that Asbury drew from the day of Pentecost, when a great number of illiterate men became fluent in foreign languages, was that "in all ages to come, unlettered men should be raised up to preach the gospel with the power of the Holy Ghost sent down from heaven." The divine call could descend upon persons of any rank: "a plowman, a tailor, a carpenter, or a shoemaker." "The learned may smile in Saul's armor," he quipped, "but give me the sling and the stone, and the gigantic Goliath falls."[52]

Asbury's second claim to authority was that the Methodists had restored an episcopate that was genuinely apostolic. This system was characterized by the bishop's firm resolve to travel permanently on behalf of his flock and to share the deprivation of the itinerant preachers—and thus to partake of genuine apostolic suffering. Asbury's episcopal vision, premised on the idea that the first should become last, was a radical inversion of worldly power. Reminding his audience that apostles were fundamentally "persons sent," Asbury distanced himself from other hierarchical church orders and challenged their bishops to imitate his grueling pace: "Would their bishops ride five or six thousand miles in nine months for eighty dollars a year, with their traveling expense less or more, preach daily when opportunity serves, meet a number of camp meetings in the year, make arrangements for stationing seven hundred preachers, ordain a hundred more annually, ride through all kinds of weather, and long roads in the worst state, at our time of life—the one sixty-nine, the other in his fifty-sixth year?"[53]

This austere vision was anything but the idle boast of a churchman in the twilight of his career. In an unmistakable sense, Asbury's forty-five-

Fig. 8. Bishop Francis Asbury, by Charles Peale Polk, 1794

year pilgrimage in America is the embodiment of this stern ideal, the use of authoritarian means to build an organization that would not be a respecter of persons. While the structure of the Methodist Episcopal church may have seemed conspicuously out of accord with the democratic stirrings of the times, the vital spring of Methodism under Asbury was to make Christianity profoundly a faith of the people. It was the church's "duty," he said, "to condescend to men of low estate," and he worked tirelessly to embrace the lowly, white and black, and to transfer resources from the center to the periphery of the movement.[54] In a more ruthless manner even than Wesley and Whitefield, Asbury pursued converts wherever they could be found, opened leadership to all, and allowed popular idioms to color worship and preaching. At the precise moment that a market revolution was rending many traditional ties of place and family, the Methodists offered a new plan for people to integrate their lives. From preachers like themselves, people received an invitation to join a movement promising them dignity of choice and beckoning them to involvement as a class leader, exhorter, local preacher, and circuit rider. In these forms, lay preaching became the hallmark of American Methodism and served as a powerful symbol that the wall between gentleman and commoner had been shattered. In fact, Asbury insisted that a ministerial calling required that one lay aside all the trappings of a gentleman—the dress, the deportment, and the financial security. "We must suffer *with* if we labor *for* the poor," he said.[55]

Asbury's presence itself was the cement in this system. Confronted at the start of his American ministry in 1771 with a parish the size of continental Europe (excluding Russia), Asbury found that early Methodist leaders such as Richard Boardman and Joseph Pilmore had a definite preference for a city ministry and looked down upon the countryside. Asbury immediately recognized the limitations of a stationed ministry that catered to New York and Philadelphia. He served notice that he would stand against those "who had manifested a desire to abide in the cities and live like gentlemen" and that he would promote "a circulation of preachers, to avoid partiality and popularity."[56] "My brethren seem unwilling to leave the cities," Asbury complained in November of 1771, "but I think that I shall show them the way."[57] By 1792, Asbury had driven the refined Joseph Pilmore into the ranks of the Episcopalians and had discarded Wesley's sacramental forms of worship for a more informal style that emphasized preaching.[58] When the Methodist itinerants met together in Conference, they authorized the *"travelling plan"* as the only *"primitive and apostolic plan"* sanctioned in the New Testament, continuing to underscore their commitment to the circumference rather than to the center:

Our grand plan, in all its parts, leads to an *itinerant* ministry. Our bishops are *travelling* bishops. All the different order which compose our conferences are employed in the *travelling* line; and our local preachers are, *in some degree*, travelling preachers. Every thing is kept moving as far as possible; and we will be bold to say, that, next to the grace of God, there is nothing *like this* for keeping the whole body alive from the centre to the circumference, and for the continual extension of that circumference on every hand.[59]

Asbury's life is a heroic testament to the outworking of this plan. A relentless recruiter, Asbury introduced Methodism to thousands of young itinerants during his thirty-one years as bishop.[60] Yet he never asked a preacher to endure a hardship that he did not undertake regularly. Asbury's labors claimed him so completely that he never found time to marry, to build a home, or to accumulate possessions beyond what a horse could carry. He shared the same subsistence allotment from the churches as any Methodist itinerant. For three decades he pursued an annual pilgrimage that rarely omitted any state of the union or any out-of-the-way hamlet where a cell of Methodist believers gathered. This circuit averaged five thousand miles annually and took him across the Alleghenies sixty-two different times.[61] He preached daily, slept in the crudest of hovels, maintained a massive correspondence, and was responsible for the annual placement of the entire army of itinerants—some seven hundred strong by the time of his death.[62] When a critic compared him to the pope, Asbury answered,

For myself, I pity those who cannot distinguish between a pope of Rome, and an old, worn man of about sixty years, who has the *power given him* of riding five thousand miles a year, at a salary of eighty dollars, through summer's heat and winter's cold, traveling in all weather, preaching in all places; his best covering from rain often but a blanket; the surest sharpener of his wit, hunger—from fasts, voluntary and involuntary; his best fare, for six months of the twelve, coarse kindness; and his reward, suspicion, envy, and murmurings all the year round.[63]

Beyond his personal example, what is remarkable about Asbury's career is his success in stamping personal convictions indelibly upon an emerging movement. This translation of ideals into reality was largely due to sustained efforts on two fronts: a relentless recruitment of like-minded young itinerants, and a persistent pressure to expand the organization from the center to the periphery and to do so, in Asbury's words, "like a well disciplined army."[64] In America, the Methodists transformed itinerancy from a phenomenon of self-directed individuals, coming and going as the spirit led, into a disciplined way of life. This disciplined itinerancy was an approach tilted decidedly in favor of the unchurched rather than the churched and allowed the Methodists within a quarter century to penetrate every populated region of the country and to bring with them means to sustain interest and to increase personal involvement in the movement.[65]

Scholars know surprisingly little about the Methodist circuit rider, for all his larger-than-life place in popular folklore and denominational hagiography. We do know that, like the Puritan "saint," this stern fraternity has been especially easy to caricature.[66] Yet the very image that abounds in popular culture—a mettlesome figure of gaunt visage, plain black clothes, perpetual motion, and relentless preaching—gives us important clues about who these people were and the life that was demanded of them.[67] We also know that almost twenty-five hundred itinerants had come to serve the Methodists by 1828 and that this stern fraternity held exclusive claim to the reins of the church's government.[68] Asbury's system simply did not allow halfhearted participation. If a preacher chose to "locate" for reasons of marriage or convenience or was forced to do so for reasons of health, he forfeited the right to full membership in the Methodist Connection. Local preachers, however fervent and valuable, simply were not accorded rights as members of the Annual Conference. In 1855 Abel Stevens made a statistical study of the Methodist ministry and found that, of 672 circuit riders he was able to quantify, four-sevenths had lasted less than twelve years.[69] The system kept the church dominated by young men who, according to a critic in the 1820s, were inexperienced, rustic, wanting in "social intercourse," and contemptuous of their elder colleagues who had been forced to locate.[70] If Americans first became susceptible to a cult of youth in this period, as David Hackett Fischer has argued, then it may be very significant that the Methodists advanced by means of a youth cadre and that power within the church constitutionally remained in the hands of the young rather than with those who could claim age and experience.[71]

There is also considerable evidence to suggest that living on horseback was a hazardous occupation. Early diaries refer repeatedly to the reality of "worn-out" circuit riders. Abel Stevens estimated in the 1860s that nearly half of the first six hundred fifty preachers died before they were thirty years old, almost two hundred of them in the first five years of service.[72] My own study shows that over 60 percent of itinerants who died in Methodist service before 1819 did so under forty years of age. (See table 1.) In view of such evidence, W. R. Ward has concluded that the American Methodist ministry was really a militarily organized mission, largely composed of

Table 1. Age at death and length of service of
itinerants who died while probationers or full
members of the traveling connection, 1780–1818
(total = 159).

Age	Number	%
23–29	33	35.9
30–39	25	27.2
40–49	12	13.0
50–59	9	9.8
60+	13	14.1
Total ages known	92	100.0

Years served	Number	%
1–5	67	42.4
6–10	49	31.0
11–15	18	11.4
16–25	10	6.3
26+	14	8.9
Total years known	158	100.0

Average age at death = 39   Average years served = 9.3

Source: Jesse Lee, *A Short History of the Methodists* (Baltimore,
1810); Methodist Episcopal Church, *Minutes Taken at Several
Annual Conferences* (New York, 1810–19).

short-service agents who were not pastorally related to the flock in the
traditional European sense.[73]

There is also evidence to suggest that these itinerants were characteristically poor, single, and self-educated. The Virginia Conference of
1809 was attended by eighty-four preachers, of whom all but three were
single; during Asbury's lifetime probably not more than a quarter of the
functioning itinerants were married. These figures are striking when, by
contrast, only one-fourth of Methodist ministers in Britain remained single
in the same period. The high rate of single preachers in America was directly related to the severe financial constraints of the office.[74] From top to
bottom, Methodist ministers were allowed a maximum allowance of sixty-
four dollars until 1800, and eighty dollars thereafter, at a time when the
average yearly income of a Congregationalist minister was approximately
four hundred dollars.[75] Even this small pittance was not a guaranteed
salary, and few itinerants received their allowance in full. At the end of his
life, Asbury reckoned that not more than one-sixth of the preachers, even
in the wealthy circuits, had regularly received the stipulated amount.[76]

Formal education was equally scarce among Asbury's traveling preachers. His explicit goal was to use the instrument of lay preaching to wake up a slumbering world. The *Discipline* of 1784 made it clear that study and learning should not interfere with soul-saving: "If you can do but one, let your Studies alone. I would throw by all the Libraries in the World rather than be guilty of the Loss of one Soul."[77] There is little reason to disagree with Peter Cartwright's estimate that, of the thousands of preachers that the Methodists recruited in the early republic, not more than fifty had more than a common English education, and scores of preachers did not have even that much. The first college graduate among the circuit riders of Indiana found his education an actual disadvantage and gave up the regular ministry because of prejudice against him.[78]

If the traveling preacher was one key to Methodism's success, another was its accordionlike power of expansion into every corner of the country. The connection was continually expanding into new circuits, new districts, and new conferences. Just as the circuit rider was to minister to people of his charge irrespective of social position, so the organization emphasized building up new societies rather than merely cultivating established churches. Asbury's mapping of circuits seemed to reflect potential rather than actual membership.[79] While Methodism retained a stronghold in the seaports of the middle colonies, Asbury hammered its organization into one that had a distinct rural orientation adept at expanding into thinly populated areas.[80] "We must draw resources from the centre to the circumference," Asbury wrote to Jesse Lee in 1797. Asbury combined this plan for horizontal expansion with an equally effective mandate that the gospel proclaimed by Methodist preachers transcend the boundaries of class, race, ethnic group, and ecclesiastical tradition. He feared almost nothing save the movement's stagnation and took consolation from little else than word of the pervasive embrace of new converts.[81] It was this systematic Methodist infiltration of popular culture in the West that two Congregationalists reported back to New England in 1814:

> This denomination has greatly increased within a few years, and this must chiefly be attributed to their complete system of missions, which is by far the best for domestic missions ever yet adopted. They send their laborers into every corner of the country; if they hear of any particular attention to religion in a place, they double the number of laborers in those circuits, and place their best men there, and endeavor generally, to adapt the character of their preachers, to the character of the people among whom they are to labor.[82]

Asbury's signal achievement was that for so long he preserved the movement from the inevitable allure of respectability. His burning desire

HARPER'S WEEKLY.

A JOURNAL OF CIVILIZATION

VOL. XI.—No. 563.]   NEW YORK, SATURDAY, OCTOBER 12, 1867.   [SINGLE COPIES TEN CENTS. $4.00 PER YEAR IN ADVANCE.

Entered according to Act of Congress, in the Year 1867, by Harper & Brothers, in the Clerk's Office of the District Court for the Southern District of New York.

THE CIRCUIT PREACHER.—DRAWN BY A. R. WAUD.—[SEE NEXT PAGE.]

Fig. 9. "The Circuit Preacher," from a drawing by A. R. Waud in *Harper's Weekly*, October 12, 1867

to reach people led him to jettison much of the churchly and liturgical elements of Wesleyanism (such as Wesley's *Sunday Service* and formal clerical attire) and to remain open to the roaring extemporaneous ethos of the camp meeting. For all his authoritarian demeanor, Asbury gave the benefit of the doubt to the people rather than to patrons of order. His concern was not to squelch popular excess but to crack down on "locality," gentility, and smug complacency.[83]

By doing so, this "man who rambled America" fathered a distinct variant of Methodism that retained for a full generation Wesley's original intent that Methodism advance as a people's movement. Nothing makes the point clearer than to note the quest for respectability and the exaggerated concern for institutional discipline that characterized leadership of English Methodism after 1789. The Methodist Conference in Britain in 1796 expelled the democratic Methodist Alexander Kilham as "a Painite and a Leveller" and thereafter was willing to accept numerical losses in order to preserve connectional discipline. Pressured for support by a nervous civil administration during the first decade of the new century, the Methodists banned camp meetings and expelled the "Primitives" who insisted upon them. In the next decade they confronted convulsive social strife in the industrial midlands—exactly the strongest area of their own growth—and reacted by aligning Methodism with the forces of stability and order. The rising leader Jabez Bunting, stationed at Halifax, stood against the Luddites resolutely and came away steeled in the conviction that what was needed was less revival and more denomination drill: "However solicitous to make the best of this, it is after all an *awful* fact—and it confirms me in my fixed opinion, that the progress of Methodism in the West of Riding of Yorkshire has been more swift than solid; more extensive than deep, more in the increase of numbers, than in diffusion of that kind of piety which shines as brightly & operates as visibly *at home* as in the prayer meeting and the crowded love feast."[84] In the words of E. P. Thompson, Bunting was intent upon ushering Methodism to a seat on the right hand of the Establishment.[85]

With a yardstick of success that resembled Timothy Dwight's more than Francis Asbury's, Bunting assumed prominence in Methodism as the leader of a younger cohort who thrived on the prestige of urban congregations, defined a "high" doctrine of the pastoral office, and put as much distance as possible between themselves and popular enthusiasm.[86] These were not men who wrung their hands over the fact that rural itinerancy and the circuit horse were almost extinct in England by 1815; that urban congregations witnessed a great social division between preachers and the wealthy, on the one side, and the poor and radical, on the other; and that, in

Fig. 10. Log church in which Bishop Francis Asbury held the first Methodist conference in Kentucky in 1790, date of picture unknown

this process, one-third of Methodist members had been expelled or lost to various reform secessions.[87] By 1820 mainstream Wesleyanism had largely purged itself of popular radicalism and had banished unrestrained revivalism to the fringes of English religious life. But the cost was a serious loss of contact with the working class of town and country.[88]

American Methodism, like other popular religious movements in America, was strangely immune from this convulsive political era. The movement was free to develop according to its own momentum, unimpeded by the political and social polarization that forced European churchmen into doctrinaire positions. Revivalists such as Asbury could pursue a program closely identified with popular interests without incurring the wrath of a nervous establishment or alienating his own flock, which was overwhelmingly Jeffersonian at the turn of the century. In short, American Methodism experienced a rare incubation period that permitted it to establish its own agenda without sharp class antagonism blunting the force of the movement. In English society the fault line of class severed the Methodist fold, greatly weakening the force of religion among the lower classes.

By the 1840s, the Methodist church in America had undertaken its own pilgrimage to respectability and was losing its own innocence in strident political controversy. Yet Methodist ministers maintained a diverse political profile, disagreeing with each other as much as any of them did with their parishioners.[89] The divisive issue of slavery cut through the Methodist Church and the entire society in a way that did not discredit ministers north or south. Preachers who defended slavery, were able to invoke the Almighty with as much fervor and appeal as those who strove to break slavery's yoke; and in the slave community itself black preachers adopted their own version of Methodist faith. This pluralism allowed Christianity to flourish as a popular force north and south, slave and free. Long after the stern itinerancy of Francis Asbury had given way to more refined and educated versions of Methodism, its preachers could never quite turn their backs on the movement's original birthright of being a haven for ordinary people.

The Independent Conscience of John Leland

American Baptists have always viewed the General Missionary Convention in Philadelphia in 1814 as a watershed event in their history. Organized to facilitate the "adoption" of Congregationalist missionaries Adoniram Judson and Luther Rice—both of whom had shifted to Baptist convictions upon arriving in India—the meeting was also the first step in creating a national denomination out of hundreds of autonomous Baptist churches scattered along the Atlantic seaboard. For the thirty-two delegates at the organizing session of "the Triennial Convention," this national undertaking was an important sign that the Baptist movement was coming of age. Baptist membership had grown tenfold since the Revolution, and its two thousand churches, sixteen hundred ministers, and one hundred associations could no longer be overlooked.[90]

Already Baptists had begun to taste a measure of respectability. Many delegates vividly remembered Baptists being ostracized, taxed, and jailed for their beliefs. Against this backdrop, the distinguished list of convention delegates signified how far Baptists had come in a single generation and foreshadowed a day when Baptists would not have to bear the reproach of inferior social position. Robert B. Semple, a delegate from Virginia, had been offered the presidency of Transylvania University and had recently completed a history of the Baptists in the Old Dominion. In his work he proudly noted that Baptists had become the largest denomination in the state and that "they were joined by persons of much greater weight in civil society."[91] William Staughton, pastor of Philadelphia's First Baptist Church and corresponding secretary for the new missions organization, received a doctor of divinity degree from Princeton in 1801. Another influential delegate, Thomas Baldwin, pastor of Boston's Second Baptist Church, delivered the annual election sermon before the Massachusetts legislature in 1802. The following year he received a doctor of divinity from Union College and in 1807 joined the trustees of Brown University. When the rustic preacher Elias Smith was called to pastor the Baptist church in Woburn, Massachusetts, in 1798, the "very fashionable" Baldwin tried to persuade the young man to put aside his plain attire and dress "in fashionable black, a large three cornered hat, and black silk gloves." Shocked by this emphasis on externals, Smith asked Baldwin if Baptists "were going back to the place from whence we came out." Baldwin replied, "We wish to make our denomination respectable as well as the rest."[92]

The convention elected Richard Furman as its president. Minister of Charleston's First Baptist Church, Furman was also a Federalist, a plantation owner, and a founder of the Baptist college that would eventually become Furman University. One of the most eloquent orators in Charleston, Furman had given the city's principal eulogy upon the deaths of George Washington and Alexander Hamilton—both at the request of the elitist Society of the Cincinnati. Furman traveled to the Philadelphia convention with his good friend, Judge Matthias B. Tallmadge, a Yale graduate and federal judge in New York, who wintered in Charleston and shared Furman's interests in foreign missions.[93]

For all their interest in supporting far-off missionaries, the influential

Baptists who convened in Philadelphia in 1814 also had other agendas in mind. They saw the occasion as a splendid opportunity to centralize the amorphous collection of churches and associations variously identified as General Baptist, Regular Baptist, Separate Baptist, Permanent Baptist, or Freewill Baptist. Men such as Richard Furman smarted at their inferior social position and the condescension of established churches. They wanted to set the denomination firmly on the road to order and respectability through vigorous national efforts. The leading spirits of the meeting were urbanites from Boston, Philadelphia, Baltimore, and Charleston. Seventeen of the thirty-two delegates came from the established, dignified Philadelphia Association.[94] The principals were men of cosmopolitan outlook—not unlike the delegates to a more famous Philadelphia convention three decades earlier. They believed in strength through unity of action and envisioned national solutions to national problems. Richard Furman saw the convention as an agent to promote change in ministerial education and domestic missions. The published proceedings of the meeting, which he coauthored, expressed deep regret that "no more attention is paid to the improvement of the minds of pious youth who are called to the gospel ministry."[95]

At the second Triennial Convention in 1817, Richard Furman used his presidential address to present an education plan to create a "national seminary of learning" that would provide young men with "classical studies" and theology in its various branches: church history, oriental languages, biblical criticism, and pulpit eloquence.[96] Within five years this dynamic group of Baptist leaders, hungry for respectability and national influence, established "the Columbian College in the District of Columbia"—now George Washington University—a stone's throw from the White House.[97] When the Triennial Convention met in Washington in 1823, it obtained an audience with President James Monroe in the White House. The same centralizing impulse led Furman, Staughton, Baldwin, Semple, and others to be involved with numerous interlocking ventures to promote the beginning of colleges, the professionalization of the clergy, the increase of associational power, the publication of denominational journals, and the formation of home missions and other benevolent associations.[98]

At least one prominent Baptist took exception to this quest for respectability. Like Patrick Henry in his reaction to the energetic designs of Federalists, John Leland "smelt a rat." In 1814 Leland was one of the most popular and controversial Baptists in America. He was most famous as a protagonist of religious freedom. As a leader among Virginia Baptists in the 1780s, Leland had been influential in petitioning the legislature on behalf of Jefferson's bill for religious freedom and for the bill to end the incorporation of the Protestant Episcopal church. There is strong evidence that James Madison personally sought his support of the federal constitution, which Leland had first opposed. At the same time, Leland also marshaled Baptist opposition to slavery in Virginia. After returning to New England in 1791, he became the outstanding proponent of religious freedom as preacher, lecturer, and publicist and served two terms in the Massachusetts legislature representing the town of Cheshire.[99]

On a national level Leland was best known for the 1235-pound "Mammoth Cheese" he presented to President Thomas Jefferson. In New York and Baltimore crowds flocked to see this phenomenal creation, molded in a cider press supposedly from the milk of nine hundred cows and bearing the motto "Rebellion to tyrants is obedience to God." Leland made the presentation to Mr. Jefferson at the White House on New Year's Day, 1802, as a token of esteem from the staunchly Republican citizens of Cheshire. Two days later, at the president's invitation, he preached before both houses of Congress on the text, "And behold a greater than Solomon is here." One congressman who heard that sermon, Manasseh Cutler, a Massachusetts Federalist and Congregationalist clergyman, had few kind words to say about Leland's politics or his religion, dismissing "the cheesemonger" as a "poor ignorant, illiterate, clownish creature." "Such a farrago, bawled with stunning voice, horrid tone, frightful grimaces, and extravagant gestures, I believe, was never heard by any decent auditory before. . . . Such an outrage upon religion, the Sabbath, and common decency, was extremely painful to every sober, thinking person present."[100]

Leland's political notoriety has often masked the fact that he was principally a preacher and itinerant evangelist. In 1824 he recorded that he had preached eight thousand times, had baptized over thirteen hundred persons, had met nearly a thousand Baptist preachers, and had traveled an equivalent of three times round the world.[101] Given Leland's stature and connections, it is not surprising that he attended the first Triennial Convention in Philadelphia and preached at William Staughton's church the night before the first session. That sermon sounded a sharp alarm for Baptists who were hungry for respectability. Even before any decisions had been made about forming a missions organization, Leland warned against the danger of "Israel" insisting on having a king so that it could be like other nations: "like the people now-a-days; they form societies, and they must have a president and two or three vice-presidents, to be like their neighbors around them."[102] When the Baptists decided to join the Protestant quest for voluntary association, Leland stepped up his attacks upon missionary agencies and their clerical supporters. For the next fifteen years, he opposed the clerical professionalism at the core of American Protestant denominations. Leland ridiculed the mercenary foundation of foreign and domestic missions, the oppression of "a hierarchical clergy—despotic judiciary—[and] an aristocratic host of lawyers," the mechanical operations of theological seminaries, the tyranny of formal structures, and the burden of creedalism—"this Virgin Mary between the souls of men and the Scriptures." In an 1830 letter to John Taylor, the stalwart foe of mission activity from Kentucky, Leland confessed that his calling had been "to watch and check *clerical hierarchy*, which assumes as many shades as a chameleon."[103]

John Leland had every reason to take up the path of order and decorum that appealed to other Baptist leaders. But the era of the Revolution had stirred a different set of impulses within him. Rather than promoting central government and policies, Leland sought at every step to restrain the accumulation of power. "I would as soon give my vote to a wolf to be a shepherd," he said in an 1802 oration celebrating American independence, "as to a man, who is always contending for the energy of government, to be a ruler."[104] John Leland's dissent flowed out of a passion for religious liberty that exalted the individual conscience over creedal systems, local control over powerful ecclesiastical structures, and popular sensibility over the instincts of the educated and powerful. A prolific publicist, popular hymn-writer, and amusing and satirical preacher, Leland strongly advocated freedom in every sphere of life. Self-reliant to an eccentric degree, Leland is fascinating and important in his own right. He also serves as an important bridge between the Revolutionary era and the quest for localism and independence that confounded Baptist history throughout the Jacksonian period. The importance of this story, played out on the fringes of denominational life, is not fully appreciated, given its lack of coherence and the penchant for early denominational historians to celebrate the growth of respectability and organizational coherence.[105]

Brought up as a fervent New Light, John Leland found resources to accept, even defend, his own "rusticity of manners."[106] Chief among these was a Jeffersonian view of conscience that championed intellectual self-reliance. In a pamphlet published in 1792 attacking the New England Standing Order, Leland explained how he came to trust his own reasoning rather than the conclusions of great men. Having once had "profound reverence" for leading civic figures, Leland discovered that in reality "not two of them agreed." "What, said I, do *great* men differ? boys, women and little souls do; but can learned, wise patriots disagree so much in judgment? If so, they cannot all be right, but they may all be wrong, and therefore *Jack Nips for himself*."[107] Leland hammered out his view of conscience as he battled the state-church tradition of Virginia during the 1780s and of New England thereafter. In over thirty pamphlets and regular contributions to

Phinehas Allen's Jeffersonian *Pittsfield Sun*, Leland spelled out a vision of personal autonomy that colored his personal life, his theological views, and his conception of society.

As early as 1790, Leland began to sound his clarion call that conscience should be "free from human control." His passion was to protect the "empire of conscience," the court of judgment in every human soul, from the inevitable encroachments of state-church traditions, oppressive creeds, ambitious and greedy clergymen, and even family tradition. "For a man to contend for religious liberty on the court-house green, and deny his wife, children and servants, the liberty of conscience at home, is a paradox not easily reconciled. . . . [E]ach one must give an account of himself to God."[108] Upon returning to New England in 1791, Leland assailed the Standing Order in a pamphlet, *The Rights of Conscience Inalienable . . . or, The High-flying Churchman, Stripped of his Legal Robe, Appears a Yaho*. With language borrowed directly from Jefferson's *Notes on the State of Virginia*, he argued that truth can stand on its own without the props of legal or creedal defense. He reiterated the theme that "religion is a matter between God and individuals."[109] In addition to repeating his warning to parents that it was "iniquitous to bind the consciences" of children, Leland clarified his explicitly democratic view of conscience: that the so-called wise and learned were actually less capable of mediating truth than were common people. Leland dismissed the common objection that "the ignorant part of the community are not capacitated to judge for themselves":

> Did many of the rulers believe in Christ when he was upon earth? Were not the learned clergy (the scribes) his most inveterate enemies? Do not great men differ as much as little men in judgment? Have not almost all lawless errors crept into the world through the means of wise men (so called)? Is not a simple man, who makes nature and reason his study, a competent judge of things? Is the Bible written (like Caligula's laws) so intricate and high, that none but the letter learned (according to the common phrase) can read it? Is not the vision written so plain that he that runs may read it?[110]

In an 1801 sermon, *A Blow at the Root*, published in five editions in four different states from Vermont to Georgia, Leland continued to project the image of the autonomous person besieged by coercive forces of state, creed, tradition, and clerical hierarchy. The political triumph of Jefferson, the *"Man of the People,"* convinced Leland that the "genius of America" had finally "arisen, like a lion, from the swelling of Jordon, and roared like thunder in the states, 'we will be free; we will rule ourselves; our officers shall be honorable servants, but not mean masters.'"[111]

Leland's credo of liberal individualism differs in several respects from the outlook of his older Baptist colleague Isaac Backus. Backus and Leland were linked in their efforts to gain full legal standing for Baptist churches in New England, but their concerns diverged because of their differing ages. Converted in 1741 under George Whitefield, Backus clung to the theology of Jonathan Edwards, the issue of infant Baptism excepted. Leland, however, could never reconcile the problem of predestination and free will and sneered at "polemical divinity" as futile and coercive. "When I hear a long harangue of metaphysical reasoning on abstruse questions," Leland declared in 1830, "I feel more like calling for my night-cap than anything else." Earlier he had written, "Confessions of faith often check any further pursuit after truth, confine the mind into a particular way of reasoning, and give rise to frequent separations."[112]

Leland's opposition to creeds and confessions was also a function of his firm identification with a popular audience, an instinct that Backus did not appreciate. Backus had defended his positions with learned tracts addressed to civil and religious elites. He opposed "high and new things" in religion and was suspicious of rallying popular opinion. Leland relished a common audience, peppering his speeches and writings with blunt common sense and earthy humor. Robert Semple, the historian of Virginia Baptists, criticized Leland for being "theatrical" and "jocund" but admitted that he "was probably the most popular preacher of any who ever resided in this State." Few preachers in his memory had "so great command of the attention and of the feelings of their auditory."[113] Leland's message and style reflected popular sentiment. He was fiercely anticlerical, mocking the pretension, greed, and genteel living of the clergy. He depicted clerics as "no great friends to sun-burnt faces and hard hands."[114] "Preaching is now a science and a trade," Leland wrote in a satirical poem on the professionalization of the ministry, "And by it many grand estates are made."[115]

The greatest difference between Backus and Leland was their contrasting views of the social order. While Backus never doubted the right of all to worship as they pleased, he was unconvinced that laymen could articulate their own theology. He defended the primacy of Calvinism and reminisced about "the most eminent fathers of New England." Leland, on the other hand, rejected the idea of natural inequality in society—as if some were set apart to lead and others to follow. He depicted the typical clergyman as venal and conniving, rather than capable of rising above self-interest. Like Jefferson, he perceived the organized church as corrupted by "priest-craft," which he defined as the clerical quest for "self-advantage." Young men chose the ministry as a profession "for the sake of ease, wealth, honor and ecclesiastical dignity." Leland devoted a whole sermon to rebut the Yankee truism that "Schools, Academies and Colleges, are the inexhaustible fountains of true piety, morality and literature." Moral virtue and the pursuit of a liberal arts curriculum were not intimately linked in his opinion, but often incompatible—"as well may cold iron and hot be welded together." Nothing offended Leland more than the symbolic trappings of authority that clergymen and other professionals used to set themselves apart from ordinary people. He reserved his most scathing satire for the mannerisms, clothing, and learned style of the clerical *persona*. That which Isaac Backus accepted as necessary to define the authority of a clergyman's station and calling, Leland dismissed as "pharisaic pomp."[116]

This democratic resistance to prescribed clerical authority is crucial to understanding Leland's continuing role in the religious affairs of the nation until his death in 1841. Leland was too iconoclastic to permit a religious structure to form around him; even his relationship with his own congregation was troubled over his refusal, as a matter of conscience, to administer the Lord's Supper. Leland defended his position by saying that in thirty years of practical experience he had never seen the ordinance move a single sinner to conversion. Despite this unchecked self-reliance, what Lyman Butterfield called his "roving temperament," Leland was a diligent publicist whose ideas had broad circulation. For the last two decades of his life he used his influence to thwart the organizational schemes of established Protestantism: mission boards, benevolent societies, theological seminaries, and the highly organized Sabbatarian campaign by Protestant denominations. Leland preached a message of localism, simplicity, and aversion to wealth:

> Religion is become the most fashionable thing among us. Moral societies, Sunday schools—tract societies—Bible societies—missionary societies, and funds to educate and make preachers, are now in the full tide of operation. . . . In barbarous times, when men were in the dark, it was believed that the success of the gospel was according to the outpourings of the Holy Spirit, but in the age of light and improvement, it is estimated according to the pourings out of the purse.[117]

Throughout the 1820s and 1830s Leland continued to stand against the *organized* character of American Protestantism. He played a direct role in influencing Senator Richard M. Johnson of Kentucky to thwart the organized agitation against Sunday mail, corresponded with antimission leaders, and contributed to various dissenting journals such as Theophilus Gates's *The Reformer*.[118]

Leland's legacy is an exaggerated opposition to official Christianity. He articulated a twofold persuasion that operated powerfully in the hinterland of Baptist church life: an aversion to central control and a quest for self-reliance. One reason that it is so difficult to write a history of the Baptists in the early republic is that centrifugal forces were so powerfully at work, giving free reign to regional distinctives and take-charge entrepreneurs. Whatever success such cosmopolitan leaders as Richard Furman or Francis Wayland had in building central institutions, their way was dogged at every step by serious defections to the antiformalist appeals of Alexander Campbell and later of William Miller;[119] by the rise of significant antimission Baptist associations in regions as diverse as New York, Pennsylvania, Illinois, Kentucky, and North Carolina; and by the appearance of charismatic dissenters such as J. R. Graves and his Landmark Baptists.[120] Equally important was the entrenched opposition to central authority among those who remained within the regular Baptist fold. The Triennial Convention, after all, had never represented Baptist churches themselves, but only individuals and societies willing to pay appropriate dues to the organization. After 1826 it was virtually disbanded when representatives from different regions locked horns over issues of authority and control.[121]

All the while, the majority of Baptists away from the eastern seaboard and urban centers clung to local customs and institutions. Baptists in Tennessee, for instance, organized a state convention in 1833, but after two years it broke into three sectional conventions. The constitution of the Mississippi state convention read that the group "shall never possess a single attribute of power or authority over any church or association." Similarly, the Illinois Association claimed in 1830 that it exercised no authority and that each church was "independent and influenced by none."[122] As many of the early republic's most visible Baptist leaders inched toward influence and respectability, a considerable network of lesser lights continued to champion local control. To cope with a confusing world and to define their place in it, they fell back upon the kind of vital and persuasive ideology that John Leland had broadcast into the marketplace of ideas.

John Leland is also important because he turned a quest for self-reliance into a godly crusade. He believed that individuals had to make a studied effort to free themselves of natural authorities: church, state, college, seminary, even family. Leland's message carried the combined ideological leverage of evangelical urgency and Jeffersonian promise. Using plain language and avoiding doctrinal refinements, he proclaimed a divine economy that was atomistic and competitive rather than wholistic and hierarchical. This kind of liberal individualism could be easily embraced at the grass roots. Ordinary people gladly championed the promise of personal autonomy as a message they could understand and a cause to which they could subscribe—in God's name, no less.

Black Preachers and the Flowering of
African-American Christianity

At the time of the War of Independence, few blacks, slave or free, were Christians. In the next three decades, thousands of African-Americans turned to the gospel. That pilgrimage, coming almost a century after the Church of England began missionary efforts in the southern colonies, did not represent a late harvest of Anglican labors. Instead, the flowering of Christianity among blacks—90 percent of whom were slaves in the first federal census—grew out of the insurgent religious movements in the early republic and their ability to wed the gospel to popular culture.

Well into the nineteenth century Episcopalians and Presbyterians were still wringing their hands about their failure to Christianize their own slaves. Charles Colcock Jones, the Presbyterian most vitally concerned about this issue, reported a total of less than three hundred black Presbyterians in 1848, when black Methodists and Baptists numbered almost 125,000. Earlier he had noted the explosive growth of Methodism among blacks in the Revolutionary era, from less than two thousand in 1787 to over forty thousand by 1815. He also estimated an equal number of black Baptists by the second decade of the century. These mass movements were a stark contrast to efforts of more established churches. He noted ruefully that the Episcopalians in South Carolina had reported a meagre 199 black members in the year 1810.[123]

There are at least three obvious reasons why blacks, slave and free, swarmed into Methodist and Baptist folds, spurning more churchly traditions. First, early Baptists and Methodists earned the right to be heard. They welcomed African-Americans as full participants in their communions and condemned the institution of slavery. However severe their eventual retreat on these issues, Baptists and Methodists in the last quarter of the eighteenth century—the generation of John Leland, Elias Smith, Francis Asbury, Freeborn Garrettson, James O'Kelly, and Lorenzo Dow—embraced slaves as brothers and sisters as vigorously as they opposed slavery by their precept and example. "I had recently joined the Methodist Church," one slave reported, "and from the sermon I heard, I felt that God had made all men free and equal, and that I ought not be a slave."[124]

Unlike earlier evangelicals such as George Whitefield and Samuel Davies, Methodists and Baptists of the Revolutionary era challenged slavery as an institution. Their stance on this issue broke sharply with that of the traditional gentry. They were militant about converting slaves, they forthrightly identified with the slaves' plight, and they gave clear antislavery testimony. The Methodists under Asbury made African-Americans a special target of their efforts. The Conference of 1787 required preachers to leave nothing undone "for the spiritual benefit and salvation of the negroes." "Religion is reviving here among the Africans. . . ," Asbury noted a decade later, "these are the poor, these are the people we are more immediately called to preach to."[125] Throughout the Revolutionary period, Methodists and Baptists aligned their cause with that of the slave despite continuing resistance of the gentry, who doubted the compatibility of slavery and evangelical Christianity. Outcasts from fashionable society themselves, white evangelical preachers in the South found common ground with African-Americans and virtue in their religious expression. After listening to a black preacher in Westmoreland County, Virginia, in 1789, the Baptist Richard Dozier commented, "Oh, see God choosing the weak things of the world to confound the things that are mighty."[126]

What made this witness to slaves credible was the number of white preachers willing to preach against slavery in the face of entrenched opposition. After freeing his own slaves in 1775, Freeborn Garrettson, a native of Virginia, faced regular threats because he laced his evangelistic preaching with attempts to "inculcate the doctrine of freedom." "Twice the clubs have been raised to beat me," James O'Kelly stated about his antislavery stance, "once the pointed dagger was presented against me . . . yet I must defend this truth, and hope that my testimony will be received among you, my brethren." In the *Virginia Chronicle*, John Leland demanded "liberty of conscience" for slaves to attend night meetings and linked slaveholding and religious persecution as two expressions of the same oppressive spirit.[127]

However shallow and short-lived this evangelical attack on slavery appears in light of events after 1800, it must be seen for what it was in its own time and place: a radical challenge to the doctrines of paternalism and absolute slave obedience that Anglican evangelizers had so actively formulated.[128] Even "the Grand Itinerant" George Whitefield and his most devoted disciple in South Carolina, Hugh Bryan, promoted the evangelism of slaves in ways that made peace with slavery as an enduring institution.[129] By contrast, the trumpet call against slavery in the last quarter of the century had serious repercussions, including a wave of manumissions in the upper South, even if it did not topple the walls of slavery itself.[130] Most important, the message resonated authentically with the slaves whose company these preachers chose to keep. It is no accident that by 1800 nearly twenty thousand African-Americans were Methodist, representing almost one-third of the American Methodist population. One historian has estimated that in 1810 the Methodist church could claim one in four adult blacks on the Delmarva Peninsula.[131]

The second reason for the enormous influx of black converts was that the Methodists and Baptists proclaimed Christianity that was fresh, capable of being readily understood and immediately experienced. African-Americans converted under its influence testified to its transparent appeal. John Thompson, born a slave in Maryland in 1812, explained how easily he could fathom the sound of Methodism:

> My mistress and her family were all Episcopalians. The nearest church was five miles from our plantation, and there was no Methodist church nearer than ten miles. So we went to the Episcopal church, but always came home as we went, for the preaching was above our comprehension, so that we could understand but little that was said. But soon the Methodist religion was brought among us, and preached in a manner so plain that the way faring man, though a fool, could not err therein. The new doctrine produced great consternation among the slaveholders. It was something which they could not understand. It brought glad tidings to the poor bondman; it bound up the broken-hearted; it opened the prison doors to them that were bound, and let the captive go free. As soon as it got among the slaves, it spread from plantation to plantation, until it reached ours, where there were but few who did not experience religion.[132]

Richard Allen, the founder of the African Methodist Church, gave a similar explanation of Methodist success: "the unlearned can understand. . . . The Methodists were the first people that brought glad tidings to the colored people. . . . for all other denominations preached so high-flown that we were not able to comprehend their doctrine. Sure am I that reading sermons will never prove so beneficial to the colored people as spiritual or extempore preaching."[133]

The evangelical message spread infectiously because it had redefined the most crucial step in the missionary endeavor: how to cross the threshold into the Christian church. Anglicans and Presbyterians had stressed religious instruction in their efforts to convert slaves. They thought of conversion as a process of religious nurturing, expecting catechumens to learn the Creed, the Lord's Prayer, and the Ten Commandments.[134] The individual convert had to conform to the objective standards of an authoritative church. Evangelical Presbyterians such as Samuel Davies in the eighteenth century and Charles Colcock Jones in the nineteenth emphasized the experience of conversion but always linked it to order and decorum: Sabbath observance, sober church music, formal catechism, and "grave, solemn, dignified" clergymen. Even as Charles Colcock Jones went the second mile to communicate with slave communities, his approach evinced the vast social and cultural chasm separating orthodox churches from the experience of African-American slaves:

> The *strictest order* should be preserved at all the religious meetings of the Negroes, especially those held on the Sabbath day, and *punctuality* observed in commencing them at the appointed hour. No *audible* expressions of feeling in the way of groanings, cries, or noises of any kind, should be allowed. To encourage such things among ignorant people, such as they are, would be to jeopardize the interests of true religion, and open the door to downright fanaticism. . . .
>
> The tunes should not be intricate but plain and awakening. One great advantage in teaching them good psalms and hymns, is that they are thereby induced to lay aside the extravagant and nonsensical chants, and catches and hallelujah songs of their own composing.[135]

In contrast to the didactic and condescending approach, Baptist and Methodist exhorters focused attention on the promise of immediate conversion. Making the drama of sin and salvation visual and personal, they invited the unconverted to claim the power of grace immediately rather than waiting for lengthy instruction or arduous preparation. Toward that end, evangelical preachers reveled in meetings that swept the audience along on powerful waves of emotion. Both Baptists and Methodists, James Essig has noted, measured the depth of worship experience by the amount of tears shed at their meetings. They were not afraid to trigger deep emotional reactions in their hearers, convinced from their own experience that such a process was the only way to produce genuine conversion.[136] They encouraged joyful responses to the proclamation of the good news. It is no accident that the enduring links between blacks and the insurgent evangelical groups of the early republic were forged by a generation of preachers who nurtured the outpouring of communal ecstasy and championed spontaneous shouting, chanting, and singing. In this climate, conversion did not suppress the rich heritage of folk belief and expression among African-Americans. Doris Elizabett Andrews has suggested that the revival provided a style of religious expression and communal engagement that represented a kind of Christian "mirror-image" of a religious heritage that Africans long had known.[137]

This open-ended environment culminated in the third and most critical reason that African-Americans became Christians: the emergence of black preachers and exhorters. The surge of African-Americans into the Christian faith between the Revolution and the War of 1812 paralleled the decisive rise of the black preacher. Virtually unknown in colonial America, black preaching exploded in the experimental climate generated by passionate Baptists and Methodists. As early as 1766 an Anglican missionary in Brunswick, Virginia, was disturbed because "New light baptist are very numerous in the southern parts of this parish—The most illiterate among them are their Teachers even Negroes speak in their Meetings."[138] Exercising the gift of exhorting opened the promise of a permanent call to preach to many African-American converts. For a brief interlude, white evangelicals endorsed the desire of converts to exercise their preaching talents, and black preaching became a regular occurrence in Baptist and Methodist communions. In a variety of churches at the end of the century, black pastors even served racially mixed congregations.

More to the point, African-Americans' interest in the gospel began to soar. John Leland noted in the *Virginia Chronicle* in 1790 that it was not strange to see slaves "walk twenty miles on Sunday morning to meeting, and back again at night." Leland also noted that slaves "put more confidence in their own color, than they do in the whites." "Their language is broken," Leland noted of black preachers, "but they understand each other." A half-century later Charles Colcock Jones looked back on the effect of black Baptist preaching: "In general the Negroes were followers of the Baptists in Virginia, and after a while, as they permitted many colored men to preach, the great majority of them went to hear preachers of their own color."[139]

Methodists were equally inclined to grant blacks the right to preach the gospel. Harry Hosier, or "Black Harry," traveled with Methodist ministers Francis Asbury, Thomas Coke, Freeborn Garrettson, and Richard Whatcoat. An illiterate who feared losing "the gift of preaching" when Asbury tried to teach him to read, Hosier was a far more popular speaker than Asbury. A free black shoemaker, Henry Evans, helped to establish Methodism in Fayetteville, North Carolina.[140] By 1810, the black Methodist leader Daniel Coker of Baltimore could list the names of thirteen ordained black ministers and another eleven Methodist local preachers.[141]

The emergence of black religious leadership was related to a fundamental paradox within evangelical Protestantism: its egalitarian character and its racism.[142] The initial enthusiasm of Baptist and Methodist communions to welcome black church members and preachers was countered by increasing white discomfort with integrated worship and by mounting opposition to any hint that blacks would exercise authority in the church.[143] Even as the first Methodist *Discipline* emphasized the importance of activity among slaves, it also limited the office of class leader to white persons. Faced with increasing proslavery sentiment, Bishop Asbury and the General Conferences of 1804 and 1808 approved versions of the *Discipline* that omitted the chapter on slavery. Similarly, the Dover Baptist Association in Virginia decided in 1802 that although all members were entitled to certain privileges, none but free male members could exercise any authority in the local church. The Portsmouth Baptist Association, which in 1794 had permitted free black men to represent churches, ruled in 1828 that black churches must be represented through white men.[144] By the 1830s most southern evangelicals had thoroughly repudiated a heritage that valued blacks as fellow church members. In an ugly incident in Charleston, South Carolina, in 1833, some arrogant young white men physically removed two free blacks from the Methodist church for sitting on the main floor—a right they had always exercised. Instead of disciplining the white ruffians, the quarterly meeting conference successfully convinced the trustees of the church to alter seating arrangements in order to prevent blacks from "intermixing with whites."[145]

By attempting to take back with one hand what had been granted by the other, white evangelicals unwittingly enhanced the leadership potential of black preachers both free and slave. Pushed to the fringes of white churches, African-American preachers asserted the autonomy of black Christianity overtly and in secret. Against all odds they struggled to preserve their right to proclaim the gospel, to order their forms of worship, and to maintain some degree of autonomy and control. "Our only design is to secure to our selves our rights and privileges," Richard Allen asserted in forming an independent black Methodist church in Philadelphia, "to regulate our affairs, temporal and spiritual, the same as if we were white people."[146] A unique set of ideological, religious, and social conditions in the Revolutionary era bequeathed the gift of preaching to the African-American community, something that all the repressive actions in the world could not take away. What preserved the black church as the first public institution over which blacks exercised control was nothing but the courage, foresight, and determination of "The Preacher," a figure that W. E. B. Du Bois later praised as "the most unique personality developed by the Negro on American soil. A leader, a politician, an orator, a 'boss,' an intriguer, an idealist,—all these he is, and ever too, the center of a group of men, now twenty, now a thousand in number."[147]

The determination and vision of this cadre of black preachers gave rise to a remarkable movement of independent black churches from 1790 to 1810. In over a score of locations from Boston to Charleston, from Philadelphia to Louisiana, black preachers successfully organized Baptist and Methodist congregations that were distinctly African. In Philadelphia, two black leaders, Absalom Jones and Richard Allen, left St. George's Methodist Church in 1794 to establish two African churches, St. Thomas's African

Fig. 11. Richard Allen, first bishop of the African Methodist Episcopal Church

Episcopal Church and Bethel Methodist Church. While Jones and Allen had already laid plans for a separate African church, a dramatic confrontation in 1792 sealed the issue. On the first Sunday after the renovation of St. George's Methodist Church—a project to which black members had contributed—white elders informed them that they were relegated to a segregated section of the new gallery. Allen later recalled:

> We expected to take the seats over the ones we formerly occupied below, not knowing any better. We took those seats; meeting had begun, and they were nearly done singing, and just as we got to the seats, the Elder said, "Let us pray." We had not been long upon our knees before I heard considerable scuffling and loud talking. I raised my head up and saw one of the trustees, H—— M——, having hold of the Rev. Absalom Jones, pulling him off his knees, and saying, "You must get up, you must not kneel here." Mr. Jones replied, "Wait until the prayer is over, and I will get up, and trouble you no more." With that he beckoned to one of the trustees, Mr. L—— S——, to come to his assistance. By this time prayer was over, and we all went out of the church in a body, and they were no more plagued by us in the church. [148]

In the face of such rude treatment, blacks warmly embraced the two churches of their own making. An estimated 40 percent of Philadelphia's fifteen hundred adult blacks had joined one or the other by the turn of the century, a level of church participation possibly twice that of comparable white laboring classes. [149]

In remaining a part of the Methodist Episcopal church, Richard Allen shrewdly negotiated a high degree of autonomy for Bethel Church. In a "public statement" issued in 1794, Allen asserted the independence of the congregation by limiting membership to "descendents of the African race," empowering Bethel's own trustees with "temporal concerns," and declaring the "right" of the majority of voting members "to call any brother that appears to us adequate to the task to preach or exhort as a local preacher, without the interference of the Conference or any other person or persons whatsoever." [150] Yet Methodist authorities were persistent in trying to curb Bethel's independence: they refused to ordain Allen an elder and a member of the traveling conference, thus preventing him from celebrating the sacraments. After 1810 an increasingly bitter struggle over control of property and the right to name preachers for Bethel pitted Methodist authorities against the thirteen hundred African-American members of Bethel Church, a congregation that had grown into one of the largest in the denomination. On two occasions the congregation actually blocked the aisles to prevent white Methodist officials from mounting the pulpit. In the end, the bitter controversy could only be resolved by the action of a state court, a decision that ruled in favor of Richard Allen and his people. Within months of this court decision, which ensured the church's full independence, Allen joined other black Methodists from Baltimore, Salem (New Jersey), and Attleborough (Pennsylvania), to form the African Methodist Episcopal denomination.

Allen's struggle points to a much broader movement for religious independence among African-Americans. In Philadelphia, blacks built fourteen churches of their own during the first third of the nineteenth century, twelve of them Methodist or Baptist. Fortified by the charismatic appeal of black leaders, these churches claimed nearly four thousand adherents by 1837 and constituted the very backbone of African-American community life.[151]

Similar contests over spiritual and temporal authority led to the formation of black churches and denominations elsewhere. Debates over the rights and privileges of black class meetings in Wilmington and New York City triggered the creation of two other African Methodist denominations during the second decade of the century.[152] In Charleston, South Carolina, the four thousand black members of the Methodist society were allowed their own separate quarterly conference until 1815. At that time, whites abolished this conference and denied blacks the right to maintain their own financial and disciplinary affairs. In response, black Methodists began to plan secretly for a separate church, sending two of their own preachers to Philadelphia to be ordained by Bishop Richard Allen. When white authorities made the decision to construct a building on the burial lot used by black Methodists, the blacks left the Methodist church en masse. "At one fell swoop," one contemporary reported, "nearly every leader delivered up his class papers, and four thousand three hundred and sixty-seven of the members withdrew." The African Church of Charleston existed until 1822, when it was suppressed and the church building demolished after civil authorities discovered that the church membership included a majority of the slaves implicated in the Denmark Vesey conspiracy, including two class leaders and the religious firebrand Vesey himself.[153]

Black Baptist preachers also pioneered independent African-American congregations in this period. The disruption caused by the outbreak of the Revolution provided the freedom for black converts David George and George Liele to found the first separate black church in Silver Bluff, South Carolina. One of Liele's converts, Andrew Bryan, a slave, was converted in 1782 and began gathering with other blacks near Savannah, Georgia. Twice Bryan and his brother Sampson were whipped and imprisoned by

Fig. 12. "Negro Methodists Holding a Meeting in Philadelphia," watercolor by Pavel (Paul) Petrovich Svinin, between 1811 and 1813

authorities for holding their own services. By 1790, the First African Church numbered 225 full members and about 350 other converts. During the 1780s two black preachers in the vicinity of Williamsburg, one named Gowan Pamphlet, the other simply Moses, organized a black church that grew to five hundred members by 1791. Similarly, a slave named "Old Captain" gathered a church in Lexington, Kentucky, in 1801 that was soon said to have three hundred members.[154] In Virginia, a wave of black Baptist congregations also came into existence at the turn of the century by separating from mixed congregations.[155] The pattern was unmistakable: increasingly suppressed in white congregations, black preachers seized every opportunity to organize distinct African-American religious communities.[156]

Even when black preaching was severely curbed during the nineteenth century, the preachers won the confidence of white Methodists and Baptists as "assistants" or retreated to their own private meetings in the slave quarters. The Swedish traveler Fredrika Bemer tells of slaves on a South Carolina rice plantation listening to a dull white Methodist on Sunday morning and then assembling at night to hear a black exhorter who preached "with great fervor and great gesticulation, thumping on the table with his clinched fists." She noted that black preaching manifested a "talent of improvisation, and of strikingly applying theoretical truths to the occurrences of daily life." "Law or no," Eugene Genovese has concluded, "repression or no repression, the slaves heard their own black preachers, if not regularly, then at least frequently enough to make a difference in their lives."[157]

The most striking evidence of the democratization of Christianity in the early republic was that black preachers successfully laid claim to "the sacred desk." Even slaves who could not read became renowned for their ability to infuse ordinary existence with profound spiritual meaning. On the basis of these demonstrated gifts, African-Americans recognized them as the natural leaders of their communities—a telling inversion of the Puritan legacy that had linked spiritual perception to common literacy and "natural" leadership to virtues gained through classical education. Just as the black spiritual severed the intimate ties between church music and high culture (a subject to be treated in a later chapter), so black preaching treated sacred subjects with a "strange familiarity . . . almost profane."[158]

The particular social and religious configurations of the early republic allowed those at the very bottom of the social scale to formulate their own compelling versions of the gospel. Independent black churches, nurtured by biblical stories of consolation and hope, by visions of a promised land, by captivating songs of joy and sorrow, and by the warm embrace of brothers and sisters, forged a folk Christianity that constituted the core of an African-American identity.[159] Particularly effective in keeping paternalistic Christian masters at arm's length, these fellowships permitted African-Americans to nurture their own leaders, sustain networks of communication, express racial strength, and reach out to enfold other sisters and brothers in the fellowship of Christian community. By its democratization in black hands, the church served as the major rallying point for human dignity, freedom, and equality among those who bore slavery's cruel yoke.[160]

The Populist Vision of Joseph Smith

The young Joseph Smith, Jr., had every reason in the world to know keen alienation from mainstream values. In a land of democratic promise and burgeoning capitalist expectation, Smith was born into a family in 1805 that never was able to break the grip of poverty, wearisome toil, and chronic dislocation. His parents, Joseph and Lucy Smith, were habitually destitute despite an ample measure of economic ambition, steady habits, and serious religious faith. To make matters worse, the family once had stood on the brink of modest prosperity. Three years before the birth of Joseph, Jr., in fact, his parents owned a farm in rural Tunbridge, Vermont, and ran a store in neighboring Randolph. From that base, they launched a venture in petty capitalism to sell a shipment of the Vermont root ginseng to the China market. Instead of reaping a handsome return on their investment, however, the Smiths were cheated out of their profit entirely and financially destroyed. Resulting debts forced the family into the ranks of the propertyless, a fate that led to seven moves in the following fourteen years. Typhoid ravaged the family in 1812, leaving seven-year-old Joseph in bed or on crutches for the next three years. From 1814 to 1816 consecutive barren harvests forced the destitute family of eleven to abandon their extended family in Vermont in order to try their luck in central New York. But even there, as Joseph Smith, Jr., came into manhood, a bitter turn thwarted the family's struggle to make ends meet. In 1825, a conniving land agent evicted his parents—now in their fifties—from the farm in Palmyra, shattering their last hope of regaining a foothold of land.[161]

In the face of such wretched luck, the Smith family looked in vain for solace from the institutional church. The church was not absent from their lives; in fact, it was all too present—but in shrill and competing forms. The experience of this intensely religious family is evidence that the proliferation of religious options in the first two decades of the nineteenth century only compounded the crisis of religious authority already so prevalent in popular culture. The swift retreat of religious coercion that Jefferson's election symbolized promised a purer and more powerful church, one that would strip away the centuries of human invention and restore primitive power and simplicity. Instead, people like the Smiths found their hopes for experiencing the divine confused by a cacophony of voices. Like his mother Lucy, who had sampled an array of denominations while doubting the efficacy of them all, Joseph was dismayed by sectarianism, particularly that which followed the supposed bliss of the revivals sweeping New York:

> For, notwithstanding the great love which the converts to these different faiths expressed at the time of their conversion, and the great zeal manifested by the respective clergy . . . it was seen that the seemingly good feelings of both the priests and the converts were more pretended than real; for a scene of great confusion and bad feelings ensued; priest contending against priest, and convert against convert; so that all their good feelings one for another, if they ever had any, were entirely lost in a strife of words and a contest about opinions.[162]

Smith's bleak conclusion was that this "war of words" destroyed all hope for an authoritative religious voice. Like Roger Williams, his own quest for divine reality led him to the conclusion that God had withdrawn his presence from churches in the modern world, all of them having "apostatized from the true and living faith . . . that built upon the Gospel of Jesus Christ as recorded in the new testament."[163]

This severe skepticism about external institutions did not deter Joseph's own intense search for salvation but turned it inward, toward a firmer reliance on religious dreams and visions that were typical of the Smith family. By 1820, he was convinced that only a new outpouring of divine revelation could pierce the spiritual darkness and confusion that gripped his own soul and that of the modern church. He was quite willing to stay away from the orthodox Christianity of his day and to search for truth in unorthodox places, including various forms of folk magic and occult sciences.[164] Smith evinced clearly his skill as a charismatic seer, a spiritual gift he and his family hoped would lead to the discovery of treasure as well as to more important spiritual insight. His growing reputation as a youth with unusual spiritual powers put him at the center of several treasure-seeking escapades, one of them in South Bainbridge, New York, where he was arrested by a justice of the peace on the charge that his "glasslooking" disturbed the peace. At his trial, Smith testified that when he looked at the seer stone he "discovered that time, place and distance were annihilated; that all the intervening obstacles were removed, and that he possessed one of the attributes of Deity, an All-Seeing Eye."[165]

By 1827, this twenty-two-year-old prophet began to claim that he had gained possession of a cache of gold plates and the Urim and Thummim, an Old Testament seer-stone-like instrument that gave him access to a long-lost story about God's wonder-working providence in America. In 1830, Smith published his translation of these gold plates as a six-hundred-page tome, the *Book of Mormon*. A work in biblical prose, it retold the entire sweep of salvation history, underscoring America's role in the scheme of redemption through a fifth or "American" Gospel. This "Gospel" was a radically reconstituted history of the New World, a drama indicting America's churches as lifeless shells, blind and deaf to the real meaning of their own history and to the divine intent for the latter days, which were swiftly approaching.[166]

For all the recent attention given to the study of Mormonism, surprisingly little has been devoted to the *Book of Mormon* itself. What are the patterns deep in the grain of this extraordinary work and what do they reveal about the perceptions and intentions of the prophet Joseph Smith?[167] Mormon historians, of course, have been more interested in pointing out the ways in which the book transcends the provincial opinions of the man Joseph Smith, thus establishing its uniquely biblical and revelatory character. Mormon detractors, on the other hand, have attempted to reduce the book to an inert mirror of the popular culture of New York during the 1820s, thus overlooking elements that are unique and original.[168] More problematic, however, is sheer neglect due to the work's unusual complexity and presumed dullness—following Mark Twain's quip that it was "chloroform in print." Scholars have not taken seriously Joseph Smith's original rationale about the nature of his prophetic mission. The pivotal document of the Mormon church, "an extraordinary work of popular imagination," still receives scant attention from cultural historians, while scholars rush to explore more exotic themes, such as the influence upon Joseph Smith of magic, alchemy, and the occult.[169] As Jan Shipps has argued, historians need to return to the centrality of the "gold bible," Joseph Smith's original testament to the world, which certified the prophet's leadership and first attracted adherents to the movement.[170]

Recent interpretations of the *Book of Mormon* have emphasized its rationality in contrast to the religious enthusiasm of American revivalism, its calm millennial hope in contrast to Millerite enthusiasm, its progressive optimism in contrast to Calvinist determinism, and its quest for order in contrast to romanticism.[171] Unfortunately, these interpretations miss the animating spirit of the book. They view it as one intellectual document among others, as if Joseph Smith were sipping tea in a drawing room, engaged in polite theological debate with Nathaniel William Taylor and William Ellery Channing. These interpretations fail to see that the *Book of Mormon* is a document of profound social protest, an impassioned manifesto by a hostile outsider against the smug complacency of those in power and the reality of social distinctions based on wealth, class, and education. In attempting to define his alienation from the world around him, Smith resorted to a biblical frame of reference rather than to one of conventional politics, a point that Richard Bushman has emphasized. Yet in constructing a grand and complex narrative account of the ancient world, he chose to employ a distinct set of biblical themes: divine judgment upon proud oppressors, blindness to those wise in their own eyes, mercy for the humble, and spiritual authority to the unlearned. This book is a stern and sober depiction of reality.[172]

Like the biblical prophets whose message it champions, the work abounds in divine mercy for an upright remnant. But it also presents a God who is both good and terrible. Surging through its pages are unmistakable undercurrents of divine rage: destruction, famine, pestilence, thunder, earthquakes, tempests, melting elements, flames of devouring fire, and chains from which there is no deliverance. In 1828, the prophet wrote a letter to his cousin declaring that "the sword of vengeance of the Almighty hung over this generation and except they repent and obeyed the Gospel, and turned from their wicked ways, humbling themselves before the Lord, it would fall upon the wicked, and sweep them from the earth as with the beacon of destruction."[173] In the *Book of Mormon*, Smith chose to quote extensively from Old Testament prophets, Isaiah and Malachi, both standing on the brink of cultural desolation and calling a few to repent before the onslaught of brutal judgment. "For behold, the day cometh that shall burn as an oven," says Malachi in 3 Nephi 25:1, "and all the proud, yea, and all that do wickedly, shall be stubble; and the day that cometh shall burn them up, saith the Lord of Hosts, that it shall leave them neither root nor branch."[174] The godly prophet Mormon, a lonely voice to God's people in the new world in the fourth century A.D., found his own Nephite civilization on the same brink of destruction. And from that vantage point, he prophesied that shortly before the final judgment the people of God would know a similar divine winnowing. To those who rejected Christ's latter-day messengers came this warning: "And it would be better for them if they had not been born. For do ye suppose that ye can get rid of the justice of an offended God, who hath been trampled under feet of men, that thereby salvation might come?"[175] The danger of an offended God clearly troubled Joseph Smith no less than it had Jonathan Edwards. What is significant is the way the *Book of Mormon* depicts the occasion of divine wrath.

The single most striking theme in the *Book of Mormon* is that it is the rich, the proud, and the learned who find themselves in the hands of an angry God. Throughout the book, evil is most often depicted as the result of pride and worldliness that comes from economic success and results in oppression of the poor. The message of Jacob is clear to the pre-Columbian Hebrews in the sixth century B.C.:

> But wo unto the rich, who are rich as to the things of the world. For because they are rich they despise the poor, and they persecute the meek, and their hearts are upon their treasures; wherefore, their treasure is their God. And behold, their treasure shall perish with them also.[176]

The prophet Nephi makes the same indictment of churches that will appear in the latter day:

> Because of pride, and because of false teachers, and false doctrine, their churches have become corrupted, and their churches are lifted up; because of pride they are puffed up.
>
> They rob the poor because of their fine sanctuaries; they rob the poor because of their fine clothing; and they persecute the meek and the poor in heart, because in their pride they are puffed up.
>
> They wear stiff necks and high heads; yea, and because of pride, and wickedness, and abominations, and whoredoms, they have all gone astray save it be a few, who are the humble followers of Christ; nevertheless, they are led, that in many instances they do err because they are taught by the precepts of men.
>
> O the wise, and the learned, and the rich, that are puffed up in the pride of their hearts, and all those who preach false doctrines, and all those who commit whoredoms, and pervert the right way of the Lord, wo, wo, wo be unto them, saith the Lord God Almighty, for they shall be thrust down to hell![177]

In two other striking ways, the author of the *Book of Mormon* portrays apocalyptic judgment as the lot of the rich and the proud. In the fourth book of Nephi, the resurrected Christ appears in the New World and establishes a two-hundred-year reign of apostolic power and bliss. But the prophet Mormon explains the reasons for a rapid apostasy and decline after this time:

And now in this two hundred and first year there began to be among them those who were lifted up in pride, such as the wearing of costly apparel, and all manner of fine pearls, and of the fine things of the world.

And from that time forth they did have their goods and their substance no more common among them.

And they began to be divided into classes; and they began to build up churches unto themselves to get gain, and began to deny the true church of Christ.

And it came to pass that when two hundred and ten years had passed away there were many churches in the land; yea, there were many churches which professed to know the Christ, and yet they did deny the more parts of his gospel, insomuch that they did receive all manner of wickedness, and did administer that which was sacred unto him to whom it had been forbidden because of unworthiness.[178]

Equally striking is the choice to employ the prophet Isaiah (chapters 2–14) as the one lengthy portion of Scripture used verbatim in the *Book of Mormon* (2 Nephi 12–24).[179] These chapters include some of holy writ's most appealing prophecies of the end times: that the mountain of the Lord's house will be exalted, that swords will be beat into plowshares, that the wolf shall lie down with the lamb, and that the earth will be full of the knowledge of the Lord, as the waters cover the sea. Yet these blissful scenes constitute a last and merciful chapter to a story that centers on the swift and sure destruction that awaits the oppressive and unjust society of Judah.

The prophet Isaiah indicts God's wayward people on two counts: their arrogant pretension and their oppression of the poor. The prophet thunders against a society of self-importance:

> The lofty looks of man shall be humbled, and the haughtiness of men shall be bowed down, and the Lord alone shall be exalted in that day.
>
> For the day of the Lord of Hosts soon cometh upon all nations, yea, upon every one; yea, upon the proud and lofty, and upon every one who is lifted up, and he shall be brought low. . . .
>
> And the loftiness of man shall be bowed down, and the haughtiness of men shall be made low; and the Lord alone shall be exalted in that day.[180]

Isaiah takes particular note of the way people distance themselves from others using fine apparel, and warns that the Lord will replace jewelry, rings, headbands, bonnets, bracelets, fine linen, veils, and perfume with sackcloth, baldness, burning, and stench.[181]

The reason for this severity is God's identification with the poor and downtrodden. "What mean ye?" the Lord demands of the wealthy. "Ye beat my people to pieces, and grind the faces of the poor." God condemns the rich for accumulating houses while oppressing the poor, preying on widows, and robbing the fatherless.[182] The interlocking themes of pride, wealth, learning, fine clothing, and oppression of the poor reappear throughout the *Book of Mormon* as the principal objects of divine displeasure.[183] And it is clergymen and their priestcraft which are said to be the chief sources of these sins.[184] What compounds the foolishness of these clergymen is their smug denial that a God of the miraculous is still powerfully at work.

In one of the most moving passages in the book, the prophet Moroni, the single remaining survivor of a godly civilization, predicts that these accumulated evils will characterize the end times—when a new prophet will discover the golden plates hidden in the Hill Cumorah and proclaim the reopening of the brazen heavens. "Search the prophecies of Isaiah," Moroni counsels that latter-day generation that is drunk with pride and callous religiosity. He proclaims that a flame of unquenchable fire will be kindled in that day because church leaders will have risen in the pride of their hearts, built churches for material gain, denied the reality of God's miraculous power, and loved to adorn themselves and their churches more than to care for the poor and needy:

> Why do ye adorn yourselves with that which hath no life, and yet suffer the hungry, and the needy, and the naked, and the sick and the afflicted to pass by you, and notice them not?
>
> Why do ye build up your secret abominations to get gain, and cause that widows should mourn before the Lord, and also orphans to mourn before the Lord, and also the blood of their fathers and their husbands to cry unto the Lord from the ground, for vengeance upon your heads?
>
> Behold, the sword of vengeance hangeth over you; and the time soon cometh that he avengeth the blood of the saints upon you, for he will not suffer their cries any longer.[185]

The final element in this litany of judgment refers to the pervasive naturalism of the end times, the orthodox teaching that the age of miraculous wonders has long since passed away and that there will no longer be "revelations, nor prophecies, nor gifts, nor healing, nor speaking with tongues, and the interpretation of tongues." Other churches and other reformers will deny the religion of the Bible because they are callous to the inspiration, revelation, and apostolic gifts that accompany genuine divine presence. "And if there were miracles wrought then," the prophet Moroni asks, "why had God ceased to be a God of miracles and yet be an unchangeable Being?"[186] His conclusion, like that of Old Testament prophets after the annihilation of the temple, is simply that the glory of God's presence will depart.[187]

The vision of Joseph Smith is intensely populist in its rejection of the religious conventions of his day and in its hostility to the orthodox clergy, its distrust of reason as an exclusive guide, and its rage at the oppression of the poor. In a more positive vein, Smith also projects a distinctly populist vision that suggests how God will restore the ancient order of things. He is violently anticlerical but confident that God will reconstitute the church according to popular norms. The *Book of Mormon* has its own preferential option for the poor, not as persons to be pitied, but as those whom God has chosen to empower. The Book of Alma, chapter 32, contains an extended account of how "the poor class of people" are cast out of the synagogues for wearing coarse apparel. Instead of despising them as the priests did, the prophet Alma blesses them because their physical poverty and the burden of being ostracized has taught them poverty of spirit. Such lowliness of heart puts them in the enviable position of learning true wisdom. In the same spirit, the prophet Nephi says that in the latter days all churches will be given over to abominations and whoredoms except "a few, who are the humble followers of Christ." In the latter days, God would again choose plain and ordinary instruments.[188]

In the most dramatic example of God using the weak things of the world to confound the wise, Nephi predicted the opening of a new word of revelation. The sealed book is first offered to a man of learning, whose efforts are thwarted by greed and ambition. The Lord then turns to an unlearned man to reveal the book to the world, declaring that "a God of miracles" would not be bound by human conventions: "Therefore, I will proceed to do a marvelous work among this people, yea a work and a wonder, for the wisdom of their wise and learned shall perish, and the understanding of their prudent shall be hid."[189] Like the unschooled prophet who revealed that book to America in 1830, Nephi declared, "I glory in plainness."[190] The *Book of Mormon* anticipated a restored church that would maintain "an equality among all men," calling preachers to work with their hands and earn their bread like everyone else.[191]

Upon the publication of the *Book of Mormon*, Joseph Smith and a tiny band of followers went forth with the compelling message that God was restoring the one true fold, the ancient order of things. By revealing an up-to-date Bible and insisting upon God's active supernatural presence, Smith gave authoritative answers to many seeking secure moorings.[192] More striking is the evidence that Smith's overall vision also had a distinct class bias. It conveyed the unmistakable claim that common people had the right to shape their own faith and to take charge of their own religious destiny.

These populist themes resonated powerfully with Smith's earliest disciples, young men who were characteristically poor, uprooted, unschooled, and unsophisticated like himself.[193] Brigham and Lorenzo Dow Young were raised in such desperate poverty that their family was broken up when their mother died of tuberculosis in 1815. They were fourteen and eight years old at the time. Denied the opportunity of formal schooling and occasions to cultivate the social graces, Brigham Young retained deep resentment against the social distinctions of the churches of his youth.[194] Orson and Parley Pratt, both in Smith's original group of Twelve Apostles, also grew up in a family trying to break a cycle of poverty and wandering. As teenagers, both were boarded out to other farmers after the family flax farm had failed when a water-powered carding mill nearby made their efforts unprofitable.[195] Parley later reflected on his experience as a wage earner:

> The next spring found me in the employment of a wealthy farmer, by the name of Eliphet Bristol. . . . I was then but a lad—being only seventeen years of age—and stood in need of fatherly and motherly care and comfort. But they treated a laborer as a machine; not as a human being, possessed of feelings and sympathies in common with his species. *Work!* work! WORK! you are hired to work. . . . I was glad when the time expired; I felt like one released from prison.[196]

Heber C. Kimball, Joseph Smith's greatest missionary, grew up in equally humble and insecure circumstances. The Kimball family had moved to Ontario County, New York, after their farm failed in Vermont in 1809. But their financial reverses continued, and Heber's father, Solomon, who worked as a blacksmith, went to jail for debts in 1815. After 1820, Heber suffered his own financial woes as an unemployed blacksmith "cast upon the world without a friend to console my grief." He was working as a potter, making simple kitchen and table implements, when he met Brigham Young.[197]

Likewise, the legendary preacher Jedediah Morgan Grant, who came to be known as "Mormon Thunder," was one of twelve children of dirt-poor farmers and shinglemakers who had been forced to pull up stakes on several occasions. In 1833, Mormon elders shared the blessings of the restored gospel with the Grant family in their farmhouse in Erie, Pennsylvania, and successfully applied healing hands to Jedediah's mother, who was bedridden with rheumatism. Jedediah was baptized that year at seventeen; two years later he was selected as one of the First Quorum of Seventy and sent forth preaching in this select cadre of missionaries. Thomas B. Marsh, the first president of the Council of Twelve Apostles, had been a waiter in a public house, a groomsman, and an unsuccessful grocer. He had withdrawn from the Methodists when that church did not seem to correspond with the Bible and when a spirit of prophecy led him to anticipate the rise of a new church.[198]

None of these seven young men cut an impressive figure in a culture that deferred to wealth and idealized upward mobility. When they heard the call of the prophet Joseph Smith, these semiliterate young men—a painter and glazier, two blacksmiths, a potter, a farm hand, a shinglemaker, and a waiter—had virtually no stake in society. Their formative years gave them every reason to forego worldly ambition and throw their considerable energy into building a spiritual kingdom in opposition to the competitive and capitalist mores of Jacksonian America. All remained unconvinced by the fervor of emotional revivals and nursed deep resentments against orthodox modes of Christianity. According to Heber C. Kimball, soon to be Brigham Young's closest friend, the members of the Young family "were in low circumstances and seemed to be an afflicted people in consequence of having a great deal of sickness and sorrow to pass through; and of course were looked down upon by the flourishing church where we lived."[199]

Kimball, Young, and their colleagues, ranging in age from nineteen to thirty, jumped at the opportunity to follow a prophet who spoke with authority and not like the scribes. They gladly assumed the roles of full-time saint and missionary and, in time, of apostle and patriarch, high priest and president. They exulted in a gospel whose cornerstone the builders had rejected and that promised to use the weak things of the world to confound the mighty. Severing ties of place and, when necessary, of family, they pursued relentlessly the cause of a church that had returned power— as in apostolic days—to illiterate men such as themselves.

III. Audience

CHAPTER FIVE

The Sovereign Audience

Lorenzo [Dow] was not only uncouth in his person and appearance, but his voice was harsh, his action hard and rectangular. It is scarcely possible to conceive of a person more entirely destitute of all natural eloquence. But he understood common life, and especially vulgar life—its tastes, prejudices, and weaknesses; and he possessed a cunning knack of adapting his discourses to such audiences. He told stories with considerable art, and his memory being stored with them, he could always point a moral or clinch a proposition by an anecdote. He knew that with simple people an illustration is better than logic, and when he ran short of Scripture, or argument failed, he usually resorted to some pertinent story or adapted allegory. . . .

Who could argue down such telling logic with the million?

SAMUEL GOODRICH, *1856*

Networks of religious communication were altered in two profound ways in the generation after the American Revolution. First, clergymen lost their unrivaled position as authoritative sources of information. In Massachusetts as a whole, for instance, clergymen had constituted 70 percent of all learned professionals in 1740; by 1800 they were only 45 percent, despite the fact that their number had doubled. The turnover rate of clergymen everywhere mounted sharply; other professionals, most noticeably lawyers, competed as sources of information, narrowing the scope of clerical authority; printers, newspapers, and post offices multiplied at a geometric rate after 1780. By 1820, Massachusetts had 443 post offices, virtually all of them established after the Revolution. Bemoaning the decline in clerical status, David Daggett, nephew of a Yale president and clergyman, contrasted the old pattern—"the minister, with two or three principal characters were supreme in each town"—with the new—"knowledge has induced the laity to think and act for themselves."[1]

A second change in networks of religious communication was an explosion of popular printed material. "A RELIGIOUS NEWSPAPER would have been a phenomenon not many years since," a Methodist journal noted in 1823, "but now the groaning press throws them out in almost every direction." Virtually nonexistent in 1800, religious periodicals had, by 1830, become the grand engine of a burgeoning religious culture, the primary means of promotion for, and bond of union within, competing religious groups. The Universalist denomination alone cranked out 138 different periodicals in the three decades after 1820. Between 1826 and 1834, Anti-Masons reached nearly every New York hamlet through over one hundred of their newspapers.[2] The Methodists turned every circuit rider into a colporteur and by 1840 claimed fifteen thousand subscribers to their weekly periodical, the *Western Christian Advocate*. A decade later the Western Methodist Book Concern in Cincinnati employed twenty-five printers and forty-six binders to produce five different periodicals with a combined circulation of eighty-five thousand. But even these figures paled before the extraordinary publishing exploits of William Miller and the Adventists, who blanketed the nation with an estimated four million pieces of literature within four years, including prophetic charts that illustrated how this world would end in 1843. The early promoters of the missionary movement were also transfixed by publishing, as were reformers Alexander Campbell and John Humphrey Noyes. Noyes made it clear that he would have sacrificed his communal experiment rather than his newspaper. Bemused by this infatuation with the printed word, Horace Bushnell observed that Americans operated "as if God would offer man a mechanical engine for converting the world, . . . or as if types of lead and sheets of paper may be the light of the world."[3]

Boston publisher Samuel Goodrich recalled that for the previous generation books and newspapers "had been scarce, and were read respectfully, as if they were grave matters, demanding thought and attention." Spectacles, he noted, were made and used differently then: "These instruments were not as now, little tortoise-shell hooks, attached to a ribbon, and put off and on with a jerk; but they were of silver or steel, substantially made, and calculated to hold on with a firm and steady grasp, showing the gravity of the uses to which they were devoted. Even the young approached a book with reverence, and a newspaper with awe. How the world has changed."[4]

A shift from a relatively coherent Christian culture to a pluralistic one was a central consequence of these changes. This competitive marketplace of diverse values diluted, if it did not destroy, the old common print culture. Printing, earlier addressed to the tastes of gentlemen and clergymen, now appealed to the masses. What had once been an instrument of cultural cohesion now became an agent of fragmentation and competition.

These changes inaugurated an age of mass communications in which religious movements remained at the cutting edge. The shift was evident in the quantity of published material and in the changed nature of communication networks and intended audiences; it was also reflected in the kind of persons stepping into the pulpit and breaking into print, in the variety of mediums, formats, and language styles employed, and in the willingness of many Christians to use any successful means of persuasion.[5] Despite their wide diversity, Methodists, Baptists, Universalists, Disciples, Mormons, and Millerites were all communication entrepreneurs, and their movements were crusades for broadcasting the truth. Each was wedded to the transforming power of the word, spoken, written, and sung; each was passionate about short-circuiting a hierarchical flow of information; each was supremely confident that the vernacular and the colloquial were the most fitting channels for religious expression; and each was content to measure the success of individuals and movements by their ability to persuade. By systematically employing lay preachers, by exploiting a golden age of local publishing, and by spreading new forms of religious folk music, they ensured the forceful delivery of their message.

This intense commitment to effective communication grew out of a dual heritage. First, the genius of evangelicals in the eighteenth century had been their firm identification with people. While others excelled in articulating and defending the truth and in building institutions to weather the storms of time, evangelicals were passionate about communicating a message. The enduring legacy of the first Great Awakening, Harry S. Stout suggests, was a new mode of persuasion. Defying a church callous to its common folk, John Wesley thundered that he would preach nothing but "plain truth for plain people." While Wesley and George Whitefield were concerned about theology, their primary interest was that each person have a profound experience with God. This required an idiom in touch with people. By the time of the American Revolution, the warmth of such evangelical appeals and their ability to draw the unchurched into cohesive fellowships made evangelicalism a major social force on both sides of the Atlantic.[6]

Yet until the last two decades of the eighteenth century, Americans were still severely limited in the amount and type of information they could receive, and much of its dispersal was still hierarchical. The intensive communication potential of itinerancy, which set off such a firestorm in the Great Awakening, remained sporadic and diffuse prior to the Revolution. And the American colonies had nothing that could be construed as a democratic religious press. The printing of sermons, even those of an evangelical stalwart such as the Baptist Isaac Backus, remained largely an intramural exchange among the clergy. The extemporaneous preaching of Wesley and Whitefield had a popular audience in view, but their sermons retained a spine of classically defined theological categories. Similarly, the

new style of evangelical hymnody proposed by Isaac Watts and champ-
pioned by Jonathan Edwards and George Whitefield was an attempt to
communicate the traditional message of evangelical Calvinism to a broader
audience.[7] In short, eighteenth-century evangelicals—the Watts, White-
fields, and Wesleys, men of proper learning and character—struggled to
reorient an elitist communications structure in their quest to infuse the
gospel with new meaning and purpose for ordinary people. Yet even their
efforts retained a clear distinction between those who had the authority to
speak and write and those who were to listen and learn.

On the eve of the Revolution, obscure Baptist preachers in Virginia
mounted a direct attack on this distinction. During the Revolution itself,
the challenge became more intense. The "New Light Stir" in the hill
country of New England, the work of Henry Alline in the Canadian
maritime provinces, and the activity of Methodists in the South continued
to undercut the cultural dominance of elites in the pulpit.[8] This evangelical
challenge was sharpened by the democratization of print that grew out of
political culture at the end of the eighteenth century. The Jeffersonian press
linked many who were suspicious of power with many who were powerless
in a common effort to open the press to all Americans. In this vein, the
unlettered Massachusetts farmer, William Manning, declared that the first
responsibility of a people intent on self-determination was to bypass the
regular press and "to invent the cheapest & most expeditious method of
conveying" knowledge to the people.[9]

A useful window on these developments is the strategy employed by
Elias Smith and Lorenzo Dow. Both were enthralled with the potential of
vernacular speaking, publishing, and song-making. Despite styles that
were clearly eccentric and exaggerated, these two illustrate by their success
how rapidly the control of religious communications could slip into the
hands of ordinary folk—whom the gentry dismissed as "destitute at once of
the urbanity of gentlemen, the information of scholars, and the principles
of virtue."[10] Both became relentless itinerants and went about discomfiting
respectable churches by reinforcing the spoken word with bundles of their
own books, pamphlets, tracts, and volumes of spiritual song. In short,
these shrewd, self-anointed preachers were clear heralds of an age of mass
media.

In 1800 a regular exposure to popular newspapers altered decisively
the spiritual pilgrimage of Elias Smith. Self-consciously imitating Benjamin Austin and the radical Jeffersonian press, Smith cranked out an
avalanche of pamphlets, tracts, books, songs, and newspaper copy that, in
form and content, conspired against social distinction. Noting with displeasure the following that Smith was building in Essex County, Mas-

sachusetts, the diarist William Bentley wrote in 1805 that "the press has lately vomited out many nauseous things from this writer." Other members of the Standing Order lashed out at the "poison of his writings," calling it "the most wretched trash that ever issued from the press."[11]

Brimming with confidence in the beneficent power of the press, Smith turned his energy toward John Adams's goal during the Stamp Act crisis of letting "every sluice-gate of knowledge be opened and set a-flowing."[12] "As truth is no private man's property," Smith contended, "and all Christians have a right to propagate it, I do also declare, that every *Christian* has a right to publish and vindicate what he believes."[13] And publish he did. In 1803, after stirring up considerable controversy with a biting satire on the clergy in the *New Hampshire Gazette*, he followed up with four different pamphlet editions of this attack, *The Clergyman's Looking-Glass*, two editions of a well-received political speech, and two pamphlets of doctrinal controversy.[14] The next year he brought out three new editions of *The Clergyman's Looking-Glass*, three new controversial pieces, and a substantial hymnbook.[15] In addition to publishing five new pamphlets and two more hymnbooks in 1805, Smith began his career as a journalist with a quarterly, the *Christian's Magazine, Reviewer, and Religious Intelligencer*, which he later said had "greatly enraged the clergy and their subjects."[16] This magazine gave way in 1808 to the keystone of Smith's career in print, the *Herald of Gospel Liberty*, a fortnightly newspaper that he edited for a decade and that served as the primary means of communication among his followers as well as a forum for a wide variety of religious radicals throughout the country. In the meantime, he continued flooding the market with pamphlets and issued several lengthy books.[17]

After 1818 Smith moved beyond the Christian Connection, which he had founded, to embrace Universalism and sectarian medicine. As a promoter of Universalism he began two short-lived journals, the *Herald of Life and Immortality* (1818–19) and the *Morning Star and City Watchman* (1827–29).[18] As a rebel against conventional medicine, Smith became the hired publicist of Samuel Thomson, the most effective proponent of sectarian medicine in Jacksonian America. In addition, Smith avidly published new forms of colloquial religious music, producing at least fifteen different editions of songbooks between 1804 and 1817. Many of these songs he composed himself.[19]

Smith brazenly held the Enlightenment conviction that truth was self-evident. The process of clearing away superstition and ecclesiastical privilege would bring truth, simple and undefiled, into plain view. Because people were capable of discerning truth for themselves, they would flock to its standard if only rightly informed. Popular enlightenment simply lacked communication. Smith saw the task before him with penetrating clarity: the very act of publishing the good news was to liberate people from the grasp of ignorance.[20]

Lorenzo Dow was an equally gifted and prodigious communicator. A bold-and-bluff preacher of daring originality, Dow combined an explicit ideology of mass communications, a rare genius for communicating that bordered on a cult of personality, and a relentless pace that made his name a household word from the streets of New York to the wilds of Alabama. By 1820, moreover, his numerous writings had been published in cities all over America. One Methodist minister noted that "he was not learned, but very intelligent," a figure whose conversation was "extremely interesting" and whose eccentricities "took well with the public." "All who have attempted to imitate him have made an utter failure."[21]

Dow's preaching was spellbinding. A theatrical performer, he might begin a sermon with a humorous tale, or an ad hominem attack on a notorious sinner in the audience. An unseen trumpet might blow at a precisely-timed moment, or he might smash a chair to the floor for effect. He could wax comical or doleful and could sustain a mood of love and affection or acrimony and condemnation. He encouraged displays of religious ecstasy which observers called "the jerking exercise." (See figure 13.) Always ready with a rejoinder, he drew adroitly upon his stock in trade of "repartee, humor, wit, irony." He responded typically when a doubter in the audience questioned whether Dow even knew what Calvinism was. "Yes," he promptly replied:

> You can and you can't,
>   You will and you won't;
> You'll be damned if you do,
>   And you'll be damned if you don't.[22]

William Winans, who later emerged as a principal leader of Methodists in antebellum Mississippi, recalled traveling ten miles to hear the celebrated Lorenzo. Expecting to see a man of "Apostolic dignity and piety," Winans was instantly repulsed by Dow's doggerel about someone who supposedly "vomited three black crows" and "the Fable of the Old Man, his Son, and their Ass." In light of this performance, Winans mused that fame was not necessarily a mark of merit or greatness.[23]

Like Elias Smith, Dow refused to be trammeled by any church structure. But his phenomenal success made Methodist authorities very wary about curtailing his activity.[24] Francis Asbury claimed that an unruly camp meeting would hush to silence "at the sound of his voice or at the sight of his fragile but awe-inspiring presence."[25] One report noted that the effect of

Fig. 13. Lorenzo Dow and the Jerking Exercise, from Samuel G. Goodrich,
Recollections of a Lifetime (New York, 1856), vol. 1

listening to a sermon was "tenfold more impressive from the lips of Lorenzo Dow himself" than merely hearing an account of it. Another commented that years later the text from Ezekiel that Dow brought to bear upon his audience "was stamped on my mind never to be forgotten."[26] The large number of children named Lorenzo attests to the powerful rapport this original preacher had with the public.[27]

Dow's frenetic pace, both preaching and printing, amplified his influence into the nooks and crannies of American popular culture. Despite chronic illness, he barnstormed the back roads of the United States for the first two decades of the nineteenth century, rivaling Frances Asbury in the thousands of miles traveled and the hundreds of sermons preached. A chaotic torrent of broadsides, pamphlets, journals, and books accompanied his travels. In the decade after 1804, over twenty of his writings were published in seventeen different locations including New York; Philadelphia; Baltimore; Augusta, Georgia; Lexington, Kentucky; Nashville, Tennessee; Lynchburg, Virginia; Salisbury and Newbern, North Carolina; Washington, Pennsylvania; Poughkeepsie, New York; and Winchester, Vermont.

This attempt to deluge popular culture with the spoken and the printed word was motivated by acute anger at the orthodox churches for withholding knowledge from ordinary folk. Intermingled with spiritual and practical advice was an anger at the oppression of lower classes, the differing lots of "Gentlemen of Nobility" and "Peasants" or "commonality." Lorenzo Dow pondered why some command while others have to obey, no matter how imperious the command; why some claim the country as their own while others are put on a level with the animals and have to bow and scrape; why "one hath thousands, gained by the labour of others, while another hath not the assurance of a days' provision, nor the money to procure the coarsest raiment." Perceiving the same kind of inequity and injustice in the church, Dow thundered against "the despotic government too much exercised everywhere among the clergy over the commonality." Dow was exercised to break the restrictions imposed by parish lines, standing orders, circuits, and bounds fixed by "a great man, or number of great men."[28]

In his pamphlet "Defense of Camp Meetings," Dow claimed that the orthodox opposition to camp meetings was not principally theological but sociological, the unwillingness of "men of self-importance" and the "self-exalted" to lower themselves and mix with ordinary people:

> You may support your distinction and feed your pride, but in a religious point of view all men are on a level, and the good man feels it

so. The very fact, your aversion to worship your Creator with the poor and despised, proves to me that you have neither part nor lot in the matter; that you know not God nor his worship, and that to follow your advice would be the sure road to perdition. The Lord hath declared his intention and purpose to exalt the humble whilst he will pull down high looks.[29]

This ideology of communications was driven by the exhilarating sense that people could break free of elite domination and speak and write whenever they felt led. This keen sense of liberation and expectancy grew out of dramatic changes that were multiplying the audience of American preaching, publication, and song-making in the new nation.

The Triumph of Vernacular Preaching

With the era of the democratic revolutions came the end of the classic age of the American sermon that had dominated the Reformed churches of New England and the middle colonies for a century and a half: stylized texts delivered on a regular occasion by a university-trained clergyman in a settled parish. Down to the Revolution most clergymen, evangelical and liberal, still earned the veneration of their congregations by sermons that "smelled of the lamp." The preaching legacy of George Whitefield certainly pushed at the boundaries of these accepted conventions, but it did not undercut their legitimacy. In 1776, Congregational ministers still dominated public communications throughout New England, their mouthpiece a sermonic form as traditional in structure and content as the Puritan errand itself.[30]

In the next generation, those who preserved this tradition of genteel and doctrinal sermons faced an unprecedented challenge from those who preferred the vernacular. "Mechanic" preachers and zealous sectarians were nothing new to Protestant churches. Yet what ruffled the orthodox in Jeffersonian America was their own impotence in the face of an explosive growth of unschooled preachers. These loud and unrestrained exhorters honed the sermon into a razor-sharp recruiting device, drummed out theological subtlety and complication, and incorporated personal idiosyncrasies and dramatic flare. They retained, in the words of an Episcopalian critic, an "irregular ministry" and "a perverse zeal for the propagation of truth."[31] Literary preaching retained vitality for citizens of the new republic—at least for those in cities and towns. But for Americans in the hinterland, away from cosmopolitan centers, the most accessible preaching was increasingly folk- rather than clergy-dominated.

A firm commitment to lay preaching constituted the foundation of the insurgent religious movements of the early republic. All rested their claims to authority on the validity of lay proclamation. They dared to raise preachers from obscurity and send them forth armed only with a sense of divine calling and the sheer talent of being able to move people. Whether Methodist, Baptist, Christian, Universalist, Millerite, or Mormon, these preachers had little else to fall back on if their presence and charisma were unconvincing. This radical dependence upon audience raised to prominence preachers who were often the inverse of the pulpit's traditional decorum. James McGready, a leader in Kentucky's Great Revival, used gestures described as "the very reverse of elegance." The Methodist itinerant Billy Hibbard convulsed audiences with his eccentricities and then pierced their hearts with arrows of divine judgment and conviction of sin. The black evangelist Harry Hosier gave riveting vernacular dramatizations of the Bible. The Virginia Baptist John Jasper had a remarkable talent for "stringing together picture after picture." The Methodist Jesse Lee preferred to portray the "torments of the damned" rather than present "velvet-mouth preaching." Baptist Jacob Knapp's "sledge-hammer" style of preaching always created a stir. Joshua Thomas, the Methodist "Parson of the Islands," raised huge crowds in Baltimore, making "people laugh and cry every time he talks." The Latter-Day Saint Brigham Young kept audiences enthralled by the hour with his rich vocabulary of provincial expressions.[32] Samuel Goodrich argued that the Methodists actually derived aid from that which was the greatest offense to their enemies, the use of "illiterate propagandists." He suggested that defects of grammar and rhetoric actually attracted rather than offended the "rude" audiences they addressed.[33]

This communication system was premised upon a firm link between speaker and audience. Authority flowed to those claimants whose person, language, and deportment best resonated with the interests of common people. At the very time that elites were finding the ministry less attractive as a profession, the opportunity opened for any American to preach. This free environment multiplied the potential of the sermon as a mass medium: it elicited new and bold strategies of persuasion, freed preaching from ecclesiastical encumbrance and from restrictions of space and time, and linked proclamation to equally vernacular forms of printing and singing.

As communicators, upstarts such as Elias Smith, Lorenzo Dow, William Miller, and Joseph Smith were folk geniuses. They projected a presence that people found inviting, compelling, and authoritative. At the same time, their approach successfully befuddled the traditional clergy, who dismissed them as mindless demagogues but could not restrain people from flocking to their cause. Brilliant debaters who refused to abide by traditional theological etiquette, these populist preachers were often "not learned but very intelligent."[34] Their coarse language, earthy humor, biting sarcasm, and commonsense reasoning appealed to the uneducated but left the professional clergy without a ready defense. In an 1817 pamphlet written to combat Elias Smith's influence, the Congregationalist Thomas Andros summed up the new tactics:

> Ridicule, sneer, malignant sarcasm and reproach, are the armour in which he goes forth. On this ground, and not on sober argumentation, he knows the success of his cause depends. . . . If he knows the doctrine of original sin is not true, let him sit down and write a manly and candid answer to President Edwards' great work on that subject. . . . Were he a dignified, candid, and intelligent controversialist, there would be enough to answer him, but who would wish to attack a windmill? Who can refute a sneer?

Andros also recognized that popularity rather than virtue was the clarion call of the movement: "They measure the progress of religion by the numbers, who flock to their standard; not by the prevalence of faith, and piety, justice and charity, and the public virtues in society in general."[35]

This vernacular preaching represents more than emotional harangue, however. Just as historians have inaccurately depicted Populism as a mass popular movement unencumbered by serious intellectual content, so they have characterized the revivalistic culture of the early nineteenth century as an emotional binge that "effectively scuttled much of the intellectual structure of Protestantism."[36] While preachers believed in fervent emotion and had no interest in allowing one generation to rule another, they were also capable of devastating logic to achieve their own purposes. They sought to build new religious cultures, free of the domination of learned theologians. Whether or not one found their arguments compelling had as much to do with where one was located on the social scale as with the inherent rationality of the case. Take, for example, the Standing Order's critique of sectarians in New Hampshire who were making "such easy and rapid progress":

> Liberty is a great cant word with them. They promise their hearers to set them at liberty. And to effect this, they advise them to give up all their old prejudices and traditions which they have received from their fathers and their ministers; who, they say, are hirelings, keeping poor souls in bondage, and under oppression. Hence to use their own

language, they say, "Break all those yokes and trammels from off you, and come out of prison; and dare to think, and speak, and act for yourselves."[37]

A compelling theme in popular preaching throughout this era was the Jeffersonian notion that people should shake off all servile prejudice and learn to prove things for themselves. Alexander Campbell and William Miller argued vehemently that self-made students of Scripture should eschew speculation and draw principles inductively from what Campbell called the "facts of the Bible." William Miller claimed to avoid speculation entirely: "We have sought to spread the truth, not by fanatical prophecies arising out of our own hearts, but by the light of the scriptures, history and sober argument. We appeal only to the Bible, and give you our rules of interpretation." While Miller had no use for academic theology, his arguments were surprisingly sophisticated, demanding rigorous thought and calculation. He invited common folk to ply clergymen with questions about the interpretation of prophecy and then trust their own intellectual abilities rather than depending on answers that descended from colleges and seminaries.[38] The devilish strategy in this appeal, of course, was that any Christian using New Testament words could fend off the most brilliant theological argument with the simple retort that one was using God's word against human opinion. All the weight of church history could not begin to tip the scale against the simple declaration that the New Testament did not contain such phrases as *total depravity* and *perseverance of the saints*. For the early republic's gentlemen theologians, this ingenious argument was both perverse and frustrating.

This rationale for individual self-respect grew out of an intense concern for audience, however humble and isolated. One great advantage of recruiting common people to preach, as Asbury found, was that most were immune from hungering and thirsting for fashionable and refined Christianity. They could retain a deep empathy for their audience, what Philip Schaff called "a decided aptness for popular discourse and exhortation."[39] The goal was to couch the sermon in homely, colloquial language, readily understood. The first two pieces of advice of the original Methodist *Discipline* were, "Always suit your subjects to your audience," and "Choose the plainest texts you can." In this vein, the Methodist itinerant Billy Hibbard remarked that people judged one of his sermons to be the best they had ever heard "because they could remember so much of it." This is exactly the kind of preaching that Brigham Young found impressive in his colleague Heber Kimball in Britain in 1837 and 1838:

Br. Kimball would say, "come my friend, do not be in a hurry," and he would begin and preach the gospel in a plain familiar manner, and make his hearers believe everything that he said, and make them testify to its truth, whether they would believe or not, asking them "now ain't that so?" and they would say "yes," and he would take scripture as he needed it out of his own bible and ask, "now ain't that so?" the reply would be "yes." He would say, "Now you believe this? You see how plain the Gospel is? Come along now" and he would lead them into the waters of Baptism. The people would want to come to see him early in the morning, and stay with him until noon, and from that until night.[40]

This kind of preaching required an approach that was personal rather than abstract.[41] Sermons were most effective which expressed a preacher's deepest personal feelings. Frequently preachers, overcome by emotion, would weep and cry aloud.[42] A hearer found it difficult to keep this kind of sermon at arm's length. Francis Asbury criticized the learned preaching of Presbyterian Patrick Allison because "if he had studied to pass by the conscience of his hearers, he could not have done it more effectually."[43] Instead, Asbury called for demonstrated energy or "Godly vehemence" in preaching that was inherently convincing. "Preach as if you had seen heaven and its celestial inhabitants and had hovered over the bottomless pit and beheld the tortures and heard the groans of the damned."[44]

Sidney Rigdon, the son of a poor farmer, embodied this kind of preaching. His magnetic presence made him a chief spokesperson for two different restoration movements: the Disciples of Christ in the late 1820s, and the Latter-Day Saints after 1830. He had a talent for enabling each individual in an audience to apply his ideas to themselves. Late in 1830, newly baptized and ordained in Smith's movement, Rigdon conducted a service on the banks of the Chagrin River in northern Ohio. Overlooking the scene were two curious observers, John Barr, the sheriff of Cuyahoga County, and Varnem J. Card, an unorthodox lawyer. Barr recalled that Rigdon went into the water, baptized one person, and from the water delivered a "powerful exhortation," after which thirty people came forward to be immersed:

> While the exciting scene was transpiring below us in the valley and in the pool, the faces of the crowd expressing the most intense emotion, Mr. Card suddenly seized my arm and said, "Take me away!" Taking his arm, I saw that his face was so pale that he seemed to be about to faint. His frame trembled as we walked away and mounted our

horses. We rode a mile toward Willoughby before a word was said. Rising the hill out of the valley, he seemed to recover, and said, "Mr., if you had not been there I certainly should have gone into the water." He said the impulse was irresistible.[45]

This was an age of communication entrepreneurs who stripped the sermon of its doctrinal spine and its rhetorical dress and opened it to a wide spectrum of fresh idioms: true-to-life passion, simplicity of structure, and dramatic creativity. Most noticeable were the uses of storytelling and overt humor. Harvard graduate Timothy Flint was sent out by the Missionary Society of Connecticut to help establish Presbyterian churches in the West. In 1826 he reported that "the ten thousand" dislike preachers who "dogmatize, and define, and dispute," but respond to those who use "many low words, images and illustrations." Similarly, Peter Cartwright advised a young Presbyterian minister that if he did not put away manuscript sermons—logically arranged according to conventional scheme of text, exposition, and proof—the Methodists would set the western world on fire while he was still lighting his match.[46] The shift from doctrinal to narrative preaching introduced a powerful tool of persuasion. Stories are rich sources of belief precisely because they are just stories and are therefore immune from falsehood and from logical fallacy. "You can refute Hegel," said W. B. Yeats, "but not . . . the Song of Sixpence."[47] According to Samuel Goodrich, this was exactly the impact that the storytelling of Lorenzo Dow had upon the people of Ridgefield, Connecticut. Dow told them a parable about a certain "Major Smith," an upstanding church member and one of the elect, "safe as a codfish, pickled, packed, and in port." The major's conversion, reformation, and subsequent fall back into drunkenness effectively undercut the doctrine of election in the minds of Dow's audience, moving Goodrich to exclaim, "Who could argue down such telling logic with the million?"[48]

Another strong index that preaching was becoming an integral function of popular culture was the wholesale introduction of humor: jokes, sarcasm, biting ridicule, witty anecdotes, clever plays on words, and irreverent doggerel.[49] Elias Smith, Lorenzo Dow, Billy Hibbard, Joshua Thomas, John Strange, Peter Cartwright, John Leland, and Brigham Young all had reputations as very amusing preachers.[50] According to one contemporary, John Leland "seldom held a congregation long without exciting a smile." After beginning one sermon with a funny anecdote, Peter Cartwright was interrupted by someone in the audience who said, "Make us cry—make us cry; don't make us laugh." Whereupon Cartwright answered that he didn't "hold the puckering strings" of their mouths.[51] No theme drew more humorous barbs from Methodists, Christians, and Mormons alike than the conundrums of Calvinist orthodoxy. Typical was one example of Elias Smith's doggerel, "On Predestination":

> If all things succeed
> Because they're decreed
> And immutable impulses rule us;
> Then praying and preaching,
> And all such like teaching,
> Is nought but a plan to befool us.

> If destiny and fate,
> Guide us this way and that,
> *As the coachman with bits guides his horses;*
> There's no man can stray,
> But all go the right way,
> As the stars in their different courses.

> . . . .

> If this be the way,
> As some preachers say,
> That all things were order'd by fate;
> I'll not spend my pence,
> To pay for nonsense,
> If nothing will alter my state.

> . . . .

> Then with all he must pass
> For a dull, senseless ass,
> Who depends upon predestination.[52]

For all the diversity of preaching styles among Baptists, Methodists, Disciples, Millerites, and Mormons, their preaching shared a fundamental impulse to convert the unconverted. All emphasized an urgent missionary purpose as the principal reason for their existence and tailored preaching to warn people of the wrath to come and to "draw in the net." More important, they yoked the drive to proselytize to relentless and systematic efforts to deluge the country with preaching. Unlike the young itinerants of the Great Awakening, whose efforts were largely uncoordinated and short-lived, these movements developed regimented and ongoing schemes for sending out gospel preaching to even the most remote pockets of American civilization. A Baptist clergyman overlooked partisanship to praise the

Methodists in 1816: "their complete system of mission circuits is by far the ablest domestic missionary effort ever yet adopted. They send their labourers into every corner of the country."[53]

Equally committed to sending forth a cadre of lay preachers, the Mormons had enlisted a preaching force of nineteen hundred young men by 1845. The earliest men sent forth on missions included hatters, carpenters, cobblers, glaziers, potters, farmers, school teachers, and former preachers from other denominations. As outlined in Joseph Smith's 1835 work, *Doctrine and Covenants*, Mormon preaching, like Methodist and Baptist preaching, resisted the Puritan tradition of painstaking study, advising preachers against using careful forethought, written notes, and detailed plans. The overriding theme was convincing the unconvinced of the new restoration. According to an ex-Mormon preacher, the approach was to employ "the most plausible means" available "to get people to unite with them."[54]

What was particularly striking about Methodists and Mormons was their relentless drive to spread their message as widely as possible, what the Methodist *Discipline* called "the continual extension of that circumference on every hand."[55] Both movements did this by a strategy of transforming earnest converts into preachers with unprecedented speed and urging them to sustain a relentless pace of engagements in order to confront people with preaching everywhere, at any hour of the day or night. The Methodist commitment to leave no circuit unattended forced their leadership to channel young converts into preaching assignments very quickly. Education for eager young Methodist recruits was a hands-on experience. They moved into exhorting and preaching while they served apprenticeships as class leaders, and they moved into circuits as understudies to more experienced preachers. The early Mormons were even less concerned about ministerial training. On several occasions, a man heard a discourse, submitted to baptism and confirmation, received a call to priesthood, and was sent on a mission—all on the same day. Canadian Samuel Hall, for instance, found a Latter-Day Saint tract on a Montreal street and traveled to Nauvoo to hear the teachings of Joseph Smith himself. On the day of his arrival, he heard a sermon by Smith, requested baptism, received ordination, and started on a mission—without ever pausing to change his wet clothes.[56]

Methodists and Mormons also multiplied the number of hearers by making preaching a daily occurrence. They moved house-to-house, if necessary, to gain an audience and purposely sought out those people who would not ordinarily be reached. The New England circuit rider Dan Young described this approach: "My practice was to commence on Monday morning as soon as I had taken breakfast, make my first call at the first house, say to them, 'I am the preacher sent to this charge; I have called to make you a religious visit; will you please to call your family together; I wish to talk with them, and to pray with and for you. . . . ' I left no house unvisited in my way, but took them of all sects and no sect."[57] The result was that preaching assumed an almost omnipresent quality, extending from the intimacy of the house to the mass audience of the camp meeting. It was this pervasive presence of Methodism that confounded a Roman Catholic priest attempting to minister in Maryland in 1821: "How can one priest attend so many different places at such great distances from each other? There are Swarms of false teachers all through the Country—at every Crossroad, in every School house, in every private house—you hear nothing but night meetings, Class meetings, love feasts &c &c."[58]

The early mission efforts of the Mormons were characterized by the same mass proclamation of the word: a relentless pace, the manifest intent to allow no one to escape the sound of the gospel, and the unending quest to convince hearers to join the new fold. Like the Methodists, the Mormons mounted a communications crusade springing from the deepest commitments of young missionaries such as Brigham Young: "I wanted to thunder and roar out the Gospel to the nations. It burned in my bones like fire pent up. . . . nothing would satisfy me but to cry abroad in the world, what the Lord was doing in the latter-days."[59]

Creating a Mass Religious Culture in Print

This transformation of the religious press is a central theme in the growth of popular literature in the early republic. The fruits of this transformation—millions of tracts, pamphlets, hymnbooks, and devotional books, as well as journals, magazines, and newspapers of every description—represent a flood of print "more numbing than illuminating," as Richard Altick has noted about the volume of evangelical print in early Victorian England.[60] Using the latest in printing technology, the American Bible Society and the American Tract Society by 1830 were annually producing over one million Bibles and six million tracts, respectively.[61] By the same year, the Methodist weekly *Christian Advocate and Journal and Zion's Herald* and the monthly interdenominational *American National Preacher* each claimed a circulation of twenty-five thousand, among the largest of any journalistic work in the world. In 1835, the American Antislavery Society flooded the mails with more than a million pieces of antislavery literature, sent free to people all over the country. In the same year, the American Baptist Dr. Samuel Bolles announced that Baptists that year had used "2500 reams of paper" and "produced 7,000,000 pages" in their missionary efforts at home and abroad. By the end of the same decade, William Miller and the Adventists had begun an unprecedented media blitz, producing an estimated four million pieces of literature within four years. The most thorough student of religious journalism in early America, Gaylord P. Albaugh, estimates that of the 605 distinct religious journals that were founded in America by 1830, only fourteen of them were in existence before 1790. In the three decades following 1800, he estimates that the number of subscribers to such journals jumped from five thousand to some four hundred thousand.[62]

In mapping the revolution in popular reading habits in the first half of the nineteenth century, historians have been more adept at tracing the rise of the popular novel and daily newspaper than the emergence of a democratic religious culture in print.[63] In the first place, it is not clear how the intense evangelical commitment to the printed word relates to this larger cultural process. To understand who wrote what, for whom, and with what effect, one must begin by considering the devotion to print resulting from a Protestant commitment to the written word and a democratic urge to multiply authors and readers.[64] As an editorial argued in the *Christian Herald* in 1823, "The kingdom of God is a kingdom of means. . . . Preaching of the gospel is a Divine institution—'printing' is no less so. . . . They are kindred offices. The PULPIT AND THE PRESS are inseparably connected. . . . The Press, then, is to be regarded with a sacred veneration and supported with religious care. The press must be supported or the pulpit falls."[65]

The Methodists were the most conscientious about implementing these strategies, giving each circuit rider the charge to serve as both preacher and bookseller. John Wesley himself had been tireless in his commitments "to furnish poor people with cheaper, shorter, and plainer books." The Methodists in America institutionalized these commitments by requiring their ministers to sell printed material. The key was that the church offered a percentage of the sale to the circuit rider, to the presiding elder, and, after 1824, to the bishop. In 1816, for instance, the average book bonus for ministers in the Ohio conference was seventy-five dollars, at a time when the annual salary was only one hundred dollars for a single minister. "The leading characters of the Methodist Society are very active, in supplying the western country with religious books," two jealous Congregationalists reported in 1815. "This energetic Society sends out an immense quantity of these books. We found them almost every where. In the possession of the obscurest families, we often found a number of volumes." The Methodist *Christian Advocate and Journal* was one of the first papers to have a national circulation. It began publication in New York in 1826, and within two years it had a weekly circulation of fifteen thousand copies—one of the largest circulation figures in the world at that time.[66]

At the turn of the century, the explosion of popular print intensified the distinctive evangelical faith in the printed word. The impetus for establishing many new religious periodicals after 1800 came, paradoxically, from Congregational and Presbyterian clergymen such as Jedediah Morse, who searched for ways to counter popular radical appeals.[67] Yet in America, the voice of these conservatives faded dramatically with time, much as did the appeals of their Federalist counterparts. In England, by contrast, it is intriguing to note that class considerations continued to govern popular reading materials produced by evangelicals. The millions of religious tracts and pamphlets that poured from the Religious Tract Society carried a clear note of social condescension, a point relished by radical journalists such as William Cobbett. According to Charles Knight, the Victorian pioneer of cheap fiction, the tracts insisted on talking to thinking beings in the language of the nursery. In *Bleak House*, Dickens captured the common resentment of this kind of literature. A slum-dweller responds to the tract-distributor, Mrs. Pardiggle: "Have I read the little book wot you left? No, I an't read the little book wot you left. There an't nobody here as knows how to read it; and if there wos, it wouldn't be suitable to me. It's a book fit for a babby, and I'm not a babby. If you was to leave me a doll, I shouldn't nuss it."[68]

For all its imitation of British sources, popular evangelical literature in America maintained a much firmer identification with its intended audience. Many authors emerged from uneducated and less-than-respectable ranks to produce forms of genuinely popular print—Elias Smith, Joseph Smith, Barton Stone, and William Miller, for instance. But even more scholarly religious literature catered to a broader, less restrictive audience. This was partly a result of the ferment to reform republican society, as in the case of antislavery and partly a result of an intense drive to communicate, as in the case of Charles G. Finney. Even the conservative Presbyterian minister William Holmes McGuffey, whose publishing exploits with the *Eclectic Reader* were unsurpassed at the time of the Civil War, took his audience seriously, challenging the ability of common folk to come to terms with a measure of substantive literature, poetry, and theology.[69] A fluid social and educational structure in America encouraged popular Christian literature that did not talk down to its intended readers. A result was that common people, eager to read, had little reason to explore literature outside the boundaries of evangelicalism.

Evangelical belief in the power of print was also reinforced by the arresting possibilities of a new technology of printing. After the American Bible Society was founded in May of 1816, its board determined that their "first exertions ought to be directed toward the procurement of well-executed stereotype plates." Similarly, the availability of inexpensive stereotyping was a principal reason for the consolidation of several societies into the American Tract Society in 1825 and for its locating in New York City. The same bent for innovation is evident in the introduction of steam-powered printing. The American Tract Society installed its original steam-powered Treadwell press in 1826, the first in New York. By 1829, the American Bible Society had sixteen Treadwell presses in operation, four years before Harper Brothers introduced their first. These societies were also pioneer supporters of machine papermaking in the United States. Amos H. Hubbard, the owner of the first Fourdrinier papermaking machine to be built in America, became the chief paper supplier to the Bible Society. As a life member, he made his donations in reams of paper rather than in money.[70] These incidents are striking and possibly atypical, given the local nature of much religious printing in the 1830s. Yet neither the Abolitionists, the Millerites, nor the Methodists could have carried out their communication strategies without exploiting these technologies.[71]

Despite the outpouring of religious print from eastern cities, particularly New York, the first half of the nineteenth century was indeed the golden age of regional printing.[72] Almost anyone could set up a printing shop, and publishing was ephemeral, genuinely popular, and virtually uncontrolled. Alexander Campbell, for instance, the founder of the Disciples of Christ, sought to transform American religion from the mountains of western Virginia by two means: an educational institution, Bethany College, and his own printing shop. An inveterate journalist, Campbell endeavored throughout his career to rise early enough in the morning to write an amount sufficient to keep his printer setting type for the entire day. In his study of the popular press in Cincinnati, John Nerone counted over forty different religious periodicals published in that city alone before 1848. Before 1789, all religious journals had issued from either Boston, New York, or Philadelphia (including Germantown), but by 1830, religious journals had been published in 195 different cities and towns and in every state but Mississippi. Of the seventy locations with such publications still active in 1830, over half were west of the Alleghenies.[73]

The hallmark of religious publishing in this era was a marked pluralism. Power, influence, and authority were dispersed, and most came by way of democratic means: popular appeal by the printed word. This climate favored religious insurgents willing to employ fresh strategies to capture public attention. An excellent case in point is the communications crusade developed by Joshua V. Himes to spread the Adventist message of William Miller. A close associate of Elias Smith, himself a key innovator in developing a democratic religious press, Himes was a formative influence in the Christian Connection in New England for two decades after 1820. Himes made the Chardon Street Chapel in Boston a hotbed of social reform, becoming closely associated with William Lloyd Garrison, Bronson Alcott, Henry C. Wright, and Edmund Quincy. In 1839, Himes met William Miller and became enamored of the "humble farmer of Low Hampton" who, discarding learned theology, interpreted Scripture as saying that Christ's advent was imminent. Along with two other influential Christian leaders, Joseph Marsh and L. D. Fleming, Himes led scores of Christian Connection churches into the Adventist camp.[74]

More important, he turned his relentless energy to making Miller's predictions a national cause. To that end, he launched an unprecedented communications crusade. Prior to meeting Himes, Miller had been an obscure lay preacher known only in pockets of rural New York and New England. Himes extended his influence in rural areas with large camp meetings. He opened the cities to Miller by pioneering in the use of a tent with a seating capacity of approximately four thousand—reportedly the largest of its kind ever seen in America.[75]

Himes also flooded the country with cheap literature and pioneered in the use of such visual aids as prophetic charts. He claimed to have distributed fifty thousand copies of the Boston fortnightly *Sign of the Times* in 1840 alone and six hundred thousand copies of his New York–based *Mid-Night Cry*, a daily two-cent newspaper, in five months of 1842, sending at least one copy to every minister in the state of New York. These and other papers were sent regularly to postmasters throughout the country, spreading the Adventist message and advertising the vast array of pamphlets, tracts, and books that Himes brought forth from the press. Many of these were collected into the "Second Advent" or "Cheap" Library, which could be purchased for under ten dollars to circulate in local communities. Those who opposed the Adventist movement poured endless ridicule upon Himes for his insistence upon hawking cheap and popular literature.[76]

Alexis de Tocqueville noted that the popular newspaper in America facilitated a new form of association that allowed individuals, keenly aware of their own autonomy, to pursue common purposes. Only the newspaper, he said, could drop "the same thought into a thousand minds at the same moment . . . without distracting men from their private affairs."[77] In a similar way, the absence of strong ecclesiastical institutions in the American republic exalted the role of the religious press. Editors and publicists found themselves with de facto authority among churches that favored local and democratic control. They could impart a sense of coherence and direction to widely scattered congregations. Blessed with a public hungry for religious discussion, they could extend the art of persuasion, and thus their own authority, far beyond the reach of personal charisma.

Inventing American Gospel Music

This chapter has argued implicitly that the reordering of preaching and print communications at the opening of the nineteenth century is related to a more fundamental reality—a complex process of democratization. Deeper and broader than any single denominational or regional current, this shift in values and behavior helps to explain how a number of insurgent religious movements, despite profound differences, came to speak and to write in similar terms. A variety of pilgrims sought to recover primitive Christianity by avoiding external influence. All, however, eventually expressed themselves in similar tones to similar audiences.

The hymnodic revolution that swept through America during this period underscores this underlying ferment. The foremost modern student of American religious folk music identifies 1780–1830 as the period in which the majority of folk texts first appeared.[78] A wide number of discrete individuals and movements broke free of the constraints of formal church music and created indigenous folk alternatives. At the turn of the nineteenth century a groundswell of self-made tunesmiths, indifferent to authorized hymnody, created their own simple verses and set them to rousing popular tunes. This outpouring of native folk lyricism, or what George Pullen Jackson has termed "indigenous country religious songs," borrowed indiscriminately from a wide variety of secular tunes of love, war, homesickness, piracy, robbery, and murder. The melodies and rhythms of fiddle tunes, marches, reels, and jigs were adopted as well. Rural Baptist dissidents in New England were the first to create a significant body of these "spiritual songs." Their wholesale commitment to the effort is revealed in the 1805 song of a Yankee farmer, tavern keeper, and folk-hymnist, Jeremiah Ingalls. Entitled "Innocent Sounds," his song urges the godly to rescue music too long employed for evil ends:

> Enlisted in the cause of sin,
> Why should a good be evil?
> Music, alas, too long has been
> Press'd to obey the devil.
> Drunken or lewd or light the lay,
> Flows to their souls' undoing,

Widen'd and strewn with flow'rs the way,
Down to eternal ruin.

Who on the part of God will rise
Innocent sounds recover?
Fly on the prey and seize the prize,
Plunder the carnal lover?
Strip him of ev'ry moving strain,
Of ev'ry melting measure?
Music in virtue's cause retain,
Risk the holy pleasure?[79]

What are the dimensions in the early republic of this popular gospel music—the "numerous ditties" that the respectable churchman Nathan Bangs claimed had "almost deluged" the Methodist Church, and that Philip Schaff decried as "a rude singing of the most vulgar street songs, so that it must be loathing to an educated man"?[80] A definitive answer is impossible, because this homespun, religious music began as an oral phenomenon, was taken up by scores of rustic and anonymous song-makers, and was only later compiled and printed. Yet the importance of the process itself has gone largely undetected by historians because its manifestations do not conform to regional or denominational boundaries and fall outside the normal purview of church music history. One historian, in fact, character-ized this period as the "musical dark ages"—a time when "men of correct taste . . . let go their hold, and the multitude had the management of it and sung what and when they pleased."[81] It is clear that this upsurge in religious folk music is yet another aspect of the democratic impulse in American Christianity. The same imperative that sent many ordinary folk into preaching and writing compelled some to express themselves in song. In all the populist religious movements with which this study deals—from Christians to Baptists to Mormons—people developed their own traditions of religious folk music. The public, in turn, seemed to have an insatiable appetite for new strains of spontaneous and lively gospel music.

At least four waves of indigenous folk religious music are evident between 1780 and 1830: from dissenting Baptists of rural New England; from proponents of camp meetings, principally Methodists, who spread these idioms throughout the country; from black communities, who for-mulated a vibrant tradition of spirituals as they came to own Christianity; and from other groups, such as Mormons and Adventists, who remained wedded to vernacular song as a way to advance their own purposes.

The first major influx of spiritual songs came from dissenters in rural New England. As early as 1766, Separatist Baptists published their own collection of locally composed tests, but it was after 1780 that a widespread movement developed.[82] In 1784, New Hampshire layman Joshua Smith published the collection *Divine Hymns, or Spiritual Songs* (Norwich, N.H.), which went through at least eleven printings by 1803. It contained some hymns from such well-known composers as Isaac Watts, but most indicated folk origin, such as the song "Christ the Appletree":

> The tree of life, my soul hath seen,
> Laden with fruit, and always green;
> The trees of nature fruitless be,
> Compar'd with Christ the Appletree.[83]

Two years later the Nova Scotia tanner-farmer and firebrand evangelist Henry Alline published his 381-page *Hymns and Spiritual Songs* in Boston. Composer of over five hundred songs, Alline was the most prolific American hymn writer of his day. His book served as the main hymnal of Freewill Baptists for a generation. Alline's common style encouraged the downtrodden "New-lights" to fortify their identity:

> Come all who are New-Lights indeed,
> Who are from sin and bondage freed;
> From Egypts land we've took our flight,
> For God has given us a New-light.
>
> Long we with the wicked trod,
> And madly ran the sinful road;
> Against the gospel we did fight,
> Scar'd at the name of a New-light.
>
> At length the Lord in mercy call'd,
> And gave us strength to give up all;
> He gave us grace to choose aright,
> A portion with despised New-lights.
>
> Though by the world we are disdain'd,
> And have our names cast out by men;
> Yet Christ our captain for us fights,
> Nor death, nor hell, can hurt New Lights.[84]

Elias Smith also turned his hand to song-making and published a torrent of hymnbooks between 1804 and 1820. Growing up in poverty in Woodstock, Vermont, Smith's family owned only four books, one of them a Watts hymnbook that Smith found of spiritual value in his teens.[85] Smith also had a smattering of musical instruction—eight classes, to be exact—

from a neighbor, Jasen Smith, who taught a simple method of reading notes and keeping time. In music, Elias Smith charted the same independent path that characterized his approach to church, politics, and society. He did not use a single hymn from Watts in his books, and there is almost no overlap with the accepted hymnals of the day, such as *The Worcester Collection* (Worcester, 1786) or *A Selection of Sacred Harmony* (Philadelphia, 1788). While Smith did include several songs by Henry Alline and John Leland, most of the work bore his distinct imprint, such as his ballad "The Christian Union":

> More than ten years have roll'd away,
> Since I did testify and say,
> Aside all party names I'll lay,
> And make the name of Christ my stay,
> And join in Christian Union.
>
> And at that time I did not know,
> One on this earthly hall below,
> That thus with me would join and go,
> I ask'd some brethren, they said No,
> We can't join such Union.
>
> My name is dear, said brother P; [Presbyterian]
> And so is mine said brother C; [Congregationalist]
> Then loud spake out my brother B; [Baptist]
> My name's the dearest of the three,
> Away with such a Union.
>
> . . . .
>
> Brother of ev'ry name to thee,
> Who do inquire if good there be
> In Christian conference, come and see,
> In Christ there is true liberty,
> Enjoying Christian Union.[86]

This country dissident tradition was widespread in rural New England and premised on linking original and catchy lyrics to popular folk tunes. Examples of these songs are found in a remarkable songbook, *The Christian Harmony; or, Songster's Companion* (Exeter, N.H., 1805), compiled by Jeremiah Ingalls, a farmer, tavern keeper, and self-taught musician. Ingalls set out to furnish a tune book of popular religious songs to circulate in rural New England. The book's 139 songs and eighty tunes relied heavily on indigenous folk and folk-like melodies—such as the song of elegy, "Farewell Hymn," based on a broadside poem on the death of a young woman, Polly Gould; and a tune in the sea chantey tradition.[87] Many of Ingalls's songs passed into the stream of American folk hymnody. George Pullen Jackson identified forty-eight of them in later collections of spirituals, many of which were used in the South and the West.[88]

The second and most enduring wave of popular song to break upon American culture in this era is that associated with Methodist revivalism. The remarkable growth of Methodism on both sides of the Atlantic has often been attributed to singing as much as to preaching or church organization. The English Unitarian James Martineau once commented that after Scripture itself the Methodist hymnal was "the grandest instrument of popular culture that Christendom ever produced." "How I long for the good old Methodist thunder," Henry Ward Beecher reflected in a similar vein. "One good burst of old-fashioned music would have blown this modern singing out of the window like wadding from a gun."[89]

American Methodists inherited a dual musical legacy from the brothers John and Charles Wesley. The Wesleys were emphatic that music should invite the participation of all people, and to that end they crafted a lively hymnody to replace the dreary psalm tunes that Joseph Addison had called "Metrical monstrosities."[90] But the Wesleys also insisted that hymns maintain dignity and reverence. In the preface to the Methodist hymnal of 1780, John Wesley wrote that he had used language of "utmost simplicity and plainness, suited to every capacity." At the same time, he boasted that he had been animated by a genuine spirit of poetry: "In these Hymns there is no doggerel, no botches, nothing put in to patch up the rhyme, no feeble expletives. Here is nothing turgid or bombast on the one hand, or low and creeping on the other. Here are no cant expressions, no words without meaning."[91] At the outset of American Methodism, the assumption was that the necessary popular revolution in singing had already been fully achieved. "How shall we reform our singing?" the first *Discipline* asked. "Let all our preachers who have any knowledge in the notes, improve it by learning to sing true themselves, and keeping close to Mr. Wesley's tunes and hymns."[92]

American Methodists took these words to heart and made the official Methodist hymnal one of the best-sellers of the early republic. By 1805, thirty-five different editions of the hymnal had been published. Yet during these same years, Methodist singing also moved in new and uncontrolled directions. The spread of the Methodist camp meeting led to an explosion of exuberant folk singing of "rough and ready rhymes set to rousing popular music." Promoters of camp meetings found that vernacular song could play a role as significant as preaching itself. The Methodist itinerant

James Finley recounted the force of musical expression in the singing of a spiritual by the Reverend Robert Manley at a camp meeting in Ohio: "Before he had finished singing the fourth verse, the *power of God* came down, and pervaded the vast assembly, and it became agitated—swelling and surging like the sea in a storm."[93] Lorenzo Dow, who originally doubted the effectiveness of singing, became a committed promoter of lively song after he witnessed its inherent power.

Like the camp meeting itself, these new and expressive forms of music spread of their own momentum, without blessing or censure from Methodist authorities. After 1800, the rash of published books collecting "spiritual songs" and "camp meeting songs" is evidence of the number of plain people who took it upon themselves to write religious music and of the broad demand for their work. These collections included songs by religious novices on subjects such as the thoughts of a young minister before preaching his first sermon or those of a woman on being baptized.[94] Those who seriously took up songwriting were often obscure figures. The two most prolific Methodist writers, John A. Granade and Caleb Jarvis Taylor, were preachers from the backcountry of Tennessee and Kentucky, respectively, not even well known in Methodist circles. They were responsible for more than half the songs in the immensely popular collection, *A Pilgrim's Songster*, and yet on the eve of the Civil War, a writer for the *Methodist Quarterly Review* searching for information on Granade could find nothing beyond a few anecdotes.[95]

Methodist revivalism removed elitist constraints on music by accepting spontaneous song, exuberant shouting, and unrestrained musical enthusiasm as natural to a vibrant spiritual community. The movement allowed an audience to join the leader in setting the style and tempo of musical expression, helping to build what Don Yoder has called "a substitute folk culture." This is what the editor of a Schuylkill County, Pennsylvania, newspaper found at a camp meeting in 1825:

When this [preaching] has continued a sufficient length of time, the officiating preacher commences singing in a loud voice, some well known hymn or chorus, in which the members one after another join, until the whole are upon their feet again. The hymn is generally a song of exultation and triumph, calculated to excite the passions, which is continued for a considerable length of time, accompanied with jumping and clapping of hands, in which the ministers partake, and sometimes to heighten the scene, join in by blowing a horn. The degree of sincerity and enthusiasm exhibited during these periods of their worship, is beyond description; each individual sings or rather shouts with all his might, clapping hands and jumping, until he falls down exhausted. A singularity remarkable in the devotions of these people is, every person seems at liberty to express his satisfaction in any way he thinks proper.[96]

One of the most popular of these songs was "Shout Old Satan's Kingdom Down," which probably came from New England at the turn of the century and later gained widespread acceptance in the South:

> This day my soul has caught new fire, Halle, hallelujah!
> I feel that heav'n is coming nigh'r, Glory hallelujah!
>
> I long to drop this cumbrous clay, Halle, hallelujah!
> And shout with saints in endless day, Glory hallelujah!
>
> [chorus]
> Shout, shout, we're gaining ground, Halle, hallelujah!
> We'll shout old Satan's kingdom down, O glory hallelujah![97]

This gospel music ranged from intensely personal testimonies of individual religious experiences to rousing march songs of collective solidarity, from songs of bereavement to "shouting" songs of exaltation and triumph, from humorous ballads to fire-and-brimstone appeals for repentance. The classic gospel song was simple and easily remembered. Its two most common features were a repeated chorus or refrain and verses written in rhyming pairs. Tunes that succeeded were catchy and contagious—the kind that could be hummed or whistled behind the plow or at the anvil. Many songs also used a pattern of call and response, such as the following from an early Methodist songbook:

> O brothers will you meet me,
> O sisters will you meet me,
> O mourners will you meet me
> On Canaan's happy shore?

Then the response:

> By the grace of God I'll meet you [thrice]
> Where parting is no more.[98]

By 1820 the genre of spiritual song was so well ingrained in popular culture that a new wave of compilers, many from the southern uplands, did a land-office business. "Singin' Billy" Walker, compiler of *The Southern Harmony*, first published in Philadelphia in 1835, claimed to have sold six hundred thousand copies between 1835 and 1860. Starke Dupuy's *Hymns and Spiritual Songs, Selected and Original* (Louisville, 1818) went through over twenty editions by 1841—one copy of which was the family hymnal in the boyhood home of Abraham Lincoln. In the North, Joshua Leavitt's *The Christian Lyre* (New York, 1831) sold eighteen thousand copies the first year and ran up sales of fifty-two thousand over a decade in twenty-six editions.[99] Between 1820 and the Civil War, scores of popular songbooks were compiled by self-taught singing teachers whose rush to publish gospel songs indicated the musical preference of potential buyers. Allen Carden's *The Missouri Harmony* (Cincinnati, 1820) is typical. Put together by a self-confessed amateur for the purpose of introducing "the rudiments of music and plain rules for beginners," this popular and widely available songbook was composed mainly of religious music. Dickson D. Bruce, Jr., has noted that most of these compilers hailed not from the seats of power but from such places as Spartanburg, South Carolina; Hamilton and Andersonville, Georgia; Maryville and Madisonville, Tennessee; Lexington, Kentucky; and Harrisonburg and Lebanon, Virginia. Another indication of this music's popularity was that compilers of more conservative hymnbooks felt obliged to include gospel songs, frequently apologizing for publishing music that was below their standards.[100]

The core of this music clearly transcended denominational distinctives. Its popularity relied on neither clergy nor ecclesiastical institutions. Much of it gained a following in different sections of the country, not unlike the overall influence of Methodist revivalism and the camp meeting. Many religious folk songs originated in rural New England but became widely known in the upland South and the West. The song "The Lord into His Garden Comes," for instance, first came to light in Abner Jones's *The Melody of the Heart* (Boston, 1804), reappeared in Jeremiah Ingalls's *The Christian Harmony*, and then became a standard in many southern compilations of gospel songs.[101]

Popular gospel music became a pervasive reality in Jacksonian culture because people wrested singing from churchly control. The music created a spontaneous, moving medium, capable of capturing the identity of plain people. The result was that official literary hymns had difficulty competing with lively gospel music. An excellent illustration of this point is the invasion of revivalism and its folk music into the world of German-speaking Lutheran and Reformed churches in Pennsylvania. During the second decade of the nineteenth century, young people in these communities tired of the complicated German chorale tradition, with its solemn tunes and baroque wording. They welcomed the rousing songs and vernacular preaching of the revivalists, who came from such Methodist sects as the United Brethren in Christ, founded in 1800 by William Otterbein, the Evangelical Association, commonly called the Albright Brethren, and the Church of God (Winebrennerian). These groups developed a significant tradition of "bush-meeting spirituals," which were little more than translations into German of the American folk music of the revival.[102] The success of these folk traditions among Pennsylvania Germans raised the ire of the churchman Philip Schaff, who commented in 1849, "There is a stamping and bouncing, jumping and falling, crying and howling, groaning and sighing, all praying in confusion, a rude singing of the most vulgar street songs, so that it must be loathing to an educated man, and fill the serious Christian with painful emotions."[103]

The most devoted advocate of revival singing was John Winebrenner, founder of the Church of God. His earliest biographer noted that he "possessed the very rare facility of striking the popular chord in hymnology." In 1825, Winebrenner published the first English camp-meeting songbook to appear among the Bush-Meeting Dutch, a work that went through twenty-seven editions. This book was instrumental in the transition from English-language originals to the fully developed Pennsylvania Dutch spiritual. In keeping with their folk singing, revivalists such as Winebrenner also were willing to preach in vernacular German, unlike their college-trained Lutheran and Reformed counterparts, who insisted on maintaining literary German.[104]

A third major wave of religious folk music that gained momentum in the early republic was the black spiritual. Like the development of the indigenous black church and of black preaching, the widespread tradition of Christian spirituals in black communities is directly linked to the evangelistic efforts of Baptists and Methodists between 1760 and 1820. It is no accident that the Christianization of African slaves, which had been a haphazard and sporadic affair throughout the history of the colonies, proceeded apace under the sound of the gospel that black and white Baptists and Methodists preached and sang.[105] These churches recast Christianity as a popular medium. Instead of yoking people to orthodox traditions of worship, they encouraged lively spiritual expansion that sprang from daily experience. Above all, these churches affirmed vernacular expression as the preferred means of communication with God and among his people. Thus, Baptist and Methodist Christianity allowed blacks to participate on their own terms in ways that sustained and renewed their own African heritage, its distinct notions of sacredness, and its exuberant spontaneity.

The experimental climate of the Baptists and Methodists accorded blacks freedom of expression that traditional churches would not tolerate. Anglicans, Presbyterians, and Congregationalists refused to abide the exuberance the environment of the camp meeting offered to the black community: songs of their own composing, songfests away from proper supervision, and tunes more appropriate for dance rather than for solemn worship.[106] This was precisely the churchly criticism of black worship itself and of its potential to corrupt the worship practices of those who had made the camp meeting an interracial institution. The Presbyterian Charles Colcock Jones, known for his mission efforts among the slaves of Georgia, tried valiantly to curtail spontaneity in black congregations: "The public worship of God should be conducted *with reverence and stillness on the part of the congregation*; nor should the minister—whatever may have been the previous habits and training of the people—encourage demonstrations of approbation or disapprobation, or exclamations, or responses, or noises, or outcries of any kind during the progress of divine worship." Jones also preferred that black congregations sing only approved hymns: "One great advantage in teaching them good psalms and hymns is that they are thereby induced to lay aside the extravagant and nonsensical chants, and catches and hallelujah songs of their own composing."[107] Similarly, a white South Carolinian suggested that revolt was improbable among Episcopalian slaves

> because the coloured leaders in that Church were not permitted to expound the Scriptures, or to exhort, in words of their own; to use extemporary prayer, and to utter at such times, whatever nonsense and profanity might happen to come into their minds. . . . they were accustomed to use *no other worship* than the regular course prescribed in the Book of Common Prayer, for the day. Hymns, or Psalms out of the same book were sung, and a printed sermon read. . . . No extemporary address, exhortation, or prayer, was permitted, or used.[108]

After observing camp meetings around Philadelphia in 1817, Methodist John F. Watson offered an equally revealing statement about the radical implications of the camp meeting, a forum that encouraged blacks to express themselves musically.

> We have too, a growing evil, in the practice of singing in our places of public and society worship, *merry* airs, adapted from old *songs*, to hymns of our composing: often miserable as poetry, and senseless as matter, and most frequently composed and first sung by the illiterate *blacks* of the society. Thus instead of inculcating sober christianity in them who have least wisdom to govern themselves; lifting them into spiritual pride and to an undue estimation of their usefulness. . . . Here ought to be considered too, a most exceptionable error, which has the tolerance at least of the rulers of our camp meetings. In the

Fig. 14. "A Negro Camp-meeting in the South," from wood engraving by Sol Eytinge, Jr., in *Harper's Weekly*, August 10, 1872

blacks' quarter, the coloured people get together, and sing for hours together, short scraps of disjointed affirmations, pledges, or prayers, lengthened out with long repetition [sic] *choruses*. These are all sung in the merry chorus-manner of the southern harvest field, or husking-frolic method, of the slave blacks; and also very greatly like the Indian dances. With every word so sung, they have a sinking of one or other leg of the body alternately; producing an audible sound of the feet at every step, and as manifest as the steps of actual negro dancing in Virginia, &tc.[109]

Whites and blacks worshiping together made mutual influence inescapable.[110] By 1820, over one-fifth of Methodist membership was black. While the exact nature of this process of cultural diffusion has yet to be clarified, two matters are clear about the development of the black spiritual. The first is that musical influence was clearly black to white as well as vice versa. Lawrence W. Levine has noted the probability that black spirituals significantly influenced white music insofar as Methodists and Baptists, departing from traditional Protestant hymnody, employed "the complex rhythmic structure, the percussive qualities, the polymeter, the syncopation, the emphasis on overlapping call and response patterns that characterized Negro music both in West Africa and the New World."[111] The innovative quality of black religious music was evident in a hymnbook published by Richard Allen, founder of the African Methodist Episcopal church. The hymnal was the first to employ the "wandering refrain"—choruses that could be randomly attached to any hymn.

A second and more important function of the black spiritual was its crucial place in the formation of Afro-American identity. By the early nineteenth century, blacks championed spirituals as their own distinctive music, a treasure external restraints could not take away. Quantitatively and qualitatively, spirituals became the slaves' most significant musical expression. For people who were illiterate or semiliterate, appealing, singable music played an integral part in structuring the world—a way of giving coherence and meaning to experience.[112] Unconfined by time or place, the spiritual served as a powerful and spontaneous bond of communal identity, imparting hope to the despairing and dignity to the oppressed, as in this moving hymn of Richard Allen:

> What poor despised company
> Of travellers are these,
> That's walking yonder narrow way,
> Along that rugged maze?

Why they are of a royal line,
They're children of a King;
Heirs of immortal crown divine,
And loud for joy they sing.

Why do they then appear so mean,
And why so much despised?
Because of their rich robes unseen
The world is not appriz'd.

Why some of them seem poor distress'd
And lacking daily bread;
Heirs of immortal wealth possess'd
With hidden Manna fed.[113]

The Mormons were equally given to exploiting the potential of popular song. The strength of early Mormon hymnody, Michael Hicks has argued, came from their easy familiarity with popular culture and their ability to transform folk music, ballads, and patriotic songs into something peculiar to the Saints—"to turn the water of popular culture into the wine of the Kingdom." W. W. Phelps, who dominated early Mormon hymnody, borrowed liberally from popular lyrics and tunes. His best-known song, "The Spirit of God Like a Fire Is Burning," borrows freely from the patriotic folk song "The American Star," which Phelps intended as the original tune.[114]

A similar pattern of adaptation is evident in *A Collection of Hymns for the Church of the Latter Day Saints* (Kirtland, Ohio, 1835), edited by Emma Smith, Joseph's wife. More important was the hymnbook issued in 1840 in Great Britain by Brigham Young, Parley P. Pratt, and John Taylor, a work that went through twenty-five editions and was also used extensively by the Saints in Utah. One of them, "A Church Without Apostles is not a Church for Me," was an explicit parody of the popular song "The Rose that All are Praising":

A Church without a prophet is not the church for me;
It has no head to lead it, in it I would not be;
But I've a church not built by man,
Out from the mountain without hand,
A Church with gifts and blessings, oh, that's the church for me.

The God that others worship is not the God for me;
He has no parts nor body, and can not hear nor see;

But I've a God that lives above,
A God of Power and of Love,
A God of Revelation, oh, that's the God for me.

A church without apostles is not the church for me;
It's like a ship dismasted afloat upon the sea;
But I've a church that's always led
By the twelve stars around its head,
A church with good foundations, oh, that's the church for me.

The hope that Gentiles cherish is not the hope for me;
It has no hope for knowledge, far from it I would be;
But I've a hope that will not fail,
That reaches safe within the veil,
Which hope is like an anchor, oh, that's the hope for me.[115]

The Mormons also excelled at martial music. As early as 1834, on the trek from Ohio to Missouri, Brigham and Joseph Young led a favorite anthem of the camp accompanied by a fife:

Heark! listen to the trumpeters!
They sound for volunteers;
On Zion's knight and flowery mount
Behold the officers.

Their horses white, their armor bright,
With courage bold they stand,
Enlisting soldiers for the king,
To march to Zion's land.

. . . .

We want no cowards in our bands,
Who will our colors fly:
We call for valiant-hearted men,
Who're not afraid to die![116]

The Adventist followers of William Miller also used rousing popular music to advance their movement. Joshua V. Himes, who had been active with Elias Smith in the Christian Connection, broadcast a variety of songbooks for use in Adventist meetings. The dominant theme of these songs, many of them adapted from older choruses, was a longing for the last day or a plea to be ready for the coming judgment. One of the most infectious and lasting of the Millerite songs was "The Old Church Yard":

You will see your Lord a-coming
While the old Church yards
Hear the band of Music
Which is sounding through the air.

Gabriel sounds his mighty trumpet
Through the old Church yards,
While the band of Music
Shall be sounding through the air

. . . .

O Sinner, you will tremble
At the old Church yards,
While the band of Music
Shall be sounding through the air.

You will flee to rocks and mountains
From the old Church yards,
While the band of Music
Shall be sounding through the air.[117]

In attempting to assess the Christianization of so much of popular culture in the antebellum period, it is impossible to overestimate the revolution in church music that unleashed religious folk music into America's highways and byways. Never has the Christian church been blessed with such a furious and creative outpouring of vernacular song. This music of the people, displayed across a wide spectrum of idioms and traditions, entered popular culture in countless ways. What other types of antebellum song could compete with those of gospel music: doleful tunes of comfort to the oppressed, rousing marches of exaltation and triumph, realistic ballads of struggle and hope, antiphonal chants of communal solidarity, triumphant rounds of ecstasy, moving choruses of familial love and affirmation—and all sung to melodies catchy enough to be hummed and whistled at work or play?

This was not church music that required folk to worship in unfamiliar forms—those fashioned for their improvement by their "betters," eminent musicians and poets. Instead, American gospel music reveled in the fact that the Lord had chosen to use earthen vessels without plating in gold or silver. The phenomenal success of the spiritual—black and white—was proof positive that the wise held no monopoly on musical talent. Ordinary people crafted spiritual folk songs to assist the flock in weeping with the brokenhearted, shouting with the joyful, and proclaiming the good news of the gospel. The outpouring of these strains in the early republic worked to make religious folk cultures resistant to the influence of formal ecclesiastical authority and immune to the allure of egalitarian movements of secular persuasion. At the same time, the infectious quality of American gospel music has permeated the entire tradition of American folk song. The pilgrimage of the wayfaring stranger, bound for the promised land, is an image that continues to stir the American soul.

CHAPTER SIX

The Right to Think for Oneself

[W]e are persuaded that it is high time for us not only to think, but also to act for ourselves; to see with our own eyes, and to take all our measures directly and immediately from the Divine Standard. . . . We are also persuaded that as no man can be judged *for his brother, so no man can* judge *for his brother. . . . That every such judgment is an express violation of the law of Christ, a daring usurpation of his throne, and a gross intrusion upon the rights and liberties of his subjects.*
DECLARATION AND ADDRESS OF THE CHRISTIAN
ASSOCIATION OF WASHINGTON [PENNSYLVANIA], *1809*

Unless we grant to the many the privilege of thinking for themselves, we must grant to the few, or one, the power of infallibility.
HERSCHEL S. PORTER OF
THE CUMBERLAND PRESBYTERIAN CHURCH, *1848*

American churches' profound commitment to audience in the early decades of the nineteenth century shaped the way religious thinking was organized and carried out. When the commoner rose in power, people of ideas found their authority circumscribed. As a result, democratic America has never produced another theologian like Jonathan Edwards, just as it has never elected statesmen of the caliber of Adams, Jefferson, and Madison. Insurgent religious leaders were not so much anti-intellectual as intent on destroying the monopoly of classically educated and university-trained clergymen. The insurgents considered people's common sense more reliable, even in theology, than the judgement of an educated few.[1]

This shift involved new faith in public opinion as an arbiter of truth. Common folk were no longer thought to be irresponsible and willful; rather, they were deemed ready to embrace truth if only it was retrieved from academic speculation and the heavy hand of the past. These new ground rules measured theology by its acceptance in the marketplace. It flattened out uncomfortable complexity and often resolved issues by a simple choice of alternatives.

This quest for a free marketplace of ideas fueled the severe anticlericalism of leaders such as Alexander Campbell. In 1840, Campbell gained a charter for Bethany College from the state of Virginia with the curious provision that no professorship of theology should ever be established. Campbell's disdain for the clerical monopoly over learning led to this ironclad prohibition in a school that hoped to train a cadre of Disciples ministers. In Campbell's view, "the kingdom of the clergy," both Protestant and Catholic, had attempted to exercise "sovereign dominion over the Bible." They had claimed a monopoly of interpretation that made it seem presumptuous for the laity to define their own convictions. By the clergy's scheme, "people have been shrewdly taught to put out their own eyes, to fetter their own feet, and to bind the yoke upon their own necks."[2]

Campbell's solution was to undermine theological orthodoxies, to disentangle "the Holy Scriptures from the perplexities of the commentators and system-makers of the dark ages." To this end, he demanded that the traditional distinction between laity and clergy be abolished. He argued that it is wrong "to constitute different orders of men, or to divide the church into the common classes of clergy and laity. . . . Nothing is more essentially opposite to the genius and spirit of Christianity."[3] Well aware that "knowledge is power," Campbell founded Bethany College upon the Bible, not for its prescriptive theology, but as a book of "plain facts" to be read and apprehended by all: "The Bible is every day read publicly by one student in the hearing of all the other students. It is then lectured upon for nearly one hour. . . . Its science or doctrine being but the meaning of its facts, and the precepts and promises founded upon them, inductively gathered and arranged by every student for himself."[4]

Like many of his generation, Campbell believed that stripping away the accretions of theology and tradition would restore peace, harmony, and vitality to the Christian church. Only slightly tempered by a sense of their own limitations, these reformers espoused private judgment as the sure route to coherence and harmony. Unfortunately, the more confidently they attacked the traditional order and espoused individual autonomy, the more confusing their limitless world became. In one of the early republic's severest ironies, the determination to quiet theological wrangling resulted in a proliferation of voices. The Presbyterian David Rice described these impulses at work among people in Kentucky: "They were then prepared to imbibe every new notion, advanced by a popular warm preacher, which he said was agreeable to Scripture. They were like a parcel of boys suddenly tumbled out of a boat, who had been unaccustomed to swim, and knew not the way to shore. Some fixed upon one error, and some upon another."[5]

No one was more painfully aware of this fragmenting ethos than

Philip Schaff and John W. Nevin, the brilliant pair of theologians who served the German Reformed church at its fledgling seminary in south central Pennsylvania during the 1840s and 1850s. Serious losses among the German Reformed to four successive Methodist-oriented sects made Nevin and Schaff acutely aware of the atomistic tendencies in American Christianity. They developed the Mercersburg Theology, which promoted a wholistic and mystical view of the church, as strong medicine for America's "sect plague," which they perceived as "endless disintegration" of the religious community. Recently arrived from Germany, Schaff used the occasion of his inaugural lecture at the seminary to sound an alarm against America's characteristic defect, its "variegated sampler of all conceivable religious chimeras and dreams": "Every theological vagabond and peddler may drive here his bungling trade, without passport or license, and sell his false ware at pleasure. What is to come of such confusion is not now to be seen."[6]

The first issue of the new *Mercersburg Review* in 1849 contained John W. Nevin's two-part article "The Sect System," which provided a thorough diagnosis of this disorder. The occasion of the article was the publication of John Winebrenner's *History of All the Religious Denominations in the United States* (Harrisburg, Pa., 1848). Nevin found the book offensive because it represented the epitome of everything he struggled against, allowing authors from fifty-three different denominations to expound the distinctive elements of their own beliefs. But what raised his ire to fever pitch was that its compiler was none other than John Winebrenner, with whom Nevin had carried on a bitter correspondence five years before and against whom, in some measure, he had addressed his polemics *The Anxious Bench* (1843) and *Anti-Christ; Or the Spirit of Sect and Schism* (1848). Winebrenner and the revivalistic Church of God, which he began in 1825 within the fold of the German Reformed church, represented for Nevin what was most typical and pernicious about American sectarianism.[7]

The Mercersburg Theology represents far more than dispassionate theological analysis. The sarcasm, anger, and frustration in Nevin's prose are clear evidence that higher and more personal stakes were involved. Nevin's attack against Winebrenner implied a struggle for power and influence between a learned theologian and a religious neophyte. Nevin did not accord Winebrenner the right to speak in God's name. He depicted Winebrenner as a religious entrepreneur, daring to invent a new and competing church: "It is felt to be as easy to start a new Church, as it is to get up a new moral or political association under any other name." Nevin mocked Winebrenner for daring to include himself among the gallery of "splendid portraits of distinguished men" included in the compendium of denominations. With equal sarcasm, he maligned the portrait of Jacob Albright, another sectarian bugbear of German Reformed church life: "But, alas, what a countenance for a Moses of God's Israel, as compared with the face of Luther!"[8] Nevin and Schaff directed their attack at upstart little "popes" who in the name of private opinion promoted their self-made systems: "The most dangerous foe with which we are called to contend, is again not the Church of Rome but the sect plague in our own midst; not the single pope of the city of seven hills, but the numberless popes—German, English, and American—who would fain enslave Protestants once more to human authority, not as embodied in the church indeed, but as holding in the form of mere private judgment and private will." In this vein, Philip Schaff described German Methodism as "barbarous Christianity" that sprang "from an overbearing contempt of others, and from intellectual imbecility."[9]

The success of these independent religious promoters was particularly galling to the learned theologians of Mercersburg. Their belief in the church's authority, stemming from and steeped in tradition and learning, did not comport with the free-wheeling marketplace of religious ideas of provincial America. Any upstart with "a ready tongue" could kindle the true light "in an obscure corner of the New World" and witness immediate response. This caused Schaff to conclude that "the deceived multitude, having no power to discern spirits, is converted not to Christ and his truth, but to the arbitrary fancies and baseless opinion of an individual, who is only of yesterday."[10]

The Mercersburg Theology perceived American popular religion as centrifugal and atomistic. From Schaff's European point of view, the American scene was a riot of sects engaged in unholy competition. Nevin argued that, despite what sectarians said about the importance of the church and mutual cooperation and respect, the very system of which they were a part showed itself to be "at war with all the attributes that enter into its [the church's] constitution." An unstable compound of religious zeal and private judgment kept the door open "indefinitely for the lawful introduction of as many more [sects], as religious ingenuity or stupidity may have power to invent." For Nevin and Schaff, the sect system and the American religious entrepreneur were intimately linked: "Anyone who has, or fancies that he has, some inward experience and a ready tongue, may persuade himself that he is called to be a reformer; and so proceed at once, in his spiritual vanity and pride, to a revolutionary rupture with the historical life of the church, to which he holds himself immeasurably superior." They lamented the host of new churches that latched onto "incidental expressions" of Scripture and made them into "a peg on which to hang the whole weight of a doctrine or institution."[11]

Nevin and Schaff also discerned certain common intellectual patterns and reflexes beneath the rampant pluralism of American Protestantism. They attributed the breakdown of theological coherence to attitudes that American Christians had assumed. These two felt that a radical Bible-centeredness was the reigning theory among Protestant sects. After surveying the statements of belief of fifty-three American denominations, Nevin surmised that the principle "no creed but the Bible" was the distinctive feature of American religion. Nevin saw this linking of the Bible with private judgment as deemphasizing the role of tradition and ecclesiastical authority. He related this phenomenon to a quest for primitive or apostolic Christianity, an emphatic revolt against theological systems—most noticeably Calvinist orthodoxy—and a practical rationalism that made the ultimate measure of Christianity consist in "the exercises of the single mind separately considered."[12]

These themes, along with a set of related attitudes about the approaching millennium and the providential role of America, constitute a useful way to approach the kinds of worldviews sustained by popular religious movements as they explained for themselves the providential movement of history and their own place in that unfolding drama. This is not to diminish the pulsating diversity that set Methodists apart from Mormons, Disciples from Baptists, Universalists from Adventists. But it is an attempt to grapple with certain defining characteristics of belief systems that in this culture were broadly communicated and enthusiastically owned. Theologies of the people could be coherent and compelling, even if theologians such as John W. Nevin and Philip Schaff railed at their authors as "patrons of ignorance."[13] Pennsylvania Methodists, the recipients of this caustic dismissal, were quick to reply that the only problem with the much-heralded Mercersburg Theology was that it was a "concealed treasure" understood only by "its two great leaders." The German Reformed ministers, the Methodists claimed, were "befogged" in a haze of German doctrinalism, and the Reformed rank-and-file had consigned themselves "in unreasoning and dutiful silence to the guidance of authority."[14]

This communication gap between the Mercersburg theologians and popular Methodist preachers is evidence that America's theological discussion has proceeded on at least two levels: academic and popular. The people have not been willing to relinquish their right to decide basic theological issues to religious experts; they have kept matters in their own hands by networks of popular education, personal influence, and a broad range of periodicals and books, biblical, theological, and devotional. J. F. C. Harrison's description of the Millerites as self-educated people with a thirst for knowledge seems an apt description of a broad range of popular Christian movements in America.[15] In this sense, the theology crafted in divinity schools has faced stiff competition from popular theologies whose authors felt no compulsion to check their interpretations with those ruling the academic roost.

The Quest for the Ancient Order

Despite the variety of Christian idioms that flowered in the early republic, most seemed to spring from the common conception that Christian tradition since the time of the apostles was a tale of sordid corruption in which kingcraft and priestcraft wielded orthodoxy to enslave the minds of the people. Ties with Catholic and Protestant traditions were severed, with a heady sense that a restoration of the primitive church was at hand. Men such as Benjamin Randal, founder of the Freewill Baptists, called for a new dispensation of gospel liberty. According to Francis Asbury, the apostolic order of things was lost in the first century, and the Reformers had beat off only part of the rubbish of intervening centuries. Methodism claimed emphatically to reinstate the apostolic form of the church in doctrine, discipline, conversion, and sanctification. In John W. Nevin's view, the American republic had given free reign to an "abstract supernaturalism" empowering believers to transcend the corruptions of eighteen hundred years and return to the simplicity, authority, and power of the age of the apostles. "Every congregation has power to originate a new Christianity for its own use," Nevin concluded, "and so may well afford to let that of all other ages pass for a grand apostasy."[16]

Elias Smith, Lorenzo Dow, Alexander Campbell, Francis Asbury, Barton Stone, Joseph Smith, and William Miller all believed that, since the age of the apostles, a great falling away had severed the relationship between God and man, leaving the visible church virtually extinct during the Dark Ages. They also agreed that, whatever good the Protestant Reformation had done, it had not reopened the heavens or restored authentic Christianity. "The stream of Christianity has become polluted," wrote Alexander Campbell, "and it is useless to temporize and try experiments. All the reformations that have occurred and the religious chymistry [sic] of the schools have failed to purify it."[17] Each was also convinced that he was a divine channel of purity for the primitive gospel.

In Alexander Campbell's first journal, *The Christian Baptist*, published from 1823 to 1830, his regular column, "A Restoration of the Ancient

Order of Things," gave practical advice to congregations about how they could strip away human invention and restore New Testament practice. Matters such as the order of worship, leadership, singing, and discipline were discussed. In his first column he applauded a Baptist association in Fayette County, Kentucky, which proposed a general conference for reform, to "bring the christianity and the church of the present day" up to the standards of "the state of christianity and of the church of the New Testament." Campbell warned, however, that authentic Christianity required far more than the kind of reform undertaken by Wycliffe, Luther, and Calvin. These had only continued a futile cycle of human effort. Restoring the church life of the New Testament required casting off human creeds and traditions, Catholic and Protestant. Campbell premised his advice column on the people's ability to transcend history, to duplicate the primitive pattern, and thus to ensure the coming of Christ's kingdom: "Just in so far as the ancient order of things, or the religion of the New Testament, is restored, just so far has the Millennium commenced."[18]

Joseph Smith and the Mormons were even more strident in their conviction that the corrupt, diseased ecclesiastical order tottered on the brink of destruction. Saints of the latter day had the opportunity to witness the unfolding of the apostolic order in all its fullness. For the first time in eighteen hundred years, the heavens had reopened. The reconvening of the Quorum of the Twelve Apostles by the prophet Joseph symbolized this restoration, as did the words of a popular Mormon hymn:

> The Spirit of God like fire is burning!
> The latter-day glory begins to come forth;
> The visions and blessings of old are returning,
> And angels are coming to visit the earth.[19]

Joseph Smith appealed to rootless religious seekers such as Parley Pratt by claiming to restore the essence of apostolic power and authority. The preaching of the Disciple Sidney Rigdon almost convinced Pratt that Rigdon embodied "the *ancient gospel* in due form." Yet he sensed one "great link was wanting to complete the chain of the ancient order of things—the apostleship, the power which should accompany the form." It was only after reading the *Book of Mormon* and conversing with Joseph Smith that he became convinced that a new dispensation had shattered the divine silence. Here, Pratt felt, was an answer for a world that had languished "without baptism, without the ministry and ordinances of God—since the days that inspiration and revelation had ceased."[20]

Why did the early republic give rise to so many varieties of restorationism, each intent on bringing the New Testament church back to life?

How could such resolute confidence and grand expectation characterize endeavors that often were halting and meager? Christian restorationism has been a recurring phenomena in the history of the Church, and its manifestations among early immigrants to North America had been particularly intense. Yet the decisive expatriation from the past evident at the turn of the nineteenth century has few parallels among eighteenth-century evangelicals, either British or American. It reflects at least two new conditions that moved popular reformers to rethink their own place in the historical process and to inject into it a note of crisis and discontinuity: the sharp blows of the democratic revolutions in severing taproots of orthodoxy and the disconcerting reality of intense religious pluralism.

The confidence that one could break the firm grip of custom and precedent rested on the conviction that people were witnessing in the flourishing of democracy the most momentous historical events in two millennia—a *novus ordo seclorum*. The opening line of Elias Smith's *Herald of Gospel Liberty* proclaimed that, due to the universal quest for liberty, "the age in which we live may certainly be distinguished from others in the history of Man." Alexander Campbell argued that the War of Independence unveiled a new epoch that would deliver the world from "the melancholy thraldom of relentless systems." America's "political regeneration" gave her the responsibility to lead a comparable "ecclesiastical renovation."[21] Both Smith and Campbell were explicitly Jeffersonian in their hostility to the heavy hand of the past and perfectly in accord with Jeffersonian assumptions, as recently portrayed by Joyce Appleby.[22]

At the same time, the bewildering array of religious options in the new nation heightened the sense that something had gone awry. The "great clash of religious sentiment" pushed the teenage Joseph Smith to despair because "God could not be the author of so much confusion."[23] Amidst such flux, each new insurgent movement—whether Methodist, Baptist, Christian, or Mormon—could confidently claim to be *the* heaven-sent solution to the riddle of sectarianism.[24]

That such resolute confidence and grand expectation gained a wide currency among disparate groups attests to the allure of self-made Christianity. Nevin and Schaff were correct to emphasize the radical implications in the ambition of a fledgling sect to appear "self-sprung from the Bible, or through the Bible from the skies."[25] This popular ideology endowed groups on the fringes of society with the conviction that the essence of the faith was not creeds drawn up at magnificent assemblies, liturgies handed down from age to age, or even sermons delivered by worthy divines. Instead, the quest for the ancient order shifted their own efforts to the center stage of cosmic drama. Restoring the apostolic order—and thus heralding the millennial kingdom—could only be done by the re-creative power of handfuls of faithful believers intent on following the New Testament pattern. Saints on that mission had no reason to bow to the wishes of well-placed graduates of colleges and seminaries, of large and prosperous urban congregations, or of councils and synods—particularly those trying to uphold Calvinist orthodoxy.

The Crusade against Calvinist Orthodoxy and Control

To the rebellious leaders of populist religious movements, inspired by the rhetoric of the Revolution, nothing represented ecclesiastical tyranny more than the Calvinist clergy with their zeal for theological systems, doctrinal correctness, organizational control, and cultural influence. The Congregationalist Standing Order had long enjoyed a privileged position in New England towns, a position it maintained well into the nineteenth century. In 1801 Congregationalists and Presbyterians joined forces in the Plan of Union to expand Reformed influence into the western missionary field. In addition, this coalition of moderate Calvinist leaders forged a chain of voluntary associations to further extend its influence, among which were the American Board of Commissioners for Foreign Missions (1810), the American Home Missionary Society (1826), the American Tract Society (1825), and the American Sunday School Union (1824).

Whatever the real power and influence of Calvinism, its enemies feared a menacing hydra, much as Jacksonians were obsessed with the power of a "monster" bank. No theme united the interests of insurgent groups between 1780 and 1830 more than an exaggerated opposition to official Christianity. In the face of the efforts of Calvinist coalitions to buttress Christian civilization, populist religious leaders worked with equal determination to withstand the control that Lyman Beecher and others worked to exert over the religious affairs of the nation. Many Methodists, Baptists, Christians, Universalists, and Disciples perceived tyrannical intent in the coordinated Calvinist schemes and launched a ferocious crusade against every facet of Calvinist orthodoxy. They fought its ordered and predictable form of religious experience, its rigid theological systems, its high-toned clericalism (what John Leland called "pharisaic pomp"), its penchant for cultural domination (what Freeborn Garrettson called a "thirst for preeminence"), and its attempt to legislate morality.[26]

The organization and rhetoric of this revolt against Calvinism remains elusive and neglected. Lacking the wealth, education, and reputation of Calvinist leaders, the dissidents were self-consciously provincial, fiercely independent, and culturally marginal. Their simultaneous attacks against Calvinism did not imply a willingness to collaborate in other matters. Despite these obstacles, dissident leaders were remarkably strong in challenging such Calvinist goals as home and foreign missions, the regulation of Sabbath observance, the education of ministers, and the forbidding of Sunday mail. These efforts to sabotage the elites' influence reveal the most savage and sustained anticlericalism in the early republic. These populist blueprints for church and nation also present striking evidence of a class division between opposing religious leaders.[27]

People nursed at least four related complaints against Reformed orthodoxy: its implicit endorsement of the status quo, its tyranny over personal religious experience, its preoccupation with complicated and arcane dogma, and its clerical pretension and quest for control. People at the bottom end of the social scale have rarely warmed to the doctrines of predestination. The anguish of injustice and poverty makes unacceptable the implication that God is ordaining, and taking pleasure in, whatever happens. African-Americans, for instance, found little place for predestination in their understanding of Christianity. In Wilkinson County, Mississippi, a slave gravedigger, with a younger helper, asked a white stranger a question:

"Massa, may I ask you something?"
"Ask what you please."
"Can you 'splain how it happened in the fust place, that the white folks got the start of the black folks, so as to make dem slaves and do all de work?"
The younger helper, fearing the white man's wrath, broke in: "Uncle Pete, it's no use talking. It's fo'ordained. The Bible tells you that. The Lord fo'ordained the Nigger to work, and the white man to boss."
"Dat's so. Dat's so. But if dat's so, then God's no fair man!"

The forms of Christianity that prospered among African-Americans were not accepting of the status quo. They supported a moral revulsion of slavery and promised eventual deliverance, putting God on the side of change and freedom.[28]

For many white people, on the other hand, Calvinist assumptions seemed as pervasive as the air they breathed. Numerous accounts of Methodist, Universalist, and Christian conversions indicate that common folk had internalized guilt and unworthiness, prompted by predestinarian preaching. But Calvinist sermons seemed to offer few means of spiritual release. Caleb Rich, an early proponent of Universalism, described the fear that plagued him as he grew up in rural New England. His Congregational minister in Sutton, Massachusetts, taught that Christ would have but few "trophies of his Mission into the world, while his antagonist would have his countless millions." "My situation appeared more precarious than a ticket in a lottery, where there was an hundred blanks to one prize."[29] Theophilus Gates, who grew up in an impoverished Connecticut farm family at the turn of the century, recounted that his preoccupation with being saved or lost led him on at least a thousand occasions to test his election by throwing a stone at a tree: "If I hit it, it was to signify that I should be saved; but if I missed the tree or stake, it was to be a sign to me that I was to be lost."[30]

The Methodists were particularly effective in attacking the Calvinist implication that pilgrims seeking salvation had to wait for the movings of an inscrutable and arbitrary God. After listening to Jesse Lee attack the notion of "unconditional election" before a crowd in Lynn, Massachusetts, one listener was said to exclaim, "Why, then, I can be saved! I have been taught that only a part of the race could be saved, but if this man's singing be true, all may be saved."[31] Similarly, the New Jersey farmer and eventual Methodist itinerant Benjamin Abbott tried to square his conversion experience under the Methodists with the Calvinist orthodoxy he had been taught. After a Presbyterian minister told him that his experience was a delusion and handed him a copy of Bellamy's *New Divinity*, Abbott tried to sort out the conflicting schemes: "I went a little out of the road, and kneeled down and prayed to God, that if I was deceived, to undeceive me; and the Lord said to me, 'Why do you doubt? Is not Christ all-sufficient? is he not able? Have you not felt his blood applied?' I then sprang upon my feet, and cried out, not all the devils in hell, nor all the predestinarians on earth, should make me doubt; for I knew that I was converted: at that instant I was filled with unspeakable raptures of joy."[32]

While Methodists, Disciples, and Mormons disagreed radically on what constituted belief in the gospel, they all shared an intense hostility to the passive quality of Calvinist religious experience, and they all made salvation imminently accessible and immediately available. Methodists, Universalists, Freewill Baptists, and Christians all described conversion as finding gospel liberty. The renegade Presbyterian Barton W. Stone recounted that he and other pioneers of the Christian church preached emphatically that the individual could exercise faith at any time: "We urged upon the sinner to believe *now*, and receive salvation—that in vain they looked for the Spirit to be given them, while they remained in unbelief . . . that no previous qualification was required, or necessary in order to believe in Jesus, and come to him. . . . When we began first to preach these things, the people appeared as just awakened from the sleep of ages—they seemed to see for the first time that they were responsible beings."[33]

The doctrinal orientation of Calvinism drew equal fire. The heady concepts of liberty that led people to renounce individual predestination also made objectionable the concepts of unconditional election and limited atonement. Numerous journals and autobiographies depicted great intellectual turmoil as young converts attempted to harmonize theology with experience. As a fledgling preacher, the Baptist convert Benjamin Randal was asked in 1779 why he did not preach election "as Mr. Calvin held it." "Because I do not believe it," he replied, a conclusion reached by his own personal experience and reading of Scripture. When arraigned before a Baptist association and threatened with being disowned, Randal responded, "It makes no odds with me, who disowns me, as long as I know that the Lord owns me. And now let that God be God, who answers by fire; and that people, be God's people, whom he owneth and blesseth."[34] As a young Calvinist minister, Barton W. Stone confessed that he was "embarrassed with many abstruse doctrines": "Scores of objections would continually roll across my mind." What he called the "labyrinth of Calvinism" left his mind "distressed," "perplexed," and "bewildered." He found relief from this dissonance of values only when he came to attack Calvinism as falsehood.[35]

The argument against Calvinism pitted enlightened common sense against scholastic metaphysics of the educated elite. As people became more insistent on thinking theologically for themselves, the carefully wrought dogmas of Calvin, Edwards, and Hopkins were dismissed as "the senseless jargon of election and reprobation." The unbridled Freewill Baptist William Smythe Babcock identified these eminent divines as the three frogs in the Book of Revelation.[36] The Methodist itinerant Tobias Spicer recounted an incident in Warren County, New York, in 1812 that illustrates the plight of Calvinism among self-educated and self-directed people. One of his first converts was Samuel Crane, who had been a devout Calvinist but was deeply perplexed by the apparent contradiction between the idea of an eternally fixed number of elect and reprobate and the idea that salvation was free for anyone to take:

> He supposed it must be as the [Calvinist] minister said, for he was a good man, and a very learned man; and of course it must be owing to his own ignorance and dulness that he could not understand it. On one occasion, as he was returning home from church, meditating on what

he had heard, he became so vexed with himself, on account of his dulness of apprehension, that he suddenly stopped and commenced pounding his head with his fist, for he really thought his stupidity must be owing to his having an uncommonly thick skull.

When Crane finally accepted Methodism, "he found a system that seemed to harmonize with itself, with the Scriptures, with common sense, and with experience."[37] Billy Hibbard had the same reaction when he first heard a Methodist explain the gospel: "I heard for the first time, a doctrine that I could understand. There was no contradiction, but he could prove his doctrine from scripture and reason."[38]

These attacks were not against Calvinism in a narrow sense, as if Arminianism or Lutheranism were the preferred rendering of scholastic theology. Instead, the attacks were directed against forms of Christianity that were preoccupied with theology. Two of Barton Stone's colleagues in Kentucky issued a symbolic epitaph for the fate of high Calvinism in American popular culture: "We are not personally acquainted with the writings of John Calvin," wrote Robert Marshall and J. Thompson, "nor are we certain how nearly we agree with his views of divine truth; neither do we care."[39]

The revolt against Calvinism sprang from issues that were personal and intellectual, yet the fundamental debate over the exercise of authority breathed fire into this opposition, turning complaints into an enduring crusade. The violently anticlerical rhetoric that hounded Calvinists for the half-century after the Revolution showed deep-seated class hostility more than the mere posturing of rival groups.[40] Populist leaders such as Elias Smith, John Leland, Freeborn Garrettson, Lorenzo Dow, and John Taylor all gave serious attention to the energetic advance of Calvinist seminaries, missionary societies, and benevolent organizations. In these efforts they sensed a self-appointed aristocracy trying to control the soul of the nation and to crush simple congregational freedom.

These Methodists, Christians, and Baptists were obsessed with Calvinist designs for social control.[41] Taking careful note of each new strategy and endeavor, they filled popular journals with anticlerical invectives for the first three decades of the nineteenth century. Elias Smith, whom one Congregationalist christened as "the Champion of reviling, railing, and slander,"[42] stormed against "priestcraft," "law religion," seminaries, and missionary societies for a quarter of a century. He denounced seminaries as "Religious Manufactories," which were "established for explaining that which is plain, and for the purpose of making easy things hard." Smith called the orthodox seminary at Andover the "New Factory" and compared it to Sanballat's rival temple on Gerizim, "from which, *fundamentals* are to flow, in annual streams, to every part where *large salaries* can be raised, or large sums given per month, for *missionary labors.*"[43] In an attack on Lyman Beecher's disdain for simple Christian folk like the Methodists, Freeborn Garrettson noted Beecher's thirst for preeminence and his insinuating tone. (Beecher had called the Hudson River Valley a "moral wilderness" despite obvious Methodist presence.) Returning the favor, Garrettson sharpened his pen of sarcasm to note the smug professionalism of the so-called settled clergy, those "who make a trade of the gospel, and want to crush every other denomination."[44]

The Baptist John Leland took up the same themes throughout the 1820s, when Calvinist organizing seemed to be reaching high tide. Leland satirized seminaries as a design of the clerical hierarchy to channel more of their sons into positions of wealth, ease, and status. In his poem "The Modern Priest," a young man named Ignatius decides to enter the ministry instead of law, medicine, or government because the work is easy, the pay high:

> Preaching is now a science and a trade,
> and by it many grand estates are made;
>
> . . . .
>
> From this, the preacher travell'd all around,
> To see where glebes and salaries were found;
>
> Many loud calls he had where land was poor,
> People were indigent, and had no store.
> The calls he heard, but gravely answer'd, "no;
> To other places God calls me to go!"
>
> At length a vacant place Ignatius found,
> Where land was good, and wealth did much abound:
> A call they gave him which he did embrace,
> "Vox populi, vox Dei," was the case.[45]

Leland saw the new machinations of "the clerical hierarchy" as an extension of the same enemy that had attempted to suppress the simplicity of the gospel throughout the ages—Byzantium, Rome, Canterbury, the New England Standing Order and Federalist Party:

> The missionary establishment, in its various departments, is a stupendous institution. Literary and theological schools, Bible and tract societies, foreign and domestic missions, general, State, country, and

district conventions, Sunday School Unions, etc., are all included in it. To keep it in motion, missionary boards, presidents, treasurers, corresponding secretaries, agents, printers, buildings, teachers, runners, collectors, mendicants, etc., are all in requisition. The cloud of these witnesses is so great that one who doubts the divinity of the measure is naturally led to think of the locusts in Egypt that darkened the *Heavens* and ate up every green thing on *earth*. This machine is propelled by steam (money), and does not sail by the wind of heaven.[46]

The most fascinating and influential watchdog of Calvinist expansion was the impoverished Connecticut farmer and self-appointed preacher Theophilus Ransom Gates. A starving and footsore pilgrim, Gates felt called to become a preacher in Virginia in 1809 at the age of twenty-two after stumbling into the house of a Baptist preacher. He ended up in Philadelphia, where he peddled an account of his spiritual struggles and several other interpretations of prophecy.[47] In Philadelphia, Gates was influenced both by Elias Smith, who for a time published the *Herald of Gospel Liberty* there, and by Lorenzo Dow, whom he joined in a land investment scheme in the Northwest Territory in 1816.

Like many of his generation, Gates was preoccupied with the Book of Revelation and was convinced that all churches were mired in apostasy. He interpreted the beast of Revelation 13 to include not only papal Rome and the Protestant church-state system, but also "every sect or constituted body of people in Christendom."[48] Gates proposed a millennium that was explicitly individualist. The age of ecclesiastical corruption would be supplanted neither by the personal advent of Christ (as William Miller later suggested), by the patterning of churches on New Testament models, nor by the restoration of divine power to a new prophet such as Joseph Smith. Instead, Christians should shun all institutions, soon to topple around them, and allow the Spirit to work within. It was the disappearance of the church and the unmediated operation of the Spirit upon the individual soul that would mark the advent of the millennium. Christ would not return in visible person, "but by the invisible, yet enlightening and powerful operations of his holy Spirit, in the hearts of many individuals; by whom, as set forth in the vision, all error, sin and delusion, of every kind, will be consumed and destroyed. . . . Indeed, when the millenium shall have fully taken place, I believe every man will be as a prophet, in point of knowledge and attainments."[49]

In 1820 Theophilus Gates founded a monthly journal, *The Reformer*, that for fifteen years brandished steel-tipped invectives against clericalism of any stripe: Methodist "hierarchy," theological schools, church buildings, degrees, clothes, creeds, and catechisms. Gates's caustic anticlericalism knew no bounds, but he offered no positive formula for the church's reconstruction. He ridiculed clerical efforts as ludicrous, wasteful, tyrannical, avaricious, crafty, and self-serving.[50] His extremist publication gained national attention by vilifying the "national establishment" represented by sabbath societies, Sunday schools, mission agencies, and seminaries. Gates's office at 290 North Third Street, Philadelphia, became a central exchange for books, tracts, and correspondence by antimission forces. The *Reformer* served as the primary agent for spreading propaganda against the missionary societies. Byran Cecil Lambert has estimated that in 1825 alone Gates used seventy-two antimission items from thirty-five different papers. Typical of these articles were reprints from the *American Eagle* (Litchfield, Connecticut), attacking the accumulation of money by the "monster" societies led by Lyman Beecher; from the *Mechanics Free Press* of Philadelphia, warning the laboring class of the danger of the Sunday School Union; and from the Universalist *Christian Intelligencer* (Portland, Maine), identifying the unified conspiracy of various reform societies:

> We entertain not a shadow of doubt that the leaders of the orthodox party . . . are determined on governing the nation. The supreme power is the grand end and aim of all their plans and labors. Every society which they have formed, from the American Education Society down to the ten thousand cent and mite societies throughout the land, are but so many strings, pulled by every person whether man, woman, or child, whom they can press or persuade into their service, the ultimate design of which is to draw them into power.[51]

Gates stood for no sect in particular but published the widely diverse voices that scorned Calvinist orthodoxy. He included articles from Methodists, Baptists, Universalists, Quakers, Disciples, and various free-thinkers. One of the *Reformer*'s chief functions seems to have been to stimulate interest in and communication about antimission efforts among western and southern Baptists. Gates reported antimission activity among Baptists in North Carolina, Mississippi, Alabama, Missouri, Illinois, and Maine.[52]

The two most significant leaders in this diverse movement, Daniel Parker and John Taylor, both had writings included in the *Reformer* and, in turn, drew strength from its combative tone. A product of the Georgia frontier, Parker founded the first Baptist churches in southern Illinois; John Taylor, a native of Virginia, became a fiercely independent Baptist preacher in Kentucky. Both men bristled with resentment against eastern missionaries, Presbyterian and Baptist, who came to the backcountry with a vision to "improve" the poor folk there and "uplift" them with moral instruction and education. As early as 1819, John Taylor wrote a pamphlet, *Thoughts on Missions*, that recalled the missionary reconnaissance trip of Congregationalists John F. Schermerhorn and Samuel J. Mills a decade earlier. Taylor remembered the Easterners' shock when they learned that he took no salary. They advised him that people should get in the habit of giving "for all sacred purposes." At that point, Taylor said he began to smell "*the New England Rat*."[53] Taylor's pamphlet, which was taken up and enthusiastically marketed by Theophilus Gates in Philadelphia for twelve and one-half cents a copy, denounced home and foreign missionaries as "high-minded" aristocrats who sought "a large empire" of personal influence. He scorned the hardship that "white-handed gentry" from the East complained of, and he denounced fancy school-made theologians who loved to be called "Rabbi" and to have the "chief rooms" in the synagogue.[54] Taylor's most memorable image, which became a commonplace in antimission circles, decried missionaries as horse leeches, always crying for more but never being satisfied.[55]

Daniel Parker was an equally rawboned backwoodsman. He had lived in Tennessee and Kentucky before beginning the first Baptist churches in Illinois after the War of 1812. Although he was barely literate—by his own admission he could read but could not write—Parker responded to the intrusion of educated Baptist missionaries from the East in 1817 by publishing a sixty-four-page pamphlet, *A Public Address to the Baptist Society* (Vincennes, Indiana, 1820). Apologizing for poor grammar, Parker proceeded to lash the "wise and learned" of the Baptist Mission Board for the "missionary plan" that he deemed high-handed interference in the work that was a matter between God and the individual. Throughout the 1820s, Parker fought against the Baptist missionary John Mason Peck, who had settled in St. Louis. Parker's antimission efforts culminated in the *Church Advocate*, which he published between 1829 and 1831. The paper's caustic tone and use of ridicule was similar to that of the *Reformer*. Using Elias Smith's terminology, Parker accused John Peck of having been "manufactured in some of the eastern man-made manufacturing machines." Parker wanted none of the condescension evidenced by Peck and his ilk: "[T]he preaching manufactories of the east appear to be engaged in sending hirelings to the west, and should any of those *man-made, devil sent*, place-hunting gentry come into our country, and read in our places, we shall likely raise against *them* seven shepards [sic], and eight principle [sic] men."[56]

The rollicking irony of the attack of grassroots Baptist leaders John Taylor and Daniel Parker upon the pretensions of moderate Calvinism was that it was done in the name of extreme predestinarian or "Hard-Shell" Calvinism. Both men believed in the conversion of the lost but took exception to "new-fangled" methods for reaching them. They believed the local church was the organizational limit for evangelical efforts. Taylor and Parker stood shoulder to shoulder against the missionary menace, as did Elias Smith, Theophilus Gates, and Alexander Campbell, profaners of the Calvinist temple every one. Yet they found more in common with these bitter opponents of predestination than with those who professed Calvinism as part of a system of elite control. People intent on breaking the expansive designs of moderate Calvinists could do so in the name of extreme liberty or extreme dependence on primitive models. Either way, this populist crusade indicates how intense was the competition for cultural power in the early republic. Grass-roots leaders of the church went to great lengths to shelter their flocks from indoctrination emanating from the seats of orthodoxy.[57] John Leland was typical when he admitted to Senator Richard M. Johnson in 1834 that for him to acknowledge any clerical power "to hold dominion over my faith and direct my conscience, is making a bow too great for my stiff neck."[58]

Sola Scriptura

The most telling evidence of the revolt against history and against Calvinist control is the distinctive way that many populists chose to read the Bible. Any number of denominations, sects, movements, and individuals between 1780 and 1830 claimed to be restoring a pristine biblical Christianity free from all human devices. "In religious faith we have but one Father and one Master," noted the Universalist spokesmen A. B. Grosh, "and the Bible, *the Bible*, is our only acknowledged creed-book."[59] "I have endeavored to read the scriptures as though no one had read them before me," claimed Alexander Campbell, "and I am as much on my guard against reading them to-day, through the medium of my own views yesterday, or a week ago, as I am against being influenced by any foreign name, authority, or system whatever."[60]

Protestants from Luther to Wesley had been forced to define carefully what they meant by *sola scriptura*. They found it an effective banner to unfurl when attacking Catholics but always a bit troublesome when common people began to take the teaching seriously. For the Reformers, popular translations of the Bible did not imply that people were to understand the Scriptures apart from ministerial guidance. Thus when dealing with a scholar such as Erasmus, Luther could champion boldly the perspicuity of Scripture, its clarity for all: "Who will maintain that the public fountain does not stand in the light, because some people in a back alley cannot see it, when everybody in the market place can see it quite plainly?" Yet when confronted with headstrong sectarians, he withdrew such democratic interpretations and admitted the danger of proving anything by Scripture: "Now I learn that it suffices to throw many passages together helterskelter whether they fit or not. If this is the way to do it, I certainly shall prove with Scripture that Rastrum beer is better than Malmsey wine."[61]

Calvin similarly charted a careful middle course in defining what biblical authority should mean: "I acknowledge that Scripture is a most rich and inexhaustible fountain of all wisdom; but I deny that its fertility consists in the various meanings which any man, at his pleasure, may assign." In the same vein, the Westminster Divines defended their flank against the Anglicans by arguing in the 1640s that on matters of church government and forms of worship the Scriptures contained all that a person needed to know. With the sectarians of the English Civil War in mind, however, they included in the Westminster Confession the statement that the whole counsel of God was "either expressly set down in Scriptures, or by good and necessary consequence may be deduced from Scriptures."[62]

It is equally clear that the eighteenth-century evangelicals John Wesley, George Whitefield, Jonathan Edwards, Isaac Backus, and others did not think of viewing the Bible as a source of authority independent of theology and the mediations of clergymen. Wesley called himself a *homo unius libri*, a man of one book, and Whitefield repeatedly exhorted his charges to return to the simplicity of Scripture. Yet they came to verbal blows, and soon the Methodists divided over abstract theology in the Calvinist-Arminian debate. Similarly, even the "high-flying" New Lights of New England and the South never sustained a convincing case that theology per se, the good and the bad, should be discarded in favor of Scripture alone. Jonathan Edwards lauded the spiritual perception of common folk, but he also noted that "the less knowing and considerate sort of people" could easily be deceived in the very process of studying the Bible.[63] The Great Awakening, then, failed to set the Bible against theology, history, and tradition. In the middle of the eighteenth century, however, rumblings of this kind came from an unexpected quarter.

The first Americans to underscore the right of private judgment in handling Scripture were, oddly enough, ministers who opposed the evangelical tenets of the Great Awakening. As New Lights in New England worked to make people more theologically self-conscious, often by rewriting church covenants to include strict doctrinal standards, theological liberals increasingly resisted strict creedal definitions of Christianity. The future president of the United States, John Adams, like many of his generation, came to despise theological argumentation. He reported in his diary in 1756, "Where do we find a precept in the Gospel requiring

Ecclesiastical Synods? Convocations? Councils? Decrees? Creeds? Confessions? Oaths? Subscriptions? and the whole cart-loads of other trumpery that we find religion encumbered with in these days?"[64]

To gain leverage against the entrenched Calvinism of the Great Awakening, theological liberals redoubled their appeal to depend on the Scriptures alone. "Why may not I go to the Bible to learn the doctrines of Christianity as well as the Assembly of Divines?" the prominent Boston clergyman Jeremy Belknap asked in 1784. Simeon Howard, a more liberal minister, exhorted his colleagues to "keep close to the Bible" and to "avoid metaphysical additions." He also advised clergymen to "lay aside all attachment to human systems, all partiality to names, councils and churches, and honestly inquire, 'what saith the scriptures.'"[65]

Charles Chauncy, pastor of Boston's First Church for sixty years (1727–87), is the most prominent example of an exclusive appeal to Biblical authority in order to unravel theological orthodoxy. Chauncy was persuaded to emphasize Bible study by reading the works of English divines, such as Samuel Clarke's *The Scripture-Doctrine of the Trinity* (London, 1712) and John Taylor's *The Scripture-Doctrine of Original Sin* (London, 1740). Both authors used a "free, impartial and diligent" method of examining Scripture to jettison, respectively, the doctrines of the Trinity and of Original Sin.[66]

During the 1750s, after the Great Awakening, Charles Chauncy spent seven years engaged in the approach to Bible study expounded by these English authors. In the spring of 1754 he wrote to a friend, "I have made the Scriptures my sole study for about two years; and I think I have attained to a clearer understanding of them than I ever had before." His studies led him to draft a lengthy manuscript in which he rejected the idea of eternal punishment and embraced universalism. He kept this work in his desk for over a quarter-century, its conclusions, he confessed, too controversial "to admit of publication in this country." He was nearly eighty when he finally allowed a London publisher in 1784 to print *The Mystery Hid from Ages and Generations . . . or, The Salvation of All Men.* To justify his conclusions, Chauncy relied on the biblical force of his argument, "a long and diligent comparing of *scripture with scripture*." He explained to Ezra Stiles, "The whole is written from the scripture account of the thing and not from any human scheme." This unorthodox biblicist would have been gratified indeed by the reaction of one minister who, finding the book's arguments convincing, wrote, "He has placed many texts and passages of Scripture in a light altogether new to me, and I cannot help thinking his system not only rational, but Scriptural."[67]

Well into the nineteenth century, rationalistic Christians—many of them Unitarians and Universalists—argued against evangelical orthodoxy by appealing to the Bible. Unitarian Noah Worcester's arguments were typical. He challenged people to think for themselves, to slough off a "passive state of mind" that deferred to great names in theology. "The scriptures," he declared, "were designed for the great mass of mankind and are in general adapted to their capacities." Worcester assumed that mysteries such as the Trinity would be discarded by a disbelieving public once people learned to explore the Bible for themselves. He recounted his Unitarian conversion in a book appropriately entitled *Bible News of the Father, Son, and Holy Spirit* (Concord, N.H., 1810).[68] In the same vein, Charles Beecher defended his rejection of his father Lyman's orthodoxy by renouncing "creed-power" and raising the banner of "the Bible, the whole Bible, and nothing but the Bible."[69] By the 1840s, however, when Charles Beecher had moved beyond the pale of orthodoxy, a different and decidedly more evangelical notion of biblicism had taken root within American culture.

Change in Christian thought, as Edmund S. Morgan has suggested, is usually a matter of emphasis. Certain ideas are given greater weight than was previously accorded them, or one idea is carried to its logical conclusion at the expense of others. "One age slides into the next," he says, "and an intellectual revolution may be achieved by the expression of ideas that everyone had always professed to accept."[70] The study of the religious convictions of self-taught Americans in the early years of the republic reveals how much weight was placed on private judgment and how little on the roles of history, theology, and the collective will of the church. In a culture that mounted a frontal assault upon tradition, mediating elites, and institutions, the Bible very easily became, as John W. Nevin complained, "a book dropped from the skies for all sorts of men to use in their own way."[71] This shift occurred gradually and without fanfare because innovators could exploit arguments as old and as trusted as Protestantism itself. Luther, Calvin, Wesley, and Backus had all argued for the principle of *sola scriptura*; unschooled Americans merely argued that they were fulfilling that same mandate. Yet, in the assertion that private judgment should be the ultimate tribunal in religious matters, common people started a revolution.

This populist hermeneutics had considerable appeal because it spoke to several pressing issues. It proclaimed a new ground of certainty for a generation distressed that it could no longer hear the voice of God above the din of sectarian confusion. This approach to Scripture also dared common people to open the Bible and think for themselves. It even challenged them to limit religious discussion to the language of the Bible. Finally, this approach freed people from staid ecclesiastical traditions, thus befuddling the respectable clergy.

This is exactly what John W. Nevin and Philip Schaff found so galling about America's "sect system." Powerful ideas such as "no creed but the Bible" took hold in popular religious movements, even if they seemed to bear little meaningful relation to the evolution of those groups. Nevin was particularly aware of the gap between a rhetoric that promised to calm sectarian strife and the actual practice of following the Bible—which seemed to multiply denominations endlessly:

> But what are we to think of it when we find such a motley mass of protesting systems, all laying claim so vigorously here to one and the same watchword? If the Bible be at once so clear and full as a formulary of Christian doctrine and practice, how does it come to pass that where men are left most free to use it in this way, and have the greatest mind to do so, according to their own profession, they are flung asunder so perpetually in their religious faith, instead of being brought together, by its influence.[72]

He was equally struck with the dichotomy between the rhetoric of people going to the Bible for themselves and the reality of a few strong figures imposing their own will. Nevin claimed that the "high-sounding phrases" of liberty, free inquiry, and an open Bible masked a new kind of ecclesiastical domination that would "kill all independent thought and all free life":

> The liberty of the sect consists at last, in thinking its particular notions, shouting its shibboleths and passwords, dancing its religious hornpipes, and reading the Bible only through its theological goggles. These restrictions, at same time, are so many wires, that lead back at last into the hands of a few leading spirits, enabling them to wield a true hierarchical despotism over all who are thus brought within their power.[73]

This divorce of democratic aspiration from the realities of an emerging capitalist society was endemic to Jacksonian America, as John Murrin and Rowland Berthoff have noted. Because of their Revolutionary heritage, Americans had trouble admitting that competition could undermine freedom of opportunity as well as freedom of thought.[74] Yet common people, Bibles in hand, relished the right to shape their own faith and submit to leaders of their own choosing. Folk who were given acceptance, dignity, and meaning by the Methodists, Mormons, and Millerites found precious few occasions to complain about religious authoritarianism.

America, Democracy, and the Millennium

For all that has been written describing millennial movements as outbursts of popular protest, eighteenth-century millennialism in the Anglo-American world remained largely the preserve of gentlemen and scholars. The popular movements of Methodism and the Great Awakening produced no offspring comparable to the socially radical Ranters, Diggers, and Fifth-Monarchy Men of the seventeenth century. In fact, with the exception of Jonathan Edwards, it was men of the Enlightenment—Isaac Newton, Joseph Priestley, Benjamin Rush—who were known for their interpretations of prophecy. The study of prophecy offered rational men the opportunity to see God's plan unfold in history and produced tangible and coherent proof of religious doctrine.[75] By the end of the eighteenth century, millennialism was nearly the inverse of Norman Cohn's sociological stereotype of a millennial movement. Unlike mystical prophets who whipped up the landless poor, students of the end times were men such as Universalist Elhanan Winchester, whom Benjamin Rush called "a theological Newton," scientist and judge James Winthrop of Harvard, and Loyalist Joseph Galloway of Pennsylvania, who spent the final years of his London exile writing a massive commentary on the Book of Revelation.[76]

Yet the age of democratic revolutions had the effect of giving awesome reality to what had been polite and respectable speculation. Americans of all ranks sensed that events of truly apocalyptic significance were unfolding before their eyes. Judging by the number of sermons, books, and pamphlets that addressed prophetic themes, the first generation of United States citizens may have lived in the shadow of Christ's second coming more intensely than any generation since.[77]

Many Congregationalists and Presbyterians associated democratic advance with the Antichrist of French revolutionary zeal. But other Americans, especially those without formal education or high social standing, interpreted the signs of the times very differently. To them a potent dose of liberty and equality seemed just the tonic for church and state. In a sermon after Jefferson's second election, Elias Smith stated that God had raised up Jefferson, like Cyrus, "to dry up the Euphrates of mystery Babylon." Firmly grounded on the principles of liberty and equality, Jefferson's administration seemed to foreshadow the millennium.[78] On the front page of the first edition of the *Herald of Gospel Liberty*, Elias Smith declared that the struggle for liberty and the rights of mankind set this age apart from all previous ages in history. According to Smith, the foundations of Christ's millennial kingdom were laid in the American and French revolutions.

"The time will come," he said, "when there will not be a *crowned head* on earth. Every attempt which is made to keep up a Kingly government, and to pull down a Republican one, will . . . serve to destroy monarchy."[79]

The following year in Washington, Pennsylvania, Thomas Campbell published the first manifesto of the Disciple movement, in which he discussed the same state of revolutionary and apocalyptic affairs: "Do ye not discern the signs of the times? Have not the two witnesses arisen from their state of political death, from under the long proscription of ages? . . . Who amongst us has not heard the report of these things—of these lightnings and thunderings, and voices, of this tremendous earthquake and great hail; of these awful convulsions and revolutions that have dashed and are dashing the nations like a potter's vessel?"[80] A sense of expectancy and an overt respect for novelty also characterized the Christians. Two of Stone's associates confessed, "We confidently thought that the Millennium was just at hand, and that a glorious church would soon be formed; we thought, also, that we had found the very plan for its formation and growth." Opponents of the movement agreed, moreover, that this apocalyptic urgency had fueled the movement from the start.[81] Two early hymns also sounded a prophetic note of expectancy.[82]

Dissident Methodist Lorenzo Dow refused to obtain a preaching license in England because it involved an oath of loyalty to the King. He linked the swiftly approaching termination of history to the downfall of privilege and rise of equality. In two pamphlets first published in 1811 and 1813, Dow spelled out an interpretation of history built on the rise of the inalienable rights of life, liberty, property, and private judgment.[83] His discussion, entitled "The Dawn of Liberty," foreshadowed the *Book of Mormon* in stating that salvation history was shifting to the New World: "America lay undiscovered for several thousand years, as if reserved for the era, when common sense began to awake her long slumber. As if the Creator's wisdom and goodness had a 'NEW WORLD,' in reversion for a new theatre for the exhibition of new things."

Dow listed specific reasons for this change in the divine economy. Europe remained bound to "the galling yoke of Tyranny and priest-craft," the minds of its people "so degraded . . . so debased" that they were not prepared to start over politically and religiously. America, however, had been settled by persons "pregnant with the spirit of freedom in embryo." The character of America's people made it the only place "that opened a fair prospect for a beginning": "From all these considerations, such persons who had the clearest heads and best hearts which those days afforded, fled to America. Determined not to receive things as matters of fact on the bare say-so of others, when repugnant to common sense; they were men—they had the spirit of inquiry: and took the liberty to think, and judge, and act for themselves."[84]

Dow's view suggests that the age of democratic revolutions both gave believers good reasons to sever ties with the past and suggested egalitarian models for a new age. Alexander Campbell referred to his movement for church reformation as a "declaration of independence of the kingdom of Jesus." Elias Smith and Barton Stone used the same words to describe their withdrawal from the Baptists and Presbyterians, respectively. Similarly, James O'Kelly claimed that he broke with the Methodists because they left him no option but "unlimited submission" or separation.[85] The extent to which some allowed political idioms to color their thinking is difficult to comprehend. Some even referred to the early church as a republican society with a New Testament constitution. In 1807, one maverick Christian in Marietta, Ohio, outdid them all by claiming that "the great potentate of the world, in principle, is the most *genuine* REPUBLICAN that ever existed."[86]

From a modern viewpoint, it seems odd that men so committed to the separation of church and state used political structures as a church model. These dissidents endowed the republic with the same divine authority as did such defenders of the Standing Order as Timothy Dwight and Noah Webster, but for opposite reasons. The republic became a new city on a hill, not because it kept faith with Puritan tradition, but because it sounded the death knell for corporate and hierarchic conceptions of the social order. In sum, a government so enlightened as to tell the churches to go their own way must also have prophetic power to tell them which way to go.[87]

Millennialism, then, served different functions in the period between 1790 and 1840 than it had during the Great Awakening. Revivals of the 1740s drew upon millennial themes to challenge believers to a greater commitment to traditional values.[88] Democratic ferment in the early republic, however, convinced many that they should erase the memory of the past and learn all they could of the gospel of equality.

This is not to suggest that political idioms uniformly colored the thinking of popular preachers in the early republic, or that the message these preachers proclaimed was not profoundly religious in purpose and scope. Early Methodist preachers, for instance, were preeminently soul savers and revivalists. They considered political involvement a distraction at best.[89] Yet even Francis Asbury was given to affectionate reflections on the religious privileges offered in his adopted land. He repeatedly contrasted Methodism in America with Methodism in Great Britain, noting the success of the offspring in outstripping the parent. Lacking sustained interest in politics or millennium, Asbury still marveled that Providence had so graciously prospered the designs of *American* Methodists.

Even the Mormons, who apparently rejected American values and imposed biblical models upon politics, developed an eschatology that was explicitly American. Joseph Smith's Garden of Eden was a New World paradise, with America as the cradle of civilization. In due time, the *Book of Mormon* recounts, God prevailed upon Columbus "to venture across the sea to the Promised Land, to open it for a new race of free men."[90] A variety of Mormon authors suggested that the free institutions of America had prepared the way for the new prophet, Joseph Smith. Early Mormon missionaries to Great Britain appealed to converts to leave the Old World, which was bound in tyranny and awaiting destruction, and travel to the new. An early song by missionary John Taylor shows the contrast between British society and the New World:

> O! This is the land of the free!
> And this is the home of the brave;
> Where rulers and mobbers agree;
> 'Tis the home of the tyrant and slave.
>
> Here liberty's poles pierce the sky
> With her cap gaily hung on the vane;
> The gods may its glories espy,
> But poor mortals, it's out of your ken.
>
> The eagle sours proudly aloft,
> And covers the land with her wings;
> But oppression and bloodshed abound,
> She can't deign to look down on such things.
>
> All men are born equal and free,
> And their rights all nations maintain;
> But with millions it would not agree,
> They were cradled and brought up in chains.[91]

Not political in any conventional sense, the early Latter-Day Saints envisioned a theology of America more concrete than any of their rivals. The Mormons never claimed that the entire American identity, like that of the church, had become polluted. They believed there was a special character to the land and its people that would allow the kingdom of heaven to be restored despite the corruption of the current generation. On this conviction, Joseph Smith established an independent kingdom at Nauvoo and simultaneously announced his candidacy for the presidency of the

United States. One of the songs of this campaign called Mormons to "rally to the standard of Liberty" and "trample down the tyrant's rod and the oppressor's crown."[92]

American popular culture allowed self-educated people to espouse millennial hopes, hopes rife with the conviction that a *novus ordo seculorum* was unfolding. Common folk could, in this culture, challenge their betters; democracy was the cause of God. The collapse of Federalism, the last symbolic refuge of privilege, rekindled both these hopes and the conviction that the millennium was to have an intimate relationship with the "land of the free and the home of the brave." Even when political and social realities seemed to defy democratic standards, populist preachers vied with elites for the birthright of the nation. They called America back to roots that had much to do with popular sovereignty and the right to think for oneself.

Putting this another way, the alienation of insurgent groups in the early republic did not produce "sects" in a European sense, mainly because of each group's conviction that the meaning of America was integral to the beginning of their individual movement. The kingdom of God could yet be built in America if they were true to their own special calling. The pull was as much toward Providence as toward purity, toward subduing the culture as toward withdrawing from it. The call was to preach, write, convert, and to call the nation back to self-evident first principles.

Latter-Day Saints, for instance, knew intense alienation from mainstream culture, yet their response was unlike that of Roger Williams or the Quakers in the Massachusetts Bay Colony. Joseph Smith and his followers withdrew from society but did not retreat to modest aims and private ambitions. They were fired with a sense of national, even international, mission: God's kingdom would yet rise in America, they believed, and their endeavors would serve as decisive leaven. Like Puritans, they set themselves to accomplish great and mighty things. Sidney Rigdon's recollection of the charged atmosphere in a log house in 1830 captures the sense of mission that transformed farmers and artisans into thundering prophets intent on shaping the destiny of a nation:

> I met the whole church of Christ in a little log house about 20 feet square . . . and we began to talk about the kingdom of God as if we had the world at our command; we talked with great confidence, and talked big things, although we were not many people, we had big feelings . . . we began to talk like men in authority and power—we looked upon men of the earth as grasshoppers; if we did not see this people, we saw by vision, the church of God, a thousand times larger. . . . [W]e talked about the people coming as doves to the

windows, that all nations should flock unto it . . . and of whole nations being born in one day; we talked such big things that men could not bear them.[93]

A similar hunger for achievement and sense of providential mission propelled others to take up Methodist, Baptist, or Christian causes. One cannot underestimate the force of their compelling visions—their egalitarian "errands into the wilderness"—in assessing the Christianization of popular culture and the relative weakness of other ideologies of dissent. These thundering legions stormed the hinterland of the nation empowered by an incomparable ideology: their innovations were the handiwork of God and the meaning of America.

IV. Legacy

CHAPTER SEVEN

Upward Aspiration and Democratic Dissent

Thus orthodoxy was in a considerable degree methodized, and Methodism in due time became orthodoxed.

SAMUEL GOODRICH, *1856*

In 1856, seventy-one-year-old Peter Cartwright published his own story as a way to focus attention on Methodism's primitive circuit riders. Converted in a Kentucky revival in 1801 at the age of sixteen, Cartwright was licensed as an exhorter before his seventeenth birthday. After itinerating in Kentucky, Tennessee, Ohio, and Indiana, he settled in Illinois in 1824, where he farmed and preached for almost a half century. A rugged and fiery preacher, Cartwright's wit, homespun sermons, and dedication to the Methodist cause contributed significantly to the movement's progress in Illinois. He also represented the Sangamon district in the state legislature from 1824 to 1840 and was defeated by Abraham Lincoln for Congress in 1846.

In his reflections, Cartwright chafed at modern Methodists' tendency to abandon simplicity for respectability and influence. He contrasted the early circuit rider's ethic of sacrifice with younger ministers' interest in college education and a respectable parish. He lamented the fact that wealthy and fashionable Methodists were turning their back on exuberant revivals, intimate class meetings, and manifest concern for "the Lord's poor." Cartwright's jeremiad reminded "downy doctors and learned presidents and professors" that their own values contrasted sharply with the commitments that had fueled Methodism as a popular movement.[1]

By mid-century, the early republic's populist religious movements were undergoing a metamorphosis from alienation to influence. Eleven of thirteen congressmen from Indiana in 1852 were Methodists, as were the

Fig. 15. Methodist preacher Peter Cartwright, ambrotype, date unknown

governor and one senator. As Methodist and Baptist churches grew wealthier, they built substantial sanctuaries, installed organs, rented out pews and demanded college-trained ministers. In 1855, Christ Church in Pittsburgh built the first Gothic edifice of American Methodism. Daniel A. Payne, who became bishop of the African Methodist Episcopal church in 1852 and later president of Wilberforce University, worked to improve the education of black ministers and the quality of black worship. For Payne this meant suppressing such folk elements as dancing, shouting, and clapping.[2] In the South, an evangelical quest for respectability was even more successful. In many places Baptist and Methodist churches became the very pillars of the establishment. Leading citizens linked their interests with those of upwardly mobile preachers to create a ministerial ideal of learning and polish.[3]

The allure of respectability dampened the original fire of the religious populists. Many second-generation Baptists, Methodists, and Disciples yearned to recover a place of influence and respect, and they directed their finest efforts toward building educational institutions. Yet giant plates beneath the religious terrain had shifted, and the environment for churches was never the same. In three ways the denominational landscape in America bears the mark of the new nation's democratic upheavals. First, the efforts of insurgent groups leavened established churches. The "New Measures" of Charles Finney, for example, transferred aggressive Methodist techniques to the Presbyterians. Second, insurgent movements themselves could not escape the allure of respectability. Nathan Bangs, a dominant Methodist leader in the generation after Asbury, symbolized a movement's hunger for legitimation, intellectual respect, and cosmopolitan influence. Religious populism thus enhanced social mobility even if it came as an unintended consequence realized by second-generation adherents. Finally, a swing toward formalization invited a backlash of populist dissent. New generations of religious firebrands had ready access to democratic vocabularies and populist methods; and in America their efforts have rarely been denied a receptive audience.

The Leaven of Democratic Persuasions

The most surprising thing about the 1837 schism of the Presbyterian church is that the church had held together so long. No ecclesiastical structure is infinitely flexible, but during the 1820s American heirs of John Calvin stretched to the limit their system of presbyteries, synods, and assemblies. A generation before, matters had been simpler. Presbyterians such as Alexander Campbell and Barton W. Stone simply walked away from a church that attempted to impose creedal orthodoxy and synodical authority. During the first decade of the century, leaders of the Cumberland presbytery had parted company with the synod of Kentucky.[4]

By the 1830s, in addition to smoldering distrust between Southerners and Northerners, Presbyterians were also competing with wildly diverse factions of the Reformed faith. Theological issues blazed as the resurgent Old School, led by Professor Charles Hodge of Princeton Theological Seminary, called the church back to doctrinal rigor and its confessional roots. The orthodox challenged the modified Calvinism of Nathaniel William Taylor and the "New Haven" theology. In the decade before 1837, Old School confessionalists brought heresy charges against three prominent ministers of this persuasion: George Duffield, Albert Barnes, and Lyman Beecher.

Presbyterian polity might have withstood these debates had they been confined to the contrasting theologies of Princeton and Yale. Yet bold and daring innovations in practice set the Old School proponents on edge. They saw dubious theology wedded to inflammatory practice, what one Princeton stalwart called "a union between Mars and Minerva." The abstractions of New Haven theology had suddenly come to life in "the coarse, bustling fanaticism of the New Measures."[5]

Charles Grandison Finney, a young lawyer from Adams, New York, gave Princeton theologians every reason to cringe. From the time of his conversion in 1821, his unexpected maneuvers kept respectable churchmen off balance. Self-taught, blunt, and immensely persuasive, Finney was successful as a volunteer lay missionary in towns along the Erie Canal. This success led the local Saint Lawrence Presbytery to ordain him as a minister in 1824, although he refused formal ministerial training and admitted that he had not even read the Westminster Confession. From 1825 to 1830, he stormed from obscurity into national prominence as the most talked-about and sought-after preacher since Whitefield. After phenomenally successful revival campaigns in towns of western New York, he accepted invitations to preach in Philadelphia and New York and then took his revival crusade back to Rochester for a decisive six-month stint in 1830.[6]

Orthodox Presbyterians were shocked that the world beat a path to Finney's doorstep. His methods were a jarring repudiation of century-old Calvinist ideals. He spoke in crude and vernacular speech. He used techniques of hard-sell persuasion such as the "anxious seat," a special bench in the front of the meeting hall for those who were concerned for the state of their souls. An overall atmosphere of informality, including the active participation of women, was part of his frenzied religious services, night after night. Finney's "irregular" methods, which Asahel Nettleton associated with "the ignoble vulgus,"[7] seemed to undercut the entire structure of ministerial authority.

Finney brazenly promoted his new system as a general remedy for the church's ills and depicted Calvinist orthodoxy as the church's chronic ailment. In his *Lectures on Revivals of Religion*, a series of weekly lectures in New York during 1835, Finney launched a blistering critique of Calvinist orthodoxy, going straight for the jugular of the Calvinist system. He denied the implicit authority of learning, mocked the impotence of carefully crafted written sermons, assaulted the "promiscuous jumble" of Calvinist theology—even borrowing a jingle from Lorenzo Dow—and decried the detached and dignified style of educated ministers. He railed at ecclesiastical bureaucracy, particularly the theological hairsplitting and heresy-hunting that had come to characterize Presbyterian conclaves: "These things in the Presbyterian church, their contentions and janglings are so ridiculous, so wicked, so outrageous, that no doubt there is a jubilee in hell every year, about the time of the meeting of the General Assembly."[8]

Finney called for a Copernican revolution to make religious life audience-centered. He despised the formal study of divinity because it produced dull and ineffective communication. He told ministers to throw out their notes, look their audience square in the face, and preach in a style that was colloquial, repetitious, conversational, and lively—"the *language of common life*." "Nothing is more calculated to make a sinner feel that religion is some mysterious thing that he cannot understand, than this mouthing, formal, lofty style of speaking, so generally employed in the pulpit."[9] In contrast, Finney praised the Methodists' example:

> Look at the Methodists. Many of their ministers are unlearned, in the common sense of the term, many of them taken right from the shop or the farm, and yet they have gathered congregations, and pushed their way, and won souls every where. Wherever the Methodists have gone, their plain, pointed and simple, but warm and animated mode of preaching has always gathered congregations. Few Presbyterian ministers have gathered so large assemblies, or won so many souls. Now are we to be told that we must pursue the same old, formal mode of doing things, amidst all these changes? As well might the North River be rolled back, as the world converted under such preaching. . . . We must have exciting, powerful preaching, or the devil will have the people, except what the Methodists can save.

In casting about for new persuasive methods, Finney suggested exploiting good ideas wherever they could be found. "What do the politicians do?" asked Finney. "They get up meetings, circulate handbills and pamphlets,

Fig. 16. Charles Finney and Elizabeth Atkinson Finney, daguerreotype, about 1850

blaze away in the newspapers, send their ships about the streets on wheels with flags and sailors, send coaches all over town, with handbills, to bring people up to the polls, all to gain attention to their cause and elect their candidate. . . . The object of our measures is to gain attention and you *must* have something new."[10]

Charles Finney is a crucial figure in American religious history. A bridge between cultures, he conveyed the indigenous methods of popular culture to the middle class. As a transitional figure, he introduced democratic modifications into respectable institutions. This upwardly mobile lawyer from small-town New York continued the dissent begun by what he called "ignorant Methodist and Baptist exhorters." To a remarkable extent Finney's experience and convictions resonate with the themes of insurgent Christianity that had flourished in New York's "Burned-Over District."

Finney began his own religious quest by denying the force of inherited religious authority. He relied upon his own enlightened, albeit theologically untutored, reason. In prolonged arguments about predestination with his Presbyterian pastor, George W. Gale, Finney argued that nothing should intervene between his own mind and the Scriptures:

> I found myself utterly unable to accept doctrine on the ground of authority. If I tried to accept those doctrines as mere dogmas, I could not do it. I could not be honest in doing it; I could not respect myself in doing it. Often when I left Mr. Gale, I would go to my room and spend a long time on my knees over my Bible. Indeed I read my Bible on my knees a great deal during those days of conflict, beseeching the Lord to teach me his own mind on those points. I had nowhere to go but directly to the Bible, and to the philosophy or workings of my own mind. I gradually formed a view of my own mind, as revealed in consciousness.[11]

Finney was influenced by Methodist revival practices, as Richard Carwadine has shown.[12] Keenly observant of their phenomenal success and at odds with Calvinistic orthodoxy, Finney felt free to define religious success by the Methodists' criteria. Like them, he made winning souls his highest priority. Toward that end he marshaled any talent, method, or institution to reach, meet the needs of, and inspire his audience.

For middle-class audiences, however, Finney trimmed away some of revivalism's rough edges. He preached on the same themes but with less ardor. Before lawyers, millers, and manufacturers he dressed "like a lawyer . . . before a court and jury . . . in an unclerical suit of gray." His revivals bore their greatest fruit among what Finney called "the highest classes of society": "My meetings soon became thronged with that class.

The lawyers, physicians, merchants, and indeed all the most intelligent people, became more and more interested, and more and more easily influenced."[13]

Finney's fifth-column effort brought revivalism into America's citadel of theological orthodoxy. This development is typical of a much broader cultural process at work. In an aggressively competitive society, Methodist and Baptist success was contagious. Democratic persuasions corroded elite ecclesiastical traditions just as they had the Federalist idea of "standing" for office.[14] Methodist inroads into New England, for instance, led the Standing Order to oppose them with one hand and to imitate them with the other. Methodist itinerant Billy Hibbard mocked Lyman Beecher for publicly denouncing Methodists while privately exhorting the Standing Order to preach like them.[15] Samuel Goodrich recalled a similar effort in his father's Ridgefield, Connecticut, church. Realizing that the Methodist "movement could not be arrested," Pastor Goodrich decided not to "breast the shock" but to imitate the competition: "He adopted evening meetings, first at the church and afterward at private houses. No doubt, he put more fervor into his Sabbath discourses. Deacons and laymen, gifted in speech, were called upon to pray and exhort, and tell experiences in the private meetings, which were now called *conferences*. A revival of religious spirit arose even among the orthodox."[16]

In his study of church and society in Baltimore, Terry D. Bilhartz has described "new measures" that Presbyterians introduced during the 1820s to keep pace with the burgeoning Methodists. The Presbyterians introduced personal testimonies, small prayer meetings, and camp-meeting choruses. They also recognized the need for direct, plain, and personal preaching. The Third Presbyterian Church was founded in 1822 to embody these more aggressive practices. In 1826, its pastor, W. C. Walton, infuriated the Old School by publishing a defense of revival methods. Like Finney, Walton argued that revivals were to be fostered by deliberate human activity.[17]

Ironically, orthodox churches in America exercised less control of their destiny than did their European counterparts, which were still wrestling with state interference. Although not subject to prince or parliament, American church leaders could not control popular leaders and urgent causes springing up in their midst. Within a culture committed to freedom of expression, the Methodists could not harness Lorenzo Dow; the German Reformed church, the Methodist sects; or the Presbyterians, Charles Finney. Creedal and liturgical orthodoxies were shunted to the fringes of American Protestant life while they gained prominence abroad: the Oxford Movement in England; the Free Church under Thomas Chalmers in Scotland; and the *Réveil* in the Netherlands, a strong confessional and pietist movement utterly opposed to the doctrine of popular sovereignty of the French Revolution.

The piety and confessionalism of Old School leader Charles Hodge parallels, in many respects, the Dutch neo-Calvinist revival in the middle of the nineteenth century. In Holland Abraham Kuyper was able to lead this movement to national prominence later in the century.[18] The sober voice of Charles Hodge, however, was hemmed in by popular persuasions, even within his own church. In America, where the theory of equality applied even to intellectual matters, acclaim for a revivalist such as Charles Finney assured him a place as a respected theologian and college president. Only in the South did Hodge's conservative theological spirit hold full sway—for reasons linked to less worthy efforts of an elite to forestall the implications of democracy. That embattled stance later divided the Presbyterian church again as it summoned its sons to battle.

The Allure of Respectability

Although he declined election as bishop of the Methodist church in 1832, Nathan Bangs left an indelible imprint upon the church in the generation after Francis Asbury. His early career was typical of those who served in Asbury's missionary band. Largely self-educated, Bangs spent his early childhood in Connecticut and his teenage years in rural New York. At twenty-one he moved to Canada and taught school in a Dutch community near Niagara. Troubled by the perplexities of Calvinism, Bangs came under the influence of Methodist itinerant James Coleman. He experienced a life-changing conversion and sanctification. Conforming to severest Methodist custom, he removed the ruffles from his shirts and cut his fashionable long hair. In 1801, a year after he joined the church and three months after he was approved as an exhorter, he was licensed to preach and given a circuit. For the next decade Bangs rode circuits from Niagara to Quebec and became the principal force in establishing Methodism in the lower Saint Lawrence valley.[19]

The New York Conference presented a challenge to Bangs in 1810 that profoundly altered the emphasis of his ministry. He was named "preacher in charge" of the five preachers, five preaching places, and two thousand members that comprised the Methodist circuit of New York City.[20] From that strategic location Bangs became a dominant influence in Methodist affairs—until the time of the Civil War, when Methodists in New York City boasted sixty churches and seventeen thousand members. Despite the Methodist rule of biennial change of appointment, Bangs never left New

York. His career and influence typified the allure of respectability facing insurgent religious movements. As their constituencies grew in wealth and social standing, it became difficult to retain their pastoral identity as defiant, alienated prophets. Bangs envisioned Methodism as a popular establishment, faithful to the movement's original fire but tempered with virtues of middle-class propriety and urbane congeniality. If Asbury's career represented Methodism's triumph as a populist movement, with control at the cultural periphery, then Bangs's career illustrates the centripetal tug of respectable culture. Dissenting paths have often, in America, doubled back toward learning, decorum, professionalism, and social standing.

From the time Nathan Bangs arrived in New York City, he worked to dampen the popular spontaneity of Methodist worship. "I witnessed," he said, "a spirit of pride, presumption, and bigotry, impatience of scriptural restraint and moderation, clapping of the hands, screaming, and even jumping, which marred and disgraced the work of God."[21] Bangs called the Methodists of New York together in the John Street Church and exhorted them to be more orderly in their social meetings. Later Bangs also opposed the spiritual songs of the camp meeting. He referred to them as "ditties" that "possessed little of the spirit of poetry and therefore added nothing to true intellectual taste."[22] He viewed his role much as his British counterpart Jabez Bunting did—as an overseer of a garden beset with the dangerous snake of disorder. Bangs's charge was to strike harder and harder with the whip of the *Discipline*. More order and decorum at the John Street Church prompted a large faction, led by Samuel and William Stillwell, to break away and to set up its own church. The occasion for the split was a plan, backed by Bangs, to rebuild the church in a grand, expensive style. It was a controversial move at best, as the *Discipline* instructed that church buildings "be built plain and decent . . . not more expensive than is absolutely necessary." The costly style of the building, which contained even a carpeted altar, rekindled the tension between what Bangs called downtown and uptown members. The plainer uptown folk, led by the Stillwells, rallied against the new building. They denounced the heavy-handed tactics of its clerical supporters as "departure from the primitive simplicity of Methodism."[23]

Bangs also threw his remarkable energy and political savvy into building powerful central agencies for the expanding Methodist church. After serving two years as the presiding elder for the New York Conference, he was elected in 1820 to be the agent of the Methodist Book Concern. This position kept him permanently in New York and provided a strategic base from which to promote Methodist publications, missions, Sunday schools, and educational institutions. Under his direction the Book Concern grew

Fig. 17. "The Rev. Nathan Bangs D.D.," engraving by Durand in *The Methodist Magazine and Quarterly Review*, 1830

from a struggling, debt-ridden agency without premises of its own to the largest publishing house in the world by 1860. Bangs reinvigorated the monthly *Methodist Magazine* and in 1826 launched the *Christian Advocate and Journal*. This weekly newspaper became an official organ of the church in 1828. It rapidly developed the largest circulation of any paper in the country—an estimated twenty-five thousand subscriptions. He helped found the missionary society of the Methodist Episcopal church and guided it for twenty years. He was also tireless in his efforts for the church's Sunday school union and was the first to use the powerful agency of the denominational press to promote required ministerial education.[24]

As Methodism's first major polemicist, theological editor, and historian, Nathan Bangs relentlessly advanced the cause of higher intellectual standards for the church. He was determined to "redeem its character from the foul blot cast upon it, not without some reason, that it had been indifferent to the cause of literature and science."[25] Bangs deplored Asbury's conclusion that the failure of early Methodist schools was a providential sign against Methodist attempts to found colleges. Embarrassed and apologetic for the "little progress we have hitherto made in general literature," Bangs aimed to make the church "'not be a whit behind the very chiefest' of the Churches in Christendom in the literary and theological eminence of her ministers." In 1830 Bangs transformed the monthly *Methodist Magazine* into a more serious and literary *Methodist Quarterly Review*. In this journal he hoped to "draw forth the most matured efforts of our best writers . . . and lead others to the cultivation of a similar taste." During his tenure as doorkeeper of Methodist thinking, Bangs's efforts accelerated the process by which many Methodists, particularly those in urban settings, shed their populist elements for the ranks of "influential" Christians. By 1844, even the bishops confessed that the church had all but sold its original birthright: "in some of the Conferences little or nothing remains of the itinerant system."[26]

This quest for respectability worked powerfully among second-generation leadership of insurgent movements such as the Methodists, the Baptists, and the Disciples. The uneducated Methodist itinerant Hope Hull (1785–1818), for instance, settled in Athens, Georgia, after its selection as the seat for the state university, so that his sons could have a liberal education. One of his sons became a lawyer and eventually Speaker of the Georgia House of Representatives; the other two sons became professors at Franklin College. With similar intent, Methodists domesticated the camp meeting, deemphasized its emotional exercises, and restricted its spontaneous exuberance. By the middle of the nineteenth century, Methodists removed their proscriptions on pew rentals, a move Peter Cartwright lamented as "a Yankee triumph."[27] Most important, in the three decades before the Civil War, the Methodists founded over thirty colleges in nineteen different states, the Baptists over twenty colleges in sixteen states. Many of these institutions provided a rudely democratic version of liberal-arts education. Although they held collegiate charters, they provided secondary-level instruction. Even so, the passion of Methodists and Baptists to have their own colleges reflects the quest for respect that could drive whole denominations.[28]

This growing civility in popular denominations increased interdenominational cooperation but accentuated internal differentiation. Respectable Methodists and Baptists found they had much in common with revivalist Presbyterians even if they achieved common ground by different routes. At the same time, this shift toward formality had great potential for creating controversy and strife within popular denominations. The antimission movement is a good illustration of how increased respectability and centralization reinforced tensions between localists and cosmopolitans, primitivists and centralizers, and rural and urban interests.

In the long run, fault lines of class, education, and social status within a single denomination may have been more significant than sectional tensions, even between northern and southern churches. Despite the regional schisms in their churches, differences between the Methodist Nathan Bangs, the Baptist Whig Francis Wayland, and the "gentlemen theologians" of the South were not that great, as Wayland ruefully noted concerning the 1845 division in the Baptist church. He observed that the Southern Baptist Convention was led by men representing the very best of enlightened southern life: "governors, judges, congressmen, and other functionaries of the highest dignity." Churches and religious leaders that flourished on the fringes of southern society, for example, those upland whites who defiantly retained their own councils, deserve greater study. Bertram Wyatt-Brown suggests that exploring their religious convictions will reveal the "confused internal cleavage between the folkways of the poor and their social betters, a conflict that belies the notion of a monolithic southern cultural unity in opposition to a northern counterpart."[29]

In the North, similar tensions related to social status played a key role in the political upheaval within the Methodist church during the 1820s. This turmoil led to the formation of the Methodist Protestant church. In Massachusetts, for example, a local preacher was expelled for clashing with a congregation over the construction of a new chapel. Claiming to speak for the "plain, meek, humble, and old-fashioned Methodist," as opposed to the "gay, assuming proud, new-fashioned" ones, he thundered against ostentation.[30] Furthermore, Nicholas Snethen and other leaders of the Methodist

Protestants employed the rhetoric of democracy with telling effect to stigmatize the hierarchy of Methodism. Similarly, an intense commitment to local autonomy kept Baptists in such states as Kentucky, Tennessee, and Missouri absolutely opposed to state, much less national, organization. When infrequent conventions were held, "sovereign and independent" churches sent messengers rather than delegates to ensure that the convention could not claim "a single attribute of power or authority over any church or association."[31] In the American religious economy, moves toward dignity, solemnity, and gentility were sure to bring a swift and strident challenge. New sets of insurgents had ready access to the visions of apostolic simplicity that had inspired their parents and grandparents in the faith.

Firebrands of Democracy

The formalization of revivalistic Protestantism in the two decades before the Civil War was part of a larger trend to bring discipline and consolidation to a culture marked by experimentation and novelty.[32] The creative ferment that had given rise to a welter of new movements began to cool. Religious denominations went about the process of establishing routines and precedents and resolving questions of jurisdiction and doctrine. Second-generation ministers such as Nathan Bangs were eager to clamp a lid on the box of youthful enthusiasm that had been opened. Even Alexander Campbell came to the conclusion that one could not simply hand the Bible to a congregation and leave it to its own devices. "A book is not sufficient to govern the church," he confessed in 1841.[33] Bangs and Campbell reckoned that democracy in the church had gone far enough.

Yet in a country where democratic aspirations prevailed, holding the line was easier said than done. Powerful, self-made leaders continued to rise within their movements. They came to prominence on a wave of popular acclaim, and their democratic appeal was difficult to squelch. These firebrands called their followers back to the first principles of the movement and noted how far the current generation had fallen. Their language and tone matched that of their audience and of its local concerns. In these respects they competed far more effectively than could far-away and cosmopolitan denominational leaders.

A backlash of democratic firebrands confronted respectable Baptists, Methodists, and Disciples throughout the middle decades of the nineteenth century. David L. Rowe has suggested that the Millerites were able to sweep so many Baptists into Adventism because the Millerites' indictment of Baptist luxury and clericalism. "What a great change in our ministry within 30 years," observed William Miller in 1837, "The present are no more like the past than a dandy is like a farmer in a striped shirt and woolen frock. . . . What do we see? A modern dandy dressed 'cap a pie.' A 50 dollar cloak. A 30$ cap. A 20$ vest. 15$ boots and a safety chain worth 75$ or 100$. This is a modern Baptist classical Priest. O God!" Miller went on to say that preaching had become "no more than a trade" peopled by the "great, the learned, the eloquent, the popular, the man pleasing" and that the graduates of Hamilton College embellished their sermons with classical phrases but knew little of the Bible.[34]

The Methodists were also not immune to disruption from dissenting charismatic leaders. The crusading abolitionists Orange Scott and La Roy Sunderland defied the bishops' authority to their faces with a journal, the *True Methodist*. When Scott, Sunderland, and several thousand followers withdrew from the church in 1842 to found the Wesleyan Methodist church, they rallied around the causes of antislavery and pure Wesleyanism, especially sanctification. A decade later, Benjamin Titus Roberts, a powerful preacher in Buffalo, New York, championed the cause of plain rural people, or "Nazarites," against the urban establishment, the so-called Regency. Roberts denounced the church's pew-rental system, its intellectualism, and its clerical tyranny. When he was censored by the church in 1858, lay "bands" sprang to his defense. On the eve of the Civil War, Roberts formed the Free Methodist church and was joined in that effort by the forces of another popular prophet, John Wesley Redfield. A holiness revival preacher from Illinois, Redfield sought to preserve the original emotional fire of the camp meeting.[35] In the southern highlands an equally fiery Methodist parson and editor, William G. Brownlow, railed against Presbyterians, Baptists, missionary societies, and in the end slaveholders in his self-proclaimed pursuit of life, liberty, and the pursuit of happiness.[36] Independent-minded leaders such as these kept Methodism's undercurrents churning even as the mainstream flowed calmly toward respectability.

The loose coalition of Disciple churches associated with Alexander Campbell retained an even more unstable ethos in the second generation. One participant described it as "a morbid fondness for controversy."[37] Campbell's two most promising heirs, Robert Richardson of Bethany College and the *Millennial Harbinger*, and Tolbert Fanning of Franklin College and the *Christian Review*, disagreed so violently over the movement's direction that they broke off all discussion. Two other second-generation leaders, Jesse B. Ferguson and John Thomas, were hounded out of the Disciples after the one taught spiritualism and the second, novel views on baptism.[38]

Even the Mormons were beset with a spate of strong-minded individualists jostling for leadership. This culminated in a revolt against Joseph
Smith in Kirtland, Ohio, and a scramble for power after his assassination.
Brigham Young prevailed in Nauvoo in 1844, using the democratic art of
persuasion to its full advantage. In doing so he consigned to historical
shadows a fascinating, if eccentric, set of characters that refused to brook
his authority. Among them were Sidney Rigdon, James J. Strang, John C.
Bennett, Lyman Wight, and Benjamin Winchester.[39]

The presence of such magnetic figures, often at the periphery of
denominational traditions, underscores two realities about the character of
popular religion in a democratic culture. The first is the ambivalent, even
paradoxical, character of democratic leadership. Whether in politics or
religion, self-made leaders who gained prominence by appealing to the
hopes, fears, and interests of plain folks have walked a fine line between
authentic servanthood and exploitive demagoguery. More accurately, a
tradition of populist leaders embodied these qualities in complex, intermingled ways. Alexander Campbell championed the interests of simple
Christians and insignificant congregations against concentrated ecclesiastical privilege, yet he became one of the wealthiest men in western Virginia
and ruled with an iron hand. The conjunction of democratic aspiration and
authoritarian style is a characteristic pattern of populist cultures, religious
and political, both in the North and the South. The paradoxically admi-
rable and destructive careers of Tom Watson, Huey Long, and Father
Coughlin, like those of early Fundamentalist and Pentecostal spellbinders,
illustrates the depth of this strain within American popular culture and its
leaders.[40]

The presence of these democratic religious leaders also points to the
pervasive quality of dissent in American Christianity. Their rise to influence, often premised on appeals to a sense of embattled localism, reflects
cultures that have been highly diverse, loosely structured, and greatly
decentralized. In building centers of power within specific denominations,
populist preachers have been able to draw on fears of concentrated and
hidden power that fueled the American Revolution and the Jeffersonian
and Jacksonian assault on monopoly. This persistent localism in religion
has blunted the characteristic affinity of Western Christianity for the mores
of high culture. In America fragments of the church have been strewn up
and down the social ladder. David Martin has suggested that Americans
took a British invention, the dissenting denomination, and transformed it
from a minor motif into a dominant theme. He argues that the vitality of
American Christianity can be correlated with this high degree of pluralism
and dissent: "Disassociate religion from social authority and high culture,

let religion adapt to every status group through every variety of pulsating sectarianism. The result is that nobody feels ill at ease with his religion, that faith is distributed along the political spectrum, that church is never the axis of dispute."[41]

From this vantage point, one can more easily understand how popular culture in the early republic became manifestly Christian, even if in diverse and unexpected ways. Tocqueville understood well the difference between Christianity in America, firmly linked to democracy, and that of Europe, which after the French Revolution dismissed any taint of liberty, equality, and fraternity. "By allying itself with political power," he said of European Christianity, "religion augments its authority over a few and forfeits the hope of reigning over all. . . . The unbelievers of Europe attack the Christians as their political opponents rather than as their religious adversaries; they hate the Christian religion as the opinion of a party much more than as an error of belief; and they reject the clergy less because they are representatives of the Deity than because they are the allies of government."[42]

The democratic orientation of American Christianity, audience centered, intellectually open to all, organizationally fragmented, and popularly led, meant that the church prospered in this vast expanse of land, even as loud and competing preachers stormed America's once-hallowed sanctuary. With exuberance and novelty, in word and song, they reshaped Christianity's solemn message in idioms that people cherished as their own.

CHAPTER EIGHT

Epilogue: The Recurring Populist Impulse in American Christianity

They are willing to have religion, as they are willing to have laws; but they choose to make it for themselves. They do not object to paying for it, but they like to have the handling of the article for which they pay. As the descendants of the Puritans and other godly Protestants, they will submit to religious teaching, but as Republicans they will have no priestcraft. . . . They say their prayers, and then seem to apologize for doing so, as though it were hardly the act of a free and enlightened citizen, justified in ruling himself as he pleases. All this to me is rowdy. I know no other word by which I can so well describe it.

ANTHONY TROLLOPE, *1863*

The vengeance with which religious issues have again entered the public arena illustrates what pollsters long have known: the United States contains more citizens who value religion than other western industrial societies. This odd combination of modernity and religion defies conventional wisdom, which suggests that secularity and socioeconomic development are positively related. Such manifest religiosity in an advanced industrial and technological society raises interesting questions about the nature of popular religious movements in the United States and about the contrast between American popular culture and that of other western industrial nations.[1]

Studies show that two out of three adults in America still maintain fairly strong religious beliefs. In a recent Gallup poll that asked how important religion should be in life, 41 percent of young Americans (ages eighteen to twenty-four) answered "very important." In France, Germany, and Great Britain, fewer than 10 percent of young people gave the same response. On any given Sunday morning, over 40 percent of the population in the United States attends religious services. In Canada and Australia this number tails off to about 25 percent; in England to about 10 percent; and in Scandinavia to around 5 percent—despite the fact that 95 percent of the Scandinavian population is confirmed in the church. Statistically, at least, the United States is God's country.[2]

In comparing the United States and other western democracies, particularly England, three features about this country stand out: the vitality of religion among ordinary people, the continuing prominence of populist religious leaders, and the vitality of mass democratic movements that reflect the charisma and organizational skills of these leaders. In the realms of high culture—in the best universities, in the arts, and in literary circles—religious values are probably no more pervasive in the United States than in England. And plausible arguments can be made that, at all levels of American society, the juggernaut of secularism rolls on, pressing religious belief into smaller, less consequential territory. As one moves down the social scale, however, the contrast between American religious vitality and British secularity becomes greater. During the twentieth century Britain has experienced what Alan Gilbert has called "the almost complete dechristianization of the British working classes"—the thorough estrangement of most common folk from the Anglican church and other denominations.[3] Among working and lower-middle-class Americans, however, religion seems to be thriving. The recent comprehensive study of religion in Muncie, Indiana, "Middletown III," carried out forty years after the classic study *Middletown* by Robert and Helen Lynd, reveals a striking increase over this time in the religious practices of working-class people. The study shows a dramatic gain in the per capita numbers of largely working-class churches, a rise in regular church attendance, and a two hundred percent increase in working-class family income contributed to churches. This evidence led Theodore Caplow to conclude that at a popular level America is more pious than it was two generations ago.[4]

An equally distinctive feature of the religious scene in modern America is the presence of a remarkable set of popular leaders, persons who derive their authority not from their education or stature within major denominations, but from the democratic art of persuasion. These gospel ministers, remarkably attuned to popular opinion, continue to rise from obscurity to command significant audiences and to organize movements and churches around them. Modern American populist religious leaders such as Billy Graham, Kathryn Kuhlman, Oral Roberts, Robert Schuller, Jimmy Swaggart, Jerry Falwell, and Pat Robertson continue a long tradition of democratic religious authority. The significance of these individuals is less their own rise to prominence and more the decentralized, grassroots, and populist religious cultures of which they are the most visible representatives. The English sociologist David Martin comments that while both England and America share an anti-intellectual populism, in

America such populists have worked within rather than without the walls of the church.[5]

In the eighteenth century, the dissenting priest George Whitefield electrified American as well as English audiences. After 1800 this pattern reversed, and Americans crossed the Atlantic to gain a hearing among the British. American Methodists Lorenzo Dow, James Caughey, and others were highly effective in Great Britain, as were numerous Millerite and Mormon preachers. This tradition has continued through the travels of American revivalists spanning from Charles Finney and Dwight Moody to Billy Graham.[6] While English intellectuals such as G. K. Chesterton, C. S. Lewis, J. B. Phillips, and John A. T. Robinson have written books read widely by American Christians, it is American preachers who have mastered the common touch on both sides of the Atlantic.

The presence of these popular religious leaders reflects a third characteristic of American Christianity: the recurring phenomenon of religious movements firmly identified with popular culture. As in American social and political movements, American Christianity has gained strength from opposition to centralized authority and demands for a dispersal of power.[7] Baptist, Methodist, Millerite, Mormon, Holiness, Pentecostal, Jehovah's Witness, and Fundamentalist movements have all shared an anti-elitist and anticentralist ideology. In their passion to communicate with and mobilize ordinary people, to challenge them to take responsibility for their destiny and to educate themselves, these movements resemble a mass democratic movement such as Populism.[8] American Christianity has always been most dynamic at the periphery of high culture, where these movements are fed by the passions of ordinary people and express traditional values of localism, direct democracy, ruralism, and individualism. The inherent power of these decentralized movements springs from their ability to communicate with people at the culture's edge and to give them a sense of personal access to knowledge, truth, and power.[9]

How does one begin to explain the ongoing religious vitality found in America and the continuity of populist religious leadership and democratic movement-building? What kind of long-term cultural mores have allowed the roots of Christianity to sink so deeply within popular culture? It is certainly not that Americans have developed a genius for ecclesiastical organization. The United States Army and General Motors may attribute their success to a centrally directed, well-honed bureaucracy, but American Christianity has muddled along in a state of anarchic, free-market pluralism. Dietrich Bonhoeffer once commented that it had been granted to America, less than to any nation on earth, to realize the visible unity of the church of God. Nor can the success of American Christianity be attributed to the prestige of its clergy. Although such modern religious leaders as Billy Graham and Theodore Hesburgh have been able to win respect, American clergymen have less prestige than do their colleagues in other western democracies.[10] The shadow of Elmer Gantry still lingers. Neither can Christianity here attribute its strength to an ability to make faith plausible to the modern world. European Protestant churches for at least a century have made it possible for their parishioners to embrace modern ways of thinking without a twinge of conscience. American churchleaders who attempt to make peace with intellectual currents of this age, however, may find their parishioners still fretting about evolution, secular humanism, prayer in the schools, and the kinds of books that libraries should own.

What then is the driving force behind American Christianity if it is not the quality of its organization, the status of its clergy, or the power of its intellectual life? I have suggested that a central force has been its democratic or populist orientation. America has lived in the shadow of a democratic revolution and the liberal, competitive culture that followed in its wake. Forms of popular religion characteristic of that cultural system bound paradoxical extremes together: a reassertion of the reality of the supernatural in everyday life linked to the quintessentially modern values of autonomy and popular sovereignty.[11] American Christians reveled in freedom of expression, refused to bow to tradition or hierarchy, jumped at opportunities for innovative communication, and propounded popular theologies tied to modern notions of historical development. No less than Tom Paine or Thomas Jefferson, populist Christians of the early republic sought to start the world over again. By raising the standard "no creed but the Bible," Christians in America were the foremost proponents of individualism even as they expected the open Bible to replace an age of sectarian rivalry with one of primitive harmony. Like the egalitarian credo of the early republic, this vision has taken a powerful hold on the American imagination despite the disparity between the quest for unity and actual religious fragmentation and authoritarianism.

These democratic impulses were also resurgent at the turn of the twentieth century when the American nation shifted sharply toward bureaucratic order and centralized professional authority.[12] Mainstream Protestants quickly adjusted to the spirit of a new age. Taking cues from academics and other professionals they increasingly defined leadership as an academic or bureaucratic function. With Progressivism's penchant for rational study, efficient planning, and the role of the learned professional, liberal Protestants attempted to sweep the sawdust of folk traditions and rural backwardness from the church, preferring instead toleration, respectability, and professional esprit.[13]

As America stood on the brink of the modern world, other Protestants resisted these efforts to consolidate and rationalize the church. The constellation of groups that came to be known as Fundamentalism, the Holiness movement, and Pentecostalism all shared certain outlooks. They were dismissed by pundits of the modern world as a vanishing breed, holdovers from an age of rural simplicity. For all their theological quarrels with liberalism—and with each other—these insurgent movements challenged the spirit of the age using a common resource, perhaps the only one available as their influence waned in the centers of mainline denominational life: by instinct and conviction they reverted to those populist techniques that had characterized American popular religion for over a century. Their power in the modern world lies in their character as democratic persuasions.

Fundamentalism, the Holiness movement, and Pentecostalism were grass-roots movements with democratic structure and spirit. All were extremely diverse coalitions, dominated by scores of self-appointed and independent-minded religious leaders. Had not dominant personalities sounded an alarm and begun building their own popular constituencies, these movements would not have come into existence.[14] The generic name that came to be associated with each of these coalitions masks their pluralism and decentralization. In the United States alone, Pentecostalism, "*the popular movement*" of the twentieth century, has expressed itself in some three hundred denominational varieties. Even the larger Pentecostal denominations, such as the Assemblies of God, began as diverse coalitions that tended to view church organization as necessary evils and that retained power largely in local hands.[15]

Similarly, Fundamentalism emerged as a federation of cobelligerents opposed to centralizing ecclesiastical authority. Their institutional legacy was a loose network of independent churches, conferences, foreign mission agencies, Bible colleges, publishers, and radio stations. In Fundamentalist hands, even Presbyterian polity veered sharply toward congregational autonomy.[16] Likewise, the confluence of Holiness associations that formed the Church of the Nazarene in Pilot Point, Texas, in 1908 departed from Methodist tradition by giving final authority to the local congregation. Because of their goal to preach holiness to the poor, the Nazarenes protested expensive church buildings and promoted aggressive evangelism and exuberant religious services, using simple choruses and popular hymns that would be successful in "getting the glory down."[17] Bishop William

Taylor, for whom Taylor University was named in 1890, carried out his far-flung missionary enterprises in opposition to official Methodist agencies. Labeled an "incorrigible individualist" by Methodist authorities, Taylor gained support and new missionary recruits at Holiness camp meetings from Maine to Oregon.[18]

At the same time, these movements went the second mile to make the Christian faith fully accessible to common people. Theology was not to be an arcane science mediated by an educated elite. "We have the Bible for everything," claimed the Pentecostal leader A. J. Tomlinson, "and we have no creeds, rituals, or articles of faith."[19] "This is a layman age," declared the Fundamentalist C. I. Scofield, whose notes to the King James Bible became a best-seller for Oxford University Press; they offered to tens of thousands the hope of understanding the Bible for themselves. A common Fundamentalist complaint about higher criticism of the Bible was that it removed "the Word of God from the common people by assuming that only scholars can interpret it."[20] Even when Fundamentalists set out to defend the truth, their temptation was to rally large constituencies to the cause rather than to prepare for scholarly exchange. William Hutchison has noted that the movement's signal attempt to defend supernatural Christianity, *The Fundamentals*, published between 1910 and 1915, was more a warning to the general Christian public than a scholarly grappling with the roots of modernism. It seemed more important to the project's backers to distribute three hundred thousand copies of *The Fundamentals* free of charge than to meet the liberals on their own ground in theological debate.[21]

Each of these movements also explained its own significance in familiar terms, drawing heavily upon restorationist and millenarian themes. However differently they defined the essence of "New Testament" Christianity, the Holiness movement, Fundamentalists, and Pentecostals shared a passion for recovering the "pure fountain" and were equally dismissive of the church's legacy over twenty centuries. Renouncing all denominations and creeds, the Holiness preacher Daniel S. Warner forged a new movement, the Church of God (Anderson, Indiana), in order to restore the apostolic church. Similarly, the Pentecostal leader A. J. Tomlinson proclaimed that for centuries the truth "has been buried beneath the debris of custom, tradition, and unbelief." "Creeds, articles of faith, systems doctrines, false churches are even now quivering, ready to fall. The True Church of God is going to rise soon above the great host of modern churchianity, and shine out in her glory and beauty with conquering tread."[22] This ahistorical bent is reflected in an intense millenarian expectancy common to all three movements.[23]

These groups also centered their life around the issue of popular communication. Although their constituents ranged from the lower middle class to the desperately poor and from the rural south to midwestern cities, their message and style resonated to the rhythms of popular culture and appealed to audiences drawn from the lower half of the social scale. While Progressive prophets attacked structures that permitted poverty and need, it was Pentecostals, Nazarenes, and Fundamentalists that founded churches among the dirt-poor farmers of Oklahoma, the automobile workers of Detroit, and the millhands of Gastonia.[24] Although these movements had their share of charlatans and autocrats, they were remarkably effective in forging moral communities among the poor, the sick, the ignorant, and the elderly—those most vulnerable in a rapidly industrializing society. Pentecostalism was eminently successful, Grant Wacker has argued, because it made "meaning for this world and salvation for the next . . . available to everyone, however ignoble."[25]

Like early Methodism, these movements opened educational and leadership opportunities to common people. The movements initiated a massive, if largely unnoticed, educational effort by founding at least two-hundred-fifty Bible schools in the twentieth century. Seldom barring anyone who possessed a rudimentary education, these schools replenished churches with leaders who bypassed normal professional certification. These institutions of popular education ensured that the ministry in America would remain an extremely diverse profession not subject to the self-regulation of an educated elite bent on common standards of certification.[26] In the heartland, furthermore, many Americans retained an abiding conviction that preachers, above all, should be persons blessed with the common touch rather than with oracles of high culture. "Don't use big words for show," advised the founder of a Churches of Christ Bible college, "make the weakest understand you. . . . Don't be haughty; be a man of the people."[27]

These populist instincts were only reinforced by Fundamentalism's loss of influence within mainline denominations and by the ridicule it received in centers of high culture—most noticeably after the Scopes trial concerning evolution in 1925.[28] Antagonistic to modern intellectual and institutional arrangements, populist Protestants built their own extensive networks of seminaries, liberal arts colleges, Bible schools, youth organizations, foreign mission boards, publishing houses, conferences, and camps. These vital subcultures nourished communities of believers as cognitive minorities, self-consciously standing against the bastions of high culture but thoroughly in tune with the attitudes of average Americans. Above all, the leaders of these movements excelled as communicators and entrepreneurial organizers. In spite of its aloofness from twentieth-century thought and its disparagement of church traditions, populist Protestantism was immensely energetic, resourceful, and inventive; in an increasingly bureaucratic society, it grew in response to the appeals of inspired individualists.

These tendencies were most evident in the Fundamentalist and Pentecostal use of radio broadcasting. From the 1920s onward, such minority religious groups outdid mainline Protestants and Catholics in taking to the airways. Their efforts were largely a grass-roots phenomenon. The radio station of Pentecostal leader Aimee Semple McPherson, the first American woman to hold a broadcast license, maintained the second largest listening audience in Los Angeles during the 1920s. Similarly, a study of broadcasting in Chicago in 1932 determined that Fundamentalists accounted for 246 of 290 weekly quarter-hours of religious programming. By 1940, Charles E. Fuller carried his "Old Fashioned Revival Hour" on 456 stations—the largest prime-time distribution of any radio program in the country—with an estimated weekly audience of twenty million people. By the end of World War II, Fundamentalists and Pentecostals sustained over sixteen hundred different radio programs, most of them productions of individual preachers on local radio stations.[29] These efforts certainly laid the foundation for the dominance of American evangelicals in modern religious broadcasting—the movement currently responsible for an estimated 85 percent of all Protestant religious broadcasting in the United States and for 75 percent of Protestant broadcasting worldwide.[30]

Populist strains have also been resilient among black Christian groups in the twentieth century. The Church of God in Christ, founded in Memphis in 1897, has become the largest black Pentecostal sect in the world and the second largest Pentecostal denomination in the United States. Equally significant has been the continuing presence of self-made preachers whose independent or loosely affiliated churches resist the embrace of modern bureaucracy and intellectual respectability. The pioneering study *The Negro's Church* by Benjamin Elijah Mays and Joseph William Nicholson (1933) indicates that black Christianity remained a dynamic popular movement as blacks moved into urban areas. Churches were decentralized and unsophisticated but keenly attuned to the religious expressions of ordinary people. Among two thousand black church buildings identified in twelve cities, Mays and Nicholson found that almost eight hundred were storefront churches. Less than ten of these were identified with the three regularly established Methodist denominations. The study's examination of 425 urban black pastors revealed less than 20 percent with a college education. Twenty percent of these ministers had previously worked as farmers or laborers; a number of others listed previous occupations as carpenters, porters, mechanics, waiters, tailors, and barbers. Mays and Nicholson found that, despite repeated schisms and a heavy burden of debt, the black churches retained a "thorough democratic spirit." Under local control, black churches offered, above all, a haven for the downtrodden: "The opportunity found in the Negro church to be recognized, and to be 'somebody,' has stimulated the pride and preserved the self-respect of many Negroes who would have been entirely beaten down by life, and possibly completely submerged."[31]

The resurgence of Fundamentalism in the last twenty years is a further example of a populist crusade, a revolt of people who feel they are being disfranchised from the core institutions of American culture. Robert Wuthnow has noted that the changing relation between religious commitment and educational attainment has been an important ingredient in this upsurge. At the very time that science, technology, and advanced education have gained a more prominent role in American society, educated persons have become more likely to turn their backs on traditional religious values. Studies show that those most ready to jettison traditional religious constraints are precisely those whose cultural authority is rising. These are the so-called new class of professionals that generate the symbols that define social reality—writers, artists, intellectuals, professors, journalists, and media people. As late as the 1950s, studies show that college-educated people held about the same level of religious belief and levels of participation as the less educated. Since the 1960s, however, social division has arisen along educational lines. Now the college-educated are less likely to hold strongly to tenets of their faith. The correlation between advanced education and nontraditional views on abortion, homosexuality, prayer in the schools, and the teaching of evolution has only intensified agitation over these concerns in the religious heartland.[32]

Seismic changes in the treatment of these issues in the public arena has stirred up a new generation of populist religious leaders. Believing that they have little reason to trust scholars and experts to clarify important religious and ethical issues, religious populists spend their energies rallying the faithful and inviting them to arbitrate complicated religious and moral questions for themselves. In this sense, the people continue to serve as custodians of their own beliefs, communicating them in understandable terms. Those who most vigorously protest the danger of secular humanism or the teaching of evolution in the schools are often least capable of winning the right to be heard by twentieth-century intellectuals.

It is these populist forms of Christianity that are so foreign to European and British Christians: the gospel music, colloquial preaching, unrefined preachers, aggressive communication, unsanctioned institutions, dynamic growth, and, recently, overt political mobilization. These groups continue to define themselves against the mainstream even if they have occupied a position of social and political dissent to the right rather than to the left of learned and respectable culture. They assume a conservative stand in opposition to liberal secular and church elites. Yet their instincts are clearly populist rather than those of upper-class conservatism.

The resulting polarization in American Christianity is deeper and more pervasive than the most sharply defined theological debate. These are contrasting systems that define leadership by different criteria and that shape their values in different social orbits. One system is oriented to the norms of high culture, while the other defines itself in relation to popular values.[33] The leadership of mainline Protestant denominations is irresistibly pulled toward values and attitudes prevalent in the modern academic world. It values respectable, progressive, and inclusive faiths that can achieve plausibility in that environment. In the world of higher education, theologians and church leaders no longer operate from a position of strength. To avoid being considered second-class citizens, they are pressured to make accommodations to the secular definition of values at the core of the university.

By contrast, Fundamentalists and Pentecostals share all the virtues and vices of popular culture. They have sustained their own coherent subcultures that excel in popular mobilization, leadership training, mass education (from kindergarten through college), family counseling, publications of every description, and mass media—films, radio, and television. These systems are still populist through and through, reflecting the deepest convictions of their own constituencies and anointing new leaders by virtue of their popular appeal. Following the long tradition of democratic Christianity in America, Fundamentalists and Pentecostals reject modernity as it is expressed in high culture but remain stalwart defenders of modern attitudes as they build popular constituencies with the most innovative techniques. They will not surrender to learned experts the right to think for themselves. For two centuries Americans have refused to defer sensitive matters of conscience to the staid graduates of Harvard, Yale, and Princeton. They have taken faith into their own hands and molded it according to the aspirations of everyday life. American Christianity continues to be powered by ordinary people and by the contagious spirit of their efforts to storm heaven by the back door.

Redefining the Second Great Awakening: A Note on the Study of Christianity in the Early Republic

Gordon S. Wood has called the early republic "the time of greatest religious chaos and originality in American history." W. R. Ward has written that the period 1790 to 1830 is "the most important single generation in the modern history not merely of English religion but of the whole Christian world."[1] Unfortunately, there are more generalizations and less solid data on the dynamics of American religion in this period than in any other in our history. The most dramatic contours of the landscape remain to be sketched: the rise of the camp meeting, the African-American embrace of Christianity, and the explosive rise of the popular religious press. Scant attention has been paid to the rise of religious folk music in American culture, northern and southern, black and white. Why do we have no modern critical biography of the indomitable Francis Asbury, one of the most revered and influential figures in the early republic? Neither are there serious biographies of Alexander Campbell or Barton W. Stone, and the story of the Disciples of Christ, that most American of denominations, has been left to the province of denominational history.

The most striking void concerns Methodism's rise to prominence. The Methodist Episcopal Church grew from fourteen thousand members and forty-two circuits in 1784 to over a million members served by 3,988 itinerants and 7,730 local preachers in 1844. As a denomination it was nearly one-half size larger than any other Protestant body.[2] Interpreting such a movement is a daunting task, but American religious historians have devoted surprisingly little attention to the subject. Their British counterparts, however, in the wake of historians Elie Halévy and E. P. Thompson, continue to wrestle with the broad social and political significance of British Methodism.[3]

There are several reasons why the religious history of the early national period remains elusive and uncharted. First, until recently historians have conventionally divided up American history by making the early republic an epilogue to the era of the Revolution or a prologue to the age of Jackson. Scholars have begun to correct this imbalance, but there is still a dearth of fine-grained studies of the early republic and of powerful interpretive frameworks in which to place them. Specifically, there is a lack of works that address the questions arising from the developments of this era. Works are needed that, in the words of Robert H. Wiebe, neither "push nor pull Americans" through this period but allow them "to walk at a human pace, experiencing a full complement of apathy, insight, and uncertainty as they go."[4]

A second and related reason that the subject remains fallow ground is that so many historians have concentrated on the relationship between religion and politics before the American Revolution. Over the last two decades, no single issue in all of American history has attracted more talent than that of linking the Great Awakening and the Revolution. Historians have traced more roots or anticipations of America's future identity to evangelical revivals than to any other single eighteenth-century source: American exceptionalism, nationalism, and individualism; the language, style, and organizational form of lower-class yearning and protest; and, most decidedly, the advent of American democracy.[5]

Aside from the merits of these arguments, a simple point can be made: if a decisive pattern of change reordered American religion before the Revolution, why invest effort ironing out the details? If the Great Awakening marks the unleashing of democratic religion, there is little compelling reason to sort through the complex and disparate sources that comprise the record of churches in the time of Francis Asbury, Alexander Campbell, and Joseph Smith. Given the imaginative power of such scholars as Alan Heimert, Rhys Isaac, Harry S. Stout, and Patricia Bonomi, it is understandable why other scholars continue to follow their lead, probing every nuance of evangelical interaction in the eighteenth century. At the same time, popular religion in the early republic has failed to catch the attention or spark the curiosity of historians seeking to address large and fundamental questions about the evolution of early American culture.

A third difficulty is that conventional contemporary religious histories retain a bias toward elite churches. Institutions that were at or near the center of culture have been the focus of study rather than movements at the culture's periphery. The danger, of course, is that we have ignored the most dynamic and characteristic elements of Christianity during this time: the displacement from power of the religious people of ideas by those who leaned toward popular culture; the powerful centrifugal forces that drove churches apart and gave new significance to local and grass-roots endeavors; and the stark emotionalism, disorder, extremism, and crudeness that accompanied expressions of the faith fed by the passions of ordinary people.

Why have historians failed to appreciate the influence of popular religion in a culture shifting from classical republican values to those of a vulgar democracy and entrepreneurial individualism? There are at least two explanations. First, during the last three decades, the quickened interest in religion as a cultural force has emerged within a broader historiographical tendency to downplay the social impact of the Revolution. Assuming that the War of Independence was primarily a contest for home rule, students of religion and society have seen the early republic as remarkably free of social conflict. They joined the assault on the Progressive interpretation and its depiction of the early republic as a time of marked change and conflict.[6] Along with Perry Miller, most scholars assumed that the Second Great Awakening confirmed "the American belief that the Revolution had not been at all revolutionary, but simply a protest of native piety against foreign impiety."[7]

Most historians giving an account of religion in the early republic point to the force of revivalism or the Second Great Awakening as the decisive causal factor in a complex situation. The danger in this approach is to make revivalism, like the Reformation, a great watershed that stops inquiry into the historical process exactly where it should begin.[8] An abstract category of interpretation has displaced the quest to locate events, the meaning of documents, and the motivations of historical actors in their original historical sockets.[9] Relying on revivalism as a principal agent of change has obscured the achievements of flesh-and-blood leaders and their dramatic strategies to forge new movements. It has also blurred the vastly different social functions the revival could assume for proponents as diverse as Lyman Beecher and Francis Asbury.

Equally confusing has been the interpretation of the Second Great Awakening as the attempt by traditional religious elites to impose social order upon a disordered and secularized society. In this view, revivalism reflects the attempt of fearful church leaders to salvage Protestant solidarity. In Perry Miller's words, the Second Great Awakening was the churches' attempt to assert "the unity of culture in pressing danger of fragmentation." "Revivalism succeeded where traditionalism had failed," noted Richard Hofstadter. "Emotional upheavals took the place of the coercive sanctions of religious establishments."[10] In a similar vein, scholars such as Clifford S. Griffin, John R. Bodo, Charles I. Foster, and Charles C. Cole, Jr., understood the Second Great Awakening as a conservative assertion of authority by ministers fearful of losing their traditional roles.[11] Although the theme of social control has waned in recent years, newer studies of the ministerial profession in the early republic have focused almost exclusively on clerical elites.[12] Even the most telling critic of the "social control" school has not complained about a preoccupation with Presbyterians and Congregationalists. Instead, she called for historians to avoid misrepresenting the motives and commitments of the clerical establishment.[13]

A second reason for the elitist cast of religious history in the early national period is that church historians from the more popular denominations have had reasons to sanitize their histories. Modern church historians have focused on those aspects of their own heritage linked to cultural enrichment, institutional cohesion, and intellectual respectability. William Warren Sweet has done more than any other single scholar in the twentieth century to promote the serious study of Methodists and Baptists on the frontier. He was committed, however, to a vision of these groups as bearers of civilization to the uncouth, unrestrained society of the frontier. Emphasizing the disastrous effects of migration upon civilization and culture, Sweet depicted evangelical denominations as bringing moral order and the first seeds of culture to a rampantly individualistic society. He emphasized how the churches brought order, education, and moral discipline to the frontier. In his hands even the camp meeting became a well-regulated institution. Sweet had little interest in evidence that hinted at radical shaking within the walls of Zion—that churches served as agents of liberation as well as of control.[14]

Other mainstream Protestant church historians in the twentieth century have also emphasized themes of Protestant solidarity and the church's role in taming the frontier. An unswerving commitment to the unity of the church has made it virtually impossible for church historians from Robert Baird and Philip Schaff to H. Richard Niebuhr and Winthrop Hudson to admit that God's ultimate plans could entail the splintering of churches.[15] In his book *The Great Tradition of the American Churches*, for instance, Winthrop Hudson suggests that the meaning of the American religious experience is the overcoming of sectarian fervor. In the face of disestablishment, he suggests that Protestants closed ranks and embarked upon a powerful counteroffensive to combat the forces of irreligion. In this scheme, there is plenty of room for Baptists and Methodists, but only as they shed sectarian dogmatism, ecstatic display, and aggressive proselytizing. Modern church historians, in short, have had difficulty identifying with dimensions of their own ecclesiastical heritage that are diametrically opposed to the modern embrace of intellectual, liturgical, and ecumenical respectability. Many enduring structures of American Christianity have been slighted because they seem least worthy of historical attention.[16]

Writing about the process of secularization, the English sociologist David Martin noted that dissent in America has become universalized. This theme has certainly not escaped church historians in the twentieth century, but the implications that Martin makes are strikingly different. Church historians tend to view the atomistic structure of American Christianity as a sign of deficiency. The general impression given is that fragmentation has been the besetting sin and crippling weakness of Christianity in this land. Turning such thinking on its head, Martin argues that the vitality of American religion is in precise correlation with the degree of pluralism and dissent present here.[17]

Religion in the early republic is often pictured, then, as a tame and subdued affair. The conservative functions of revivalism in the era of the Second Great Awakening are a common theme among scholars who have concentrated on Presbyterian and Congregational sources. This theme is also found among denominational historians of the frontier who wished to establish the respectability of their respective denomination, and among church historians of an ecumenical bent who emphasized themes of consolidation and toleration.

An additional reason that popular religious movements remain unexplored is surprising given the deep commitment of a new generation of social historians to understanding common people's lives in the age of capitalist transformation. While considerable attention has been focused on the changing nature of markets, on the decline of independent artisans and farmers, and on the rise of the American working class, little energy has gone into exploring the forces of insurgent religious movements.[18] This neglect stems both from the neo-Marxist preoccupation with the formation of social classes and from the assumption that religion is generally a conservative and pernicious force.[19] These studies fail to take into account that, for better or worse, the most powerful popular movements in the early republic were expressly religious. However powerful working-class organizations became in cities such as New York and Baltimore, their presence cannot compare with the phenomenal growth and collective élan of Methodists, Baptists, Christians, Millerites, and Mormons. It was lay preachers in the early republic who most effectively constructed new frames of reference for people living in a time of profound transition. Religious leaders from the rank and file were phenomenally successful in reaching out to marginal people, in promoting self-education and sheltering participants from the indoctrination of elite orthodoxies, in binding people together in supportive communities, and in identifying the aspirations of common people with the will of God.

Unfortunately, the most notable recent attempt to study the function of religion in an emerging industrial economy reinforces the opposite stereotype: that religion is primarily a tool of control and repression. Paul E. Johnson describes Charles E. Finney's revivalism in Rochester as "order-inducing, repressive, and quintessentially bourgeois." To Johnson, it was a middle-class solution to the problem of order in a manufacturing economy, a means by which entrepreneurs imposed discipline upon themselves and their workers.[20] Revivalism may have served these social functions in Rochester, but in other contexts—in nearby Palmyra, for example—new forms of religion also offered coherence and meaning to the very people that a burgeoning capitalist economy had shunted aside. In *A Shopkeeper's Millennium*, however, Paul Johnson reinforces the historiographical tradition of understanding the Second Great Awakening as the inverse of the Great Awakening. The impulse of revivalism, which in the age of Whitefield embodied strains of radical protest, becomes the handmaiden of authority in the age of Finney.

The cumulative effect of these interpretations has been to foreclose a broad range of questions about popular Christianity in the early republic. The canon of historical literature has left a vast array of popular sources gathering dust and has masked the broad cultural ferment over the meaning of freedom. This groundswell shook churches to the foundation during these years. Traditional elites, keenly aware of the fragile authority of "college learnt merchants of the gospel," scrambled to consolidate the position of orthodox churches.[21] The crisis that they confronted as ordinary people asserted their right to act on the religious scene was mounting confusion over the nature, purpose, and function of the church. Nourished by sources as contradictory as George Whitefield and Tom Paine, many deeply religious people were set adrift from ecclesiastical establishments at the same time they demanded that the church begin living up to its spiritual promise. Many individuals and families remained deeply religious without church affiliation.[22] To appreciate the story of these people requires an understanding of the egalitarian forces powerfully at work within popular religious cultures of the new nation.

It seems appropriate to term this time of social ferment the Second Great Awakening. Christendom had probably not witnessed a comparable period of religious upheaval since the Reformation—and never such an explosion of entrepreneurial energy. This awakening developed inversely to that commonly depicted, however. Instead of fostering a unified, cohesive movement, it splintered American Christianity and magnified the diversity of institutions claiming to be the church. It sprang from a populist upsurge rather than from changing mores of established parishes. The movement captured the aspirations of society's outsiders. It was only secondarily the response of clergy nervous about eroding deference and competing churches. The heart of the movement was a revolution in communications, preaching, print, and song; and these measures were instrumental in building mass popular movements. The adjustment of staid churches was only a secondary theme in the awakening's story. Even Charles Finney's "new measures" are best seen as an aftershock of a more fundamental reordering exemplified by Francis Asbury's stern recruits.

Most important, the Second Great Awakening delineated the fault line of class within American Christianity. Clergy from both ends of the social scale battled for cultural authority. Blessed with a common touch, the insurgents enjoyed the advantage. Embodying the aspirations and values of common people, upstarts hopelessly blurred the distinction between pulpit and pew. Their success may have been the most profoundly democratic upheaval in the early republic. Using every means possible, they gave witness to the message that virtue and insight resided in ordinary people. While Lyman Beecher dismissed these efforts as "enthusiasm," Francis Asbury relished them as the mighty acts of God in the lives of humble people.

In the aftermath of the Second Great Awakening, many Americans divorced religious leadership from social position, completing a separation that had been building for a century. They ascribed authority to preachers ill qualified to stand for public office. In a new nation, premised on equality and struggling to free itself from the past, people were ready to see the hand of God upon a Lorenzo Dow, a Joseph Smith, or a William Miller. They could rejoice that, at last, the weak were confounding the mighty, the last becoming first.

A Sampling of Anticlerical and Anti-Calvinist Christian Verse

Better than any other source, popular poems and songs capture the force of the early republic's religious populism. Severely anticlerical yet overtly Christian, this verse is tangible evidence of the success of popular religious leaders in articulating the interests of ordinary people. In turn, these poems, ballads, and songs are ingenious tools of communication. They translate theological concepts into language of the marketplace, personalize theological abstractions, deflate the pretension of privileged church leaders, and instill hope and confidence in popular collective action. This verse demonstrates the full range of rhetorical weapons available to outsiders in the wake of the democratic revolutions. Using biting sarcasm and a Jeffersonian sense of history, insurgent authors wrest theological discussion from the rules of the orthodoxy in order to bring it before the court of public opinion.

"On Predestination," Elias Smith
"There is a Reprobation Plan," Lorenzo Dow
"God Will Have Mercy on Whom He Will," Lorenzo Dow
"The World Turned Upside Down," William C. Martin
"Priest-Craft Float Away," Timothy Waterous
"Freedom of the Human Will," William Smythe Babcock
"The Beauties of Predestination," Solomon Wiatt
"Against the Calvinian Doctrine," Solomon Wiatt
"Election," Elias Smith
"The Modern Priest," John Leland
"False Prophets Contrasted With the Apostle Paul," John Leland
"Methodist and Formalist," author unknown
"Bigotry Reported," Joseph Thomas

On Predestination

If all things succeed
Because they're decreed
And immutable impulses rule us;
 Then praying and preaching,
 And all such like teaching,
Is nought but a plan to befool us.

If destiny and fate,
Guide us this way and that,
As the coachman with bits guides his horses;
 There's no man can stray,
 But all go the right way,
As the stars in their different courses.

But if we may will,
To move or sit still,
As best suits our own inclination;
 'Tis an evil mistake,
 That ministers make,
To lay it to predestination.

If this be the way,
As some preachers say,
That all things were ordered by fate;
 I'll not spend my pence,
 To pay for nonsense,
If nothing will alter my state.

If preachers were wise,
Their int'rest they'd prize,
And lay aside predestination;
 And they'd live by their art,
 And not preach to a part,
But preach up a free proclamation.

That ALL if they choose,
May enjoy the GOOD NEWS,
May embrace Jesus Christ and Salvation;
 Then with all he must pass
 For a dull, senseless ass,
Who depends upon predestination.

Source: Elias Smith, *Herald of Gospel Liberty*, September 15, 1809. An earlier version of this poem is found in the *Continental Journal*, March 11, 1779.

There is a Reprobation Plan

There is a Reprobation plan,
 Some how it did arise;
By the Predestinarian clan
 Of horrid cruelties.

The plan is this, they hold a few,
  They are ordain'd for heaven,
They hold the rest accursed crew,
  That cannot be forgiven.

They do hold, God hath decreed
  Whatever comes to pass;
Some to be damned, some to be freed,
  And this they call free grace.

This iron bedstead they do fetch,
  To try our hopes upon;
And if too short, we must be stretch'd,
  Cut off, if we're too long.

This is a bold serpentine scheme,
  It suits the serpent well;
If he can make the sinner dream
  That he is doom'd to hell.

Or if he can persuade a man,
  Decree is on his side;
Then he will say without delay,
  This cannot be untied.

He tells one sinner, he's decreed
  Unto eternal bliss;
He tells another, he can't be freed,
  For he is doom'd to miss.

The first he bindeth fast in pride,
  The second in despair;
If he can only keep them tied,
  Which way he does not care.

Source: Lorenzo Dow, *All the Political Works of Lorenzo* (New York, 1814), 27.

God Will Have Mercy on Whom He Will
God will have mercy on whom he *will*,
  Come think you who they be?
'Tis every one that loves his Son,
  And from their sins do flee;

'Tis every one that doth repent,
  And truly hates his sin;
'Tis every one that is content,
  To turn to God again.

And whom he will be *hardeneth*,
  Come think you who they be?
'Tis every one that hates his Son,
  Likewise his liberty;

'Tis ev'ry one that in sin persist,
And do outstand their day;
Then God in justice leaves them to
Their own heart's lusts a prey.

Source: Lorenzo Dow, *All the Political Works of Lorenzo*, 46.

The World Turned Upside Down

When Paul went to Ephesus,
He preached to them Jesus,
Who died to redeem us,
From an Indignant frown:
They knowing not the stranger,
Once cradled in a manger,
Cry'd out our craft's in danger,
They turn the world upside down.

In the thessolonian nation,
Paul taught the great salvation,
Which rais'd the indignation,
Of those who lov'd to frown;
They being not so clever,
Conducted now as ever,
Saying these have come hither,
Who turn the world upside down.

Priests follow this example,
Although it is not ample,
That they should on us trample,
And turn us out of town;
But when a soul engaged,
The Clergy cry enraged,
They pull our churches down.

O What a sad commotion,
On Babylon's broad ocean,
The Clergy and each notion,
With their surplice and gown;
Can be no longer smother'd,
Not people by them bother'd,
Since light has now discover'd,
That they are wrong side down

. . . .

In the time of reformation,
The Clergyman's vexation,
For losing their taxation,
They often sue the town;
They hate a gospel preacher,
And cry out a false teacher,
A wolf an active creature,
Turns our church upside down.

They have found out our tinkling,
And upset infant sprinkling,
And set the people thinking,
O dear what shall we do?
If the President and Congress,
Don't have some pity on us,
And drive those run-a-gates from us,
We all to work must go.

Source: William C. Martin, *Herald of Gospel Liberty*, June 23, 1815, 694.

Priest-Craft Float Away

Why are we in such slavery, to men of that degree;
Bound to support their knavery when we might all be free;
They're nothing but a canker, we can with boldness say;
So let us hoist the anchor, let Priest-craft float away.

It is a dark confusion, that the people welters in;
To harbour such delusion, to plead for righteous sin;
If truth could just come forward, and justice bare the sway;
The Priests would sink in horror, and Priest-craft float away.

The Priests are on a nettle, to see their glory cease;
Because they cannot settle on any terms of peace:
Therefore with maze and wonder, they languish in the fray;
For truth shall fetch them under, and Priest-craft float away;
For truth and her communion, which they do soarly hate;
Shall break that horrid union, of devil, Church, and State.

Though we make our appearance, to execute this plan;
Yet we give our adherence, the sacred rights of man;
To every sect and nation, their tenets to display;
Yet may the whole creation, let Priest-craft float away.

Source: Timothy Waterous, *The Battle-Axe and Weapons of War: Discovered by the Morning Light, Aimed for the Final Destruction of Priestcraft* (Groton, Conn., 1811), 3–4.

Freedom of the Human Will

Know then that every soul is free
To choose his life and what he'll be;
For this eternal truth has giv'n,
That God will force no man to heav'n.

He'll draw, persuade, direct him right;
Bless him with wisdom, love and light;
In nameless ways be good and kind,
But never force the human mind.

Freedom and reason make us men:
Take these away, what are we then?
Mere animals, and just as well
The beasts may think of heav'n or hell.

May we no more our powers abuse,
But ways of truth and goodness choose;
Our God is pleas'd when we improve
His grace, and seek the worlds above.

It's my free will for to believe;
'Tis God's free will me to receive:
To stubborn willers this I'll tell;
It's all free grace and all free will.

Those that despise grow harder still;
Those that adhere he turns their will;
And thus despisers sink to hell,
While those that hear, in glory dwell.

But if we take the downward road,
And make in hell our last abode;
Our god is clear, and we shall know
We've plunged ourselves in endless wo.

Source: William Smythe Babcock in Elias Smith, *Hymns, Original and Selected* (Boston, 1805), 231–32.

The Beauties of Predestination

No Wonder to me,
We so often do see,
   Deism prevailed in our nation:
Since Calvins declare,
That God every where
   Is working out Predestination.

If this be the case,
All men run the race,
   Like the Devil in his fixed station:
The king, though a chief,
May get drunk with the thief,
   To comply with his fore-ordination.

'Tis truth, exclaim'd I,
With my work I'll comply,
   To the thirst for the blood of creation:
This the whoremonger pleads,
When impeach'd for his deeds,
   See the glory of Predestination.

To comport with the rest,
I'll both swear and protest,
   Right or wrong shall be my vocation:
From this I can't swerve,
Though hell I deserve,
   This I learned in my Predestination.

Thus all the black crew,
Both of Pagan and Jew,
  Turks, Popes, and the foul mouth of creation.
The tyrant's of state,
May plead up their fate,
  In the system of Predestination.

Why then don't you see,
You comply with decree,
  Find no fault with your fixed station:
'Twould astonish the world,
And the stars would be hurled,
  To oppose God-like Predestination.

Your conduct don't clash,
Though you meet with the lash,
  Of those fools you have rais'd to their station:
The contrast is great,
Which the learned do prate,
  When descanting from Predestination.

The good and the bad,
These both may be had,
  In the store house of honest probation:
These blended in one,
Is the sound of the drum,
  From the pulpit, and free ordination.

Could the Author of all,
Condemn men at all,
  Who works all in all through creation,
When no praise or blame,
On the good or prophane,
  Can be found in our Predestination.

No, the wisdom of God,
Which men spread abroad,
  No sin can be found in creation:
The Deist may laugh,
At the learned calf,
  When the thunders out hell and damnation.

Source: Solomon Wiatt, *Wiatt's Impartial Selection of Hymns and Spiritual Songs* (Philadelphia, 1809), 97–99.

Against the Calvinian Doctrine
Thou God of mercy, loving, kind,
To save the fallen race inclined;
Mercy and love are thy delight,
And all thy ways are just and right.

Can Christ our God a Moloch be,
Pleas'd with his creatures' misery?
Dooming nine-tenths of men that fell,
To burning flames and endless hell?

A God in wrath and vengeance dress'd,
In rage which cannot be express'd?
Decreeing unborn souls to death;
Long ere they sinn'd or drew their breath?

No, Lord, thy name and nature's love,
To all mankind thy bowels move;
Thy saving grace for all is free,
And none are doom'd to misery.

Those only who thy love abuse,
And madly all thy grace refuse,
Shall into endless darkness go,
'Tis all the heav'n they wish to know.

Lord, set the erring Christians right,
Teach them thy truth, thy truth is light;
Then will they know, and feel, and prove,
Thy nature and thy name is love.

Source: Solomon Wiatt, *Wiatt's Impartial Selection of Hymns and Spiritual Songs*, 159–60.

Election

Election, what a glorious plan,
To save the rebel creature, man,
    And glory bring to God.
For motives in the father's breast,
The precious Lamb elected is
    To bear the heavy load.

The Father so has lov'd the world,
To give his son, our blessed Lord,
    To save our souls from sin,
That he might shed his precious blood,
And ope the door that leads to God,
    And call us, sinners, in.

Elected he a Prophet is,
To teach us, and to make us wise
    To everlasting life.
Elected he a Priest become,
Aton'd for crimes that we have done,
    That we might pardon have.

Elected he the victory won,
And rose triumphant from the tomb
    And conquer'd death and hell.
Election, yes; this song we'll sing,

(He's Lord of lords, and King of kings,)
   While we this name can spell.

I read my Bible, this is plain,
Christ Jesus is elect, *Amen*,
   And blessed be the Lord,
But no election I can find
Of enemies to God in mind,
   Who hate his blessed word.

When we repent and turn to God,
Believe and love his blessed words,
   And hate our former sin,
Then we're elect in Jesus Christ,
Who groan'd and dy'd upon the cross,
   That we the prize might win.

Now, sinners, don't you dare to stand
And say, "if I elected am
   "From all eternity,
"Though now I fight against the Lord,
"He'll bring me by his power and word,
   "And I shall saved be."

For God may cut the brittle thread,
And number you among the dead,
   And you mistaken be.
You'll then lift up your eyes in hell,
And say, "I now remember well,
   "When Jesus call'd for me."

He said, that 'all things ready were,'
"That my poor soul might have a share,
   "If I'd forsake my sins;
"But I refus'd to hear the call,
"And barr'd my heart against them all,
   "'T' endured eternal pain."

Now glory to the Lord, *Amen*;
Christ Jesus saves us from our sin,
   When we believe in God;
Now glory to the glorious Son,
And Holy Spirit, three in one,
   Let's live upon his word.

Brethren and sisters in the Lord,
Examine this by Jesus' word,
   See if these things be so:
If thus you find it in the word,
Believe, and glory give to God,
   The gospel trumpet blow.

Source: Elias Smith, *Hymns, Original and Selected* (Boston, 1805), 237–39.

The Modern Priest

Ignatius, born somewhere, no matter where,
Trained up in school, and taught to say his prayer,
Tired with his task at the academy,
Jump'd over all to university:

The books he read, and read, then laid them down,
But little wiser when his task was done;
But college pedantry bore such a sway,
That soon he gained a soaring diploma,

Dubb'd like a knight on a commencement day,
Gladly he quit his task, and went his way.
He thought of doctor, lawyer, prince and priest,
And made remarks in earnest or in jest,

"Should I turn doctor, I must stem the cold,
And break my rest, to gain the shining gold;
Must make my patients think their lives and blood
Are in my hands, or I can do no good.

When men believe in witches, witches are;
But when they don't believe there are none there;
When men believe in doctors, doctors heal,
At sight of whom their patients easy feel.

If I'm a lawyer, I must lie and cheat,
For honest lawyers have no bread to eat;
'Tis rogues and villains feed the lawyers high,
And sue the men that gold and silver buy.

Should I be statesman, I must use disguise,
And, if a priest, hear nothing else but lies;
State tricks, intrigues, and arts would me confound,
And truth and honesty nowhere be found.

This way of getting money is a risk,
I judge it better to become a priest
Preaching is now a science and a trade,
And by it many grand estates are made;

The money which I spent at grammar school
I'll treble now by teaching sacred rule.
My prayers I'll stretch out long, my sermons short,
The last write down, the first get all by rote;

While others labor six days, I but one,
For that day's work I'll gain a pretty sum.
For fifty-two days labor in a year,
The sum of eighty pounds my heart shall cheer."

So asses heads for three score pieces sold,
When famines were severe, in days of old.

Ignatius thus resolved to rise by rule,
And to a grave divine he went to school,

The science of divinity engag'd,
And read the sacred volume page by page.
The Bible was so dark, the style so poor,
He gain'd but little from the sacred store;

Pool, Whitby, Burchett, Henry, Yorick, Gill,
He read, to find what was Jehovah's will,
Gravity, rhetoric, and pulpit airs
He studied well, and how to form his prayers.

At length his master gave him commendation,
That he was qualified to preach salvation.
And with his commendation gave him more
Than twenty notes that he had us'd before;

These for his models, and his learned guides,
Helped him to form his work with equal sides.
In composition he did pretty well,
And what he could not read, he'd softly spell.

A day appointed for him to perform,
Notice was giv'n and many took th' alarm.
At the appointed hour the people came,
To hear the will of God revealed to men.

At length Ignatius came all dress'd in black,
With sacerdotal bands and three shap'd hat.
Under his arm the holy book appeared,
And in it were the notes he had prepared:

He bow'd, and bow'd, and to the pulpit steered,
Went up the stairs, and in the desk appeared,
First he address'd the throne of God supreme;—
His master's prayer, new-moddled, did for him;

Fifty-nine minutes long, prays and repeats,—
He clos'd, and all the people took their seats.
The sacred volume next he gravely spread,
Before his eyes upon his elbow bed,

And so it happened, that Ignatius hit
The very place where all his notes were writ.
His text he told, and then began to read
What he had written, with a school-boys heed,

If he presumed to look upon the folks,
His thumb stood sentinel upon his notes.
Short were the visits that his eyes could pray;
He watch'd his notes lest he should miss his way.

At the conclusion, with an angry tone,
He said his gospel came from God alone.
From this, the preacher travell'd all around,
To see where glebes and salaries were found;

Many loud calls he had where land was poor,
People were indigent, and had no store.
The calls he heard, but gravely answer'd, 'no;
To other places God calls me to go!'

At length a vacant place Ignatius found,
Where land was good, and wealth did much abound:
A call they gave him which he did embrace,
'Vox populi, vox Dei,' was the case.

A handsome settlement they gave, a farm,
With eighty pounds, and wood to keep him warm.
All things were ready for his consecration,
A sacred council came for ordination.

The candidate was first examined well,
To see if he in knowledge did excel;
The first of John he hem'd and hammered thro,'
Some things forgot, but most he never knew,

But as he'd spent his time and money both,
To fit himself to wear the sacred cloth,
All things considered, 'twas believed that he
Was a proficient in divinity.

Lineal succession rites were then perform'd,
Their hands impos'd, Ignatius gravely warn'd
The sacred care of all the flock to take,
In love, *and not for filthy lucre's* sake.

Source: John Leland, *The Writings of the Late Elder John Leland*, ed. L. F. Green (New York, 1845), 193–95.

False Prophets Contrasted with the Apostle Paul
In sable robes with serious faces,
They mount aloft to highest places;
An hour or more employ their tongues—
Weary the throng . . . exhaust their lungs.

"Bring forth your worldly wealth," they cry,
"And barter for the joys on high!
Treasure bestow with liberal hands,
To save the souls in heathen lands.

Support our Missionary plan;
Reverend divines this scheme began,
But all must fail if you withhold
The needful silver and the gold.

Does Christ for aid his hands extend!
And will you not His cause befriend?
Your choicest idol, gold, resign,
For heavenly wealth, and bliss divine!"

"I seek not yours, but you," said Paul,
"Freely I preach to great and small;
Silver and gold I do not crave,
But all the world I long to save.

These hands my earthly wants supply:
My crown of glory waits on high.
As thus I follow Christ my Lord,
Walk in my steps with one accord."

Beware of prophets false and greedy;
Those ravening wolves who rob the needy—
Who seek pre-eminent to shine,
And dare assume titles divine!

Disguised like sheep, they seize their prey;
The wretched flock are borne away,
Deceived and fleec'd by selfish men,
Whose godliness is worldly gain.

'Tis by the fruit the tree we know;
Nor grapes or figs on brambles grow,
Tho long and loud in formal prayer,
Their fruits designate who they are.

'Tis not by money, might or power,
Hirelings who sermonize their hour,—
Nor all the men-made priests combin'd,
Can renovate the carnal mind.

The power and grace of God alone,
Can win and melt our hearts of stone,
And save the world from sin and guilt:
Employ O Lord, whoe'er thou wilt.

Ye whom the Lord hath sent to preach
His great salvation, we beseech,
Like Paul make Christ your trust and guide,
And all your wants will be supply'd.

Source: John Leland, *The Reformer*, vol. 2, no. 23 (October 25, 1821), 240.

Methodist and Formalist

Methodist

Good morning, brother Pilgrim! What, trav'ling to Zion?
What doubts and what dangers have you met today?
Have you gain'd a blessing, then pray without ceasing,
Press forward, my brother and make no delay;

Is your heart now glowing, your comforts now flowing,
And have you an evidence now bright and clear?
Have you a desire that burns like a fire,
And longs for the hour when Christ shall appear?

Formalist

I came out this morning, and now I'm returning,
Perhaps little better than when I first came,
Such groaning and shouting, it sets me to doubting,
I fear such religion is only a dream.
The preachers were stamping, the people were jumping,
And screaming so loud that I nothing could hear,
Either praying or preaching—such horrible shrieking!
I was truly offended at all that was there.

Methodist

Perhaps, my dear brother, while they prayed together
You sat and considered, but prayed not at all:
Would you find a blessing, then pray without ceasing,
Obey the advice that was given by Paul.
For if you should reason at any such season,
No wonder if Satan should tell in your ear,
That preachers and people are only a rabble,
And this is no place for reflection and prayer.

Formalist

No place for reflection—I'm filled with distraction,
I wonder that people could bear for to stay,
The men they were bawling, the women were squalling,
I know not for my part how any could pray.
Such horrid confusion—if this be religion
I'm sure that it's something that never was seen,
For the sacred pages that speak of all ages,
Do nowhere declare that such ever has been.

Methodist

Don't be so soon shaken—if I'm not mistaken
Such things were perform'd by believers of old;
When the ark was coming, King David came running,
And dancing before it, in Scripture we're told.
When the Jewish nation had laid the foundation,
To rebuild the temple at Ezra's command,
Some wept and some praised, such noise there was raised,
'Twas heard afar off and perhaps through the land.

And as for the preacher, Ezekiel the teacher,
God taught him to stamp and to smite with the hand,
To show the transgressions of what wicked nation
To bid them repent and obey the command.
For Scripture collation in this dispensation,

The blessed Redeemer has handed it out—
"If these cease from praising," we hear him there saying,
"The stones to reprove them would quickly cry out."

Formalist

Then Scripture's contrasted, for Paul has protested
That order should reign in the house of the Lord—
Amid such a clatter who knows what's the matter?
Or who can attend unto what is declared?
To see them behaving like drunkards, all raving,
And lying and rolling prostrate on the ground,
I really felt awful, and sometimes felt fearful
That I'd be the next that would come tumbling down.

Methodist

You say you felt-awful—you ought to be careful
Lest you grieve the Spirit, and so he depart,
By your own confession you've felt some impression,
The sweet melting showers have soften'd your heart.
You fear persecution, and that's a delusion
Brought in by the devil to stop up your way.
Be careful, my brother, for blest are no other
Than persons that "are not offended in Me."

As Peter was preaching, and bold in his teaching,
The plan of salvation in Jesus's name,
The Spirit descended and some were offended,
And said of these men, "They're filled with new wine."
I never yet doubted that some of them shouted,
While others lay prostrate, by power struck down;
Some weeping, some praising, while others were saying:
"They're drunkards or fools, or in falsehood abound."

As time is now flying and moments are dying,
We're call'd to improve them, and quickly prepare
For that awful hour when Jesus, in power
And glory is coming—'tis now drawing near.
Methinks there'll be shouting, and I'm not a-doubting,
But crying and screaming for mercy in vain;
Therefore, my dear brother, let us pray together,
That your precious soul may be fill'd with the flame.

Formalist

I own prayer's now needful, I really feel awful
That I've grieved the Spirit in time that is past;
But I'll strive for the blessing, and pray without ceasing,
His mercy is sure unto all that believe.—
My heart is now glowing! I feel his love flowing!
Peace, pardon, and comfort I now do receive!

Source: Author unknown, *Hesperian Harp*, compiled by William Hauser (Philadelphia, 1848), 454.

Bigotry Reported

A horrid thing pervades the land,
The priests and prophets in a band,
  (Called by the name of preachers,)
Direct the superstitious mind,
What man shall do his God to find,
  He must obey his teachers.

Those leaders, differing in their mode,
Each traveling in a different road,
  Create a sad division;
Each one believes he must be right,
And vents at others all his spite,
  Contemns them with derision.

Their proselytes around them wait,
To hear them preach, and pray, and prate,
  And tell their growing numbers;
They love to hear their preachers tell,
The adverse sects will go to hell,
  All laid in guilt and slumbers.

Each party has its special rules,
Borrowed from bishops, popes and schools,
  And thinks them best of any;
And yet they change to suit the times,
And differ in the different climes,
  To catch the passing penny.

They are directed to obey,
And never tread another way,
  All others are deceivers;
All those who do dissent from this,
Are not within the road to bliss,
  Nor can be true believers.

Some thousands thus are dup'd and led,
By prejudice and priestcraft fed,
  Who love to hold contention;
Their old confessions they defend,
For human rules do strong contend,
  The ground of much dissention.

Is this religion? God forbid,
The light within the cloud is hid,
  My soul be not deceived;
The Great Redeemer never told
The priests to separate his fold,
  And this I've long believed.

I love religion—do declare,
That peace and love are ever there,

And universal kindness;
The Bible is my rule for this,
It points me to eternal bliss,
  Dispels Sectarian blindness.

Let Christians now unite and say,
We'll throw all human rules away,
  And take God's word to rule us;
King Jesus shall our leader be,
And in his name we will agree,
  The priests no more shall fool us.

Source: Joseph Thomas, *Life, Travels and Gospel Labors of Elder Joseph Thomas* (New York, 1861), 173–75.

Notes

Chapter One

1. Richard Carwardine, "Methodist Ministers and the Second Party System," in *Rethinking Methodist History: A Bicentennial Historical Consultation*, ed. Russell E. Richey and Kenneth E. Rowe (Nashville, 1985), 134; David Benedict, *A General History of the Baptist Denomination* (Boston, 1813), 2:552–53; Timothy L. Smith, *Revivalism and Social Reform: American Protestantism on the Eve of the Civil War* (Nashville, 1957), 22; C. C. Goss, *Statistical History of the First Century of American Methodism* (New York, 1866), 106.

2. Walter Nugent, *Structures of American Social History* (Bloomington, Ind., 1981), 54–86; E. A. Wrigley and R. S. Schofield, *The Population History of England 1541–1871* (Cambridge, Mass., 1981); and *Historical Statistics of the United States: Colonial Times to 1957* (Washington, D.C., 1960).

3. I have estimated that the British colonies that became the United States had about eighteen hundred clergy serving twenty-three denominations in the year 1775. See Frederic Lewis Weis, *The Colonial Clergy and the Colonial Churches of New England* (Lancaster, Mass., 1936), *The Colonial Clergy of Maryland, Delaware, and Georgia* (Lancaster, Mass., 1950), *The Colonial Clergy of Virginia, North Carolina, and South Carolina* (Boston, 1955), *The Colonial Clergy of the Middle Colonies: New York, New Jersey, and Pennsylvania 1628–1776* (Worcester, Mass., 1957). I have estimated 38,540 preachers serving 49 denominations in 1845 using John Winebrenner's 600-page study of American denominations, *History of All the Religious Denominations in the United States* (Harrisburg, Penn., 1848). The following estimates are given for the number of clergy in certain denominations: 1015 Freewill Baptists, 1023 Antimission Baptists, 1323 Episcopalians, 540 Lutherans, 834 Roman Catholics, 1412 Congregationalists, and 14,556 Methodists.

4. I have chosen to use the word *populist* because it suggests leadership that is

deliberate in championing the interests of common people against professional expertise and elite institutions.

5. Three recent books are superb on these themes: Robert H. Wiebe, *The Opening of American Society: From the Adoption of the Constitution to the Eve of Disunion* (New York, 1984), particularly chap. 8, "Revolution in Choices," 143–67; Sean Wilentz, *Chants Democratic: New York City and the Rise of the American Working Class, 1788–1850;* and Joyce Appleby, *Capitalism and a New Social Order: The Republican Vision of the 1790s* (New York, 1984).

6. Henry Mayer, *A Son of Thunder: Patrick Henry and the American Republic* (New York, 1986), 444–45. On the rise of public opinion as an authority, see Gordon S. Wood, "The Democratization of Mind in the American Revolution," in *Leadership in the American Revolution,* ed. Gordon S. Wood (Washington, D.C., 1974), 63–89.

7. Wilentz, *Chants Democratic,* 61.

8. An example of this tumultuous transition is in Charles Brockden Brown's novel *Arthur Mervyn* (1799). Daniel A. Cohen has provided an insightful interpretation of the hero as a young man struggling for survival and success in an age in which it was no longer clear how a young man was supposed to behave. Cohen sees Arthur Mervyn as caught between the conflicting demands of traditional social patterns based on landed property, ascriptive rank, authoritative moral inculcation, household apprenticeship, and ordered generational succession on the one hand; and a disordered and relentlessly competitive social world on the other. Arthur is torn between viewing morality either as an outgrowth of submission to authority or as a product of the autonomous individual's own enlightened reason. Cohen, "Arthur Mervyn and His Elders: The Ambivalence of Youth in the Early Republic," *William and Mary Quarterly,* 3d ser., 43 (1986):362–80.

9. See Ruth H. Block, *Visionary Republic: Millennial Themes in American Thought, 1756–1800* (Cambridge, England, 1985); and Nathan O. Hatch, "Millennialism and Popular Religion in the Early Republic," in *The Evangelical Tradition in America,* ed. Leonard I. Sweet (Macon, Ga., 1984), 113–30.

10. Berthoff suggests about the early nineteenth century that it is difficult to write "a coherent account of so disjunctive a history." "The assumption persists that the history of America can be written without reflecting on what was missing from its unestablished religion, self-made elite, negligible government, discontinuous literary tradition, and loyalty to lofty but impersonal abstractions." Roland Berthoff, "Writing a History of Things Left Out," *Reviews in American History* 14 (1986): 1–16.

11. The phrase is that of John Murrin in "The Great Inversion, or Court Verses Country: A Comparison of the Revolution Settlements in England (1688–1721) and America (1776–1816)," in *Three British Revolutions: 1641, 1688, 1776,* ed. J. G. A. Pocock (Princeton, 1980), 425.

12. R. Laurence Moore, *Religious Outsiders and the Making of Americans* (New York, 1986), 3–24.

13. Alan D. Gilbert, *The Making of Post-Christian Britain: A History of the Secularization of Modern Society* (London, 1980), 114.

14. David Hempton, *Methodism and Politics in British Society, 1750–1850* (Stanford, 1984), 55–115. See also W. R. Ward, *Religion and Society in England 1790–1850* (London, 1982), 70–104.

15. W. R. Ward, "The Religion of the People and the Problem of Control, 1790–1830," in *Popular Belief and Practice*, ed. G. J. Cuming and Derek Baker (Cambridge, England, 1972), 249.

16. Gordon S. Wood makes this argument in "Ideology and the Origins of Liberal America," *William and Mary Quarterly*, 3d ser., 44 (1987):637.

17. Edmund S. Morgan, *Inventing the People: The Rise of Popular Sovereignty in England and America* (New York, 1988).

18. The eighteenth-century distinction between vulgar and refined language denied the possibility of virtuous intelligence in vernacular expression. In the age of democratic revolution no change was more essential and far-reaching than the act of faith that attributed virtue to the vernacular expression of ordinary people. On this intellectual revolution, see Olivia Smith, *The Politics of Language, 1791–1819* (New York, 1984).

19. Appleby, *Capitalism and a New Social Order*, 79.

20. George A. Rawlyk, *Ravished by the Spirit: Religious Revivals, Baptists, and Henry Alline* (Kingston, Ontario, 1984), 14.

21. Doris Elizabeth Andrews, "Popular Religion and the Revolution in the Middle Atlantic Ports: The Rise of the Methodists, 1770–1800" (Ph.D. diss., Princeton University, 1986), 140. Richard L. Bushman, *Joseph Smith and the Beginnings of Mormonism* (Urbana, Ill., 1984), 59.

22. In a similar sense, Lawrence Goodwyn defines the Populist movement of the late nineteenth century in democratic terms not because of its achievement but because of the moment of intense democratic aspiration and hope in which it was born. Lawrence Goodwyn, *Democratic Promise: The Populist Moment in America* (New York, 1976).

23. Richard Hofstadter, *Anti-Intellectualism in American Life* (New York, 1962), 55–116.

24. On the democratic tensions within Roman Catholicism, see Patrick W. Carey, *People, Priests, and Prelates: Ecclesiastical Democracy and the Tensions of Trusteeism* (Notre Dame, Ind., 1987).

25. For two cogent essays that emphasize the importance of regionalism in studying American religion, see Edwin S. Gaustad, "Regionalism in American Religion," in *Religion in the South*, ed. Charles Reagan Wilson (Jackson, Miss., 1985), 155–72; and Jerald C. Brauer, "Regionalism and Religion in America," *Church History* 54 (1985):366–78.

26. Daniel W. Patterson, *The Shaker Spiritual* (Princeton, 1979), 136. On the remarkable impact of the farmer-tanner Henry Alline, whose epitaph on his gravestone also used the phrase "a burning and a shining light," see George A. Rawlyk, *Henry Alline: Selected Writings* (New York, 1987); and Rawlyk, *Ravished by the Spirit*.

27. Similarly, Nathaniel Hawthorne was singularly unimpressed with the Mormon leader Orson Pratt, whom he met in Liverpool, England. "Orson Pratt the famous Mormonite, called on me a little while ago—a short, blackhaired, dark-complexioned man; a shrewd, intelligent but unrefined countenance, expressively unprepossessing; an uncouth gait and deportment; the aspect of a person in uncomfortable circumstances and decently behaved, but of a vulgar nature and destitute of early culture. I think I should have taken him for a shoemaker, accustomed to reflect in a rude, strong, evil-disposed way on matters of this world and the next, as he sat on his bench." Breck England, *The Life and Thought of Orson Pratt* (Provo, 1985), 201.

28. Thomas Andros, *The Scriptures Liable to be Wrested to Men's Own Destruction, and an Instance of This Found, in the Writings of Elias Smith* (Taunton, Mass., 1817), 6.

29. Alexis de Tocqueville, *Democracy in America*, trans. Henry Reeve, 2 vols. (New York, 1945), 1:317.

30. I am using class simply to mean that certain groups in society perceive and articulate their interests differently than do others. Obviously, questions of wealth, education, social position, geography, family background, and religious affiliation bear upon how groups define their interests with respect to others.

31. In the same way, the struggle between Federalist and Anti-Federalist was not merely an intellectual debate but a profound struggle for authority between different classes of people. On this issue, the work of Gordon S. Wood has been immensely useful. See Wood, *The Creation of the American Republic, 1776–1787* (Chapel Hill, N.C., 1969); and "Interests and Disinterestedness in the Making of the Constitution," in *Beyond Confederation: Origins of the Constitution and American National Identity*, ed. Richard Beeman, Stephen Botein, and Edward C. Carter II (Chapel Hill, N.C., 1987), 69–109.

32. The religious sources on which this book depends bear out the contention of Gordon S. Wood that a liberal social order was not simply foisted on the country by merchants and aristocrats but that it also percolated up from the convictions of the mass of ordinary Americans. See a lively discussion on these issues in the forum of essays on Wood's *Creation of the American Republic* in the *William and Mary Quarterly*, 3d ser., 44 (1987): 549–640, particular the essays by Gary B. Nash, John M. Murrin, and Gordon S. Wood. My perspective has also been influenced by Appleby, *Capitalism and a New Social Order*.

33. As commonly used, the term encompasses many diverse, even contradictory, historical phenomena. For an explicit critique and a suggestion for redefining the term, see below, "Redefining the Second Great Awakening: A Note on the Study of Christianity in the Early Republic."

34. Studies typical of this genre include J. M Bumstead, "Religion, Finance, and Democracy in Massachusetts: The Town of Norton as a Case Study," *Journal of American History* 57 (1971):817–31; James Walsh, "The Great Awakening in the First Congregational Church of Woodbury, Connecticut," *William and Mary Quarterly*, 3d ser., 28 (1971):543–62; Gerald F. Moran, "Conditions of Religious Conversion in the First Society of Norwich, Connecticut, 1718–1744," *Journal of Social History* 5 (1972): 331–43; and Richard D. Shields, "The Second Great Awakening in Connecticut: Critique of the Traditional Interpretation," *Church History* 49 (1980): 401–15.

35. Terry D. Bilhartz, *Urban Religion and the Second Great Awakening: Church and Society in Early National Baltimore* (Rutherford, N.J., 1986), 98–99, 139.

Chapter Two

1. Bennett Tyler, *The New England Revivals . . . from Narratives First Published in the Connecticut Evangelical Magazine* (Boston, 1846), v.

2. [Lyman Beecher], *An Address to the Charitable Society for the Education of Indigent Pious Young Men for the Ministry of the Gospel* (New Haven, 1814), 7.

3. Thomas Andros, a member of the Massachusetts standing order, voiced a similar critique of unlettered preachers whose clarion call was popularity rather

than the social virtues: "They measure the progress of religion by the numbers, who flock to their standard; not by the prevalence of faith, and piety, justice and charity, and the public virtues in society in general." See Andros, *The Scriptures Liable to be Wrested to Men's Own Destruction, and an Instance of This Found, in the Writings of Elias Smith* (Taunton, Mass., 1817), 6.

4. [Beecher], *Address to the Charitable Society*, 5–8.

5. Timothy Dwight, *A Sermon Preached at the Opening of the Theological Institution in Andover* (Boston, 1808), 7–8.

6. Ibid., 9, 11. The founding of Princeton Seminary in 1812 had as one of its central aims the training of cultured and respectable ministers. The prominent New York Presbyterian Samuel Miller expressed this concern in a letter to the churches in 1810: "Without some provision of this kind [a central denomination seminary], it is in most cases, utterly impossible to bring forward candidates for the ministry, with that furniture and those qualifications for their work which the state of society now renders, in a great measure, indispensable to their respectability and usefulness." Miller argued that it would be impossible "for the religious teacher to maintain weight of character, and permanent influence, if his knowledge be scanty, and his literature circumscribed." This letter is quoted in Mark A. Noll, "The Founding of Princeton Seminary," *Westminster Theological Journal* 42 (1979): 92. For a similar quest for gentility, refined intelligence, polish, and dignity among southern urban clergymen, see E. Brooks Holifield, *The Gentlemen Theologians: American Theology in Southern Culture, 1795–1860* (Durham, N.C., 1978), 36–49.

7. Billy Hibbard, *The Life and Travels of B. Hibbard, Minister of the Gospel* (New York, 1825), 50, 331. On Hibbard, see William B. Sprague, *Annals of the American Pulpit* (New York, 1865), vol. 7, *Methodist*, 298–306.

8. [Billy Hibbard], *Philom's Address to the People of New England* (n.p., 1817), 59.

9. Lorenzo Dow, *History of Cosmopolite: or the Four Volumes of Lorenzo's Journal, Concentrated in One* (Philadelphia, 1816), 556, 574–76; Freeborn Garrettson, *A Letter to the Rev. Lyman Beecher* (New York, 1816), 7–8. Dow displayed an equally independent spirit when dealing with Methodist authority, even though he followed their discipline and spent his career largely among Methodists. In 1797, Nicholas Snethen informed him that Jesse Lee disapproved of his traveling to so many new places in New England. Dow replied, "I told him it did not belong to J. L. or any other man to say whether I should preach or not, for that was to be determined between God and my own soul; only it belonged to the Methodists to say whether I should preach in their connection; but as long as I feel so impressed, I shall travel and preach, God being my helper: and as soon as I can feel my mind released, I intend to stop, let people say what they will." Dow, *Life and Travels of Lorenzo Dow*, 72–73.

10. Samuel Goodrich, *Recollections of a Lifetime*, 2 vols. (New York, 1856), 1:209–10. In light of Beecher's and Dwight's ideal that the clergy should be known for their decorum, respectability, and refined presence, it is noteworthy that Goodrich concludes that Lorenzo Dow "had begun to be talked about chiefly on account of his eccentricities." Ibid., 205.

11. Ibid., 196–97. Goodrich noted that the Methodist movement in the region seemed to spread to epidemic proportions: "I have only a general recollection of the deep anxiety of both my parents about this time. A cloud was on their hearts and

their countenances, by day and night. The deacons were called in, and there were profound consultations as to what was to be done. The neighboring clergy were consulted, and it was soon discovered that they, too, were beset by the same dangers. In some cases, their people joined the Methodists; in others, they imitated them by evening meetings for prayer and mutual exhortation. The very air at last seemed impregnated with the electric fluid." Ibid., 216.

12. Bentley, *The Diary of William Bentley, D. D.*, 4 vols. (Salem, Mass., 1911), 3:65, 503, 515, 271.

13. Jarratt, *The Life of the Reverend Devereux Jarratt* (Baltimore, 1806), 14–15, 181.

14. The two reports of David Rice are *An Epistle to the Citizens of Kentucky, Professing Christianity; Especially Those that Are, or Have Been, Denominated Presbyterians* (Lexington, Ky., 1805) and *A Second Epistle to the Citizens of Kentucky, Professing the Christian Religion, Especially Those Who Are, or Have Been Denominated Presbyterians* (Lexington, Ky., 1808). I have used these works as they are reprinted in Robert H. Bishop, *An Outline of the History of the Church in the State of Kentucky, During a Period of Forty Years: Containing the Memoirs of Rev. David Rice* (Lexington, Ky., 1824), 321–84, quotation on 354. On David Rice, see *Princetonians, 1748–1768: A Biographical Dictionary*, ed. James McLachlan (Princeton, 1976), 354–57.

15. "This, and the high encomiums often passed on young beginners, prepared and disposed them to despise the ancient reformers, to stop their ears to age and experience, to slight creeds and confessions, which had been highly esteemed by the most pious and judicious christians for centuries, to treat old authors with contempt, and to follow new notions, by which they might be distinguished from professors of former ages." Bishop, *The Church in the State of Kentucky*, 367.

16. Ibid., 353. Rice, who had blended a Princeton education with evangelical piety, despaired that religious knowledge had come to consist "of fragments, scraps picked up here and there. . . . By many it is now thought unnecessary even for ministers thoroughly to study the system of religion before they undertake to teach." Ibid., 370.

Charles Nisbet, the first president of Dickinson College, manifested the same hostile reaction to what he perceived as rampant religious democracy in western Pennsylvania at the turn of the century. He mocked the age of the sovereign people by referring to a people's Bible: "In the Beginning the Sovereign people created Heaven & the Earth: And the Sovereign People spake to Moses, saying, Speak unto the Children of Israel, Thou shalt have no other Sovereign People before me." Nisbet to William Marshall, Oct. 3, 1800, Presbyterian Historical Society, Philadelphia. Quoted in James H. Smylie, "Charles Nisbet: Second Thoughts on a Revolutionary Generation," *Pennsylvania Magazine of History and Biography* 98 (1974): 195.

17. Donald M. Scott, *From Office to Profession: The New England Ministry, 1750–1850* (Philadelphia, 1978). Sidney Mead, "The Rise of the Evangelical Conception of the Ministry in America, 1607–1850," in *The Ministry in Historical Perspective*, ed. H. Richard Niebuhr and Daniel Williams (New York, 1956).

18. For a useful discussion of how similar issues of authority dominated the politics of the infant state of Ohio, see Andrew R. L. Cayton, *The Frontier Republic: Ideology and Politics in the Ohio Country, 1780 to 1825* (Kent, Ohio, 1986), 68–80.

19. *The Works of John Adams, Second President of the United States*, ed. Charles Francis Adams, 10 vols. (Boston, 1856), 9:375; Edmund S. Morgan, "The Great Political Fiction," *New York Review of Books* 25 (March 9, 1978):13–18.

20. James A. Henretta, *The Evolution of American Society, 1700–1815* (Lexington, Mass., 1973); Richard D. Brown, *Modernization: The Transformation of American Life, 1600–1865* (New York, 1976); Richard D. Brown, "The Emergence of Voluntary Associations in Massachusetts, 1760–1830," *Journal of Voluntary Action Research* 2 (April 1973):64–73; Jackson Turner Main, "Government by the People: The American Revolution and the Democratization of the Legislatures," *William and Mary Quarterly*, 3d ser., 23 (July 1966):391–407; Bernard Bailyn, *The Ideological Origins of the American Revolution* (Cambridge, Mass., 1967); Richard E. Ellis, *The Jeffersonian Crisis: Courts and Politics in the Young Republic* (New York, 1971); David Brion Davis, *The Problem of Slavery in the Age of Revolution, 1770–1823* (Ithaca, N.Y., 1975); David Hackett Fisher, *Growing Old in America* (New York, 1977); Robert A. Gross, *The Minutemen and Their World* (New York, 1976); and Mary Beth Norton, *The Revolutionary Experience of American Women, 1750–1800* (Boston, 1980).

21. For an insightful treatment of the ways in which three decades of political debate mobilized common people, culminating in the 1790s, see Joyce Appleby, *Capitalism and a New Social Order: The Republican Vision of the 1790s* (New York, 1984), especially 51–104. For the hyperbolic character of politics in the 1790s, see John R. Howe, "Republican Thought and the Political Violence of the 1790s," *American Quarterly* 19 (1967):147–65; and Marshall Smelser, "The Federalist Period as an Age of Passion," *American Quarterly* 10 (1958):391–419.

22. John M. Murrin, "Political Development," in *Colonial British America: Essays in the New History of the Early Modern Era*, ed. Jack P. Greene and J. R. Pole (Baltimore, 1984), 414–56. See also the introduction by Gordon S. Wood to *The Rising Glory of America, 1760–1820*, ed. Gordon S. Wood (New York, 1971), 1–22; and Sean Wilentz, "Artisan Republicanism," in *Chants Democratic: New York City and the Rise of the American Working Class, 1788–1850* (New York, 1984), 61–103.

23. For the importance of the idea of volitional allegiance in this period, see James H. Kettner, *The Development of American Citizenship, 1608–1870* (Chapel Hill, N.C., 1978), 173–209. See also Gordon S. Wood, *The Creation of the American Republic, 1776–1787* (Chapel Hill, N.C., 1969), 483–99; Alfred F. Young, *The Democratic Republicans of New York: The Origins, 1763–1797* (Chapel Hill, N.C., 1967); and Edmund S. Morgan, *The Challenge of the American Revolution* (New York, 1976), 211–18.

24. Wood, *Creation of the American Republic*, 482–83.

25. Jonathan Elliot, *The Debates, Resolutions, and Other Proceedings, in Convention on the Adoption of the Federal Constitution*, 4 vols. (Washington, D.C., 1827–1830), 1:112.

26. Young, *Democratic Republicans of New York*, 468–95.

27. Wood, *Creation of the American Republic*, 483–99.

28. Thomas C. Leonard, "News for a Revolution: The Exposé in America, 1768–1773," *Journal of American History* 67 (1980):26–40.

29. Stephen Botein, "Printers and the American Revolution," in *The Press and the American Revolution*, ed. Bernard Bailyn and John B. Hench (Worcester, Mass., 1980), 11–57.

30. Richard Buel, Jr., "Freedom of the Press in Revolutionary America: The Evolution of Libertarianism, 1760–1820," in *The Press and the American Revolution*, ed. Bailyn and Hench, 59–97.

31. *The Patriot, or Scourge of Aristocracy*, Oct. 2, 1801, 85–86.

32. Ibid., 149.

33. Gordon S. Wood, "The Democratization of Mind in the American Revolution," in *Leadership in the American Revolution*, Library of Congress Symposia on the American Revolution (Washington, D.C., 1974), 63–89.

34. Young, *Democratic Republicans of New York*; Howard B. Rock, *Artisans of the New Republic: The Tradesmen of New York City in the Age of Jefferson* (New York, 1979).

35. The explosion of the popular press in America in the two decades after 1790 contrasts sharply with the class bias of England's freedom of the press. In one celebrated case, the radical Thomas Cooper, whom Edmund Burke criticized on the floor of Parliament, countered in print but then received the following stern warning from the attorney general: "Continue if you please to publish your reply to Mr. Burke in an octavo form, so as to confine it probably to that class of readers who may consider it cooly: so soon as it is published cheaply, for dissemination among the populace, it will be my duty to prosecute." Quoted in Appleby, *Capitalism and a New Social Order*, 60.

36. For an extensive treatment of the role of Austin, see Richard E. Ellis, *The Jeffersonian Crisis: Courts and Politics in the Young Republic* (New York, 1971), 184–224. Austin's *Observations*, originally published in 1786, are reprinted in the *American Journal of Legal History* 8 (1969):244–302.

37. Benjamin Austin, Jr., *Constitutional Republicanism in Opposition to Fallacious Federalism* (Boston, 1803), 173.

38. Ibid., 212.

39. Samuel Eliot Morison, ed., "William Manning's *The Key of Libberty*," *William and Mary Quarterly*, 3d ser., 13 (1956):211.

40. Ibid., 212, 213, 218, 220, 221.

41. Ibid., 253, 232, 248.

42. Ellis, *Jeffersonian Crisis*.

43. Jesse Higgins, *Sampson Against the Philistines, or the Reformation of Lawsuits; and Justice Made Cheap, Speedy, and Brought Home to Every Man's Door; Agreeably to the Principles of the Ancient Trial by Jury, Before the Same was Innovated by Judges and Lawyers* (Philadelphia, 1805). On this movement, see G. S. Rowe, "Jesse Higgins and the Failure of Legal Reform in Delaware, 1800–1810," *Journal of the Early Republic* 3 (1983):17–43.

44. Benjamin Austin, Jr., "Observations on the Pernicious Practice of the Law" (1786), in *American Journal of Legal History* 13 (1969):258.

45. "Decius," *Independent Chronicle*, Jan. 30, 1804, 1.

46. Ellis, *Jeffersonian Crisis*, 171, 177; Austin, "Observations on the Pernicious Practice of the Law," 264.

47. For the importance in Thomas Jefferson's thought of breaking the grip of custom and precedent, see Edmund S. Morgan, *The Meaning of Independence: John Adams, George Washington, Thomas Jefferson* (Charlottesville, 1976), 71–79; and Daniel J. Boorstin, *The Lost World of Thomas Jefferson* (Boston, 1948).

48. On the Thomsonian movement, see Alex Berman, "The Thomsonian

Movement and Its Relation to American Pharmacy and Medicine," *Bulletin of the History of Medicine* 25 (1951):405–28; Joseph F. Kett, *The Formation of the American Medical Profession: The Role of Institutions, 1780–1860* (New Haven, Conn., 1968), 97–131; and Ronald L. Numbers, "Do-It-Yourself the Sectarian Way," in *Medicine Without Doctors: Home Health Care in American History*, ed. Guenter B. Risse, Ronald L. Numbers, and Judith Walzer Leavitt (New York, 1977), 49–72. For Thomson's trial, see Dudley Atkins Tyng, *Reports of the Cases Argued and Determined in the Supreme Judicial Court of the Commonwealth of Massachusetts* (Newburyport, Mass., 1811), 6:134–42.

49. Samuel Thomson, *New Guide to Health: or Botanic Family Physician* (Boston, 1825), 155; and Samuel Thomson, *An Earnest Appeal to the Public Showing the Misery Caused by the Fashionable Mode of Practice of the Doctors at the Present Day* (Boston, 1824). Elias Smith's medical publications are *The Medical Pocket-Book, Family Physician and Sick Man's Guide to Health* (Boston, 1822); and *The American Physician and Family Assistant* (Boston, 1826).

50. Numbers, "Do-It-Yourself the Sectarian Way," 50.

51. Ibid., 107, 131.

52. *Boston Thomsonian Manual* 1 (1835):8.

53. Samuel Thomson, *New Guide to Health*, 6–9, 165; Samuel Thomson, *Earnest Appeal*, 2.

54. John Thomson, *A Vindication of the Thomsonian System of the Practice of Medicine on Botanical Principles* (Albany, N.Y., 1825), 73.

55. Samuel Thomson, *Earnest Appeal*, 7.

56. Leland, *The Writings of the Late Elder John Leland*, ed. L. F. Greene (New York, 1845), 431–32. Adam Wallace, *The Parson of the Islands; A Biography of the Rev. Joshua Thomas* (Philadelphia, 1861), 197. Leonard J. Arrington, *Brigham Young: American Moses* (New York, 1985), 311; Robert T. Divett, *Medicine and the Mormons* (Bountiful, Utah, 1981).

57. See Alan Taylor, "The Backcountry Conclusion to the American Revolution: Agrarian Unrest in the Northeast, 1750–1820," in *The American Revolution: Further Explorations in the History of American Radicalism*, ed. Alfred F. Young (DeKalb, Ill., forthcoming), manuscript p. 21. The figures for Pennsylvania are from Thomas P. Slaughter, *The Whiskey Rebellion: Frontier Epilogue to the American Revolution* (New York, 1986), 65; for Kentucky and Tennessee from Malcolm J. Rohrbough, *The Trans-Appalachian Frontier: People, Societies, and Institutions 1775–1850* (New York, 1978), 25.

58. This argument is developed persuasively by Alan Taylor in "The Early Republic's Supernatural Economy: Treasure Seeking in the American Northeast, 1780–1830," *American Quarterly* 38 (1986):18–19.

59. Slaughter, *Whiskey Rebellion*, 65–66, 84–85.

60. Ibid., 37.

61. Marion L. Starkey, *A Little Rebellion* (New York, 1955), 18. David P. Szatmary, *Shays' Rebellion: The Making of an Aquarian Insurrection*, (Amherst, Mass., 1980).

62. This petition, which was written by the radical preacher Samuel Ely, is quoted in Robert E. Moody, "Samuel Ely: Forerunner of Shays," *New England Quarterly* 5 (1932):127.

63. Ann Grant, *Memoirs of an American Lady*, 2 vols. (New York, 1903). For

the intensely religious dimension to these struggles over land in New York, see David J. Goodall, "New Light on the Border: New England Squatter Settlements in New York during the American Revolution" (Ph.D. diss., State University of New York at Albany, 1984), especially 263–308. Baptist preacher James Finn moderated a July 20, 1786, meeting of Yankee settlers that declared, "Equal distribution of property, and not engrossing large domains, is the basis of free and equal government, founded on republican principles . . . the labours bestowed in subduing a rugged wilderness were our own, and can never be wrested from us without infringing the eternal rules of right." Minutes of a settlers' meeting, July 20, 1786, quoted in Taylor, "Backcountry Conclusion to the American Revolution," manuscript pp. 22–23.

A principal leader of the "Wild Yankees" was Matthew Adgate, who served in the last provincial congress and in the State Assembly. A bitter opponent of Philip Schuyler and of Schuyler's father-in-law John Van Rensselaer over land policy, Adgate published at the turn of the century *A Northern Light: or a New Index to the Bible* (Troy, N.Y., 1800), an interpretation of biblical prophecy that conflates the "doctrine taught by our Saviour when on earth" and the "first and great truth" of the Declaration of Independence that all men are created equal; and sees the republican government of the United States foretold in chapters 11 and 19 of the book of Revelation. Adgate, *Northern Light*, 71, 80.

64. For a description of the religious underpinnings of agrarian unrest in Vermont, see Chilton Williamson, *Vermont in Quandary: 1763–1825* (Montpelier, Vt., 1949), 21.

65. "In order to gain our present liberty from upper powers of tyranny, the powers of kings was first reduced to a mere shadow, and then, by our independence, abolished altogether . . . to reduce us again to tyranny, the power of our legislatures is reduced to shadows; for what little is left them may, by the same hasty proceedings, be taken from them the next month or two, or in ten or a dozen years. . . . The new constitution breaks through all the sacred ties, oaths, and obligations, by which we were united together under our former constitutions." Herman Husband, *A Sermon to the Bucks and Hinds of America* (Philadelphia, 1788), 13–14. The most comprehensive study of Husband is Mark H. Jones, "Herman Husband: Millenarian, Carolina Regulator, and Whiskey Rebel" (Ph.D. diss., Northern Illinois University, 1982).

66. Herman Husband, *Fourteen Sermons on the Characters of Jacob's Fourteen Sons* (Philadelphia, 1789), v; sermon 7:25–26, 30–33.

67. Ibid., sermon 10:13. Ruth Bloch discusses this shift in *Visionary Republic: Millennial Themes in American Thought, 1756–1800* (Cambridge, England, 1985), 113–14.

68. Husband's attack against Hamilton's financial program is found in *A Dialogue Between an Assembly-Man and a Convention-Man* (Philadelphia, 1790). He condemned the creation of a national debt because of the advantage given to speculators: "If all men are to be born free and to purchase this freedom, all martyrs of Christianity spilt their blood; then it will follow that public credit, established on the subjecting of our children, to be born with a burden on their backs . . . that it is the curse of all curses, and is as unjust as if by law to oblige insolvent debtors to black their children in infancy and sell them slaves for life." Ibid., 11–12.

69. Timothy Dwight, *Travels in New England and New York*, ed. Barbara

Miller Solomon, 4 vols. (Cambridge, Mass., 1969), 2:189. For an overview of Ely's life, see Moody, "Samuel Ely."

70. Samuel Ely, *The Deformity of a Hideous Monster, Discovered in the Province of Maine, by a Man in the Woods, Looking after Liberty. Printed near Liberty Tree, for the Good of the Commonwealth* (Boston, 1797). See also Ely, *The Unmasked Nabob of Hancock County or the Scales Dropt from the Eyes of the People* (Portsmouth, N.H., 1796) and [Samuel Ely and James David], *The Appeal of the Two Counties of Lincoln and Hancock from the Forlorn Hope, or Mount of Distress; to the General Court, or to All the World* (Portsmouth, N.H., 1796).

71. Nathan Barlow, *A Vision Seen by Nathan Barlow, of Freetown (Called so by the Inhabitants) Adjacent to the North-End of Harlem, in the County of Kennebec, District of Maine, January 8, 1801* (Boston, 1802).

72. On Brackett and his activities, see Alan Taylor, "'Stopping the Progres of Rogues and Deceivers': A White Indian Recruiting Notice of 1808," *William and Mary Quarterly*, 3d ser., 42 (1985):90–103, quotation on 102.

73. Scales became a Shaker and led an eccentric itinerant life. His pilgrimage is described in the chap. on religion in Alan Taylor, *Liberty-Men and Great Proprietors* (Chapel Hill, N.C., forthcoming). Scales's works include *The Confusion of Babel Discovered: Or, an Answer to Jeremy Belknap's Discourse upon the Lawfulness of War, or Military Duty* ("America," 1780); and *Priestcraft Exposed from its Foundation: or, Religious Freedom Defended; in Nine Chapters* (Danvers, Mass., 1781).

74. William Jones, *A True Account of All the Presbyterian and Congregational Ministers That Were Settled or Preached for a Year or More from Kennebec to St. George's Fort* (Bristol, Maine, 1808), and *The Inconsistency and Deception of the Methodist Ministers Together with the Abuses Exercised Towards their Church Members, Exposed* (Bristol, Maine, 1810).

75. James Shurtleff, *The Substance of a Late Remarkable Dream in Which was Presented the Celestial Worlds and the Internal Regions With the Arch Enemy of Mankind With His Legions Paraded* (Hallowell, Maine, 1800), 8–9. See also Shurtleff, *A Concise Review of the Spirit Which Seemed to Govern in the Time of the Late American War, Compared with the Spirit Which Now Prevails* (Augusta, Maine, 1798).

76. Backus, *The Diary of Isaac Backus*, ed. William G. McLoughlin, 3 vols. (Providence, R.I., 1980). See my review of this edition in *William and Mary Quarterly*, 3d ser., 40 (1983):141–42.

77. George A. Rawlyk, *Ravished By the Spirit: Religious Revivals, Baptists, and Henry Alline* (Kingston, Ontario, 1984), 145.

78. Perry Miller, *The Life of the Mind in America: From the Revolution to the Civil War* (New York, 1965), 7.

79. Works that make this general assumption include Richard Hofstadter, *Anti-Intellectualism in American Life* (New York, 1962); Miller, *Life of the Mind in America*; and Sidney E. Mead, *The Lively Experiment in America: The Shaping of Christianity in America* (New York, 1963).

Scholars have also had a tendency to link the advent of democratic values to the outworking of one or another of these separate traditions. For Vernon L. Parrington, American democracy represented the victory of Jeffersonians in the South and Unitarians in New England over the arch-conservative impulses of evangelical Calvinism. See Parrington, *Main Currents of American Thought*, 2 vols. (New York, 1927; rev. ed., 1954), 2:313–14. Inverting these categories, Alan Heimert attributed the most durable democratic current to evangelical Calvinists and their disposition to adopt Jeffersonian ideas. See Heimert, *Religion and the American Mind from the Great Awakening to the Revolution* (Cambridge, Mass., 1966), 510–52.

That democratic values and varieties of evangelical Christianity were mutually reinforcing in the early republic was the direct legacy of neither eighteenth-century revivals nor any other single agency or source. It was born of strange conjunctures and owes less to any single movement than to an entire historical process, in many cases a clash of wills out of which something emerged that no one had ever willed. People slipped into new points of view without knowing it and found their labors deflected to unpredictable ends. What made many evangelicals enthusiastic for democracy in the wake of the Revolution was a flowering of both the movement itself and of values grafted onto it, often unexpectedly and from alien sources.

80. For a brilliant description of the intellectual ferment of popular culture in this period, see Gordon S. Wood, "Evangelical America and Early Mormonism," *New York History* 61 (1980):359–86.

81. Goodrich, *Recollections of a Lifetime*, 1:207. On Dow, generally, see Charles Coleman Sellers, *Lorenzo Dow: The Bearer of the Word* (New York, 1928); and Richard Carwardine, *Transatlantic Revivalism: Popular Evangelicalism in Britain and America, 1790–1865* (Westport, Conn., 1978), 104–07, 134–35.

82. Benjamin Bawley, "Lorenzo Dow," *Journal of Negro History* 1 (1916):269. Dow's frenetic itinerating is recounted in the numerous editions of his journal, which began in 1804 as *The Life and Travels of Lorenzo Dow* (Hartford, 1804). By 1814, these accounts had expanded into a book of almost four hundred pages. See Dow, *History of Cosmopolite: or, the Four Volumes of Lorenzo's Journal* (New York, 1814). Later editions of Dow's complete works were over seven hundred pages long. See *History of Cosmopolite: or The Four Volumes of Lorenzo Dow's Journal . . . also his Polemical Writings* (Wheeling, Va., 1848).

83. Dow rails against the tyranny of elites in his work "Analects Upon the Rights of Man," published separately in Alexandria, Virginia, and in New York City in 1813 and then included in most subsequent editions of his journal and his polemical works. See *All the Polemical Works of Lorenzo Dow* (New York, 1814), and *History of Cosmopolite* (1814).

84. In 1805, Nicholas Snethen wrote to British Methodists warning them to have nothing to do with Dow. He criticized Dow for estimating "truth and right, not so much by principle as by success" and for his vulgarity: "His manners have been clownish in the extreme; his habit and appearance more filthy than a Savage Indian; his public discourses a mere rhapsody, the substance often an insult upon the gospel . . . frequently choosing the most vulgar saying as a motto to his discourses." Snethen also warned of Dow's assumed role as a prophet: "He has affected a recognizance of the secrets of men's hearts and lives, and even assumed the awful prerogative of prescience, and this not occasionally, but as it were habitually, pretending to foretell, in a great number of instances, the deaths or calamities of persons, &c." Dow quotes this letter in *History of Cosmopolite* (1814), 353–55. The account of his prophecy against Saint Stephen's, Alabama, is found in Richard J. Stockham, "The Misunderstood Lorenzo Dow," *Alabama Review* 16 (1963):20; see also 31–32. For Dow's reputation as a holy man with unusual powers, see Sellers, *Lorenzo Dow*, 148–51.

85. Dow, *History of Cosmopolite* (1848), 420.

86. Dow, *History of Cosmopolite* (1814), 356–57.

87. Samuel Goodrich noted Dow's unkept beard, reddish and dusty, "some six inches long—then a singularity if not an enormity, as nobody among us but old Jagger the beggar cultivated such an appendage." Goodrich, *Recollections of a Lifetime*, 1:207.

88. Dow, "Chain of Lorenzo," in *History of Cosmopolite* (1814), iii–iv. Dow claims this was the twenty-seventh printed edition of the "Chain."

89. Goodrich, *Recollections of a Lifetime*, 1:211.

90. John W. Francis, *Old New York; or Reminiscences of the Past Sixty Years* (New York, 1858), 147.

91. Caleb Rich, "A Narrative of Elder Caleb Rich," *Candid Examiner* 2 (1827):179–80. Stephen A. Marini includes a fuller discussion of Rich in *Radical Sects of Revolutionary New England* (Cambridge, Mass., 1982), 72–75.

92. Rich, "A Narrative," 205–08.

93. For a discussion of Winchester's career, see Joseph R. Sweeny, "Elhanan Winchester and the Universal Baptists" (Ph.D. diss., University of Pennsylvania, 1969).

94. Elhanan Winchester, *The Universal Restoration* (London, 1788), xvii–xviii.

95. During the 1770s, the unlearned Methodist convert Benjamin Abbott, wrestling with the complexities of Calvinism, made a similar decision: "I had to stand for myself," he concluded. He recounted his experiences as follows: "I then drew a conclusion, that I would not join any Church until I had read the Bible and compared it with their articles or confessions of faith. Accordingly I took the Westminster Confession of Faith, and compared it with the Scriptures, and found it held many things which were not in the Bible: but repugnant thereunto: I then got the Baptist Confession of Faith, and compared their articles in like manner, and found them as unscriptural and repugnant to truth as the former. I found the Bible held out free grace *to all*, and *for all*, and that Christ tasted death for *every man*, and offered Gospel salvation to *all*: therefore, I could not bear those contracted partial doctrines of unconditional election and reprobation. So I threw them both aside, and went on with the Bible, from Genesis to the Revelation, until I had read it through; by which time I was well armed with arguments against the predestinarians." Abbott, *Experience and Gospel Labours of the Rev. Benjamin Abbott* (New York, 1832), 25.

96. Smith, *The Life, Conversion, Preaching, Travels, and Sufferings of Elias Smith* (Boston, 1840), 257–58.

97. Jones, *Memoir of Elder Abner Jones*, ed. A. D. Jones (Boston, 1842), 24, 49–51.

98. See William Smythe Babcock Papers, American Antiquarian Society, Worcester, Massachusetts.

99. Miscellaneous Papers, Babcock Papers. For the entire poem, see appendix.

100. Journal of Preaching, December 1809, Babcock Papers.

101. Lucy Smith, *Biographical Sketches of Joseph Smith, the Prophet* (Liverpool, 1853; reprint, New York, 1969), 37, 46–49. The Mormon elder Parley Parker Pratt, born in Burlington, New York, in 1807, recalled that his father was an equally devout but unattached believer: "He taught us to venerate our Father in Heaven, Jesus Christ, His prophets and Apostles, as well as the Scriptures written by them;

while at the same time he belonged to no religious sect, and was careful to preserve his children free from all prejudice in favor or against any particular denomination, into which the so-called Christian world was then unhappily divided." *The Autobiography of Parley Parker Pratt, One of the Twelve Apostles*, ed. Parley P. Pratt (New York, 1874), 17.

102. Simon Hough, *The Sign of the Present Time or a Short Treatise Setting Forth What Particular Prophecies Are Now Fulfilling* (Stockbridge, Mass., 1799), 5–6. For brief discussions of Hough, who was probably the most socially radical millennialist in America during the 1790s, see Bloch, *Visionary Republic*, 138, 157; and James West Davidson, "Searching for the Millennium: Problems for the 1790's and the 1970's," *The New England Quarterly* 45 (1972):253–54. Hough's other pamphlets are *An Alarm to the World: Dedicated to All Ranks of Men* (Stockbridge, Mass., 1792) and *A True Gospel Church Organized and Disciplined* (Stockbridge, Mass., 1793).

103. Timothy Waterous, *The Battle-Axe and Weapons of War: Discovered by the Morning Light, Aimed for the Final Destruction of Priestcraft* (Groton, Conn., 1811). The poem is quoted by Elias Smith in *Herald of Gospel Liberty*, June 21, 1811, 296. On the Rogerene Quakers, see Ellen Starr Brinton, "The Rogerenes," *New England Quarterly* 16 (1943):3–11; and Brinton, "Books by and about the Rogerenes," *Bulletin of the New York Public Library* 49 (1945):627–48. The entire poem "Priest-Craft Float Away" is included in the appendix.

104. These images are found throughout Simon Hough, *Alarm to the World*, and Lorenzo Dow, "On Church Government," in *History of Cosmopolite* (1816). For the way in which the *Book of Mormon* picks up many of these same themes, see chap. 4 below.

105. Hough, *Alarm to the World*, 21–22.

106. Appleby, *Capitalism and a New Social Order*, 82.

107. The phrase is that of Fisher Ames comparing Federalists and Republicans. *Works of Fisher Ames*, ed. Seth Ames, 2 vols. (Boston, 1854), 2:113. Quoted in Wood, "The Democratization of Mind," 78. On this point Samuel Goodrich made a specific contrast between the Methodists and the Standing Order in Connecticut: "The Methodists had the advantage, however, for their preachers introduced topics in their discourses, often making pointed and personal attacks the pepper and salt of their harangues—while the more stately orthodox usually confined their discussions to private circles, or perhaps general and dignified notices in their sermons." Goodrich, *Recollections of a Lifetime*, 1:211–12.

Chapter Three

1. Asbury, *The Journal and Letters of Francis Asbury*, ed. Elmer C. Clark, J. Manning Potts, and Jacob S. Payton, 3 vols. (Nashville, 1958), 3:341–45, 453. While Asbury's estimate of camp meeting attendance was probably exaggerated, others noted that by 1811 four to five hundred meetings were being staged annually. An average attendance of three thousand persons at four hundred camp meetings would involve 1.2 million persons. Asbury's estimate of the number of camp meetings is found in a letter to Thomas Coke, ibid., 3:455.

2. Ibid., 3:343.

3. For discussions of Dow's two trips to Great Britain and his problems with Methodist authorities, see Richard Carwardine, *Trans-Atlantic Revivalism: Popular*

Evangelicalism in Britain and America, 1790–1865 (Westport, Conn., 1978), 103–07; and Julia Stewart Werner, *The Primitive Methodist Connexion: Its Background and Early History* (Madison, 1984), 45–47.

4. Dow's significant role in stimulating interest in camp meetings in England is explored in Werner, *Primitive Methodist Connexion*, 45–47, and Deborah Valenze, *Prophetic Sons and Daughters: Female Preaching and Popular Religion in Industrial England* (Princeton, 1985), 78–79.

5. David Hempton has commented that, although Methodism had earlier mounted a successful challenge to one religious establishment, at the turn of the century it was well on the way to creating another. See Hempton, *Methodism and Politics in British Society 1750–1850* (Stanford, 1984), 80. The work of W. R. Ward is also excellent on the external pressures upon the Methodists and their internal quest for order. See Ward, "The Religion of the People and the Problem of Control, 1790–1830," in *Popular Belief and Practice*, ed. G. J. Cuming and Derek Baker (Cambridge, England, 1972), 237–57; and Ward, *Religion and Society in England 1790–1850* (New York, 1973), 21–53.

6. Deborah Valenze has an insightful discussion of why British Methodists reacted so vehemently to the camp meeting. She suggests that such events "elevated the debased to the realm of the sacred and upset the hierarchy of the experience essential to conventional social order." *Prophetic Sons and Daughters*, 89–93.

7. *Journal and Letters of Francis Asbury*, 3:344. On the integration of camp meetings into the life of the Methodist Episcopal Church in America, see Russell E. Richey, "From Quarterly to Camp Meeting: A Reconsideration of Early American Methodism," *Methodist History* 23 (1985):199–213. The standard history of the subject is Charles A. Johnson, *The Frontier Camp Meeting: Religion's Harvest Time* (Dallas, 1955).

8. Bentley, *The Diary of William Bentley, D.D.*, 4 vols. (Salem, Mass., 1905–14), 3:174. Bentley makes this entry on July 21, 1805, after noting a week-long camp meeting in Lynn, Massachusetts.

9. George A. Phoebus, comp., *Beams of Light on Early Methodism in America* (New York, 1887), 142; Finley, *Autobiography of Rev. James B. Finley*, ed. W. Strickland (Cincinnati, 1853).

10. Latrobe's sketch and description of Bunn the blacksmith are together in Edward C. Carter II et al., *Latrobe's View of America, 1795–1820* (New Haven, Conn., 1985), 276–77.

11. This phrase is from the scathing critique by Frances Trollope in 1829 of a camp meeting on the border of Indiana and Ohio. Trollope, *Domestic Manners of the Americans*, ed. Donald Smalley (New York, 1949), 170.

12. John Wesley to Sarah Mallet, 15 Dec. 1789, quoted in Valenze, *Prophetic Sons and Daughters*, 83. Wesley also would not tolerate loud and spontaneous prayer. William Turner, *A Key to Unlock Methodism, or Academical Hubbub, Containing Some Remarks on Fanaticism* (Norwich, Conn., 1800); reprinted as appendix B in Edgar F. Clark, *The Methodist Episcopal Churches of Norwich, Conn.* (Norwich, Conn., 1867), 241–42; *Journal and Letters of Francis Asbury*, 3:370.

13. In a letter to Thornton Fleming on December 2, 1802, Asbury said, "I wish you would hold camp meetings; they have never been tried without success. To collect such a number of God's people together to pray, and the ministers to

preach, and the longer they stay, generally, the better—this is field fighting, this is fishing with a large net." *Journal and Letters of Francis Asbury*, 3:251.

14. Hempton, *Methodism and Politics*, 73.

15. Donald G. Mathews, "The Second Great Awakening as an Organizing Process, 1780–1830," *American Quarterly* 21 (1969):36. At times, the Methodists would preach without even a single local supporter. Jesse Lee commented in his journal that in August of 1789 he preached to a large crowd in Milford, Connecticut. "This is the third time I have preached at this place, and have not yet become acquainted with any person." Lee, *Memoir of the Rev. Jesse Lee*, ed. Minton Thrift (New York, 1823), 121.

16. *Minutes of Several Conversations between the Rev. Thomas Coke, LL.D., the Rev. Francis Asbury and Others, at a Conference, begun in Baltimore, in the State of Maryland, on Monday, the 27th of December, in the Year 1784* (Philadelphia, 1785), 12. This work, commonly called the *Discipline* of 1784, was the first in a series of works instructing Methodist preachers in doctrine and deportment. Robert Paine, *Life and Times of William M'Kendree*, 2 vols. (Nashville, 1870), 1:40.

17. Michael Walzer, *The Revolution of the Saints: A Study in the Origins of Radical Politics* (Cambridge, Mass., 1965), 1–21; and Walzer, "Puritanism as a Revolutionary Ideology," *History and Theory* 3 (1964):59–90.

18. Towle, *Vicissitudes Illustrated in the Experience of Nancy Towle* (Portsmouth, N.H., 1833), 25, 30.

19. W. R. Ward, "The Legacy of John Wesley: The Pastoral Office in Britain and America," in Anne Whiteman et al., *Statesmen, Scholars and Merchants* (Oxford, 1973), 346–48.

20. Ralph E. Morrow, "The Great Revival, the West, and the Crisis of the Church," in *The Frontier Re-examined*, ed. John F. McDermott (Urbana, Ill., 1967), 72. Another superb example of this type of visionary leader bent on movement formation is Sidney Rigdon, whose own dynamic presence led him to forceful roles, first as chief lieutenant in the Disciples under Alexander Campbell and then in the Mormons under Joseph Smith. Smith said of Rigdon's willingness to abandon all for the sake of a cause: "Truth was his pursuit, and for truth he was prepared to make every sacrifice in his power." See F. Mark McKeirnan, *The Voice of One Crying in the Wilderness: Sidney Rigdon, Religious Reformer, 1793–1876* (Lawrence, Kans., 1971), quote on 13.

21. Parsons Cooke, *A Century of Puritanism and a Century of Its Opposites* (Boston, 1855), 258; quoted in Paul G. Faler, *Mechanics and Manufacturers in the Early Industrial Revolution: Lynn, Massachusetts, 1780–1860* (Albany, N.Y., 1981), 47.

22. Richard Carwardine has argued that many of the so-called new measures supposedly introduced by the revivalist Charles Finney (the "anxious bench," women praying in public, colloquial preaching, protracted meetings) had been widely employed by the Methodists before Finney. See "The Second Great Awakening in the Urban Centers: An Examination of Methodism and the 'New Measures,'" *Journal of American History* 59 (1972):327–40. For the innovative techniques of the Methodists, see also Terry D. Bilhartz, *Urban Religion and the Second Great Awakening: Church and Society in Early National Baltimore* (Rutherford, N.J., 1986).

23. Lawrence Goodwyn, *The Populist Moment: A Short History of the Agrarian Revolt in America* (New York, 1978), vii–xxiv, 34–35, 293–96.

24. Young, *Autobiography of Dan Young, A New England Preacher of Olden Time,* ed. W. Strickland (New York, 1860), 34.

25. Gatch, *Sketch of Rev. Philip Gatch,* ed. John M'Lean (Cincinnati, 1854), 135.

26. The itinerant Methodist Joshua Thomas reports two such incidents with Dow. See Adam Wallace, *The Parson of the Islands: A Biography of the Rev. Joshua Thomas* (Philadelphia, 1861), 59, 76.

27. Michael Chevalier, *Society, Manners and Politics in the United States: Being a Series of Letters from North America* (Boston, 1839), 317.

28. Goodwyn, *Populist Moment,* xviii.

29. Alan V. Briceland, "The Philadelphia Aurora, the New England Illuminati, and the Election of 1800," *The Pennsylvania Magazine of History and Biography* 100 (1976):3–36; James M. Banner, Jr., *To the Hartford Convention: The Federalists and the Origins of Party Politics in Massachusetts, 1789–1815* (New York, 1970), 122–67; Donald H. Stewart, *The Opposition Press of the Federalist Period* (Albany, N.Y., 1969).

30. Stephen A. Marini, *Radical Sects of Revolutionary New England* (Cambridge, Mass., 1982), 36–38. The estimates from Stiles are found in *The Literary Diary of Ezra Stiles,* ed. Franklin Bowditch Dexter, 3 vols. (New York, 1901), 2:412. Alan Taylor has provided an excellent discussion of the weakness of the Standing Order in Maine in the chap. on religion in *Liberty-Men and Great Proprietors* (Chapel Hill, N.C., forthcoming).

31. For the plight of the Episcopal church in Virginia, see David Lynn Holmes, Jr., "William Meade and the Church of Virginia, 1789–1829" (Ph.D. diss., Princeton University, 1971), 166–90.

32. James Thayer Addison, *The Episcopal Church in the United States, 1789– 1931* (New York, 1951), 79.

33. William H. Williams, *The Garden of American Methodism: The Delmarva Peninsula, 1769–1820* (Wilmington, Del., 1984), 92.

34. Sarah McCulloh Lemmon, "Nathaniel Blount: Last Clergyman of the 'Old Church,'" *The North Carolina Historical Review* 50 (1973):363.

35. Morrow, "The Great Revival," 69.

36. Ibid., 78.

37. John Opie, "The Melancholy Career of 'Father' David Rice," *Journal of Presbyterian History* 47 (1969):295–319. Johnson's poem reads as follows:

On Parson R--e,
Who refused to perform divine service till his arrears were paid.
Ye fools! I told you once or twice,
You'd hear no more from canting R--e;
He cannot settle his affairs,
Nor pay attention unto pray'rs,
Unless you pay up your arrears.
O how he would in pulpit storm,
And fill all hell with dire alarm!
Vengeance pronounce against each vice,
And, more than all, curs'd avarice;
Preach'd money was the root of ill,
Consign'd each rich man unto hell;

But since he finds you will not pay,
Both rich and poor may go that way.
'Tis no more than I expected—
The meeting-house is now neglected:
All trades are subject to this chance,
No longer pipe, no longer dance.

38. Rice's two reports published in 1805 and 1808, respectively, are included in Robert H. Bishop, *An Outline of the History of the Church in the State of Kentucky, during a Period of Forty Years; Containing the Memoirs of Rev. David Rice* (Lexington, Ky., 1824). On Rice, see also the entry in *Princetonians, 1748–1768: A Biographical Dictionary*, ed. James McLachlan (Princeton, 1976), 354–57.

39. See David Hackett Fischer, *The Revolution of American Conservatism: The Federalist Party in the Era of Jeffersonian Democracy* (New York, 1965).

40. On the shift to a culture that did not recognize elite claims to disinterestedness, see Gordon S. Wood, "Interests and Disinterestedness in the Making of the Constitution," in *Beyond Confederation: Origins of the Constitution and American National Identity*, ed. Richard Beeman, Stephen Botein, and Edward C. Carter II (Chapel Hill, N.C., 1987), 69–109.

41. Historians of American religion since World War II have more or less reached consensus in their interpretations of revivalism. They have focused on its positive and integrative social roles, largely ignoring issues of social conflict and the struggle for cultural power between different kinds of Protestants. They have interpreted revivalism as a powerfully cohesive force, with evangelicalism emerging as a kind of national church or national religion. See William Warren Sweet, *Religion in the Development of American Culture 1765–1840* (New York, 1952); Timothy L. Smith, *Revivalism and Social Reform: Protestantism on the Eve of the Civil War* (Nashville, 1957); Winthrop S. Hudson, *American Protestantism* (Chicago, 1961); Sidney E. Mead, *The Lively Experiment: The Shaping of American Christianity in America* (New York, 1963); Perry Miller, *The Life of the Mind in America: From the Revolution to the Civil War* (New York, 1965); Martin E. Marty, *Righteous Empire: The Protestant Experience in America* (New York, 1970); Robert T. Handy, *A Christian America: Protestant Hopes and Historical Realities* (New York, 1971); and C. C. Goen, *Broken Churches, Broken Nation: Denominational Schisms and the Coming of the Civil War* (Macon, Ga., 1985).

42. Horace Bushnell, "Barbarism the First Danger," in Bushnell, *Work and Play* (New York, 1881), 267.

43. Horace Bushnell, "Barbarism the First Danger," 227, 230–33, 245. Lyman Beecher's obsession with unity and all his exertions to produce what he called "a more homogeneous character" grew out of his intense fear of disorder. In the 1820s he had warned in equally grave tones that if the "extravagance and disorder" of the Finney revivals were to continue, it would "roll back the wheels of time to semibarbarism" and constitute "an era of calamity never to be forgotten"—what future historians would surely call "the dark age of our republic." *Letters of the Rev. Dr. Beecher and Rev. Mr. Nettleton, on the "New Measures" in Conducting Revivals of Religion* (New York, 1828), 98–99.

44. Perry Miller, "From the Covenant to the Revival," in *The Shaping of American Religion*, ed. James Ward Smith and A. Leland Jamison (Princeton, 1961), 354.

45. Hans Kohn, *American Nationalism: An Interpretive Essay* (New York: 1957), chap. 1.

46. John M. Murrin, "A Roof without Walls: The Dilemma of American National Identity," in *Beyond Confederation*, ed. Beeman et al., 347.

47. Quoted in Michael Kammen, *A Season of Youth: The American Revolution and the Historical Imagination* (New York, 1978), 3, 4.

48. *Julian M. Sturtevant: An Autobiography*, ed. J. M. Sturtevant, Jr. (New York, 1896), 160–61. By 1860, Jacksonville had eighteen Protestant churches for a town of fewer than ten thousand people. See Don Harrison Doyle, *The Social Order of a Frontier Community: Jacksonville, Illinois, 1825–70* (Urbana, Ill., 1978), 39–61.

49. Lawrence Foster, "Free Love and Feminism: John Humphrey Noyes and the Oneida Community," *Journal of the Early Republic* 1 (1981):170.

50. Morrow, "The Great Revival," 70.

51. Josiah Quincy, *The History of Harvard University*, 2 vols. (Cambridge, Mass., 1840), 2:663.

Chapter Four

1. Luther P. Gerlach and Virgnia H. Hine have argued that the success of religious movements can actually spring from organizational fission and lack of cohesion. Splitting, combining, and proliferating can be seen as clear signs of health if recruiting new members is the goal. See Gerlach and Hine, *People, Power, Change: Movements of Social Transformation* (Indianapolis, 1970).

2. Stephen Porter, *A Discourse, in Two Parts, Addressed to the Presbyterian Congregation in Ballston* (Ballston Spa, N.Y., 1814), 2, 7, 10, 16, 42, 45. A description of the incident is found in *Herald of Gospel Liberty*, June 23, 1815, 693–94.

3. The lyrics of this song are included in the appendix.

4. Bentley, *The Diary of William Bentley, D.D.*, 4 vols. (Salem, Mass., 1905–14), 3:157–393 passim.

5. Smith, *The Life, Conversion, Preaching, Travels and Sufferings of Elias Smith* (Portsmouth, N.H., 1816), 341–42.

6. Elias Smith, *The Loving Kindness of God Displayed in the Triumph of Republicanism in America: Being a Discourse Delivered at Taunton (Mass.) July Fourth, 1809; at the Celebration of American Independence* (n.p., 1809), 32. Smith's colleague Abner Jones also experienced what he called a "disintegration" of his Calvinist beliefs and was quick to note the theological implications of demands for social equality. "In giving the reader an account of my birth and parentage," Jones wrote in 1807, "I shall not (like the celebrated Franklin and others,) strive to prove that I arose from a family of eminence; believing that all men are born equal, and that every man shall die for his own iniquity." Jones, *Memoirs of the Life and Experience, Travels and Preaching of Abner Jones* (Exeter, N.H., 1807), 3.

7. For a brief sketch of Smith's life, see William G. McLoughlin, *New England Dissent, 1630–1883: The Baptists and the Separation of Church and State*, 2 vols. (Cambridge, Mass., 1971), 2:745–49. Otherwise, no one has undertaken a serious study of Smith, despite his prominence as a religious and political radical in New

England from 1800 to 1820, his scores of publications addressed to a popular audience, his newspaper that ran for a decade, and his fascinating memoir. The number of his itinerant followers is taken from one of his Congregational assailants: Thomas Andros, *The Scriptures Liable to be Wrested to Men's Own Destruction, and an Instance of This Found in the Writings of Elias Smith* (Taunton, Mass., 1817), 18. A list of agents for Smith's newspaper is found in *Herald of Gospel Liberty*, Aug. 18, 1809, 104. For the number of subscribers, see ibid., Sept. 29, 1815, 720. On Smith's movement, which became known as the Christian Connection, see Thomas H. Olbricht, "Christian Connection and Unitarian Relations," *Restoration Quarterly* 9 (1966):160–86.

8. The best treatment of James O'Kelly is Charles Franklin Kilgore, *The James O'Kelly Schism in the Methodist Episcopal Church* (Mexico City, 1963). See also Edward J. Drinkhouse, *History of Methodist Reform*, 2 vols. (Baltimore, 1899), vol. 1; and Milo T. Morrill, *A History of the Christian Denomination in America* (Dayton, 1912). O'Kelly's primary works are *The Author's Apology for Protesting against the Methodist Episcopal Government* (Richmond, 1798); and *A Vindication of the Author's Apology* (Raleigh, 1801).

9. O'Kelly, *Author's Apology*, 4, 21.

10. O'Kelly, *Vindication*, 60–61.

11. "The Last Will and Testament of Springfield Presbytery," in John Rogers, *The Biography of Elder B. Warren Stone* (New York, 1972), 51–53. For other primary accounts of this movement, see Barton W. Stone, *An Apology for Renouncing the Jurisdiction of the Synod of Kentucky* (Lexington, Ky., 1804); [Richard McNemar], *Observations on Church Government, by the Presbytery of Springfield* (Cincinnati, 1807); Robert Marshall and James Thompson, *A Brief Historical Account of Sundry Things in the Doctrines and State of the Christian, or as It Is Commonly Called, the Newlight Church* (Cincinnati, 1811); Levi Purviance, *The Biography of Elder David Purviance* (Dayton, 1848); and Robert H. Bishop, *An Outline of the History of the Church in the State of Kentucky, During a Period of Forty Years: Containing the Memoirs of Rev. David Rice* (Lexington, Ky., 1824).

12. There is a considerable body of uncritical denominational literature on Barton W. Stone produced by the Disciples of Christ. See William Garrett West, *Barton Warren Stone: Early American Advocate of Christian Unity* (Nashville, 1954). For emphasis on Stone's contribution to the revivalist heritage of the South, see John B. Boles, *The Great Revival, 1787–1805: The Origins of the Southern Evangelical Mind* (Lexington, Ky., 1972). For appreciation of Stone in his full cultural context, see Ralph Morrow, "The Great Revival, the West, and the Crisis of the Church," in *The Frontier Re-examined*, ed. John F. McDermott (Urbana, 1967), 65–78.

13. Rogers, *Biography of Elder B. Warren Stone*, 3, 47.

14. For discussions of the origins of the Campbellites, see David Edwin Harrell, Jr., *Quest for a Christian America: The Disciples of Christ and American Society to 1866* (Nashville, 1966); Robert Frederick West, *Alexander Campbell and Natural Religion* (New Haven, Conn., 1948); Lester G. McAllister, *Thomas Campbell: Man of the Book* (St. Louis, 1954); and Errett Gates, *The Early Relation and Separation of Baptists and Disciples* (Chicago, 1904). In addition, see the extensive memoirs of father and son: Alexander Campbell, *Memoirs of Elder Thomas Campbell* (Cincinnati, 1861); and Robert Richardson, *Memoirs of Alexander Campbell*, 2 vols. (Cincinnati, 1913).

15. Richardson, *Memoirs of Alexander Campbell*, 1:465–66, 438. Many scholars have assumed that Thomas and Alexander Campbell applied to an American context beliefs that they had learned under the influence of Scottish reformers such as Robert Haldane and James Alexander Haldane. See, for example, Sydney E. Ahlstrom, *A Religious History of the American People* (New Haven, Conn., 1972), 448–49. The early documents of the Campbellite movement, however, manifest a keen awareness that the issues to be faced were, in their intensity at least, peculiarly American and demanded new solutions. See, for example, Thomas Campbell, *The Declaration and Address of the Christian Association of Washington* (Washington, Pa., 1809).

16. Lester G. McAllister and William E. Tucker, *Journey in Faith: A History of the Christian Church (Disciples of Christ)* (St. Louis, 1975), 154–55.

17. Alexander Campbell, "An Oration in Honor of the Fourth of July, 1830," *Popular Lectures and Addresses* (Philadelphia, 1863), 374–75.

18. "Elias Smith was here last week, distributing his books & pamphlets, & preached a lecture last week without sparing any of the hirelings as he calls them." Bentley, *Diary of William Bentley*, 3:388.

19. *Herald of Gospel Liberty*, Sept. 1, 1808, 1.

20. Stephen Porter, a Presbyterian clergyman, attempted to ward off the influence of Smith and his lieutenants among his congregation. Porter, *Discourse, in Two Parts*, 42–44.

21. Elias Smith, *The Clergyman's Looking-Glass: Being a History of the Birth, Life, and Death of Anti-Christ* (Porstmouth, N.H., 1803), 11. For examples of Smith's sensitivity to elitist codes of all sorts, even while he was still a Baptist, see Smith, *Life . . . of Elias Smith*, 279–80.

22. *Christian Baptist*, July 4, 1823, 280. (Pagination for *The Christian Baptist* is taken from the fifteenth edition, ed. Alexander Campbell, 7 vols. in 1 (St. Louis, [n.d.]).

23. *Herald of Gospel Liberty*, Dec. 8, 1808, 29–30.

24. Abel M. Sargent founded a radical sect in Marietta, Ohio, where he published six issues of *Halcyon Itinerary and True Millennium Messenger*. The quotation is found in *Halcyon Itinerary and True Millennium Messenger* (Dec. 1807), 147–48. For a letter from Sargent to Smith, see *Herald of Gospel Liberty*, Aug. 16, 1811, 310. On Sargent, see John W. Simpson, *A Century of Church Life* (Marietta, Ohio, 1896), 31.

25. Christians assailed the clergy as "tyrannical oppressors," "the mystery of iniquity," "friends of monarch religion," "old tories," "an *aristocratical body of uniform nobility*," and "hireling priests"; people who would submit to such tyrants they labeled priest-ridden, slavishly dependent, passively obedient. See Smith, *Life . . . of Elias Smith*, 384, 402–03; *Herald of Gospel Liberty*, Oct. 13, 1809, 117; O'Kelly, *Vindication*, 47. In 1815 Smith claimed that most people in New England from forty to seventy years old could remember the respectable clergy emphasizing apocalyptic themes such as "*Anti-Christ, mystery Babylon, the great whore* that sitteth on many waters, the *beast* with seven heads and ten horns, the man of sin &c." *Herald of Gospel Liberty*, May 20, 1815, 685. On the multivalence of language, see J. G. A. Pocock, *Politics, Language and Time: Essays on Political Thought and History* (New York, 1971), 3–41; and Harry S. Stout, "Religion, Communications, and the Ideological Or-

igins of the American Revolution," *William and Mary Quarterly*, 3d ser., 34 (1977):538.

26. Smith, *Loving Kindness of God Displayed*, 26–27; Smith, *Life . . . of Elias Smith*, 362–63. See also *Herald of Gospel Liberty*, April 14, 1809, 67.

27. *Christian Baptist*, Jan. 2, 1826, 209; Smith, *Life . . . of Elias Smith*, 402–03; *Herald of Gospel Liberty*, Sept. 15, 1808, 6. See also Richardson, *Memoirs of Alexander Campbell*, 1:382–83.

28. See David Rice, *An Epistle to the Citizens of Kentucky, Professing Christianity; Especially Those That Are, or Have Been, Denominated Presbyterians* (Lexington, Ky., 1805), as given in Bishop, *The Church in the State of Kentucky*, 332–33.

29. Rhys Isaac, "Evangelical Revolt: The Nature of the Baptists' Challenge to the Traditional Order in Virginia, 1765 to 1775," *William and Mary Quarterly*, 3d ser., 31 (1974):345–68.

30. Isaac Backus, *A History of New England with Particular Reference to the Denomination of Christians Called Baptists*, 2 vols. (Newton, Mass., 1871), 2:487. For evidence of the Baptist quest for respectability in the generation after the Great Awakening, see C. C. Goen, *Revivalism and Separatism in New England, 1740–1800* (New Haven, Conn., 1962). For the reaction of Baptists to the dissent spawned by the Revolution, see McLoughlin, *New England Dissent*, 2:710.

31. James Patrick Walsh, "The Pure Church in Eighteenth Century Connecticut" (Ph.D. diss., Columbia University, 1964), 143.

32. Rogers, *Biography of Elder B. Warren Stone*, 51–53.

33. *Christian Baptist*, Nov. 3, 1823, 25; Richardson, *Memoirs of Alexander Campbell*, 2:62.

34. [McNemar], *Observations on Church Government*, 4, 9, 15. This pamphlet, the best-developed statement of Christian ecclesiology, rejects "external rules" and insists that all human organization spring from the deliberate and uncoerced choice of the individual.

35. O'Kelly, *Vindication*, 49. For similar expressions of resistance to human mediation of divine authority by Alexander and Thomas Campbell, see *Christian Baptist*, April 3, 1826, 229; and T. Campbell, *Declaration and Address of the Christian Association*, 3. For the recurrence of this line of thought a generation later, see Lewis Perry, *Radical Abolitionism: Anarchy and the Government of God in Antislavery Thought* (Ithaca, N.Y., 1973).

36. Gilbert McMaster, *An Essay in Defence of Some Fundamental Doctrines of Christianity; including a Review of the Writings of Elias Smith and the Claims of his Female Preachers* (Schenectady, 1815), 100, 109, 111. On Cram, see J. F. Burnett, *Early Women of the Christian Church* (Dayton, 1921), 9–13.

37. Towle, *Vicissitudes Illustrated in the Experience of Nancy Towle* (Portsmouth, N.H., 1833), 44, 26, 29.

38. Richard Hughes, "Christians in the Early South: The Perspective of Joseph Thomas, 'The White Pilgrim,'" *Discipliana* 46 (1986):1, 35–37, 43.

39. Joseph Thomas, *The Travels and Gospel Labors of Joseph Thomas, Minister of the Gospel and Elder in the Christian Church* (Winchester, Va., 1812). A later edition is *The Life of the Pilgrim Joseph Thomas, Containing an Accurate Account of his Trials, Travels, and Gospel Labors, up to the Present Date* (Winchester, Va., 1817).

40. Thomas, *Life*, 132. J. W. Grant, "A Sketch of the Reformation in Ten-

nessee," 55, typescript in Center for Restoration Studies, Abilene Christian University. Cited in Hughes, "Christians in the Early South," 36.

41. Thomas, *Life*, 259–64. Thomas's songbooks include *The Pilgrims Hymn Book* (Winchester, Va., 1816) and *The Trump of Christian Union, Containing a Collection of Hymns* (Winchester, Va., 1819). A poem by Joseph Thomas, "Bigotry Reported," is included in the appendix.

42. For an excellent example of the potential for factionalism within a local Christian church, see Don Harrison Doyle, *The Social Order of a Frontier Community: Jacksonville, Illinois, 1825–70* (Urbana, Ill., 1978), 157–60.

43. Smith himself left the Christian Connection in 1818 to join the Universalists, and two of his colleagues, Joshua V. Himes and Joseph Marsh, became early advocates of William Miller. David L. Rowe, "A New Perspective on the Burned-Over District: The Millerites in Upstate New York," *Church History* 48 (1978):408–20. Of five men who signed the "Last Will and Testament of Springfield Presbytery," two returned to the Presbyterians, two became Shakers, and only Stone retained his identity as a Christian. Alexander Campbell similarly saw his best preacher, Sidney Rigdon, defect to the Mormons. Mario S. De Pillis, "The Quest for Religious Authority and the Rise of Mormonism," *Dialogue: A Journal of Mormon Thought* 1 (1966):68–88.

44. Christopher Hill, *The World Turned Upside Down: Radical Ideas during the English Revolution* (New York, 1972).

45. J. F. C. Harrison, *The Second Coming: Popular Millenarianism, 1780–1850* (New Brunswick, 1979), 163–206.

46. The phrase is that of Joseph Smith, who reacted strongly to the sectarian competition he knew as a young man. Smith, *The Pearl of Great Price* (Salt Lake City, 1891), 56–70.

47. Richard McNemar, "The Mole's Little Pathways," in Daniel W. Patterson, *The Shaker Spiritual* (Princeton, 1979), 136–37.

48. John Williamson Nevin, "Antichrist and the Sect," in *The Mercersburg Theology*, ed. James Hastings Nichols (New York, 1966), 93–119; quote on 98–99.

49. L. C. Rudolph, *Francis Asbury* (Nashville, 1966), 144–46.

50. Asbury, *The Journal and Letters of Francis Asbury*, ed. Elmer C. Clark, J. Manning Potts, and Jacob S. Payton, 3 vols. (Nashville, 1958) 3:492, 475–78.

51. Ibid., 3:475–76.

52. Ibid., 3:479–81, 487.

53. Ibid., 3:476. Asbury had made the same kind of contrast in the 1798 *Discipline*: "All the episcopal churches in the world are conscious of the dignity of the episcopal office. The greatest part of them endeavour to preserve this dignity by large salaries, splendid dresses, and other appendages of pomp and splendour." He goes on to speak of "that infinitely superior dignity which is the attendant of labour, of suffering and enduring hardship for the cause of Christ." *The Doctrines and Discipline of the Methodist Episcopal Church, in America* (Philadelphia, 1798), 44–45.

54. Robert Wiebe, *The Opening of American Society* (New York, 1984), 158.

55. Francis Asbury in *The Arminian Magazine* 7 (London, 1784):681. Quoted in Robert Emerson Coleman, "Factors in the Expansion of the Methodist Episcopal Church from 1784 to 1812" (Ph.D. diss., University of Iowa, 1954), 214–15.

56. Asbury, *Journal and Letters of Francis Asbury*, 1:85, 10. On Asbury's early and intense commitment to a "traveling plan," see Coleman, "Factors in the Expan-

sion of the Methodist Episcopal Church," 29–31. Asbury clearly felt uncomfortable in polite urban society. He wrote to his parents a year after arriving in America, "'Tis one great disadvantage to me I am not polite enough for the people. They deem me fit for the country, but not for the cities; and it is my greater misfortune I cannot, or will not, learn, and they cannot teach me. But as my father and mother were never very polite people, it is not so strange. And as I was not born so, nor educated after this sort, I cannot help it." *Journal and Letters of Francis Asbury*, 3:14.

57. Asbury, *Journal and Letters of Francis Asbury*, 1:10. On January 1, 1772, Asbury complained again: "I find that the preachers have their friends in the cities, and care not to leave them." Ibid., 1:16.

58. Asbury had little sympathy with the sacramentalism of urban chapels and played a crucial role in discarding the *Sunday Service* that John Wesley had instituted for America, with its formal prayer forms, responsive readings, creeds, and weekly observance of the Lord's Supper. Asbury despised formalism and feared that people would become overreliant on the sacraments. For a careful discussion of the striking contrast between Asbury and Joseph Pilmore on these points, see William Nash Wade, "A History of Public Worship in the Methodist Episcopal Church and the Methodist Episcopal Church, South, from 1784 to 1905" (Ph.D. diss., University of Notre Dame, 1981), 141–82.

In his valedictory address, Asbury quoted the low-church Anglican Thomas Haweis to exalt the plain worship of the apostolic community: "The simplicity of gospel truth ill accords with a *farrago* of rites and ceremonies. Nothing could be more unadorned than the primitive worship. A plain man, chosen from among his fellows, in his common garb, stood up to speak, or sat down to read the Scriptures, to as many as chose to assemble in the house appointed. A back room, and that probably a mean one, or a garret, to be out of the way of observation, was their temple." Asbury, *Journal and Letters of Francis Asbury*, 3:488.

59. *Doctrines and Discipline* (1798), 36, 42.

60. For a good example of how Asbury singled out young men for itinerant ministries, see the account of Jesse Lee, whom Asbury recruited in 1782: "At the close of the conference, Mr. Asbury came to me and asked me if I was willing to take a circuit; I told him that I could not well do it, but signified I was at a loss to know what was best for me to do. I was afraid of hurting the cause which I wished to promote; for I was very sensible of my own weakness." Asbury then announced in public, "I am going to enlist brother Lee." Menton Thrift, *Memoir of the Rev. Jesse Lee with Extracts from his Journals* (New York, 1823), 42–43.

61. Asbury's journal entry for October 26, 1799, reads as follows: "I stayed at the house, to read, write, and plan a little. I tremble and faint under my burden:—having to ride about six thousand miles annually; to preach from three to five hundred sermons a year; to write and read so many letters, and read many more:—all this and more, besides the stationing of three hundred preachers; reading many hundred pages; and spending many hours in conversation by day and by night, with preachers and people of various characters, among whom are many distressing cases." Asbury, *Journal and Letters of Francis Asbury*, 2:210.

62. Certainly one of Asbury's greatest trials was the unpredictability of his living accommodations. He reported the following in 1803: "The people, it must be confessed, are amongst the kindest souls in the world. But kindness will not make a crowded log cabin, twelve feet by ten, agreeable: without are cold and rain; and

within, six adults, and as many children, one of which is all motion; the dogs, too, must sometimes be admitted. On *Saturday*, at Felix Ernest's, I found that amongst my other trials, I had taken the itch; and, considering the filthy houses and filthy beds I have met with, in coming from the Kentucky Conference, it is perhaps strange that I have not caught it twenty times: I do not see that there is any security against it, but by sleeping in a brimstone shirt:—poor bishop! But we must bear it for the elect's sake. I wrote some letters to our local brethren, and read the book of Daniel while in the house." Ibid., 2:411.

63. Ibid., 2:417.

64. Ibid., 3:333.

65. One can speculate that being so outwardly directed had intellectual consequences that were the opposite of the tribal instincts of New England Puritanism. As Edmund S. Morgan describes them, seventeenth-century New Englanders easily lost sight of serving as a beacon to the world and became more a refuge from it, preaching, coaxing, and praying in order to save their own children. By lifting their sights to a mass audience, the Methodists suffered another danger, that of domesticating the message that they proclaimed to the mores of popular culture to which they were attempting to speak. On Puritan "tribalism," see Edmund S. Morgan, *The Puritan Family: Religion and Domestic Relations in Seventeenth-Century New England* (Boston, 1944), 161–86.

66. Michael Walzer, *The Revolution of the Saints: A Study in the Origins of Radical Politics* (Cambridge, Mass., 1965), 3.

67. Allen Wiley, an early Indiana preacher, gave this typical description of his colleague Thomas Hellum, whom he met in 1806: "He was a tall, raw-boned, hollowed-eyed man, who dressed according to the Methodist preacher fashion of that day, namely round-breasted coat, long vest with the corners cut off, short breaches, and long stockings, with his hair turned back, from about midway between the forehead and the crown, and permitted to grow down to the shoulders. He had a most solemn and impressive countenance, and his subjects of discourse were usually of a grave and pathetic cast; and they were rendered much more pathetic by his manner of delivering them. The intonations of his voice were as solemn as death, and usually the large tears dropped from his face most of the time while he was preaching. So far as I can judge, his piety was deep and abiding, and his talents I should think were above mediocrity." Wiley's reflections, originally published in 1848 in the *Western Christian Advocate*, are reprinted as "Methodism in Southeastern Indiana," *Indiana Magazine of History* 23 (1927):35–36.

68. Nathan Bangs counted 2,468 preachers received into full connection between 1769 and 1828. See Wade C. Barclay, *Early American Methodism 1769–1844*, 2 vols. (New York, 1950), 2:355.

69. Abel Stevens, *A Compendious History of American Methodism* (New York, 1867), 528. The General Conference of 1792 defined the status of "supernumerary Preacher" as one who could not preach constantly because of broken health, but was willing to do any work in the ministry that the Conference might direct or his strength allow. See William Warren Sweet, *Methodism in American History* (Nashville, 1953), 135.

70. This criticism came from Nicholas Snethen (1769–1845), one of Asbury's trusted companions whom he called the movement's "silver trumpet." After serving over a decade as a circuit rider, Snethen married in 1804 and withdrew from

the itinerancy to serve as a local preacher. In 1811 he served as chaplain to the United States House of Representatives. Snethen became the key organizer and publicist of the reform agitation of the 1820s, which eventuated in the formation of the Methodist Protestant church in 1830. This movement, which concerned the rights of local congregations and local preachers, can be seen as a power struggle between the old and the young, the local preachers and the circuit riders. *Wesleyan Repository* (August, 1822), 135–36. Steven J. Novak has a useful discussion of these issues in an unpublished paper, "The Perils of Respectability: Methodist Schisms of the 1820s." See also Emory Stevens Bucke et al., *The History of American Methodism*, 3 vols. (New York, 1964), 1:636–62.

71. David Hackett Fisher, *Growing Old in America* (New York, 1978), 77–112.

72. Stevens, *Compendious History of American Methodism*, 528.

73. W. R. Ward, "The Legacy of John Wesley: The Pastoral Office in Britain and America," in Anne Whiteman et al., *Statesmen, Scholars and Merchants* (Oxford, 1973), 347.

74. The General Conference of 1796 appealed for a chartered fund that would provide support for the superannuates and the widows and orphans: "It is to be lamented, if possible, with tears of blood, that we have lost scores of our most able married ministers . . . because they saw nothing before them for their wives and children, if they continued itinerants, but misery and ruin." *Journals of the General Conference of the Methodist Episcopal Church*, 2 vols. (New York, 1855–56), 1:22.

Asbury noted in his journal at the Virginia Conference in 1809, "The high taste of these southern folks will not permit their families to be degraded by an alliance with a Methodist traveling preacher; and thus, involuntary celibacy is imposed upon us: all the better; anxiety about worldly possessions does not stop our course." Asbury, *Journal and Letters of Francis Asbury* 2:591.

75. Edward Channing, *A History of the United States* (New York, 1923), 4:9–10. Donald M. Scott, *From Office to Profession: The New England Ministry, 1750–1850* (Philadelphia, 1978), 113.

76. Peter Cartwright joined the Western Conference in 1804; in 1807 he was compelled to return to the home of his father because he had no money for clothes or a horse. Cartwright, *Autobiography of Peter Cartwright, the Backwoods Preacher*, ed. W. P. Strickland (New York, 1856), 103–07. In 1806, Asbury found the preachers at the Western Conference in such abject poverty that he felt constrained to part with his watch, coat, and shirt. Coleman, "Factors in the Expansion of the Methodist Episcopal Church," 211.

77. *Minutes of Several Conversations between the Rev. Thomas Coke, LL.D., the Rev. Francis Asbury and Others, at a Conference, begun in Baltimore, in the State of Maryland, on Monday, the 27th of December, in the Year 1784* (Philadelphia, 1785), 8.

78. Frederick V. Mills, Sr., "Mentors of Methodism, 1784–1844," *Methodist History* 12 (1973):51–53. William Warren Sweet, *Circuit-Rider Days in Indiana* (Indianapolis, 1916), 76–77. See also Cartwright, *Autobiography of Peter Cartwright*, 78–83.

79. Coleman, "Factors in the Expansion of the Methodist Episcopal Church," 196–200.

80. The best study to date of Methodism in a given locale is the book by Dee

Andrews, *Popular Religion and the Revolution in the Middle Atlantic Ports: The Rise of the Methodists, 1770–1800* (Princeton, forthcoming).

81. In 1805, Asbury confessed to Thomas Sargent, "I console myself with an increase of about 20,000 souls Joyned to the Church annually." Six months later, in a letter to Thomas Coke, he again alluded to his own principal yardstick of success: "As judgment is begun at the house of God we mean to have no cyfers [zeros] in our connection." Asbury, *Journal and Letters of Francis Asbury*, 3:332, 343.

82. John F. Schermerhorn and Samuel J. Mills, *A Correct View of That Part of the United States Which Lies West of the Allegany Mountains, with Regard to Religion and Morals* (Hartford, Conn., 1814), 41.

83. Asbury's negative reaction in 1811 to the rising prominence of Methodist ministers is typical: "Hilliard Judge is chosen chaplain to the legislature of South Carolina; and O, great [Nicholas] Snethen is chaplain to Congress! So; we begin to partake of *the honor that cometh from man*: now is our time of danger. O Lord, keep us pure, keep us correct, keep us holy!" Asbury, *Journal and Letters of Francis Asbury*, 2:687.

84. Jabez Bunting to George Marsden, January 28, 1813. Quoted in W. R. Ward, "The Religion of the People and the Problem of Control, 1790–1830," in G. J. Cuming and Derek Baker, *Popular Belief and Practice* (Cambridge, England, 1972), 247.

85. E. P. Thompson, *The Making of the English Working Class* (New York, 1963), 397. Alan D. Gilbert suggests a corrective to Thompson's emphasis on the antiradical implications of Methodism. At a local level, he emphasizes that mildly radical forms of sociopolitical commitment were prevalent. For our purposes, it is significant that politics became a major disruptive factor within local Methodist societies. See Gilbert, "Methodism, Dissent and Political Stability in Early Industrial England," *Journal of Religious History* 10 (1978–79):381–99; and *Religion and Society in Industrial England: Church, Chapel and Social Change, 1740–1914* (London, 1976).

86. W. R. Ward has done excellent work on these matters. See his *Religion and Society in England 1790–1850* (New York, 1973), 21–104; "Religion of the People and the Problem of Control"; and his edited volumes of the correspondence of Jabez Bunting, *The Early Correspondence of Jabez Bunting 1820–1829* (London, 1972); and *Early Victorian Methodism: The Correspondence of Jabez Bunting 1830–1858* (Oxford, 1976). On the development of a "high" doctrine of the pastoral office, see John C. Bowmer, *Pastor and People: A Study of Church and Ministry in Wesleyan Methodism from the Death of John Wesley (1791) to the Death of Jabez Bunting (1858)* (London, 1976).

87. John Walsh, "Methodism at the End of the Eighteenth Century," in Rupert Davies et al., *A History of the Methodist Church in Great Britain* (London, 1965), 344.

88. David Hempton, *Methodism and Politics in British Society 1750–1850* (Stanford, 1984), 227. A Methodist pamphlet of 1821 declared the phrase "the liberties and rights of the people" to be "the cant word, or rather the watch-word of Treason and rebellion." *The Patriot; A Tale, Illustrating the Pernicious Effects of Bad Principles on the Lower Orders of Society* (London, 1821), 13, quoted in Bernard Semmel, *The Methodist Revolution* (New York, 1973), 140. After the clash at Peterloo, the Methodist superintendent in Manchester dismissed four hundred from the membership roll and proclaimed that the chief object in view was "to give the sound part of the

society the ascendency." Ward, *Religion and Society in England*, 90–92. In a similar vein, a friend of Jabez Bunting urged him to run for Parliament in 1832 because of "the noble stand you have taken against that overwhelming flood of democracy and misrule which was so recently breaking in upon us almost everywhere." See Ward, *Early Victorian Methodism*, xvi.

89. On the political diversity of Methodists in the 1830s and 1840s, see Richard Carwardine, "Methodist Ministers and the Second Party System," in *Rethinking Methodist History: A Bicentennial Historical Consultation*, ed. Russell E. Richey and Kenneth E. Rowe (Nashville, 1985), 135–47.

90. In 1813 David Benedict had published *A General History of the Baptist Denomination*, 2 vols. (Boston, 1813), which had well over two thousand subscribers, including all the major figures at the convention. In his careful assessments of Baptist strength, Benedict counted 2633 churches, 2142 ministers, and 204,185 members. This is an increase from an estimated 500 churches and 20,000 communicants at the time of the Revolution.

91. Robert B. Semple, *A History of the Rise and Progress of the Baptists in Virginia* (Richmond, 1810), 254.

92. Smith, *Life . . . of Elias Smith*, 243, 248.

93. James A. Rogers, *Richard Furman: Life and Legacy* (Macon, Ga., 1985), 135–68. When Furman moved from pastoring a church in the backcountry of South Carolina to Charleston in 1787, his former church issued a formal complaint about his adopting the fashionable dress of Charleston society. Ibid., 84–85.

94. Robert G. Torbet, *A History of the Baptists* (Chicago, 1963), 250.

95. *Proceedings of the Baptist Convention for Missionary Purposes* (Philadelphia, 1814), 42.

96. Rogers, *Richard Furman*, 179, 293–95.

97. Torbet, *History of the Baptists*, 310.

98. Within eight years of 1817, for instance, five institutions that grew into Baptist colleges or seminaries were founded at Hamilton, New York, in 1819; Waterville, Maine, in 1820; Washington, D.C., in 1822; Newton, Massachusetts, in 1825; and Georgetown, Kentucky, in 1829. Rogers, *Richard Furman*, 195.

99. The best assessments of Leland's activities are L. H. Butterfield, "Elder John Leland, Jeffersonian Itinerant," *Proceedings of the American Antiquarian Society* 62 (1953):155–242; McLoughlin, *New England Dissent*, 2:915–38; and Edwin S. Gaustad, "The Backus-Leland Tradition," *Foundations: A Baptist Journal of History and Theology* 2 (1959):131–52. On Leland's antislavery activity in Virginia, see James D. Essig, *The Bonds of Wickedness: American Evangelicals Against Slavery, 1770–1808* (Philadelphia, 1982), 67–72.

100. W. P. Cutler and J. P. Cutler, *Life, Journals and Correspondence of Rev. Manasseh Cutler*, 2 vols. (Cincinnati, 1888), 2:66–67. On the creation and presentation of the cheese, see Butterfield, "Elder John Leland," 214–29.

101. Leland, *The Writings of the Late Elder John Leland*, ed. L. F. Greene (New York, 1845), 513–15.

102. Ibid., 377.

103. On Leland's significant role in antimission activities, see Byron Cecil Lambert, *The Rise of the Anti-Mission Baptists: Sources and Leaders, 1800–1840* (New York, 1980), 116–52; "A Little Sermon Sixteen Minutes Long," in Leland, *Writings of the Late Elder John Leland*, 410. For Leland's opposition to formal theological

education, see his satirical poem "The Modern Priest" in the appendix. John Leland, *The Virginia Chronicle* (Fredericksburg, Va., 1790), 34; "Extracts from a Letter to Rev. John Taylor of Kentucky, Dated Dec. 10, 1830," in Leland, *Writings of the Late Elder John Leland*, 601.

104. John Leland, *An Oration Delivered at Cheshire, July 5, 1802, on the Celebration of Independence* (Hudson, N.Y., 1802), 12.

105. Three early historians of the Baptists in America all chronicle the rise of a movement from persecution to respectability. All make an implicit appeal that Baptists be accorded the same respect as other churches. See Semple, *History of . . . Baptists in Virginia*; Benedict, *General History of the Baptist Denomination*; and Isaac Backus, *A History of New England with Particular Reference to the Denomination of Christians Called Baptists* (Newton, Mass., 1871). The same approach is also evident in the writing of Methodist history: see Nathan Bangs's *A History of the Methodist Episcopal Church*, 4 vols. (1840–53). On Bangs, see chap. 7 below.

106. "Events in the Life of John Leland Written by Himself," in *Writings of the Late Elder John Leland*, 10.

107. "The History of Jack Nips," in ibid., 76–77.

108. See Leland's discussion of "The Right and Bonds of Conscience" in his pamphlet *The Virginia Chronicle*, 45. "Conscience," Leland wrote in 1830, "is a court of judicature, erected in every breast, to take cognizance of every action in the home department, but has nothing to do with another man's conduct. My best judgment tells me that my neighbor does wrong, but my conscience has nothing to say of it. Were I to do as he does, my conscience would arrest and condemn me, but guilt is not transferable. Every one must give an account of himself." See "Transportation of the Mail," in Leland, *Writings of the Late Elder John Leland*, 565.

109. *The Rights of Conscience Inalienable . . . or, The High-flying Churchman, Stripped of his Legal Robe, Appears a Yaho* (New London, 1791), 8. Elsewhere Leland argued explicitly that truth would prevail in a free market of ideas: "Truth is in the least danger of being lost, when free examination is allowed." Leland, *Writings of the Late Elder John Leland*, 78.

110. Leland, *The Rights of Conscience Inalienable*, 15–16. Three years later, in 1794, the Congregational minister Noah Worcester expressed the very stereotype of common folk that Leland rejected. In Worcester's view, the Baptists succeeded by their ability to engage that "class of persons . . . who possess weak judgments, fickle minds, and quick and tender passions." Worcester explained that such persons "are of such low understanding, that they are incapable of duly examining the force of arguments; and may be confounded by the length or multiplicity of them, while no real conviction is afforded to their minds." Worcester, *Impartial Inquiries Respecting the Progress of the Baptist Denomination* (Worcester, Mass., 1794), 11–12.

111. Leland, *Writings of the Late Elder John Leland*, 255. The sermon was published in New London and Suffield, Conn. (1801), Bennington, Vt. (1801), Edenton, N.C. (1803), and Washington, Ga. (1805).

112. "Letter to the Editor of the Baptist Chronicle, at Georgetown, Ky.," in Leland, *Writings of the Late Elder John Leland*, 571; Leland, *The Virginia Chronicle*, 34. In the papers of Isaac Backus there is a manuscript, "Leland's queries," which openly questions the logic of Calvinism. William G. McLoughlin has reprinted this in *The Diary of Isaac Backus*, 3 vols. (Providence, 1979), 3:1261.

113. Semple, *History of . . . Baptists in Virginia*, 206–07.

114. "Which Has Done the Most Mischief in the World, the Kings-Evil or Priest-Craft?" in Leland, *Writings of the Late Elder John Leland*, 494.

115. "The Modern Priest," in ibid., 193. This poem is included in the appendix.

116. Ibid.; Backus, *A History of New England*, 2:487; "Which Has Done the Most Mischief in the World," 484; "A Little Sermon, Sixteen Minutes Long," 408–12; "Catechism," in Leland, *Writings of the Late Elder John Leland*, 451.

117. "Part of a Speech, Delivered at Suffield, Connecticut, on the First Jubilee of the United States," in Leland, *Writings of the Late Elder John Leland*, 523–24; Butterfield, "Elder John Leland," 196.

118. Butterfield, "Elder John Leland," 236–39. For an example of Leland's contribution to *The Reformer*, see his poem "False Prophets Contrasted With the Apostle Paul" in the appendix.

119. Gates, *Early Relation and Separation of Baptists and Disciples*; David L. Rowe, *Thunder and Trumpets: Millerites and Dissenting Religion in Upstate New York, 1800–1850* (Chico, Calif., 1985).

120. Lambert, *The Rise of the Anti-Mission Baptists*; Harold L. Twiss, "Missionary Support by Baptist Churches and Associations in Western Pennsylvania, 1815–45," *Foundations: A Baptist Journal of History and Theology* 10 (1967):36–49; James E. Tull, *A History of Southern Baptist Landmarkism in the Light of Historical Baptist Ecclesiology* (New York, 1980).

121. Francis Wayland, president of Brown University and editor of the *American Baptist Magazine*, had hoped to transform the Triennial Convention of 1826 into a genuine instrument of Baptist polity. Instead, the convention was virtually dismantled. New England and New York delegates, led by Wayland, were effective in discrediting Luther Rice, whose base of operations was in Washington, D.C. They concentrated power in their own hands and moved the headquarters of the mission board to Boston. For a full discussion of these developments, see Winthrop S. Hudson, "Stumbling into Disorder," *Foundations: A Baptist Journal of History and Theology* 1 (1958):45–71.

122. Walter Brownlow Posey, *The Baptist Church in the Lower Mississippi Valley, 1776–1845* (Lexington, Ky., 1957), 126–27; Edward P. Brand, *Illinois Baptists: A History* (Bloomington, Ill., 1930), 86. On the belligerently democratic movements among Illinois Baptists in the Jacksonian era, see John F. Cady, "The Religious Environment of Lincoln's Youth," *Indiana Magazine of History* 37 (1941):16–30.

123. Charles Colcock Jones (1804–63) was a full-time Presbyterian missionary to slaves in Liberty County, Georgia, and secretary of the Presbyterian Board of Domestic Missions. See his *The Religious Instruction of the Negroes in the United States* (Savannah, 1842), 55–62; and *Thirteenth Annual Report of the Missionary to the Negroes, in Liberty County, (Ga.)* (Charleston, 1848), 45–55.

124. Benjamin Drew, *The Refugee: A North-Side View of Slavery* (Boston, 1856), 108, quoted in Milton C. Sernett, *Black Religion and American Evangelicalism: White Protestants, Plantation Missions, and the Flowering of Negro Christianity, 1787–1865* (Metuchen, N.J., 1975), 107.

125. Wesley M. Gewehr, *The Great Awakening in Virginia, 1740–1790* (Durham, N.C., 1930), 249; Asbury, *Journal and Letters of Francis Asbury*, 2:122.

126. Richard Dozier, "Text Book," April 27, 1789 (Richmond, Va.), quoted in James D. Essig, *The Bonds of Wickedness: American Evangelicals Against Slavery, 1770–1808* (Philadelphia, 1982), 34.

127. Essig, *Bonds of Wickedness*, 48–49.

128. For the Anglican role in legitimizing the slave system, see Jon Butler, "Enlarging the Body of Christ: Slavery, Evangelism, and the Christianization of the White South, 1690–1790," in *The Evangelical Tradition in America*, ed. Leonard I. Sweet (Macon, Ga., 1984), 87–112.

129. Stephen J. Stein, "George Whitefield on Slavery: Some New Evidence," *Church History* 42 (1973):243–56. See also Harvey H. Jackson, "Hugh Bryan and the Evangelical Movement in Colonial South Carolina," *William and Mary Quarterly* 3d ser., 43 (1986):594–614.

130. In 1787–88, Methodists in Sussex County, Virginia, emancipated one hundred slaves at a single session of the County Court. Luther P. Jackson, "Religious Development of the Negro in Virginia from 1760 to 1860," *The Journal of Negro History* 16 (1931):178.

131. In her perceptive study, "Popular Religion and the Revolution in the Middle Atlantic Ports: The Rise of the Methodists, 1770–1800" (Ph.D. diss., Princeton University, 1986), Doris Elizabett Andrews notes that, after the Revolutionary War, the Methodists had greater impact among blacks, slave and free, in a decade than the Anglicans had in the previous seventy-five years (p. 218). The estimate for the Delmarva Peninsula is given in William H. Williams, *The Garden of American Methodism: The Delmarva Peninsula, 1769–1820* (Wilmington, Del., 1984), 112.

132. Thompson, *The Life of John Thompson, A Fugitive Slave* (Worcester, Mass., 1856), 18–19, quoted in Albert J. Raboteau, *Slave Religion: The "Invisible Institution" in the Antebellum South* (New York, 1978), 133.

133. Allen, *The Life Experience and Gospel Labors of the Rt. Rev. Richard Allen* (New York, 1960), 29–30.

134. For an excellent discussion of this point, see Raboteau, *Slave Religion*, 115–20.

135. Jones, *Religious Instruction of the Negroes*, 255, 262, 266.

136. Essig, *Bonds of Wickedness*, 36; George A. Rawlyk, *Ravished by the Spirit: Religious Revivals, Baptists, and Henry Alline* (Kingston, Ontario, 1984), 11.

137. Andrews, "Popular Religion and the Revolution in the Middle Atlantic Ports," 251. Raboteau, *Slave Religion*, 148–50.

138. Raboteau, *Slave Religion*, 134.

139. Leland, *Writings of the Late Elder John Leland*, 98; Jones, *Religious Instruction of the Negroes*, 49.

140. Warren Thomas Smith, "Harry Hosier: Black Preacher Extraordinary," *Journal of the Interdenominational Theological Center* 7 (1980):111–28. Donald G. Mathews, *Religion in the Old South* (Chicago, 1977), 201.

141. Daniel Coker, *Dialogue Between a Virginian and an African Minister* (Baltimore, 1810), 40–41.

142. Albert J. Raboteau, "The Black Experience in American Evangelicalism: The Meaning of Slavery," in *The Evangelical Tradition in America*, ed. Sweet, 183.

143. The earliest documentary evidence of Baptists in Virginia segregating seating dates from 1811 in the First Baptist Church of Alexandria, Virginia. The

following year the Wicomico Baptist Church built a wooden partition inside the church to separate black and white members. See W. Harrison Daniel, "Virginia Baptists and the Negro in the Early Republic," *Virginia Magazine of History and Biography* 80 (1972):60.

144. Jackson, "Religious Development of the Negro in Virginia," 175; Raboteau, *Slave Religion*, 137–38.

145. Mathews, *Religion in the Old South*, 205–06. For a full discussion of the Methodist retreat from their early campaign against slavery, see Donald G. Mathews, *Slavery and Methodism: A Chapter in American Morality, 1780–1845* (Princeton, 1965).

146. Asbury, *Journal and Letters of Francis Asbury*, 3:366–67.

147. W. E. B. DuBois, *The Souls of Black Folk* (Chicago, 1937), 190.

148. Allen, *Life . . . of the Rt. Rev. Richard Allen*, 55.

149. Gary B. Nash, "To Arise Out Of The Dust": Absalom Jones and the African Church of Philadelphia, 1785–95," in Nash, *Race, Class and Politics: Essays on American Colonial and Revolutionary Society* (Urbana, Ill., 1986), 323–55.

150. Tucker Tanner, *An Outline of Our History and Government for African Methodist Churchmen* (Philadelphia, 1884), 142–48. For a full discussion of the evolution of Allen's relationship to Methodism, see Will B. Gravely, "African Methodisms and the Rise of Black Denominationalism," in *Rethinking Methodist History*, ed. Richey and Rowe, 111–24.

151. Gary B. Nash, *Forging Freedom: The Formation of Philadelphia's Black Community, 1720–1840* (Cambridge, Mass., 1988), 260–67.

152. On the formation of the Union Church of Africans in Wilmington, see Lewis V. Baldwin, *"Invisible" Strands in American Methodism: A History of the African Union Methodist Protestant and Union American Methodist Episcopal Churches, 1805–1980* (Metuchen, N.J., 1983). The founding of the African Methodist Episcopal Zion Church in New York is discussed in Gravely, "African Methodisms."

153. Raboteau, *Slave Religion*, 204–05, 163.

154. Thad W. Tate, *The Negro in Eighteenth-Century Williamsburg* (Charlottesville, 1965), 158–63; Raboteau, *Slave Religion*, 134–41.

155. These churches include the Gillfield Baptist and the Harrison Street Baptist of Petersburg, the First Baptist of Norfolk, the Elam Baptist of Charles City, and the King and Queen Baptist in the county of the same name. Jackson, "Religious Development of the Negro in Virginia," 188.

156. For a thorough examination of the emergence of distinct black churches, see Will B. Gravely, "The Rise of African Churches in America (1786–1822): Re-examining the Contexts," *Journal of Religious Thought* 41 (1984):58–73.

157. For an incisive discussion of these themes, see the section "The Black Preachers," in Eugene D. Genovese, *Roll, Jordan, Roll: The World the Slaves Made* (New York, 1972), 255–79; quote on 257. Fredrika Bremer, *The Homes of the New World*, 2 vols. (New York, 1853), 2:289–90, 490–91.

158. Sir Charles Lyell used this phrase to characterize the singing of black Christians; quoted in Genovese, *Roll, Jordan, Roll*, 271.

159. Both Eugene D. Genovese in *Roll, Jordan, Roll* (280–81) and Albert J. Raboteau in *Slave Religion* (136–37) have argued that the indigenous Christianity that came to flourish among enslaved Africans was the crucial element in the formation of a distinct African-American culture.

160. Nash, "To Arise Out Of The Dust," 347.

161. On Joseph Smith, see Richard L. Bushman, *Joseph Smith and the Beginnings of Mormonism* (Urbana, Ill., 1984); and Donna Hill, *Joseph Smith, the First Mormon* (New York, 1977). The maturing of scholarship on Mormons is evident in these works as well as in two other superb treatments of the movement, Jan Shipps, *Mormonism: The Story of a New Religious Tradition* (Urbana, Ill., 1985); and Klaus J. Hansen, *Mormonism and the American Experience* (Chicago, 1981). A subtle and insightful interpretation of the culture that gave rise to Mormonism is Gordon S. Wood, "Evangelical America and Early Mormonism," *New York History* 61 (1980): 359–86. On the dynamic and often embattled state of Mormon historical scholarship, see David Brion Davis, "Secrets of the Mormons," *New York Review of Books*, August 15, 1985, 15–19.

162. Brigham H. Roberts, ed., *History of the Church of Jesus Christ of Latter-day Saints*, 7 vols. (Salt Lake City, 1932–51), 1:3; quoted in Bushman, *Joseph Smith*, 54.

163. Joseph Smith, "History of the Life of Joseph Smith, Jr.," 156; quoted in Bushman, *Joseph Smith*, 55.

164. Shipps, *Mormonism*, 10. On Joseph Smith's extensive reliance on folk magic, see D. Michael Quinn, *Early Mormonism and the Magic World View* (Salt Lake City, 1987).

165. Alan Taylor, "The Early Republic's Supernatural Economy: Treasure Seeking in the American Northeast, 1780–1830," *American Quarterly* 38 (1986):24–25.

166. Lucy Smith reported to her brother in 1831 that the lessons she learned from reading the *Book of Mormon* were "that the eyes of the whole world are blinded; that the churches have all become corrupt, yea every church upon the face of the earth; that the Gospel of Christ is nowhere preached." Lucy Smith to Solomon Mack, January 6, 1831, Church Archives of the Church of Jesus Christ of Latter-Day Saints; quoted in Bushman, *Joseph Smith*, 140.

167. Two very suggestive treatments of the *Book of Mormon* are Richard L. Bushman, "The Book of Mormon and the American Revolution," *Brigham Young University Studies* 17 (1976):3–20; and Timothy L. Smith. "The Book of Mormon in a Biblical Culture," *Journal of Mormon History* 7(1980):3–21. A helpful overview of the content of the *Book of Mormon* is found in Thomas F. O'Dea, *The Mormons* (Chicago, 1957), 22–40.

168. Typical of this approach is Fawn M. Brodie, who suggests that the *Book of Mormon* "can best be explained, not by Joseph's ignorance nor by his delusions, but by his responsiveness to the provincial opinions of his time." See Brodie, *No Man Knows My History: The Life of Joseph Smith*, 2d ed. (New York, 1971), 69.

169. Gordon S. Wood has suggested that efforts to understand the *Book of Mormon* have foundered because of a limited and elitist understanding of early-nineteenth-century popular culture. See Wood, "Evangelical America and Early Mormonism." My point is not to dismiss the well-documented use of folk magic by Joseph Smith but to suggest that such beliefs and practices must be understood in the context of an overall ideological system, the structure of which still remains elusive. Smith's beliefs were clearly a synthesis which grew out of the Judeo-Christian scriptures, magic and the occult arts, and his experience with dreams and visions. More than anything else, Smith yearned for everyday life to recover the kind of miraculous power described in the New Testament.

170. Shipps, *Mormonism*, 32–33.

171. The first two interpretations are made by O'Dea, *The Mormons*, 31, 35; the second two are made by Hansen, *Mormonism and the American Experience*, 68–83.

172. Bushman has shown conclusively that the *Book of Mormon* was not a conventional American book reflecting the ordinary political sentiments of its time. See Bushman, "The Book of Mormon and the American Revolution." Bushman has also suggested that in their radical critique of American civilization, the Latter-Day Saints showed more affinity for premillennialist disillusionment with society than for American optimism and romantic nationalism. Bushman, *Joseph Smith*, 139.

173. George Albert Smith, "History," Church Archives of the Church of Jesus Christ of Latter-Day Saints; quoted by Hill, *Joseph Smith*, 83–84.

174. The verse is quoted from Malachi 4:1.

175. 3 Nephi 28:35.

176. 2 Nephi 9:30.

177. 2 Nephi 28:12–15.

178. 4 Nephi 1:24–27.

179. The third book of Nephi also quotes extensively from the Sermon on the Mount, Matthew chaps. 5–7. In view of Joseph Smith's basic concerns, the themes in that material are also illuminating: blessings upon the poor, the mourning, the meek, and the persecuted; denunciations of hypocrites who give alms and pray in public, admonitions to seek first the kingdom rather than food and raiment; and warnings about false prophets who are ravening wolves in sheep's clothing.

180. 2 Nephi 12:11–17 (Isaiah 2:11–17).

181. 2 Nephi 13:16–26 (Isaiah 3:16–26).

182. 2 Nephi 13:15, 15:7–8, 20:1–2 (Isaiah 3:15, 5:7–8, 10:1–2).

183. A good example of these related themes is found in Alma chap. 4: "And it came to pass in the eighth year of the reign of the judges, that the people of the church began to wax proud, because of their exceeding riches, and their fine silks, and their fine-twined linen, and because of their many flocks and herds, and their gold and their silver, and all manner of precious things, which they obtained by their industry; and in all these things were they lifted up in the pride of their eyes, for they began to wear very costly apparel. . . .

"Yea, he [Alma] saw great inequality among the people, some lifting themselves up with their pride, despising others, turning their backs upon the needy and the naked and those who were hungry, and those who were athirst, and those who were sick and afflicted." Alma 4:6–12.

2 Nephi 26:20 relates pride, learning, despising God's miracles, and grinding the faces of the poor. Alma 5:53–55 threatens unquenchable fire for those who are proud, wear costly apparel, seek riches, persecute the humble, and turn their backs on the poor and needy.

184. "For behold, ye do love money, and your substance, and your fine apparel, and the adorning of your churches, more than ye love the poor and the needy, the sick and the afflicted." Mormon 8:37. A major theme in the book is the clergy's quest for financial gain. "O ye wicked and perverse and stiffnecked people, why have ye built up churches unto yourselves to get gain?" Mormon 8:33. For attacks on priestcraft, see 2 Nephi 26:29, 3 Nephi 16:10, and 30:2.

185. Mormon 8:39–41.

186. Mormon 9:7–11, 15–20. The model saint for the prophet Mormon is one that knows the reality of supernatural gifts: "And he knoweth their faith, for in his name could they remove mountains; and in his name could they cause the earth to shake; and by the power of his word did they cause prisons to tumble to the earth; yea, even the fiery furnace could not harm them, neither wild beasts nor poisonous serpents, because of the power of his word." Mormon 8:24.

187. "Yea, wo unto him that shall deny the revelations of the Lord, and that shall say the Lord no longer worketh by revelation, or by prophecy, or by gifts, or by tongues, or by healings, or by the power of the Holy Ghost!" 3 Nephi 29:6. On this theme, see also 2 Nephi 27:23, 28:4–5, 29:3–10, and the Mormon paper from Kirtland, Ohio, *Evening and Morning Star* 2, no. 20 (May, 1834), 305–07.

188. 2 Nephi 28:14. The book of Mosiah also gives an excellent illustration of identification with the downtrodden. The injunction is given to generosity with those in need: "ye will not suffer that the beggar putteth up his petition to you in vain, and turn him out to perish." A strong indictment is also made of those who blame the poor for their plight, withholding assistance because "the man has brought upon himself his misery" and "his punishments are just." "For behold, are we not all beggars?" Mosiah 4:16–19. The prophet Alma also indicates that it was contrary to the commands of God "that there should be a law which should bring men on to unequal grounds." Alma 30:7. This theme is also prominent in Joseph Smith, *The Doctrine and Covenants of the Church of Jesus Christ of Latter-day Saints* (Salt Lake City, 1876 [1835]), 124:1 and 133:57–59.

189. 2 Nephi 27:26.

190. 2 Nephi 33:6. The theme of plainness in communication is replete in the *Book of Mormon*. See 1 Nephi 13:24, 14:23, 25:4, 32:7, Ether 12:23, Jacob 4:13.

191. Mosiah 27:3–5.

192. Mario S. De Pillis, "The Quest for Religious Authority and the Rise of Mormonism," *Dialogue: A Journal of Mormon Thought* 1 (1966):68–88.

193. Using Davis Bitton's *Guide to Mormon Diaries and Autobiographies* (Provo, Utah, 1977), Marvin S. Hill has estimated that 92 percent of those converted before 1846 whose birth and conversion dates are given (211 of 229) were under 40 at the time of baptism. The median age was between 20 and 25; more than 80 percent (182) were 30 or under. Hill, "The Rise of Mormonism in the Burned-Over District: Another View," *New York History* 61 (1980):411–30.

194. "I have seen deacons, Baptists, Presbyterians, members of the Methodist church, with long, solid, sturdy faces and a poor brother would come along and say to one of them, 'Brother, such-a-one, I have come to see if I could get a bushel of wheat, rye or corn of you. I have no money, but I will come and work for you in harvest,' and their faces would be drawn down so mournful, and they would say, 'I have none to spare.' 'Well, deacon, if you can let me have one bushel, I understand you have considerable, I will come and work for you just as long as you say, until you are satisfied, in your harvest field, or haying or anything you want done.'

"After much talk this longfaced character would get it out, 'If you will come and work for me two days in harvest, I do not know but I will spare you a bushel of rye.'

"When the harvest time comes the man could have got two bushels of rye for one day's work; but the deacon sticks him to his bargain, and makes him work two days for a bushel of wheat or rye. . . . I could not swallow such things." Quoted in

Leonard J. Arrington, *Brigham Young: American Moses* (New York, 1985), 25–26. See also Rebecca Cornwall and Richard F. Palmer, "The Religious and Family Background of Brigham Young," *Brigham Young University Studies* 18 (1978):286–310.

195. Breck England, *The Life and Thought of Orson Pratt* (Provo, Utah, 1985), 8–13.

196. Pratt, *The Autobiography of Parley Parker Pratt, One of the Twelve Apostles of the Church of Jesus Christ of Latter-Day Saints*, ed. Parley Parker Pratt (son) (New York, 1874), 20–21.

197. Stanley B. Kimball, *Heber C. Kimball: Mormon Patriarch and Pioneer* (Urbana, Ill., 1981), 1–24; quote on 10.

198. Gene A. Sessions, *Mormon Thunder: A Documentary History of Jedediah Morgan Grant* (Urbana, Ill., 1982), 3–23. On Marsh, see Andrew Jenson, *Latter-day Saint Biographical Encyclopedia*, 4 vols. (Salt Lake City, 1901), 1:74–76.

199. Heber C. Kimball, "History," manuscript, book 94–B, Heber C. Kimball Papers, Library-Archives of the Historical Department of the Church of Jesus Christ of Latter-Day Saints; quoted in Arrington, *Brigham Young*, 16.

Chapter Five

1. Richard D. Brown, "Spreading the Word: Rural Clergymen and the Communication Network of 18th Century New England," *Proceedings of the Massachusetts Historical Society* 94 (1982):10–13.

2. *Methodist Magazine* 6, no. 6 (Jan. 1823); quoted in Frank Luther Mott, *A History of American Magazines, 1741–1850* (New York, 1930), 136. On the novelty of religious newspapers around the year 1800, see David Benedict, *Fifty Years Among the Baptists* (New York, 1860), 25. For the severe difficulties that the Methodists had in sustaining a religious periodical before 1800, see Millard George Roberts, "The Methodist Book Concern in the West, 1800–1870" (Ph.D. diss., University of Chicago, 1947), 1–50. Russell E. Miller, *The Larger Hope: The First Century of the Universalist Church in America, 1770–1870* (Boston, 1979), 285–87. Milton W. Hamilton, "Anti-Masonic Newspapers, 1826–1834," *The Papers of the Bibliographical Society of America* 32 (1938):71–97.

3. John C. Nerone, "The Press and Popular Culture in the Early Republic: Cincinnati, 1793–1843" (Ph.D. diss., University of Notre Dame, 1982), 197–98. The Adventist leader Josiah Litch gave this estimate in a letter in 1843. See *Signs of the Times*, Nov. 15, 1843, 11; quoted in David Tallmadege Arthur, "Joshua V. Himes and the Cause of Adventism, 1839–1845" (M.A. thesis, University of Chicago, 1961), 106. The most sensitive study to date of the cultural significance of the rise of religious journalism is Joan Jacobs Brumberg, *Mission for Life: The Study of the Family of Adoniram Judson* (New York, 1980), esp. chap. 3, "Does the Bibliomania Rage at Tavoy?" 44–78. For the primary importance of the press for Noyes, see Lawrence Foster, "Free Love and Feminism: John Humphrey Noyes and the Oneida Community," *Journal of the Early Republic* 1 (1981):178–79; and Robert Fogarty, "Oneida: A Utopian Search for Religious Security, *Labor History* 14 (1973):202–27. Horace Bushnell, *New Englander and Yale Review* 2 (1844):605–07; quoted in Brumberg, *Mission for Life*, 67. The Abolitionist use of the press is another clear example of effective religious journalism. See Leonard L. Richards, *Gentlemen*

of Property and Standing: Anti-Abolition Mobs in Jacksonian America (Worcester, Mass., 1983), 21.

4. Samuel Goodrich, *Recollections of a Lifetime*, 2 vols. (New York, 1857), 1:86. Quoted in David D. Hall, "The Uses of Literacy in New England, 1600–1850," in *Printing and Society in Early America*, ed. William L. Joyce et al. (Worcester, Mass., 1983), 21.

5. One critic noted of Lorenzo Dow, "for such is the nature of his plan or system, that he estimates truth and right, not so much by principle as by success." Lorenzo Dow, *History of Cosmopolite; or, the Four Volumes of Lorenzo's Journal* (New York, 1814), 353–55, 81.

6. Harry S. Stout, "Religion, Communications, and the Ideological Origins of the American Revolution," *William and Mary Quarterly*, 3d ser., 34 (1977):525. Frederick Dreyer, "Faith and Experience in the Thought of John Wesley," *American Historical Review* 88 (1983):12–30. See E. P. Thompson, *The Making of the English Working Class* (New York, 1966); Rhys Isaac, "Evangelical Revolt: The Nature of the Baptists' Challenge to the Traditional Order in Virginia, 1765–1775," *William and Mary Quarterly*, 3d ser., 31 (1974):345–68.

7. On the introduction of the hymns of Isaac Watts to America and the enthusiasm for them by Edwards and Whitefield, see Stephen A Marini, "Rehearsal for Revival: Sacred Singing and the Great Awakening in America," in *Sacred Sound: Music in Religious Thought and Practice*, ed. Joyce Irwin (Chico, Calif., 1983), 71–91.

8. On these three developments, see Isaac, "Evangelical Revolt;" Stephen A. Marini, *Radical Sects of Revolutionary New England* (Cambridge, Mass., 1982), 40–59; and George A. Rawlyk, *Ravished by the Spirit: Religious Revivals, Baptists, and Henry Alline* (Kingston, Ontario, 1984).

9. Samuel Eliot Morison, ed., "William Manning's *The Key of Liberty*," *William and Mary Quarterly*, 3d ser., 13 (1956):253.

10. The phrase is that of Samuel Miller in *A Brief Retrospect of the Eighteenth Century*, 2 vols. (New York, 1803), 2:254–55; quoted in Gordon S. Wood, "The Democratization of Mind in the American Revolution," *Leadership in the American Revolution* (Washington, D.C., 1974), 80.

11. For the influence of Benjamin Austin ("Old South") upon Smith, see Smith, *The Life, Conversion, Preaching, Travels and Sufferings of Elias Smith* (Portsmouth, N.H., 1816), 341–42. Bentley, *The Diary of William Bentley, D.D.*, 4 vols. (Salem, Mass., 1905–1914), 3:157. Thomas Andros, *The Scriptures Liable to be Wrested to Men's Destruction, and an Instance of This Found, in the Writings of Elias Smith* (Taunton, Mass., 1817), 10, 21.

12. John Adams, "Dissertation on the Feudal and Canon Law," in *The Works of John Adams*, ed. Charles Francis Adams, 10 vols. (Boston, 1856), 3:447–64.

13. Smith, *Life . . . of Elias Smith*, 309.

14. Elias Smith, *The Clergyman's Looking-Glass: Being a History of the Birth, Life, and Death of Anti-Christ* (Portsmouth, N.H., 1803); Smith, *A Discourse Delivered at Jefferson Hall, Thanksgiving Day, November 25, 1802: and Redelivered (by Request) the Wednesday Evening Following, at the Same Place: The Subject, Nebuchadnezzar's Dream* (Portsmouth, N.H., 1803); Smith, *A Reply to This Congregational Methodistical Question* (Portsmouth, N.H., 1803); and Smith, *The Doctrine of the Prince of Peace and His Servants, Concerning the End of the Wicked* (Boston, 1803).

15. The new editions of *The Clergyman's Looking-Glass* were published in Boston. Elias Smith, *Five Letters* (Boston, 1804); Smith, *A Letter to Mr. Daniel Humphreys* (Portsmouth, N.H., 1804); and Smith, *A Reply to This Question, How Shall I Know That I am Born Again* (Boston, 1804).

16. Smith, *Life . . . of Elias Smith*, 309.

17. These works include *A New Testament Dictionary, Containing the New Testament Meaning of Eleven Hundred and Eight Words, Pocket Volume* (Philadelphia, 1812); *The Age of Enquiry: The Christian's Pocket Companion and Daily Assistant* (Exeter, N.H., 1807); *The History of Anti-Christ* (Portland, Me., 1811); *Sermons, Containing an Illustration of the Prophecies* (Exeter, N.H., 1808); and his memoirs, *Life . . . of Elias Smith*.

18. Smith published both of these monthly magazines in Boston.

19. These books were published in at least six different locations: in Boston; Philadelphia; Exeter, New Hampshire; Portsmouth, New Hampshire; Portland, Maine; and Poughkeepsie, New York. Smith's most widely circulated songbook, *Hymns, Original and Selected, for the Use of Christians* (Boston, 1804), went through at least eight printings. *Herald of Gospel Liberty*, September, 1808, 5.

20. Much of the preceding discussion is influenced by valuable insights in Nerone, "Press and Popular Culture."

21. Young, *Autobiography of Dan Young, a New England Preacher of Golden Time*, ed. W. P. Strickland (New York, 1860), 95–97.

22. John W. Francis, *Old New York: or Reminiscences of the Past Sixty Years* (New York, 1858), 147–49. Charles Finney also used this jingle against high Calvinism. See Charles Finney, *Sermons on Important Subjects* (New York, 1836), 81.

23. Ray Holder, *William Winans* (Jackson, Miss., 1977), 9.

24. Dow confessed on one occasion, "All that saved me in this conference from an expulsion was the blessing which had attended my labors." In another instance the General Conference of New York would have curtailed his activities but for the argument of some that "he does us no harm, but we get the fruit of his labour." Dow, *History of Cosmopolite* (1814), 81, 214.

25. Richard J. Stockham, "The Misunderstood Lorenzo Dow," *Alabama Review* 16 (1963):32.

26. Ibid., 33. Charles Coleman Sellers, *Lorenzo Dow: The Bearer of the Word* (New York, 1928), 135.

27. Dow's biographer, Charles Coleman Sellers, estimated that no figure in the early republic had more children named after him than Lorenzo Dow. I have come across at least eleven cases of the name, including three early Mormon leaders: Lorenzo Dow Hickey, one of the original twelve apostles; Lorenzo Dow Watson; and Lorenzo Dow Young, Brigham Young's brother. For the impact of Dow on the Young family, see Leonard J. Arrington, *Brigham Young: American Moses* (New York, 1985), 10, 24. Other namesakes include Lorenzo Dow McCabe, a nineteenth-century religious philosopher; Lorenzo Dow Baker, one of the founders of the United Fruit Company; Lorenzo Dow, the inventor of a waterproof cartridge during the Civil War and son of a Methodist itinerant, Huse Dow; Lorenzo Dow Johnson, author of a book on congressional chaplains; Lorenzo Dow Lewelling, the Populist governor of Kansas from 1893 to 1895; Lorenzo Dow Blackson, a leader in the Union American Protestant Episcopal church; and Lorenzo Thomas, son of the itinerant evangelist Joseph Thomas, the "White Pilgrim." My favorite namesake is

Lorenzo D. Butler, who was born in Vermont in 1807 and died in Minnesota in 1883. His nephew, James Butler Hickok, "Wild Bill," named two sons Lorenzo, the first having died in infancy. Lorenzo D. Butler's great-grandson, the source of this genealogy, is historian Jon Butler of Yale University.

28. On these themes, see in particular Dow's two pamphlets "Analects upon Natural, Social, and Moral Philosophy," in *History of Cosmopolite* (1814), 142–43; and "On Church Government" in *History of Cosmopolite; or the Four Volumes of Lorenzo's Journal, Concentrated in One* (Philadelphia, 1816), 574–75.

29. Lorenzo Dow, "Defense of Camp Meetings," in *History of Cosmopolite; or the Four Volumes of Lorenzo Dow's Journal* (Wheeling, Va., 1848), 593.

30. Harry S. Stout, *The New England Soul: Preaching and Religious Culture in Colonial New England* (New York, 1986).

31. The statement is from Episcopal bishop Samuel Horsley, quoted in Walter Brownlow Bosey, *Religious Strife on the Southern Frontier* (Baton Rouge, La., 1965), 35–36.

32. On James McGready, see Catherine C. Cleveland, *The Great Revival in the West, 1797–1805* (Chicago, 1916), 39; on Billy Hibbard: William B. Sprague, *Annals of the American Pulpit* (New York, 1865), vol. 7, *Methodist*, 302; on John Jasper and Harry Hosier: David S. Reynolds, "From Doctrine to Narrative: The Rise of Pulpit Storytelling in America," *American Quarterly* 32 (1980):486; on Jesse Lee: Minton Thrift, *Memoir of the Rev. Jesse Lee with Extracts from his Journals* (New York, 1823), 115; on Jacob Knapp: Richard Carwardine, *Transatlantic Revivalism: Popular Evangelicalism in Britain and America, 1790–1865* (Westport, Conn., 1978), 9; on Joshua Thomas: Adam Wallace, *The Parson of the Islands; A Biography of the Rev. Joshua Thomas* (Philadelphia, 1861), 269; on Brigham Young: Arrington, *Brigham Young*, 196–97.

33. Goodrich, *Recollections of a Lifetime*, 2:197. Of course the preference for unlearned leaders was sweeping the American political universe at the same time. Benjamin Latrobe, the noted architect and engineer, commented in 1806 about Pennsylvania politics, "Our state legislature does not contain one individual of superior talents. The fact is, that superior talents actually excite distrust, and the experience of the world perhaps does not encourage the people to trust men of genius." Benjamin Latrobe to Philip Mazzei, Dec. 19, 1806, in *Philip Mazzei: Selected Writings and Correspondence*, ed. Margherita Marchione et al., 3 vols. (Prato, Italy, 1983), 3:439. This citation is part of a superb treatment of this general theme in Gordon S. Wood, "Interests and Disinterestedness in the Making of the Constitution," in *Beyond Confederation: Origins of the Constitution and American National Identity*, ed. Richard Beeman, Stephen Botein, and Edward C. Carter II (Chapel Hill, N.C., 1987), 93–103, quotation on 102.

34. Young, *Autobiography*, 95–96.

35. Andros, *The Scriptures Liable to be Wrested to Men's Own Destruction*, 21, 6.

36. Sydney E. Mead, *The Lively Experiment: The Shaping of American Christianity* (New York, 1963), 54. Lawrence Goodwyn has criticized historians for assuming that the ideas of the Populists are not to be taken seriously. See *Democratic Promise: The Populist Movement in America* (New York, 1976), xvi.

37. Walter Harris, *Characteristics of False Teachers* (Concord, N.H., 1811), 19.

38. See the Adventist newspapers the *Midnight Cry*, November 17, 1842, 3;

and *Signs of the Times*, September 21, 1842, 8; September 28, 1842, 16; and October 15, 1840, 112.

39. Philip Schaff, *America: A Sketch of Its Political, Social, and Religious Character*, ed. Perry Miller (Cambridge, Mass., 1961), 137–38.

40. *Minutes of Several Conversations between the Rev. Thomas Coke, LL.D., the Rev. Francis Asbury, and Others, at a Conference, begun in Baltimore, in the State of Maryland, on Monday, the 27th of December, in the Year 1784* (Philadelphia, 1785), 18–19. Billy Hibbard, *The Life and Travels of B. Hibbard, Minister of the Gospel* (New York, 1825), 191. Orson F. Whitney, *Life of Heber C. Kimball, an Apostle: The Father and Founder of the British Mission* (Salt Lake City, 1888), 204, quoted in Barbara Joan McFarlane Higdon, "The Role of Preaching in the Early Latter Day Saint Church, 1830–1846" (Ph.D. diss., University of Missouri, 1961), 257.

41. The Methodist circuit rider Joshua Thomas used the vicissitudes of family life as a staple of his preaching: "His own family had great reason to stand in awe of some of his sallies. He felt it his privilege to introduce so much of home matters, of their blunders and faults, (in a way which they thought would do them and others good,) that they might well fear something was coming out, that they would rather he should have kept to himself; but they were so accustomed to it that they did not seem much alarmed by his disclosures, or feel apprehensive beforehand of his personalities." Wallace, *The Parson of the Islands* (1861), 28.

42. Methodist Jesse Lee's 1784 journal entry is typical of this intensely emotional preaching: "While I was speaking of the love of God, I felt so much of that love in my own soul, that I burst into a flood of tears, and could speak no more for some time, but stood and wept. I then began again; but was so much overcome, that I had to stop and weep several times before I finished my subject.—There were very few dry eyes in the house." Thrift, *Memoir of the Rev. Jesse Lee*, 64–65.

43. Asbury, *The Journal and Letters of Francis Asbury*, ed. Elmer C. Clark, J. Manning Potts, and Jacob S. Payton, 3 vols. (Nashville, 1958), 1:153.

44. Asbury, *Journal and Letters of Francis Asbury*, 2:785. Lorenzo Dow made much the same point: "The most learned lectures may be delivered to any man, or set of men, for years together, and yet if that kind of energy which urges to immediate practice be wanting, all will be vain. The tenor of the Gospel is, 'now is the accepted time, now is the day of salvation.' And the minister of the gospel, to be successful, must show by every word and every gesture that he feels it so. He must 'know the terror of the Lord,' and act consistently with the deepest sense of it, or he will never effectually persuade men. . . . Our Methodist preachers excel in this kind of earnestness or Godly vehemence, and the most astonishing effects follow their labors on these occasions, so favorable to their manner of preaching." "Defense of Camp Meetings," 599.

45. Frederic G. Mather, "The Early Days of Mormonism," *Lippincott's Magazine of Popular Literature and Science* 26 (August, 1880):206–07. The incident is recounted in Higdon, "Role of Preaching in the Early Latter Day Saint Church," 292–93; and F. Mark McKiernan, *The Voice of One Crying in the Wilderness: Sidney Rigdon, Religious Reformer, 1793–1876* (Lawrence, Kans., 1971), 49.

46. Timothy Flint, *Recollections of the Last Ten Years* (Boston, 1826), 117, 183; Cartwright, *Autobiography of Peter Cartwright, the Backwoods Preacher*, ed. W. P. Strickland (New York, 1856), 307–08.

47. W. B. Yeats to Lady Elizabeth Pelham, January 4, 1939. Quoted in Joseph M. Hone, *W. B. Yeats 1865–1939* (New York, 1943), 510. I am grateful to Dr. Anthony W. Shipps for locating this citation.

48. Goodrich, *Recollections of a Lifetime*, 2:212–14. On the general themes of narrative preaching and storytelling, see Reynolds, "From Doctrine to Narrative," 479–98.

49. The humor used by Whitefield and other revivalists of the Great Awakening seems muted and refined when compared with the earthy banter and jesting that appears at the end of the eighteenth century, paralleling, it seems, the use of humor as a political weapon. An introduction to the topic is Doug Adams, *Humor in the American Pulpit: from George Whitefield Through Henry Ward Beecher* (North Aurora, Ill., 1975).

50. Baptist historian Robert Semple admitted in 1810 that John Leland had been the most popular preacher in the state of Virginia but feared that his levity transgressed William Cowper's advice: "He that negotiates between God and man . . . must beware of lightness in his speech." Leland, after all, wrote an essay entitled "Old Pigs Want Teats as Well as the Young." See Robert B. Semple, *A History of the Rise and Progress of the Baptists in Virginia* [Revised and extended by Rev. G. W. Beale] (Philadelphia, 1894), 206–07.

Allen Wiley, a Methodist leader in Indiana, gave this recollection of the preaching of John Strange (1789–1832): "Sometimes, in his most glowing and impassioned strains, when the whole audience was greatly moved, he would stoop to queer and witty sayings, which had no dignity in them, and which would fill the minds and hearts of the hearers with levity. . . . These witty sayings, however, seemed to be spontaneous and natural to brother Strange, that they did not produce that disgust which they would do in a man who seems to labor hard to be witty." Wiley, "Introduction and Progress of Methodism in Southeastern Indiana," *Indiana Magazine of History* 23 (1927):439.

51. Cartwright, *Autobiography*, 217.

52. *Herald of Gospel Liberty*, September 15, 1809, 112. For the complete poem, see the appendix.

53. Stout, *New England Soul*, 201. John F. Schermerhorn and Samuel J. Mills, *A Correct View of That Part of the United States Which Lies West of the Allegany Mountains with Regard to Religion and Morals* (Hartford, 1814), 41.

54. Higdon, "Role of Preaching in the Early Latter Day Saint Church," 35, 56–57, 72–73. Oliver Olney, *The Absurdities of Mormonism Portrayed* (Hancock County, Ill., 1843), 28.

55. *The Doctrines and Discipline of the Methodist Episcopal Church in America* (Philadelphia, 1798), 42.

56. Higdon, "Role of Preaching in the Early Latter Day Saint Church," 58–59.

57. Young, *Autobiography*, 90.

58. Letter from James Redmond to Archbishop Maréchal of Baltimore, May 22, 1821, quoted in John Ronin Murtha, "The Life of the Most Reverend Ambrose Maréchal" (Ph.D. diss., Catholic University of America, 1965), 107.

59. Brigham Young, "The Privileges and Blessings of the Gospel," *Journal of Discourses* 1 (1854):313.

60. Richard D. Altick, *The English Common Reader: A Social History of the Mass Reading Public, 1800–1900* (Chicago, 1957), 102.

61. David Paul Nord, "The Evangelical Origins of Mass Media in America, 1815–1835," *Journalism Monographs* 88 (1984):1–30.

62. Gaylord P. Albaugh, "The Role of the Religious Press in the Development of American Christianity, 1730–1830," unpublished manuscript, 1984, 6–7. For the Abolitionist use of the Press, see Richards, *Gentlemen of Property and Standing*, 47–81. On the Baptists, see Brumberg, *Mission for Life*, 68. On the Adventists, see Arthur, "Joshua V. Himes," 106. The vast quantity of Adventist literature is evident in *The Millerites and Early Adventists: An Index to the Microfilm Collection of Rare Books and Manuscripts*, ed. Jean Hoornstra (Ann Arbor, Mich., 1978).

63. Michael Schudson, *Discovering the News: A Social History of American Newspapers* (New York, 1978); James D. Hart, *The Popular Book: A History of America's Literary Taste* (New York, 1950).

64. For excellent discussions of this point, see Altick, *English Common Reader*, 99–101; and Brumberg, *Mission for Life*, 67–78.

65. Quoted in Albaugh, "Role of the Religious Press," 16.

66. Millard George Roberts, "The Methodist Book Concern in the West, 1800–1870" (Ph.D. diss., University of Chicago, 1947), 14, 88, 124. Samuel J. Mills and Daniel Smith, *Report of a Missionary Tour through that part of the United States which lies West of the Allegany Mountains* (Andover, Mass., 1815), 49. William Warren Sweet, *Religion on the American Frontier, 1783–1840* (Chicago, 1946), vol. 4, *The Methodists*, 70.

67. Nord, "Evangelical Origins of Mass Media," 2–3.

68. Altick, *English Common Reader*, 105. Charles Knight, *Passages of a Working Life During Half a Century* (London, 1864), 242–43. Charles Dickens, *Bleak House*, chap. 8, quoted in Altick, *English Common Reader*, 107.

69. By 1859, W. B. Smith and Company of Cincinnati, McGuffey's publisher, was the largest publisher of schoolbooks in the country. More than two million copies of the "Eclectic" series were being published annually. It is estimated that as many as two-thirds of primary schools west of the Alleghenies used McGuffey. See Walter Sutton, *The Western Book Trade: Cincinnati as a Nineteenth-Century Publishing and Book-Trade Center* (Columbus, Ohio, 1961), 182–89.

70. Nord, "Evangelical Origins of Mass Media," 8–12.

71. On the Methodists, see Sutton, *Western Book Trade*, 150–65. The Abolitionist use of the new print technology is discussed in Richards, *Gentlemen of Property and Standing*, 47–81.

72. Hall, "Uses of Literacy in New England," 10.

73. For Campbell, see Robert Richardson, *Memoirs of Alexander Campbell*, 2 vols., (Cincinnati, 1913). Nerone, "Press and Popular Culture," 316–18. Albaugh, "Role of the Religious Press," 5.

74. Arthur, "Joshua V. Himes" 1–20. Thomas H. Olbricht, "Christian Connection and Unitarian Relations," *Restoration Quarterly* 9 (1986):160–86.

75. David T. Arthur, "Joshua V. Himes and the Cause of Adventism," in Ronald L. Numbers and Jonathan M. Butler, *The Disappointed: Millerism and Millenarianism in the Nineteenth Century* (Bloomington, Ind., 1987), 36–58.

76. On these developments, see David L. Rowe, *Thunder and Trumpets: Millerites and Dissenting Religion in Upstate New York, 1800–1850* (Chico, Calif., 1985); *Mid-Night Cry*, August 24, 1843, 1; and *Signs of the Times*, September 28, 1842, 16.

77. Alexis de Tocqueville, *Democracy in America*, trans. Henry Reeve, 2 vols. (New York, 1959), 2:111.

78. George Pullen Jackson, *White and Negro Spirituals: Their Life Span and Kinship* (New York, 1943), 62.

79. Ibid., 74–75; George Pullen Jackson, *Down-East Spirituals* (New York, 1943), 164–65.

80. Nathan Bangs, *A History of the Methodist Episcopal Church*, 4 vols. (New York, 1840–53), 2:105. Philip Schaff quoted in William Nast, "Dr. Schaff and Methodism," *Methodist Quarterly Review* 31 (1857):431.

81. Nathaniel D. Gould, *History of Church Music in America* (Boston, 1853), 7–8.

82. *Hymns and Spiritual Songs, Collected from the Works of Several Authors* (Newport, 1766).

83. Jackson, *White and Negro Spirituals*, 38–39; Louis F. Benson, *The English Hymn: Its Development and Use in Worship* (Richmond, Va., 1962; orig. pub. New York, 1915), 202.

84. For full discussions of the importance of Alline's folk hymnody in Nova Scotia and northern New England, see George A. Rawlyk, ed., *New Light Letters and Songs, 1778–1793* (Hantsport, Nova Scotia, 1983); and Marini, *Radical Sects of Revolutionary New England*, 156–62. Other editions of his hymnal were published in Dover, N.H., in 1795 and 1797; and in Stonington, Conn., in 1802.

85. Smith, *Life . . . of Elias Smith*, 42, 47, 54.

86. Elias Smith, *Hymns, Original and Selected for the Use of Christians* (Portsmouth, N.H., 1815). On the tune of the "Union" ballad see Jackson, *White and Negro Spirituals*, 127; and George Pullen Jackson, *Spiritual Folk-Songs of Early America* (New York, 1937), 67. Smith's version seems clearly an adaptation of a well-known song, "The New Union," which is found in Jeremiah Ingalls's *The Christian Harmony; or, Songster's Companion* (Exeter, N.H., 1805), 30, and in numerous other revivalist songbooks.

87. *Vermont Harmony* 2, University of Vermont Choral Union, directed by James Chapman, Philo 1038 (1976).

88. Jackson, *White and Negro Spirituals*, 72–73. This kind of singing, of course, was not without its severe critics. One noted in 1809, "This kind of composition has, for several years past been greatly abused—Songs have been circulated, not only in Ms. but also in print, which have been so barbarous in language, so unequal in numbers, and so defective in rhyme, as to excite disgust in all persons even of tolerable understanding in these things." See William Parkinson, *A Selection of Hymns and Spiritual Songs* (New York, 1809), preface.

89. Robert Emerson Coleman, "Factors in the Expansion of the Methodist Episcopal Church from 1784 to 1812," 349; *The History of American Methodism*, ed. Emory S. Bucke et al., 3 vols. (New York, 1964), 2:341.

90. Quoted in Jackson, *White and Negro Spirituals*, 135.

91. Benson, *The English Hymn*, 253.

92. *Minutes of the Methodist Conferences annually held in America, from 1773 to 1794, inclusive* (Philadelphia, 1795), 71.

93. Asbury, *Journal and Letters of Francis Asbury*, 3:397. Elizabeth K. Nottingham, *Methodism and the Frontier: Indiana Proving Ground* (New York, 1941), 26. Finley, *Autobiography of Rev. James B. Finley; or, Pioneer Life in the West*, ed. W. P. Strickland (Cincinnati, 1853), 228, quoted in Dickson D. Bruce, Jr., *And They All Sang Hallelujah: Plain-Folk Camp-Meeting Religion, 1800–1845* (Knoxville, 1974), 73.

94. Elias Smith, *A Collection of Hymns for the Use of Christians* (Boston, 1804), 52, 74.

95. Thomas S. Hinde, a local Methodist preacher in Newport, Kentucky, compiled *A Pilgrim's Songster; or, a Choice Collection of Spiritual Songs* (Chillicothe, Ohio, 1815) which contained one hundred twenty songs, one-third by the Methodist circuit riders Granade and Taylor, but over half composed by persons unknown to the compiler. This songbook went through at least three editions and was estimated to have sold at least ten thousand copies in the West. See "The Early Camp-Meeting Song Writers," *Methodist Quarterly Review* 41 (1859):401–13, which describes the songs as "destitute of poetical merit" (402).

96. *The Miner's Journal, And Schuylkill Coal & Navigation Register* (Pottsville, Pa.) August 27, 1825, quoted in Don Yoder, *Pennsylvania Spirituals* (Lancaster, 1961), 53. See also ibid., 110.

97. Jackson, *Down-East Spirituals*, 232, 265. Rollin H. Neale, a compiler of revival songs, commented in his *Revival Hymns* (Boston, 1842) on this song: "This hymn and the original melody, which have been so useful in revival seasons for more than half a century, and which, it is believed, have never before been published together, were lately procured after considerable search, from the diary of an ancient servant of Christ, bearing the date 1810." Quoted in Jackson, *Down-East Spirituals*, 234.

98. Jackson, *White and Negro Spirituals*, 83–85. David B. Mintz, *Hymns and Spiritual Songs* (Newbern, N.C., 1806).

99. On songbook compilers, see Bruce, *And They All Sang Hallelujah*, 92–94; and George Pullen Jackson, *White Spirituals in the Southern Uplands* (Chapel Hill, N.C., 1933). On Joshua Leavitt, see Jackson, *White and Negro Spirituals*, 73.

100. Benson, *The English Hymn*, 203, 299.

101. Charles W. Hughes, *American Hymns Old and New* (New York, 1980), vol. 2, *Notes on the Hymns and Biographies of the Authors and Composers*, 142. The publishing history of "Oh, When Shall I See Jesus?" resembled that of "The Lord into His Garden Comes": it appeared in Smith's *A Collection of Hymns*, in *The Christian Harmony*, and then in collections by a wide range of southern compilers. On the use of religious folk songs in frontier Illinois, see John Mack Faragher, *Sugar Creek: Life on the Illinois Prairie* (New Haven, Conn., 1986), 168–69.

102. On these themes, see Don Yoder, "The Bench Versus the Catechism: Revivalism and Pennsylvania's Lutheran and Reformed Churches," *Pennsylvania Folklife* 10 (1959):14–23; and his careful and illuminating study *Pennsylvania Spirituals*.

103. Philip Schaff, quoted in Nast, "Dr. Schaff and Methodism," 431.

104. George Ross, *Semi-Centennial Sketch. Biography of Elder John Winebrenner* (Harrisburg, 1880), quoted in Yoder, *Pennsylvania Spirituals*, 396–97. On the issue of vernacular versus "Pennsylvania High German," see ibid., 78–79, 114, 140–41.

105. Donald G. Mathews, *Religion in the Old South* (Chicago, 1977), 185–202.

106. Eileen Southern, *The Music of Black Americans: A History* (2d edition, New York, 1983), 85.

107. Charles Colcock Jones, *Suggestions on The Religious Instruction of the Negroes in the United States* (Philadelphia, n.d.), 39–40; Jones, *Religious Instruction of the Negroes in the Southern States* (Savannah, 1842), 265–66, quoted in Dena J. Epstein, *Sinful Tunes and Spirituals: Black Folk Music to the Civil War* (Urbana, Ill., 1977), 201.

108. *Practical Considerations Founded on the Scriptures, Relative to the Slave Population of South-Carolina* (Charleston, 1823), 33–36, quoted in Epstein, *Sinful Tunes and Spirituals*, 196.

109. [John F. Watson], *Methodist Error; or, Friendly Christian Advice, To Those Methodists, Who Indulge in Extravagant Emotions and Bodily Exercises*, rev. ed. (Trenton, N.J., 1819), 28–30.

110. Epstein, *Sinful Tunes and Spirituals*, 199; Albert J. Raboteau, *Slave Religion: The "Invisible Institution" in the Antebellum South* (New York, 1978), 243; Lawrence W. Levine, "Slave Songs and Slave Consciousness: An Exploration in Neglected Sources," in *Anonymous Americans*, ed. Tamara K. Hareven (Englewood Cliffs, N.J., 1971), 102–04.

111. Levine, "Slave Songs and Slave Consciousness," 101–02.

112. On the importance of the spirituals to antebellum black identity, see Levine, "Slave Songs and Slave Consciousness," 99–130; and Eugene D. Genovese, *Roll, Jordan, Roll: The World the Slaves Made* (New York, 1972), 233–55.

113. Richard Allen, *A Collection of Hymns and Spiritual Songs from Various Authors* (Philadelphia, 1801), 17.

114. Michael Hicks, "Poetic Borrowing in Early Mormonism," *Dialogue: A Journal of Mormon Thought* 18 (1985):132–42.

115. On the development of Mormon singing, see Levette J. Davidson, "Mormon Songs," *Journal of American Folklore* 58 (1945):273–300; Howard S. Swan, "The Music of the Mormons, 1830–1865," *The Huntington Library Quarterly* 3 (1949):223–52; and Helen Hanks Macaré, "The Singing Saints" (Ph.D. diss., U.C.L.A., 1961). For the vibrant tradition of Mormon folk songs that developed in Utah, see Thomas E. Cheney, ed., *Mormon Songs from the Rocky Mountains: A Compilation of Mormon Folksong* (Austin and London, 1968).

116. Arrington, *Brigham Young*, 40–41.

117. Joshua Himes, *The Millennial Harp; Designed for Meetings on the Second Coming of Christ* (Boston, 1843), part 2, 24. Jackson, *White and Negro Spirituals*, 107–09.

Chapter Six

1. Gordon S. Wood, "The Democratization of Mind in the American Revolution," *Leadership in the American Revolution* (Washington, D.C., 1974), 64. On the tradition of commonsense realism in America, see George M. Marsden, "Everyone One's Own Interpreter?: The Bible, Science, and Authority in Mid-Nineteenth-Century America," in *The Bible in America: Essays in Cultural History*, ed. Nathan O. Hatch and Mark A. Noll (New York, 1982), 79–100.

2. On the prohibition of a theology professorship in the charter of Bethany College, see Robert Frederick West, *Alexander Campbell and Natural Religion* (New

Haven, 1948), 196–201. *The Christian Baptist*, September 1, 1823 and October 6, 1823, 14. (Pagination for *The Christian Baptist* is taken from the fifteenth edition, ed. Alexander Campbell, 7 vols. in 1 (St. Louis, [n.d.]).

3. *Millenial Harbinger*, 1850, 1–2, quoted in West, *Alexander Campbell and Natural Religion*, 165; *Christian Baptist*, October 6, 1823, 17.

4. West, *Alexander Campbell and Natural Religion*, 29; *Millennial Harbinger*, 1850, 291, quoted in John L. Morrison, "The Centrality of the Bible in Alexander Campbell's Thought and Life," *West Virginia History* 35 (1973):196.

5. David Rice, *An Epistle to the Citizens of Kentucky, Professing Christianity; Especially Those that Are, or Have Been, Denominated Presbyterians* (Lexington, Ky., 1805), as given in Robert H. Bishop, *An Outline of the History of the Church in the State of Kentucky, During a Period of Forty Years: Containing the Memoirs of Rev. David Rice*, (Lexington, Ky., 1824), 336. The Methodists issued a similar complaint about the potential of theological anarchy among those who magnified the Bible alone: "[I]t would appear that their bible was to be their only rule and guide in faith and practice; but it was, in fact, turning every one foot-loose, as every individual had an equal right to put his own construction, in order to answer his own purposes, on every question, as to doctrine or government. . . . they ran wild." Theophilus Armenius, "An Account of the Rise and Progress of the Work of God in the Western Country, No. VI," *Methodist Magazine* 2 (1819):350.

6. Philip Schaff, *The Principle of Protestantism*, ed. Bard Thompson and George H. Bricker (1845; Philadelphia, 1964), 154, 150. On the Mercersburg Theology generally, see *The Mercersburg Theology*, ed. James Hasting Nichols (New York, 1966); *Catholic and Reformed: Selected Theological Writings of John Williamson Nevin*, ed. Charles Yrigoyen, Jr., and George H. Bricker (Pittsburg, 1978); and Charles Yrigoyen, Jr., "Mercersburg's Quarrel with Methodism," in *Rethinking Methodist History: A Bicentennial Historical Consultation*, ed. Russell E. Richey and Kenneth E. Rowe (Nashville, 1985), 194–203.

7. On John Winebrenner, see Richard Kern, *John Winebrenner: Nineteenth Century Reformer* (Harrisburg, Pa., 1974).

8. John W. Nevin, "The Sect System," in *Catholic and Reformed*, 146, 135.

9. Nevin, "Sect System," 165; Schaff, *Principle of Protestantism*, 154. Earlier in "Sect System," Nevin wrote, "The liberty of the sect consists at last, in thinking its particular notions, shouting its shibboleths and passwords, dancing its religious hornpipes, and reading the Bible only through its theological goggles. These restrictions, at the same time, are so many wires, that lead back at last into the hands of a few leading spirits, enabling them to wield a true hierarchical despotism over all who are thus brought within their power" (144). William Nast, "Dr. Schaff on Methodism," *The Methodist Quarterly Review* 17 (1857):431.

10. Schaff, *Principle of Protestantism*, 149–50.

11. See Perry Miller's introduction to Philip Schaff, *America: A Sketch of Its Political, Social, and Religious Character* (Cambridge, Mass., 1961), vii–xxxv. Nevin, "Sect System," 166. For a lament about the divisive and competitive structure of American Protestantism, see Schaff, *Principle of Protestantism*, 140, 149–52.

12. Nevin, "Sect System," 152; Schaff, *Principal of Protestantism*, 155.

13. Kern, *John Winebrenner*, 57. In "Sect System," Nevin dismissed sectarian theological efforts altogether: "No sectarian theology can ever be of any permanent value" (109).

14. B. H. Nadal, "Schaff on America," *The Methodist Quarterly Review* 16 (1856):138.

15. J. F. C. Harrison, *The Second Coming: Popular Millenarianism 1780–1850* (New Brunswick, N.J., 1979), 202.

16. John W. Nevin, "Antichrist and the Sect System," in *The Mercersburg Theology*, ed. Nichols, 111, 104.

17. *Millennial Harbinger*, 1832, 13.

18. *The Christian Baptist*, February 7, 1825, 126–28. "Human creeds may be reformed and re-reformed, and be erroneous still, like their authors; but the inspired creed needs no reformation, being, like its author, infallible. The clergy, too, may be reformed from papistical opinions, grimaces, tricks, and dresses, to protestant opinions and ceremonies; protestant clergy may be reformed . . . to independency, and yet the Pope remain in their heart. They are clergy still—and still in need of reformation. . . . The spirit of the latter is as lordly and pontifical as that of the former, though his arm and his gown are shorter. The moschetto is an animal of the same genus with the hornet, though the bite of the former is not so powerful as the sting of the latter." Ibid.

19. This hymn, written by W. W. Phelps, is quoted in Klaus J. Hansen, *Mormonism and the American Experience* (Chicago, 1981), 28.

20. Pratt, *The Autobiography of Parley Parker Pratt, One of the Twelve Apostles*, ed. Parley Parker Pratt (son) (New York, 1874), 32–39.

21. *Herald of Gospel Liberty*, September 1, 1808, 1; *The Christian Baptist*, February 6, 1826, 213.

22. "It is this rejection of the past as a repository of wisdom that constitutes the most important element in the ideology of the victorious Jeffersonian Republicans." Appleby, *Capitalism and a New Social Order: The Republican Vision of the 1790s* (New York, 1984), 79. On Jefferson, see Edmund S. Morgan, *The Meaning of Independence: John Adams, George Washington, Thomas Jefferson* (Charlottesville, 1976), 71–79.

23. Brigham H. Roberts, ed., *History of the Church of Jesus Christ of Latter-Day Saints*, 7 vols. (Salt Lake City, 1902), 1:3–4, quoted in Mario S. DePillis, "The Quest for Religious Authority and the Rise of Mormonism," *Dialogue: A Journal of Mormon Thought* 1 (1966):72.

24. A subscription paper for the first Methodist church building asked for funds to erect a house "where the gospel of Jesus Christ might be preached without distinction of sect or party." C. C. Goss, *Statistical History of the First Century of American Methodism* (New York, 1866), 172.

25. Nevin, "Antichrist and the Sect System," 104.

26. Leland, *The Writings of the Late Elder John Leland*, ed. L. F. Greene (New York, 1845), 451; Freeborn Garrettson, *A Letter to the Rev. Lyman Beecher Containing Strictures and Animadversions on a Pamphlet Entitled An Address of the Charitable Society for the Education of Indigent Pious Young Men for the Ministry of the Gospel* (New York, 1816), 7.

27. In an intriguing article on the decline of Calvinism in the modern world, Daniel Walker Howe has suggested that the move away from Calvinism was part of an alteration in the social reference group of the upper middle class, which became "aristocratized" in Boston, Geneva, Amsterdam, and other places and lost touch with the rigors of Calvinism, originally a zealous and crusading movement. The

revolt of Methodists, Freewill Baptists, Disciples, and Mormons against Calvinist orthodoxy in America represents an inverse model, as these outsiders lashed out at the aristocratic pretension of Calvinists and reasserted a religion that was extremely rigorous and demanding—"puritanical," so to speak. Most populist dissent in the early republic attempted to break the Calvinist grip entirely rather than reasserting a more orthodox form, as had often been the pattern in the Great Awakening. See Howe, "The Decline of Calvinism: An Approach to Its Study," *Comparative Studies in Society and History* 13 (1972):306–27.

28. For this incident and a helpful discussion of African-Americans and Calvinism, see Eugene D. Genovese, *Roll, Jordan, Roll: The World the Slaves Made* (New York, 1972), 243–44. Also helpful is Timothy L. Smith, "Slavery and Theology: The Emergence of Black Christian Consciousness in Nineteenth-Century America," *Church History* 41 (1972):497–512.

29. Rich, "A Narrative of Elder Caleb Rich," *Candid Examiner* 2 (1827):179.

30. Gates, *The Life and Writings of Theophilus R. Gates* (Philadelphia, 1818), 11. Deborah Millett, who grew up in Marblehead, Massachusetts, during the same time, recalled that in an orthodox environment her experience was one of deep conviction but no release: "All these years conviction followed me. I knew not what to do: I had never heard the voice of prayer, except from a minister; and the sound of 'knowing our sins forgiven' would have been the height of boasting." Gilbert Haven and Thomas Russell, *Father Taylor, the Sailor Preacher* (Boston, 1872), 73.

31. Quoted in Paul G. Faler, *Mechanics and Manufacturers in the Early Industrial Revolution: Lynn Massachusetts 1780–1860* (Albany, 1981), 46.

32. Abbott, *Experience and Gospel Labours of the Rev. Benjamin Abbott*, ed. John Ffirth (New York, 1832), 22–23.

33. Stone, *The Biography of Barton W. Stone, Written by Himself with Additions and Reflections*, ed. John Rodgers (Cincinnati, 1847), 44–45. Keith Thomas has noted that the doctrine of Providence has little appeal to those on the bottom end of the social scale because it forces them to explain misfortune in a way that jeopardizes either their own self-esteem or the benevolence of the creator. See Thomas, *Religion and the Decline of Magic* (New York, 1971), iii.

34. John Buzzell, *The Life of Benjamin Randall* (Limerick, Me., 1827), 76–79.

35. Stone, *Biography*, 14, 31, 33.

36. Miscellaneous Papers, William Smythe Babcock Papers, American Antiquarian Society, Worcester, Mass.

37. Spicer, *Autobiography of Rev. Tobias Spicer* (Boston, 1851), 32–33.

38. Hibbard, *The Life and Travels of B. Hibbard, Minister of the Gospel* (New York, 1825), 60. The itinerant Benjamin Abbott recorded the large number of people in the town of Patchogue on Long Island who scorned a Baptist preaching predestination: "The people rose and universally testified their abhorrence to the doctrine [of predestination] and one man said, Mr. C. your preaching is an abomination: I know it to be so in my family; for my children are now men and women grown and if I reprove them for sin, let it be what it will, their reply is 'it was so ordained, and if we are to be saved, we shall do what we will, and if we are not to be saved it is in vain to try; we can do nothing.'" *The Experience and Gospel Labors of the Reverend Benjamin Abbot* (New York, 1813), 224, quoted in Robert E. Cray, Jr., "Forging a Majority: The Methodist Experience on Eastern Long Island, 1789–1845," *New York History* 67 (1986):292.

39. Robert Marshall and J. Thompson, *A Brief Historical Account of Sundry Things in the Doctrines and State of the Christian, or, as It Is Historically Called, the Newlight Church* (Cincinnati, 1811), 3–4.

40. At this point I take exception to one of the arguments of the intriguing book by R. Laurence Moore, *Religious Outsiders and the Making of Americans* (New York, 1986), which suggests that outsiders such as the Mormons "invented oppositions" to the mainstream as a way to inculcate self-confidence. My own sense is that the verbal combat in the early republic between respectable and insurgent churches was much less a strategy fabricated by the latter to carve out a recognizable niche and more a reflection of the cleavage between the religious folkways of common people and those of their betters.

41. Neither those who have defended a so-called social control interpretation of the Second Great Awakening (Clifford S. Griffin, John R. Bodo, Charles I. Foster, and Charles C. Cole, Jr.) nor those who do not (Lois Banner and Ronald G. Walters) have factored into their interpretation the broad network of populist religious leaders who did perceive in moderate Calvinists a conspiracy for social control. Very helpful in comprehending these populist networks is Byron Cecil Lambert, *The Rise of the Anti-Mission Baptists: Sources and Leaders, 1800–1840* (New York, 1980).

42. The phrase is that of Joseph Buckminster, minister of the Brattle Street Church in Boston. See Elias Smith, *The Clergyman's Looking-Glass*, no. 3 (Portsmouth, N.H., 1804), 3.

43. *Herald of Gospel Liberty*, October 26, 1810, 263, 227.

44. Garrettson, *Letter to the Rev. Lyman Beecher*, 11.

45. Leland, *Writings of the Late Elder John Leland*, 193–95. For the full poem, see the appendix.

46. Cushing Biggs Hassell, *History of the Church of God* (New York, 1886), 624.

47. Gates's work included *The Trials, Experience, Exercises of Mind, and First Travels of Theophilus R. Gates* (Philadelphia, 1809); *Truth: or the Religious Sentiments of Theophilus R. Gates* (Philadelphia, 1810); *Truth Advocated, or Explanations of Parts of the Revelation and Other Prophecies* (Philadelphia, 1812); *A Measuring Reed, to Separate Between the Precious and the Vile* (Philadelphia, 1815).

48. Theophilus R. Gates, "Truth Advocated: or the Apocalyptic Beast, and Mystic Babylon," in Gates, *Life and Writings*, 235.

49. Theophilus R. Gates, "Observations on the Signs of the Times; intended as a supplement to Truth Advocated," ibid., 354.

50. For an excellent description of the tone of Gates's rhetoric, see Lambert, *Rise of the Anti-Mission Baptists*, 177–79.

51. *The Reformer* 5 (1824):134–38; *The Reformer* 8 (1827):55. Quoted in Lambert, *Rise of the Anti-Mission Baptists*, 186, 191–92.

52. Lambert, *Rise of the Anti-Mission Baptists*, 225.

53. John Taylor, *Thoughts on Missions* (Franklin County, Ky., 1820), 5.

54. Ibid., 8, 12, 17, 26–29, 25. Taylor refused to acknowledge that the mediation of theologians was necessary: "Nothing is more absurd than to say, that a man cannot understand the Scriptures, but by a knowledge of the original languages in which they were written. This is some of the doctrine of those theologians, by which they would destroy our confidence in all translations, and thereby take our Bible from us." Ibid., 23.

55. On Taylor generally, see Dorothy Brown Thompson, "John Taylor of the Ten Churches," *Register of the Kentucky Historical Society* 46 (1948):541–72; and "John Taylor and the Day of Controversy," ibid., 53 (1955), 197–233.

56. *The Church Advocate*, 2, no. 122 (1831), 286.

57. Bertram Wyatt-Brown, "The Antimission Movement in the Jacksonian South: A Study in Regional Folk Culture," *Journal of Southern History* 36 (1970):501–29.

58. Leland, *Writings of the Late Elder John Leland*, 648.

59. John L. Winebrenner, *History of all the Religious Denominations in the United States* (Harrisburg, Pa., 1853), 595.

60. *The Christian Baptist*, April 3, 1826, 229.

61. E. G. Rupp, "The Bible in the Age of the Reformation," in *The Church's Use of the Bible Past and Present*, ed. D. E. Nineham (London, 1963), 84; Martin Luther, *Works* (Philadelphia Edition), 39:75–76.

62. A. Skevington Wood, *The Principles of Biblical Interpretation: As Enunciated by Irenaeus, Origin, Augustine, Luther, and Calvin* (Grand Rapids, 1967), 92. On the Westminster approach to the Bible, see Jack Bartlett Rogers, *Scripture in the Westminster Confession* (Grand Rapids, 1967); and John G. Leith, *Assembly at Westminster: Reformed Theology in the Making* (Richmond, 1973).

63. For Wesley's use of Scripture, see Mack B. Stokes, *The Bible in the Wesleyan Heritage* (Nashville, 1979), 19–26. Edwards discusses this danger in *The Works of Jonathan Edwards: Religious Affections*, ed. John E. Smith (New Haven, Conn., 1964), 2:143–44.

64. Adams, *The Works of John Adams*, ed. Charles Francis Adams, 10 vols. (Boston, 1856), 2:5–6, quoted in Conrad Wright, *The Beginnings of Unitarianism in America* (Boston, 1955), 231.

65. Wright, *Beginnings of Unitarianism*, 235.

66. Edward M. Griffin, *Old Brick: Charles Chauncy of Boston, 1705–1787* (Minneapolis, 1980), 109–25. Henry May suggests that the Arian Samuel Clarke was one of the three most read and quoted divines in eighteenth-century America; see May, *The Enlightenment in America* (New York, 1976), 38. Chauncy acknowledged his debt to John Taylor for a method of examining the Bible in *The Mystery Hid from Ages and Generations . . . or, the Salvation of All Men* (London, 1784), xi–xii. See Wright, *Beginnings of Unitarianism*, 78.

67. Wright, *Beginnings of Unitarianism*, 176.

68. Chauncy, *Mystery Hid from Ages*, 359; Griffin, *Old Brick*, 11, 176. See Noah Worcester's article, "On Humility in the Investigation of Christian Truth," in *The Christian Disciple* 1, no. 4 (Boston, 1813), 17–22. Worcester elaborates on this hostility to human creeds and confessions in his book, *Causes and Evils of Contention Unveiled in Letters to Christians*, a favorite of the reformer Lucretia Mott. See Otelia Cromwell, *Lucretia Mott* (Cambridge, Mass., 1958), 39, 204.

69. Charles Beecher, *The Bible a Sufficient Creed* (Boston, 1850), 24, 26.

70. Edmund S. Morgan, ed., *Puritan Political Ideas* (Indianapolis, 1965), xiii.

71. John W. Nevin, "Early Christianity," in Yrigoyen and Bricker, *Catholic and Reformed*, 255.

72. Nevin, "Sect System," 137.

73. Ibid., 144.

74. Rowland Berthoff and John M. Murrin, "Feudalism, Communalism, and

the Yeoman Freeholder: The American Revolution Considered as a Social Accident," in *Essays on the American Revolution*, ed. Stephen G. Kurtz and James H. Hutson (Chapel Hill, N.C., 1973), 282–88.

75. The rational bent of eighteenth-century studies of prophecy is discussed in Margaret C. Jacob, *The Newtonians and the English Revolution, 1689–1720* (Ithaca, N.Y., 1976); Clarke Garrett, *Respectable Folly: Millenarians and the French Revolution in France and England* (Baltimore, 1975); and Donald J. D'Elia, *Benjamin Rush: Philosopher of the American Revolution* (Philadelphia, 1974).

76. Elhanan Winchester's writings include *A Course of Lectures on Prophecies that Remain to Be Fulfilled*, 4 vols. (London, 1789–90) and *The Three Woe Trumpets* (London, 1793). James Winthrop, *A Systematic Arrangement of Several Scripture Prophecies* (Boston, 1795). Joseph Galloway, *Brief Commentaries upon Such Parts of the Revelation and Other Prophecies as Immediately Refer to the Present Times*, 2 vols. (London, 1802).

77. On the outpouring of millennial writing, both radical and conservative, after the French Revolution, see Ruth H. Bloch, *Visionary Republic: Millennial Themes in American Thought, 1756–1800* (Cambridge, England, 1985), 150–231.

78. Elias Smith, *The Whole World Governed by a Jew: or the Government of the Second Adam, as King and Priest* (Exeter, N.H., 1805), 74.

79. *Herald of Gospel Liberty*, September 1, 1808, 1; Elias Smith, *A Discourse Delivered at Jefferson Hall, Thanksgiving Day, November 25, 1802; and Redelivered (by Request) the Wednesday Evening Following, at the Same Place: The Subject, Nebuchadnezzar's Dream* (Portsmouth, N.H., 1803), 30–32.

80. Thomas Campbell, *The Declaration and Address of the Christian Association of Washington* (Washington, Pa., 1809), 14; Alexander Campbell, "Oration in Honor of the Fourth of July," *Popular Lectures and Addresses* (Philadelphia, 1863), 374–75.

81. Marshall and Thompson, *A Brief Historical Account of . . . the Newlight Church*, 255. Presbyterian David Rice complained in 1805 about Stone and his followers: "Another thing that prepared the minds of many for the reception of error, was their high expectation of the speedy approach of the Millennium." Rice, *Epistle to the Citizens of Kentucky*, as quoted in Bishop, *The Church in the State of Kentucky*, 335.

82. James O'Kelly, *Hymns and Spiritual Songs, Designed for the Use of Christians* (Raleigh, 1816). See "The Vision" (p. 110) and "The Expected Reformation" (p. 12 at the back of the book), a verse of which goes as follows: "The great reform is drawing near, / Long look'd for soone will come / The time will move both earth and sea, / Just like a glorious Jubilee."

83. Lorenzo Dow, *Hint to the Public, or Thoughts on the Fulfillment of Prophecy* (Boston and Salisbury, N.C., 1811); *Analects; or, Reflections upon Natural, Moral and Political Philosophy, Including the Rights, Interest and Duties of Man, Addressed to the Different Ranks and Societies Throughout the U.S. of America* (Alexandria, 1813).

84. Lorenzo Dow, *History of Cosmopolite: or the Four Volumes of Lorenzo's Journal* (New York, 1814), 115–215; quotations on 201, 141, 169, 215, 169. Dow employed the common interpretation of this day in which the persecuted woman who flees into the wilderness (Revelation 12) prefigured the eventual prosperity of the gospel in America (pp. 122–25).

85. Alexander Campbell, "Oration in Honor of the Fourth of July," 377; Elias Smith, *The Life, Conversion, Preaching, Travels and Sufferings of Elias Smith*, 292;

Stone, *Biography*, 47; James O'Kelly, *The Author's Apology for Protesting against the Methodist Episcopal Government* (Richmond, 1798), 52.

86. Abel Sargent, *Halcyon Itinerary and True Millennium Messenger* 5 (1807): 146.

87. Elias Smith devoted a sermon of 120 pages to the subject of how republican values should be applied to the church. See his *The Whole World Governed by a Jew*.

88. James West Davidson, *The Logic of Millennial Thought: Eighteenth-Century New England* (New Haven, Conn., 1977), 122–41.

89. Richard Carwardine, "Methodist Ministers and the Second Party System," in Richey and Rowe, *Rethinking Methodist History*, 134–47.

90. W. H. Oliver, *Prophets and Millennialists: The Uses of Biblical Prophecy in England From the 1790s to the 1840s* (Oxford, 1978), 235.

91. John Taylor, *Millennial Star* (London), November 15, 1847. Quoted in Howard S. Swan, "Music of the Mormons, 1830–1965," *Huntington Library Quarterly* 12 (1949):226.

92. These phrases are from a campaign song written for Smith by Parley Pratt. Quoted in Levette J. Davidson, "Mormon Songs," *Journal of American Folklore* 58 (1945):277.

93. Rigdon's sermon was reported in a Mormon newspaper published by Joseph Smith's brother William. See *The Prophet*, June 8, 1844, 2. Quoted by Marvin S. Hill, "The Role of Christian Primitivism in the Origin and Development of the Mormon Kingdom, 1830–1844" (Ph.D. diss., University of Chicago, 1968), 72–73.

Chapter Seven

1. Cartwright, *Autobiography of Peter Cartwright, the Backwoods Preacher*, ed. W. P. Strickland (New York, 1856), 481–90, 520–23, 243.

2. Timothy L. Smith, *Revivalism and Social Reform: American Protestantism on the Eve of the Civil War* (New York, 1965), 24. Charles Edwin Jones, "The Holiness Complaint with Late-Victorian Methodism," in *Rethinking Methodist History: A Bicentennial Historical Consultation*, ed. Russell E. Richey and Kenneth E. Rowe (Nashville, 1985), 61. Henry C. Mitchell, *Black Preaching* (Philadelphia, 1970), 79–82.

3. Donald G. Mathews, *Religion in the Old South* (Chicago, 1977), 81–135. E. Brooks Holifield, *The Gentlemen Theologians: American Theology in Southern Culture, 1795–1860* (Durham, 1978).

4. On the formation of the Cumberland Presbyterian Church, see Ben M. Barrus et al., *A People Called Cumberland Presbyterians* (Memphis, 1972). George M. Marsden provides a thorough discussion of the issues underlying the 1837 Presbyterian split in *The Evangelical Mind and the New School Presbyterian Experience* (New Haven, Conn., 1970).

5. This language is from the definitive Old School critique of Charles Finney by Albert Baldwin Dod. See Dod's review, "Finney's Lectures," *Biblical Repertory and Theological Review* 7 (1835):656–57. For a full discussion of the Princeton critique of Finney, see Keith J. Hardman, *Charles Grandison Finney, 1792–1875: Revivalist and Reformer* (Syracuse, N.Y., 1987), 286–92.

6. Finney was a spellbinding orator, as the following incident in Rochester illustrates. As he described a sinner's slide to perdition, tracing the course from ceiling to floor with outstretched finger, "half his hearers . . . would rise unconsciously to their feet to see him descend into the pit below." Henry B. Stanton, *Random Recollections* (New York, 1887), 42, quoted in Whitney R. Cross, *The Burned-Over District: The Social and Intellectual History of Enthusiastic Religion in Western New York, 1800–1850* (Ithaca, N.Y., 1950), 155.

7. Benet Tyler, *Memoir of the Life and Character of the Rev. Asahel Nettleton, D.D.* (Hartford, Conn., 1844), 252, quoted in Hardman, *Charles Grandison Finney*, 147.

8. Charles Grandison Finney, *Lectures on Revivals of Religion*, ed. William G. McLoughlin (Cambridge, Mass., 1960), 291. In these lectures Finney spent almost one hundred pages attacking the methods of the respectable clergy. The following is typical: "It may be illustrated by the case of a minister that goes to sea. ⸢.⸣e may be learned in science, but he knows nothing how to sail a ship. And he begins to ask the sailors about this thing and that, and what is this rope for, and the like. 'Why,' say the sailors, 'these are not *ropes*, we have only one rope in a ship, these are the rigging, the man talks like a fool.' And so this learned man becomes a laughing-stock, perhaps, to the sailors, because he does not know how to sail a ship. But if he were to tell them one half of what he knows about science, perhaps they would think him a conjurer, to know so much. So learned students may understand their *hic, hac, hoc*, very well, and may laugh at the humble Christian, and call him ignorant, although he may know how to win more souls than five hundred of them." For the anti-Calvinist jingle from Lorenzo Dow, see ibid., 205.

9. Ibid., 208.

10. Ibid., 273, 181.

11. Charles G. Finney, *Memoirs* (New York, 1876), 54.

12. Richard Carwardine, "The Second Great Awakening in the Urban Centers: An Examination of Methodism and the 'New Measures,'" *Journal of American History* 59 (1972):327–40.

13. Ibid., 338–39. Stanton, *Random Recollections*, 40–42. On Finney's more respectable style, see Cross, *Burned-Over District*, 155. Paul E. Johnson confirms Finney's testimony about the appeal to entrepreneurial classes in *A Shopkeeper's Millennium: Society and Revivals in Rochester, New York, 1815–1837* (New York, 1978), 106.

14. The impact of democratic electioneering techniques upon the Federalists is explored in David Hackett Fischer, *The Revolution of American Conservatism: The Federalist Party in the Era of Jeffersonian Democracy* (New York, 1965), 91–109.

15. [Billy Hibbard], *Philom's Address to the People of New England* (n.p., 1817), 76.

16. Samuel Goodrich, *Recollections of a Lifetime*, 2 vols. (New York, 1856), 1:216–17.

17. Terry D. Bilhartz, *Urban Religion and the Second Great Awakening: Church and Society in Early National Baltimore* (Rutherford, N.J., 1986), 94–98. See W. C. Walton, *Narrative of a Revival of Religion in the Third Presbyterian Church in Baltimore* (Northampton, Mass., 1826).

18. On the Dutch context, see Justus M. Van der Kroef, "Abraham Kuyper and the Rise of Neo-Calvinism in the Netherlands," *Church History* 17 (1948):316–34.

19. Abel Stevens, *The Life of Nathan Bangs, D.D.* (New York, 1863), 1–65.

20. Ibid., 182.

21. Ibid., 183.

22. Nathan Bangs, *A History of the Methodist Episcopal Church*, 4 vols. (1840–53), 2:105.

23. Stevens, *Life of Nathan Bangs*, 184–85. *The Doctrines and Discipline of the Methodist Episcopal Church* (New York, 1820), 165. Samuel A. Seaman, *Annals of New York Methodism* (New York, 1892), 219. Quoted in Emory Stevens Bucke et al., eds., *The History of American Methodism*, 3 vols. (1964), 1:626.

24. Stevens, *Life of Nathan Bangs*, 239–54, 232. By 1860, the Methodist Book Concern, with eastern and western branches and five depositories, employed four "book agents," twelve editors for its periodicals, and 460 other workers and operated between twenty and thirty cylinder and power presses. Its multiple periodicals had an aggregate circulation of over one million copies per month, and its quadrennial sales for the period ending in 1860 were over one million dollars. As early as 1820 Bangs proposed a seminary in New York, a move bitterly opposed by the same people who balked at building a new John Street Church. In 1824, Bangs was also unsuccessful in persuading the General Conference of the Methodist church to establish a central college or university. Ibid., 248–49.

25. Bangs, *History of the Methodist Episcopal Church*, 70, 289, 281–82.

26. Ibid. *Journal of the General Conference of the Methodist Episcopal Church* (New York, 1844), 157.

27. William B. Sprague, *Annals of the American Pulpit* (New York, 1865), vol. 7, *Methodist*, 112–14. For a description of the domestication of camp meetings around Baltimore about 1820, see Bilhartz, *Urban Religion and the Second Great Awakening*, 93–94. Cartwright, *Autobiography of Peter Cartwright*, 481.

28. Donald G. Tewksbury, *The Founding of American Colleges and Universities Before the Civil War* (New York, 1932), 104–06, 115–17. In 1834 Indiana Baptists organized the Indiana Manual Labor Institute, which became Franklin College a decade later. Its very name reflects the fact that in the heartland a collegiate education was no longer the way that society endowed certain of its sons with the rank of a gentlemen. At Oberlin College in the 1850s, only one-eighth of the thirteen hundred students were enrolled in a regular college course, and only one-third were pursuing college work of any type. On these matters, see Timothy L. Smith, "Uncommon Schools: Christian Colleges and Social Idealism in Midwestern America, 1820–1950," in the Indiana Historical Society, *Lectures, 1976–77: The History of Education in the Middle West* (Indianapolis, 1978); and William C. Ringenberg, *The Christian College: A History of Protestant Higher Education in America* (Grand Rapids, Mich., 1984).

29. Bertram Wyatt-Brown, "The Antimission Movement in the Jacksonian South: A Study in Regional Folk Culture," *Journal of Southern History* 36 (1970):528, 503.

30. Alexander M'Lean, *An Appeal to the Public* (Belchertown, Mass., 1828), 4, 6, 54–55, quoted in Steven J. Novak, "The Perils of Respectability: Methodist Schisms of the 1820s," unpublished paper presented to the American Historical Association, 1980.

31. Walter Brownlow Posey, *The Baptist Church in the Lower Mississippi Valley, 1776–1845* (Lexington, Ky., 1957), 115–27.

32. John Higham, *From Boundlessness to Consolidation: The Transformation of American Culture, 1848–1860* (Ann Arbor, Mich., 1969).

33. Alexander Campbell, "The Nature of Christian Organization," *Millennial Harbinger* 1 (1841):532, quoted in Leroy Garrett, *The Stone-Campbell Movement: An Anecdotal History of Three Churches* (Joplin, Mo., 1981), 417.

34. William Miller to Truman Hendryx, October 26, 1837, quoted in David L. Rowe, *Thunder and Trumpets: Millerites and Dissenting Religion in Upstate New York, 1800–1850* (Chico, Calif., 1985), 90.

35. Frederick A. Norwood, *The Story of American Methodism: A History of the United Methodists and Their Relations* (Nashville, 1974), 195–96, 294–95.

36. E. Merton Coulter, *William G. Brownlow: Fighting Parson of the Southern Highlands* (Chapel Hill, N.C., 1937).

37. Lester G. McAllister and William E. Tucker, *Journey in Faith: A History of the Christian Church (Disciples of Christ)* (St. Louis, 1975), 235.

38. On the tumultuous evolution of the Disciples, a subject that deserves far more study, see Garrett, *Stone-Campbell Movement*, and David Edwin Harrell, Jr., *Quest for a Christian America: The Disciples of Christ and American Society to 1866* (Nashville, 1966).

39. On this splintering process, see Thomas F. O'Dea, *The Mormons* (Chicago, 1957), 70–71. An excellent article on Strang is Lawrence Foster, "James J. Strang: The Prophet Who Failed," *Church History* 50 (1981):182–92. A good discussion of Benjamin Winchester, an important Mormon publicist, is found in David J. Whittaker, "Early Mormon Pamphleteering" (Ph.D. diss., Brigham Young University, 1982), 139–235.

40. Two works have been immensely helpful on this point: C. Vann Woodward, *Tom Watson, Agrarian Rebel* (New York, 1938); and Alan Brinkley, *Voices of Protest: Huey Long, Father Coughlin and the Great Depression* (New York, 1982).

41. David Martin, *A General Theory of Secularization* (New York, 1978), 36, 30.

42. Alexis de Tocqueville, *Democracy in America*, trans. Henry Reeve, 2 vols. (New York, 1945), 1:321–25.

Chapter Eight

1. In a study that correlates religious belief and "development variables" in a number of countries, Walter Dean Burnham has argued that the United States presents a striking exception to the nearly linear and extremely strong connection between religious beliefs and composite measures of development. See the appendix to his article "The 1980 Earthquake: Realignment, Reaction, or What?" in *The Hidden Election: Politics and Economics in the 1980 Presidential Campaign*, ed. Thomas Ferguson and Joel Rogers (New York, 1981), 132–40.

2. Laurence Veysey, "Continuity and Decline in American Religion since 1900," Kaplan Lecture, University of Pennsylvania, 1980. The Gallup figures are taken from *Religion in America 1979–80* (Princeton, N.J., 1980).

3. Alan D. Gilbert, *The Making of Post-Christian Britain: A History of the Secularization of Modern Society* (London, 1980), 88. On the significant decline in religious practice and belief in many European countries since World War II, see Theodore Caplow, "Contrasting Trends in European and American Religion," *Sociological Analysis* 46 (1985):101–08.

4. Theodore Caplow et al., *All Faithful People: Change and Continuity in Middletown's Religion* (Minneapolis, 1983).

5. David Martin, *A General Theory of Secularization* (New York, 1978), 30.

6. On the impact of Dow, Caughey, and Finney in Great Britain, see Richard Carwardine, *Transatlantic Revivalism: Popular Evangelicalism in Britain and America, 1790–1865* (Westport, Conn., 1978). The role of Mormons and Millerites is discussed in James B. Allen and Malcolm R. Thorp, "The Mission of the Twelve to England, 1840–41: Mormon Apostles and the Working Class," *Brigham Young University Studies* 15 (1975):499–526; and Louis Billington, "The Millerite Adventists in Great Britain, 1840–1850," *Journal of American Studies* 1 (1967):191–212.

7. These themes are treated suggestively in Alan Brinkley, *Voices of Protest: Huey Long, Father Coughlin and the Great Depression* (New York, 1982), 143–68.

8. The comparison with American Populism draws upon the work of Lawrence Goodwyn, who has deep sympathy for the human meaning of the Populist movement. See *Democratic Promise: The Populist Moment in America* (New York, 1976); and an abbreviated version of the work, *The Populist Moment: A Short History of the Agrarian Revolt in America* (New York, 1978). One significant difference is that, unlike Populism itself, these religious movements have endured in American society. James Turner had made the point that Populism deserves to be viewed as a manifestation of one of the most central and venerable characteristics of the American political tradition. See Turner, "Understanding the Populists," *Journal of American History* 67 (1980):354–73.

9. Luther P. Gerlach and Virginia H. Hine, *People, Power, Change: Movements of Social Transformation* (Indianapolis, 1970).

10. Martin, *General Theory of Secularization*, 28, 35. "The clergy [in America] are assimilated to the concept of rival entrepreneurs running varied religious series on a mixed laissez-faire and oligopolistic model: their status usually is not high. Religious styles constantly adapt and accept vulgarization in accordance with the stylistic tendencies of their varied markets, sometimes in such a way as to weaken content and intellectual articulation." Ibid., 28.

11. On the importance of the values of autonomy and popular sovereignty in the early republic, see James T. Kloppenberg, "The Virtues of Liberalism: Christianity, Republicanism, and Ethics in Early American Political Discourse," *Journal of American History* 74 (1987):9–33.

12. Robert H. Wiebe, *The Search for Order, 1877–1920* (New York, 1967), xiii–xiv, 76–110.

13. The rural church reform movement among mainline Protestants reflected the essence of this spirit. In the first quarter of the twentieth century, these outside experts sought to bring the blessings of urban America to backward country folk. The study *Rural Church Life in the Middle West*, sponsored by the Institute of Social and Religious Research and written by Benson Y. Landis in 1922, called for church consolidation and for a more professional ministry in light of the vast array of small, localistic churches in rural America and in light of the fact that only 37 percent of midwestern rural Protestant ministers were college or seminary graduates. "The various denominations," Landis wrote, must "professionalize the country minister and train men to be rural social and religious engineers." In his perceptive study of this reform movement, James H. Madison concludes that most rural church folk resisted the diagnosis and advice of these outside agents of change. See Madison,

"Reformers and the Rural Church, 1900–1950," *Journal of American History* 73 (1986):645–68, quotation on 659.

14. Some of the more prominent of these leaders include Fundamentalists A. T. Pierson, Reuben A. Torrey, A. J. Gordon, John Roach Straton, and William B. Riley; Holiness leaders Henry Clay Morrison, Phineas F. Bresee, and A. .B. Simpson; and Pentecostals A. J. Tomlinson, Aimee Semple McPherson, and William H. Durham.

15. Peter W. Williams, *Popular Religion in America* (Englewood Cliffs, N.J., 1980), 144. Grant Wacker, "The Functions of Faith in Primitive Pentecostalism," *Harvard Theological Review* 77 (1984):353–75; and Wacker, "A Profile of American Pentecostalism," unpublished paper, 1981.

16. George M. Marsden, *Fundamentalists and American Culture: The Shaping of Twentieth-Century Evangelicalism, 1870–1925* (New York, 1980); and Joel Carpenter, "Fundamentalist Institutions and the Rise of Evangelical Protestantism, 1929–1942," *Church History* 49 (1980):62–75.

17. Timothy L. Smith, *Called Unto Holiness: The Story of the Nazarenes* (Kansas City, 1962), 114–18, 119. The Holiness advocate Henry Clay Morrison complained in 1899 about the smugness of the Methodist Episcopal church: "Without doubt the times are ripe in all of our large cities for just such churches as the Nazarene in Los Angeles. There is a stiffness and coldness in our city churches that freezes out the common people, and, worst of all shuts out the Christ of the common people." Quoted in "The Holiness Complaint with Late-Victorian Methodism," in *Rethinking Methodist History: A Bicentennial Historical Consultation*, ed. Russell E. Richey and Kenneth E. Rowe (Nashville, 1985), 59.

18. William C. Ringenberg, *Taylor University: The First 125 Years* (Grand Rapids, 1973), 66–70.

19. Quoted in Wacker, "Profile of American Pentecostalism," 30.

20. Virginia Lieson Brereton, "Protestant Fundamentalist Bible Schools, 1882–1940" (Ph.D. diss., Columbia University, 1981), 149. Timothy P. Weber, "The Two-Edged Sword: The Fundamentalist Use of the Bible," in *The Bible in American Culture: Essays in Cultural History*, ed. Nathan O. Hatch and Mark A. Noll (New York, 1982), 111.

21. William R. Hutchison, *The Modernist Impulse in American Protestantism* (Cambridge, Mass., 1976), 196–99.

22. Wacker, "Functions of Faith in Primitive Pentecostalism," 365.

23. A similar form of eschatology, premillennial dispensationalism, dominated both Pentecostals and Fundamentalists. See ibid., 368–75; and Timothy P. Weber, *Living in the Shadow of the Second Coming: American Premillennialism, 1875–1925* (New York, 1979). For the premillennialism of the Holiness leader Henry Clay Morrison, see his book *The Second Coming* (Louisville, 1914).

24. The classic study by Liston Pope, *Millhands and Preachers: A Study of Gastonia* (New Haven, Conn., 1942), notes that in the two decades after 1920, "newer sects" began twenty-six different churches in Gastonia, North Carolina, with an aggregate membership of nearly four thousand, and all were "firmly mill churches." He noted that these highly atomistic religious units often began with the activities of an individual minister who set out to organize a group of his own (128–29).

25. Wacker, "Functions of Faith in Primitive Pentecostalism," 363.

26. A superb study of these schools is Brereton, "Protestant Fundamentalist Bible Schools." On the tight links between higher education and professionalism in this period, see Burton J. Bledstein, *The Culture of Professionalism: The Middle Class and the Development of Higher Education in America* (New York, 1976).

27. Robert E. Black, *The Story of Johnson Bible College* (Kimberlin Heights, Tenn., 1951), 22–23, quoted in Brereton, "Protestant Fundamentalist Bible Schools," 10.

28. Marsden, *Fundamentalists and American Culture*, 184–90.

29. Quentin J. Schultze, "Evangelical Radio and the Rise of the Electronic Church, 1921–1948," *Journal of Broadcasting & the Electronic Media* 32 (1988):289–306.

30. James Davison Hunter, *Evangelicalism: The Coming Generation* (Chicago, 1987), 7.

31. Arthur E. Paris, *Black Pentecostalism: Southern Religion in an Urban World* (Amherst, 1982), 19. Benjamin Elijah Mays and Joseph William Nicholson, *The Negro's Church* (New York, 1933), 278–313.

32. Robert Wuthnow, "Religious Movements and Counter-Movements in North America," in *New Religious Movements and Rapid Social Change*, ed. James Beckford (Paris, 1987). See also Grant Wacker, "Searching for Norman Rockwell: Popular Evangelicalism in Contemporary America," in *The Evangelical Tradition in America*, ed. Leonard I. Sweet (Macon, Ga., 1984), 289–315.

33. Robert Wuthnow emphasizes that in recent years this cleavage has grown more serious. See chap. 8, "The Great Divide: Toward Religious Realignment," in Wuthnow, *The Restructuring of American Religion: Society and Faith Since World War II* (Princeton, N.J., 1988).

Redefining the Second Great Awakening

1. Gordon S. Wood, "Evangelical America and Early Mormonism," *New York History* 61 (1980), 362. W. R. Ward, "The Religion of the People and the Problem of Control., 1790–1830," in *Popular Belief and Practice*, ed. G. J. Cuming and Derek Baker (Cambridge, 1972), 237.

2. Frederick V. Mills, Sr., "Mentors of Methodism, 1784–1844," *Methodist History* 12 (1973), 43. William W. Sweet, *Religion on the American Frontier, 1783–1840* (Chicago, 1946), vol. 4, *The Methodists*, 11, 45–46.

3. See, for example, Bernard Semmel, *The Methodist Revolution* (New York, 1973); David Hempton, *Methodism and Politics in British Society 1750–1850* (Stanford, 1984); and W. R. Ward, *Religion and Society in England 1790–1850* (New York, 1973); and John Walsh, "Methodism at the End of the Eighteenth Century," in *A History of the Methodist Church in Great Britain*, ed. Rupert Davies (London, 1965).

4. See Wiebe's superb overview of the early republic, *The Opening of American Society* (New York, 1984), quotations on xii. Other useful critiques of conventional periodization include Edward Pessen, "We Are All Jeffersonians, We Are All Jacksonians: Or a Pox on Stultifying Periodizations," the lead essay in the first issue of *The Journal of the Early Republic* 1 (1981):1–26; and Sean Wilentz, "On Class and Politics in Jacksonian America," *Reviews in American History* 10 (1982):45–63.

5. The talented group of scholars includes Alan Heimert, *Religion and the American Mind from the Great Awakening to the Revolution* (Cambridge, Mass., 1966);

William G. McLoughlin, "'Enthusiasm for Liberty': The Great Awakening as the Key to the Revolution," *Proceedings of the American Antiquarian Society* 87 (1977):69–95; Harry S. Stout, "Religion, Communications, and the Ideological Origins of the American Revolution," *William and Mary Quarterly*, 3d ser., 34 (1977):519–41; Philip Greven, *The Protestant Temperament: Patterns of Child-Rearing, Religious Experience, and the Self in Early America* (New York, 1977); Gary B. Nash, *The Urban Crucible: Social Change, Political Consciousness, and the Origins of the American Revolution* (Cambridge, Mass., 1979); Rhys Isaac, *The Transformation of Virginia, 1740–1790* (Chapel Hill, N.C., 1982); and Patricia U. Bonomi, *Under the Cope of Heaven: Religion, Society, and Politics in Colonial America* (New York, 1986).

6. Gordon S. Wood, "The Significance of the Early Republic," *Journal of the Early Republic* 8 (1988):1–20.

7. Henry F. May points to the new scholarly interest in religion in "The Recovery of American Religious History," *American Historical Review* 70 (1964):79–92. Perry Miller, "From the Covenant to the Revival," in *The Shaping of American Religion*, ed. James Ward Smith and A. Leland Jamison (Princeton, N.J., 1961), 350. The broader trend to dismiss the social repercussions of the Revolution is evident in Frederick B. Tolles, "The American Revolution Considered as a Social Movement: A Re-Evaluation," *American Historical Review* 60 (1954–55):1–12.

8. In this regard, Herbert Butterfield's advice about studies of the Reformation is telling: "Sometimes it would seem we regard Protestantism as a Thing, a fixed and definite object that came into existence in 1517; and we seize upon it as a source, a cause, an origin, even of movements that were taking place concurrently; and we do this with an air of finality, as though Protestantism itself had no antecedents, as though it were a fallacy to go behind the great watershed, as though indeed it would blunt the edge of our story to admit the workings of a process instead of assuming the interposition of some direct agency." Butterfield, *The Whig Interpretation of History* (London, 1931), 51–52.

9. For a compelling statement on the importance of historians being contextualists seeking to understand the past on its own terms see Bernard Bailyn, *History and the Creative Imagination* (St. Louis, 1985).

10. Miller, "From the Covenant to the Revival," 354. Richard Hofstadter, *Anti-Intellectualism in American Life* (New York, 1962), 84.

11. Clifford S. Griffin, *Their Brothers' Keepers: Moral Stewardship in the United States, 1800–1865* (New Brunswick, 1960); John R. Bodo, *The Protestant Clergy and Public Issues, 1812–1848* (Princeton, 1954); Charles I. Foster, *An Errand of Mercy: The Evangelical United Front, 1790–1837* (Chapel Hill, N.C., 1960); and Charles C. Cole, Jr., *The Social Ideas of the Northern Evangelists, 1820–1860* (New York, 1954).

12. E. Brooks Holifield, *The Gentlemen Theologians: American Theology in Southern Culture, 1795–1860* (Durham, N.C., 1978), 36–49; Donald M. Scott, *From Office to Profession: The New England Ministry, 1750–1850* (Philadelphia, 1978); and Ann Douglas, *The Feminization of American Culture* (New York, 1977).

13. Lois W. Banner, "Religious Benevolence as Social Control: A Critique of an Interpretation," *Journal of American History* 60 (1973):23–41.

14. William Warren Sweet, *Religion in the Development of American Culture, 1765–1840* (New York, 1952), 129–60. Sweet begins his major collection of source materials on the Methodists with the assertion "no single force had more to do with bringing order out of frontier chaos than the Methodist circuit-rider." Sweet,

Religion on the American Frontier, 1783–1840 (Chicago, 1946), vol. 4, *The Methodists*, v. He defined the central theme of his book *Religion in the Development of American Culture* as the part played by groups such as the Methodists in the transit of civilization westward; thus his chapter title "Barbarism vs. Revivalism." According to James L. Ash, Jr., Sweet "patronized the multitude of sectarian groups in America as little more than institutional and theological anomalies which attracted the mentally unstable." See "American Religion and the Academy in the Early Twentieth Century: The Chicago Years of William Warren Sweet," *Church History* 50 (1981):461.

15. H. Richard Niebuhr's influential book *The Social Sources of Denominationalism* (New York, 1929) is an eloquent appeal for Christian unity premised on the assumption that "denominationalism thus represents the moral failure of Christianity" (25).

16. This paragraph draws upon R. Laurence Moore, *Religious Outsiders and the Making of Americans* (New York, 1986), 3–21. Richard Carwardine has made the same point: "Yet later denominational and local church historians often underemphasized or deliberately ignored a side of evangelical life whose emotionalism, disorder, and impropriety were an embarrassment to them." Carwardine, *Transatlantic Revivalism: Popular Evangelicalism in Britain and America, 1790–1865* (Westport, Conn., 1978), xiv.

17. David Martin, *A General Theory of Secularization* (New York, 1978), 30, 36.

18. For examples of the focus on cities and industrial workers, see Alan Dawley, *Class and Community: The Industrial Revolution in Lynn* (Cambridge, Mass., 1976). Paul G. Faler, *Mechanics and Manufacturers in the Early Industrial Revolution: Lynn Massachusetts 1780–1860* (Albany, N.Y., 1981); Charles G. Steffen, *The Mechanics of Baltimore: Workers and Politics in the Age of the Revolution, 1763–1812* (Urbana, Ill., 1984); and Sean Wilentz, *Chants Democratic: New York City and the Rise of the American Working Class, 1788–1850* (New York, 1984). Wilentz is perceptive and judicious in treating the role of popular religion in New York City, and of Methodism in particular; but popular religion is only incidental to the purposes of his work. A good example of what might be called the "new rural history" is Steven Hahn and Jonathan Prude, eds., *The Countryside in the Age of Capitalist Transformation: Essays in the Social History of Rural America* (Chapel Hill, N.C., 1987).

19. David Hempton makes this observation about the work of E. P. Thompson in Hempton, *Methodism and Politics in British Society, 1750–1850* (Stanford, 1984), 75–76.

20. Paul E. Johnson, *A Shopkeeper's Millennium: Society and Revivals in Rochester, New York, 1815–1837* (New York, 1978), 9, 136–41.

21. The quote is from a radical Christian in western Massachusetts. See Simon Hough, *An Alarm to the World: Dedicated to All Ranks of Men* (Stockbridge, Mass., 1792), 12.

22. Richard Bushman, *Joseph Smith and the Beginnings of Mormonism* (Urbana, Ill., 1984), 5. For two generations Smith's deeply religious family had minimal connection with mainstream Protestantism.

Index

Abbott, Benjamin, 172
Abolitionists, 144
Adams, John, 22, 25, 129, 162, 180–81
Adams, Samuel, 25
Adventists. *See* Millerites
African Methodist Episcopal Church, 104; founding of, 110; quest for respectability, 195
Agrarian revolt. *See* Backcountry dissent
Albright, Jacob, 154, 165
Alcott, Bronson, 145
Allen, Phinehas, 98
Allen, Richard, 11, 13, 67; on appeal of Methodism to blacks, 104; founds independent black church, 107–10; and black religious music, 157
Alline, Henry, 10, 13, 128; and popular religious music, 148, 149
Allison, Patrick, 137
America: role in populist millennialism, 186–89
American Bible Society, 141, 144
American Board of Commissioners for Foreign Missions, 170
American Education Society, 177
American Home Missionary Society, 62, 170
American Revolution, 34, 208; as democratic influence, 5–9; as cause of social upheaval, 14, 22–23; and expansion of popular press, 25; and revolt against professions, 28, 29; and backcountry dissent, 31, 33; creator of artificial national identity, 61; and Christian movement, 69, 76; influence on Barton Stone, 70–71; historiography of, 221
American Sunday School Union, 170
American Tract Society, 141, 144, 170
Andover Seminary, 17–19
Andros, Thomas, 135
Anglicanism, 8, 34; lack of appeal to slaves, 102, 104–5, 154
Antiauthoritarianism. *See* Anticlericalism; Anti-institutionalism; Egalitarian protest; Legal profession; Medical profession
Anticlericalism, 9, 12, 14, 22, 26, 44–46, 59, 75, 99–100, 135–36, 170–71, 174–79; in Christian movement, 73–76, 163
Anti-Federalists, 33, 34, 44; and egalitarian protest, 23–24
Anti-institutionalism, 100–1; in Christian movement, 77–78; continuing influence of, 214–15
Anti-Masons, 126
Antimissions protest, 97, 177–79
Arminianism, 44, 174, 180
Asbury, Francis, 11, 13, 67, 73, 106, 131, 201, 220, 222, 226; attitude toward lower classes, 8; authoritarian style of, 11, 70, 81–83; entrepreneurial method of, 57; praises camp meetings, 49–50, 55; primitivism of, 83, 167; and itinerancy, 83–89; and populist worship style, 89–91; and slavery, 102–3; on Lorenzo Dow, 130; preaching style of, 137; on American Methodism, 186–87; contrasted with Nathan Bangs, 202
Asceticism of populist preachers, 13, 82–89

305

Assemblies of God, 214
Austin, Benjamin, Jr.: egalitarian protest of, 25–26; revolt against legal profession, 27–28; anticlericalism of, 59; influence on Elias Smith, 69, 128

Babcock, William Smythe, 42–43, 173
Backcountry dissent, 30–34
Backus, Isaac, 69, 73, 77, 127; and Great Awakening, 34; contrasted with John Leland, 99; and the Bible, 180, 182
Baldwin, Thomas, 94, 95
Bangs, Nathan, 147, 195, 201–4, 205, 206
Baptist movement, 10, 21, 34, 56, 58, 59, 66, 77, 79, 212, 223, 224; growth of, 3; and democratic protest, 9; loss of intensity of, 16; Caleb Rich banished by, 40; criticized, 70; female preachers in, 79; quest for respectability of, 93–95, 195, 204, 205, 206–7; decentralizing forces in, 101; and black Christianity, 103–7, 110–12, 154–57; and religious press, 127, 141–42; lay preachers in, 134; missionary imperative of, 139; and popular religious music, 147–50, 154, 157; primitivism in, 168; and revolt against Calvinism, 170; anticlericalism in, 174, 177; antimissions protest in, 178; millennialism in, 189
Baptists, Freewill, 4, 21, 95, 167; and primacy of individual conscience, 42–43; and popular religious music, 148; and revolt against Calvinism, 172
Baptists, other: Antimission, 4; General, 95; Permanent, 95; Regular, 95; Separate, 95; Landmark, 101
Barlow, Nathan, 33
Barnes, Albert, 61, 196
Barr, John, 137
Bavarian Illuminati, 59, 77
Beecher, Charles, 182
Beecher, Henry Ward, 150
Beecher, Lyman, 62, 181, 222; conflict with populist preachers, 17–20, 35, 170, 175, 177, 226; defends clerical respectability, 35, 46; imitates populist preachers, 61; accused of heresy, 196
Bellamy, Joseph B.: New Divinity, 172
Bennett, John C., 208
Bentley, William, 21, 52, 69, 129
Bethany College, 144, 163, 207
Bible, 61; in populist theology, 16, 65, 81, 179–83, 207; literalism, 35; and primacy of conscience, 41–43; in Christian movement, 78; in liberal theology, 180–82
Bible prophecy: and social upheaval, 6; and Book of Mormon, 116–20; and populist preachers, 176. See also Millennialism
Black Christianity, 3, 4, 9, 10, 12, 220; origins and characteristics, 102–13; and

popular religious music, 154–58; and revolt against Calvinism, 171; continuing populist influence in, 217–18
Blair, Samuel, 61
Blount, Nathaniel, 59
Boardman, Richard, 85
Book of Mormon: social protest of, 115–20; and millennialism, 189
Bourne, Hugh and James, 50
Brackett, Daniel, 33
Bremer, Frederika, 112
Brownlow, William G., 207
Bryan, Andrew and Sampson, 110–12
Bryan, Hugh, 103
Bunn the Blacksmith, 52–55
Bunting, Jabez, 7, 91–93, 203
Bushnell, Horace, 62, 126

Calvin, John, 168, 173, 174, 180, 182, 195
Calvinism, 17–19, 44, 115, 180; revolt against, 10, 40–43, 130, 139, 166, 170–79, 196–97
Campbell, Alexander, 65, 67, 69, 80, 195, 207, 208, 220; role in rise of Christian movement, 71; and popular press, 74–77, 126, 144; and primacy of individual conscience, 76, 136, 179; opposes Baptist centralization, 101; and populist theology, 163; primitivism of, 167–68, 169; antimission protest of, 179; and millennialism, 186; on limits of religious democracy, 206
Campbell, Thomas, 73, 185
Camp meetings, 7, 58, 220; Methodism and, 49–56, 204
Card, Varnem, 137
Carden, Allen, 153
Cartwright, Peter, 8, 89; preaching style of, 138; and Methodist quest for respectability, 193, 204–5
Catholicism. See Roman Catholicism
Caughy, James, 212
Chalmers, Thomas, 200
Channing, William Ellery, 35, 116
Chauncy, Charles, 181
Cheese. See "Mammoth Cheese"
Chesterton, G. K., 212
Chevalier, Michael, 58
Christian Connection, 42, 57, 129, 145, 159; decline of, 80. See also Christian movement; Disciples of Christ
Christianity, American: as a popular movement, 4–5; chaos in early republic, 64–66, 80–81; continuing populist influence in, 210–19
Christianization of America, 9, 209, 210–11; accomplished through sectarian rivalry, 62–66, 68; of black America, 102–13, 154; and popular music, 160–61

Christian movement, 7, 12, 21, 58, 59, 224; number of preachers, 4; female preachers in, 56, 78–80; background and characteristics of, 68–81; lay preachers in, 134; and revolt against Calvinism, 139, 170–72; anticlericalism in, 174; millennialism in, 185–86, 189. *See also* Christian Connection; Disciples of Christ

Churches of Christ. *See* Christian Connection; Christian movement

Church of England. *See* Anglicanism

Church of God (Anderson, Indiana), 215

Church of God in Christ, 217

Church of God (Winebrenner), 154, 164

Church of the Nazarene, 214, 216

Clarke, Samuel, 181

Clergy: growth in numbers, 4; formal training of, 17–18, 171; professionalization of, 22; loss of authority, 125, 213. *See also* Preachers, populist

Cobbett, William, 143

Coke, Thomas, 50, 106

Coker, Daniel, 11, 106

Coleman, James, 201

Columbian College, 95

Communications, religious: popular revolution in, 125–33; and vernacular preaching, 133–41; role in democratization of Christianity, 146; continuing importance of, 215–16. *See also* Preachers, populist; Press, religious

Congregational Church, 4, 22, 44, 223, 224; institutional weakness of, 59–61; controversy with Christian movement, 70, 77; and religious press, 143; and black religious music, 154; extension of influence of, 170

Conscience, primacy of individual, 81, 179; in populist theology, 35, 40–43; in Christian movement, 76–78; John Leland and, 97–98, 101; in populist preaching, 135–36; Charles Finney and, 199

Constitution, U.S.: opposition to, 23–24, 26, 32

Cooper, Ezekiel, 52

Coughlin, Father Charles, 208

Cram, Nancy Gove, 78

Crane, Samuel, 173–74

Dagget, David, 125

Danforth, Clarissa H., 78

Davies, Samuel, 21, 34, 61; and African-Americans, 102, 104

Democratization of Christianity: in early republic, 3, 6, 7, 15, 210; leadership in, 5, 7, 11, 12–16, 208; definition of, 9–11; and social upheaval, 13–14; as continuing impulse, 16, 212–19; populist ideology of, 34–36; popular movement building

in, 57–58; black preachers and, 112–13; communications revolution and, 146; popular opinion and, 162–63; Charles Finney and, 197; in mid-nineteenth century, 206–9. *See also* Egalitarian protest

Denominations: growth in number of, 4, 64–66

Dickens, Charles: *Bleak House*, 143

Disciples of Christ, 56, 66, 71, 163, 220; polity, 9; loss of intensity of, 15; organizational impulse in, 80; and religious press, 127, 144; missionary imperative of, 139; anticlericalism in, 177; and quest for respectability, 195, 204; and democratic backlash, 206, 207. *See also* Christian Connection; Christian movement

Discipline (Methodist): on primacy of saving souls, 55, 89; ceases to oppose slavery, 106–7; on preaching, 136; and missionary imperative, 140; and Methodist quest for respectability, 202

Dow, Lorenzo, 78, 176, 197, 226; popularity of, 7, 130, 134–35; and religious press, 11, 128; religious doubts of, 17; controversy with Lyman Beecher, 20, 35; and revolt against medical profession, 29; characteristics of, 36–40; preaches in Great Britain, 7, 50, 212; relationship with Methodist leadership, 52, 130, 200; and emotional religion, 58; and slavery, 102; and vernacular preaching, 130–33, 138; and popular religious music, 151; primitivism of, 167; anticlericalism of, 174; millennialism of, 185–86

Dozier, Richard, 103

Duane, William, 59

Du Bois, W. E. B., 107

Duffield, George, 61, 196

Dupuy, Stark, 152

Dwight, Timothy, 17, 18, 32, 59, 91, 186; and popular religious press, 11, 25; criticizes untrained preachers, 19; defends clerical respectability, 35

Easter, John, 55

Edwards, Jonathan, 11, 17, 117, 128, 135, 162; theology of, 173; and the Bible, 180; and biblical prophecy, 184

Egalitarian protest: and populist religion, 5, 9–11, 14, 24, 26; in early republic, 23–27; and revolt against professions, 27–30; in backcountry dissent, 30–34; and anticlericalism, 44–46; in Christian movement, 75–76; in Methodism, 82–85, 93; and African-Americans, 102–3; and Mormons, 115–22; and vernacular preaching, 132–33; and popular religious music, 160–61; and millennialism, 184–86. *See also* Democratization of Christianity

Ely, Samuel, 32–33
Enlightenment thought: and Second Great Awakening, 35; in populist theology, 35–36; and Elias Smith, 129
Episcopalianism, 4, 96; institutional weakness, 60; and African-Americans, 102, 155
Erasmus, 179
Evangelical Association, 154
Evans, Henry, 106

Falwell, Jerry, 211
Fanning, Tolbert, 201
Federalists: opposition to, 24–27, 44, 70, 175–76, 188; imitate opponents, 61
Ferguson, Jesse B., 201
Finley, James B., 52, 151
Finney, Charles G., 212, 226; and populist religion, 195, 196–201
Fleming, L. D., 145
Flint, Timothy, 137
Folk religion, 10, 36; of African-Americans, 105; and popular music, 160–61. *See also* Preachers, populist; Popular culture; Populist religion; Theology, populist
Foreign missions, 65, 93, 126, 170–71
Francis, John, 40
Franklin College, 204, 207
French Revolution, 5, 8, 22, 184
Fuller, Charles E., 217
Fundamentalism, 208, 212, 214–19
Furman, Richard, 94–95, 101

Gale, George W., 199
Galloway, Joseph, 184
Garrettson, Freeborn, 10, 106; controversy with Lyman Beecher, 20; and slavery, 102–3; anticlericalism of, 170, 174, 175
Garrison, William Lloyd, 145
Gates, Theophilus, 11, 100; and revolt against Calvinism, 172; anticlericalism of, 176–77, 178; antimission protest of, 179
George, David, 110
George Washington University, 95
Goodrich, Samuel, 126, 193; criticizes populist preachers, 20, 134, 138
Graham, Billy, 211, 212, 213
Granade, John A., 151
Grant, Jedediah Morgan, 121–22
Graves, J. R., 101
Great Awakening, 59; contrasted with Second Great Awakening, 5, 34, 57, 139, 180, 186; contrasted with Christian movement, 71, 77; and legacy of popular communications, 127; and millennialism, 184; historiography of, 221
Great Britain, 36; population, 4; religious climate, 5, 7, 8, 50, 143, 211–12

Hall, Samuel, 140
Hamilton, Alexander, 32, 94
Hamilton College, 207
Hampton-Sidney College, 61
Harvard College, 33, 59, 219
Henry, Patrick, 6, 95
Hesburgh, Theodore, 213
Hibbard, Billy: controversy with Lyman Beecher, 19–20; preaching style of, 134, 136, 138; and revolt against Calvinism, 174
Higgins, Jesse, 28
Himes, Joshua V., 145, 159
Historiography, religious: stress on intellectualism and cohesive institutions, 5; traditional organizing principles of, 12; and spread of Christianity, 15; and American Revolution, 23; of Second Great Awakening, 35–36, 62–63, 135, 220–26
Hodge, Charles, 196, 201
Holiness movement, 212, 214–16
Hopkins, Samuel, 173
Hosier, Harry, 106, 134
Hough, Simon, 44–45
Hubbard, Amos H., 144
Hull, Hope, 204
Humphreys, Herman, 18
Husband, Herman, 32
Hutchinson, Anne, 21

Ingalls, Jeremiah, 146–47, 149–50, 153
Itinerants, Methodist, 11; and revolt against medical profession, 29; Lorenzo Dow, 36–40; and ethic of sacrifice, 82–89; and primacy of soul-saving, 186

Jackson, Andrew, 22
Jarratt, Devereux, 21, 82
Jasper, Harry, 134
Jefferson, Thomas, 7, 8, 76, 95, 98, 162, 184, 213; and John Leland, 96
Jeffersonian political thought, 10, 46; in populist theology, 34–36; and Lorenzo Dow, 37; and John Leland, 95–96; ahistorical assumptions of, 169. *See also* Republicanism
Jeffersonians: radical egalitarianism of, 23–27; attack clergy, 59; communication strategies of, 61, 128
Jehovah's Witnesses, 212
Johnson, Richard M., 100, 179
Johnson, Tom, 61
Jones, Abner, 42, 153
Jones, Absalom, 107–9
Jones, Charles Colcock, 102, 104–5, 106, 155
Jones, William, 33
Judson, Adoniram, 93

Keteltas, William, 24
Kilham, Alexander, 91
Kimball, Heber C.: background of poverty, 121–22; preaching style of, 136–37
King, Jabez, 68
King, Martin Luther, 58
Knapp, Jacob, 134
Knox, Henry, 31, 33
Kuhlman, Kathryn, 211
Kuyper, Abraham, 201

Latrobe, Benjamin Henry, 52–55
Latter-Day Saints. *See* Mormons
Leavitt, Joshua, 153
Lee, Jesse, 89; preaching style of, 134; and revolt against Calvinism, 172
Legal profession: monopoly of, 16; revolt against, 26–28
Leland, John, 13, 67; and revolt against medical profession, 29; Jeffersonian politics of, 95–96; populist religion of, 96–101; and slavery, 102–3; on black Christianity, 106; preaching style, 138; and popular religious music, 149; anticlericalism of, 170, 174, 175, 179
Lewis, C. S., 212
Liberalism: and populist religion, 14
Liberty, religious. *See* Conscience, primacy of individual
Liele, George, 110
Lincoln, Abraham, 153, 193
Long, Huey, 208
Luther, Martin, 59, 165, 168; and the Bible, 179–80, 182
Lutherans, 4; and popular religious music, 153; theology, 174

McGready, James, 134
McGuffey, William Holmes, 143
M'Kendree, William, 55
McMaster, Gilbert, 78
McNemer, Richard, 13, 81
McPherson, Aimee Semple, 217
Madison, James (bishop), 60
Madison, James, (president), 96, 162
"Mammoth Cheese": presented to Thomas Jefferson, 96
Manley, Robert, 52, 151
Manning, William, 26–27, 128
Marsh, Joseph, 145
Marsh, Thomas B., 121
Marshall, Robert, 174
Martineau, James, 150
Meade, William, 61
Medical profession: monopoly of, 16; revolt against, 28–30, 129
Mercersburg Theology, 164–67
Methodism, 7, 10, 12, 13, 21, 33, 56, 58, 59, 65, 66, 128, 212, 216, 223, 224;

growth of, 3, 4; polity, 9, 11; criticized, 14, 70; loss of intensity of, 16; and camp meetings, 49–56, organizational impulse of, 57; female preachers in, 79; background and characteristics, 81–93; and black Christianity, 103–10, 154–57, 217; and religious press, 126, 127, 142, 144; lay preachers in, 134; and revolt against Calvinism, 139, 170–72, 174; missionary imperative of, 139–41; and popular religious music, 147, 150; anticlericalism in, 174, 177; and Bible-only theology, 183; millennialism in, 184, 189; and quest for respectability, 193, 201–6, 207; influence on Charles Finney, 197–200; historiography of, 220–21. See also *Discipline* (Methodist); Itinerants, Methodist
Methodism, British, 59; conservative nature of, 7, 8, 50–52, 91–93; Luddite movement and, 8, 91
Methodism, German-American, 200; conflict with Mercersburg theologians, 164–67
Methodist Protestant Church, 205–6
Methodists, other: Free, 207; Wesleyan, 207
Millennialism: apocalyptic imagery and, 6, 33, 40, 45; and primitivism, 170, in populist religion, 176, 184–89; continuing influence of, 215
Miller, William, 13, 145, 159, 226; opposes Baptist centralizers, 101, 207; and religious press, 126, 142, 143; popular appeal of, 134–35; and primacy of individual conscience, 136; primitivism of, 167; millennialism of, 176
Millerites, 56, 115, 167, 212, 224; and Baptist centralizers, 101, 206–7; and religious press, 126, 142, 144, 145; and lay preachers, 134; missionary imperative of, 139; and popular religious music, 147, 159–60; and Bible-only theology, 183
Mills, Samuel J., 178
Ministers. *See* Clergy; Itinerants, Methodist; Preachers, populist
Monroe, James, 95
Moody, Dwight, 212
Mormons, 4, 7, 56, 58, 65, 212, 224; polity, 9, 11; loss of intensity of, 16; and Thomsonian medicine, 30; and appeal to the poor, 113–22; and mass publishing, 126; lay preachers, 134, 140; and revolt against Calvinism, 139, 172; missionary imperative of, 139–41; and popular religious music, 147, 158–59; primitivism of, 168; and Bible-only theology, 183; millennialism of, 187–88; and democratic backlash, 208
Morse, Jedediah, 18, 59, 143

new technology, 144; role in movement building, 145
Priestly, Joseph, 184
Primitivism: in Methodism, 82–83; in populist religion, 167–70, 179
Princeton College, 196, 219
Progressivism, 213
Puritans, 13, 59, 186

Quakers, 34, 177, 188; Rogerenes, 44
Quincy, Edmund, 145

Radio and populist religion, 217
Randall, Benjamin, 167, 173
Redfield, John Wesley, 207
Reeve, Tapping, 18
Reformed Churches, German: and popular religious music, 153; Methodist inroads into, 164, 200
Religious Tract Society, 143
Republicanism: and egalitarian protest, 28, 45–46; and Thomsonian medicine, 29; and backcountry dissent, 32
Respectability, quest for: in Methodism, 89, 93, 193, 195, 201–7; in the Baptist movement, 93–97, 195, 204–7; as continuing impulse in populist religion, 219
Restorationism. See Primitivism
Revivalists. See Clergy; Itinerants, Methodists; Preachers, populist
Revivals, 7, 56, 115; in Kentucky, 13, 70; in New England, 17; and Second Great Awakening, 62–63; and populist religion, 67; in New York, 114; and Charles Finney, 199–200; historiography of, 222, 225. See also Second Great Awakening
Revolution. See American Revolution; French Revolution
Rice, David, 21, 61, 163
Rice, Luther, 93
Rich, Caleb, 40–41, 171–72
Richardson, Robert, 207
Rigdon, Sidney: preaching style of, 137; and primitivism, 168; and millennialism, 188; and democratic backlash against Mormons, 208
Roberts, Benjamin Titus, 207
Roberts, Oral, 211
Robertson, Pat, 211
Robinson, John A. T., 212
Roman Catholicism, 4, 12
Rush, Benjamin, 184
Rutledge, John, 23

Sargent, Abel, 75–76
Scales, William, 33
Schaff, Philip, 223; criticizes populist religion, 136, 147, 154, 169, 183; and Mercersburg Theology, 164–67

Schermerhorn, John F., 178
Schuller, Robert, 211
Scofield, C. I., 215
Scott, Orange, 207
Second Great Awakening, 56; as egalitarian movement, 5; and church growth, 15; in New England, 17; contrasted with Great Awakening, 5, 34, 57, 139, 180, 186; historiography of, 35–36, 62–63, 135, 220–26
Sedition Act, 25
Semple, Robert B., 94, 95
Shakers, 65
Shays, Daniel, 31
Shays's Rebellion, 19, 31
Shurtleff, James, 33–34
Singletary, Amos, 24
Slavery, 65, 110; and populist religion, 67; and Methodism, 93, 106–7; and populist preachers, 96, 102–3. See also Black Christianity
Smith, Elias, 71, 78, 80, 159, 176; and religious press, 11; revolt against medical profession, 29; and primacy of individual conscience, 42, 139; anticlericalism of, 45, 75, 174–75; and movement building, 57; role in rise of Christian movement, 68–70; and religious press, 73–76, 128–30, 143, 145; and Baptist quest for respectability, 94; and slavery, 102–3; popular appeal of, 134–35; preaching style of, 138; and popular religious music, 148; primitivism of, 167, 169; antimission protest of, 179; millennialism of, 184–86
Smith, Emma, 158
Smith, Jasen, 149
Smith, Joseph, 67, 68, 208, 226; populist appeal of, 13, 120–22, 134–35; and Thomsonian medicine, 29–30; mysticism of, 49, 114–15; background of poverty, 113–15; and Book of Mormon, 115–17; on preaching, 140; and religious press, 143; primitivism of, 167–69; millennialism of, 176, 187–88
Smith, Joseph, Sr., 43, 113
Smith, Joshua, 148
Smith, Lucy Mack, 113, 43
Snethen, Nicholas, 82, 205–6
Social classes: and Methodism, 14, distinctions between after Revolution, 23; Mormon appeal to poor, 113–22; and vernacular preaching, 132–33. See also Egalitarian protest; Populist religion
Social upheaval in early republic, 6, 13–14, 64
Society of the Cincinnati, 27, 94
Spicer, Tobias, 173
Standing Order. See New England Standing Order